CONTINENT
ABLAZE

CONTINENT ABLAZE

The Insurgency Wars in Africa
1960 to the Present

JOHN W. TURNER

ARMS AND
ARMOUR

Arms and Armour Press
An Imprint of the Cassell Group
Wellington House, 125 Strand, London WC2R 0BB

Distributed in the USA by Sterling Publishing Co.
Inc., 387 Park Avenue South, New York,
NY 10016-8810.

British Library Cataloguing-in-Publication Data:
a catalogue record for this book is available from
the British Library

ISBN 1-85409-128-X

Designed and edited by DAG Publications Ltd.
Designed by David Gibbons; edited by Gerald
Napier; printed and bound in Great Britain.

Contents

Acknowledgements

Writing this book has been a long and often laborious process. It would not have been possible without the contributions of many people. I would like to thank many, too numerous to list here, who have assisted me and provided me with information and with analytical insights into ongoing developments in Africa.

The photographs here were used with the kind permission of several of the above. For the war in South-West Africa, I want to thank Mr Morgan Norval, of Washington, DC, who provided me with a range of pictures that document COIN warfare. For Mozambique, Mr Thomas Schaaf permitted me to use a number of photographs about RENAMO. The Free Angola Information Service in Washington, DC, provided photographs of UNITA combat operations in Angola. Mr. Nhial Deng provided photographs of SPLA operations. The Embassy of the Republic of Chad, Washington, DC, permitted me to use photographs of the 1986–7 fighting in northern Chad against Libyan forces.

I am indebted to the help of many individuals in writing this book. Among them I wish especially to thank Mike Bittrick, Margaret Calhoun, Nhial Deng, Gege Figuerada, Roger Glickson, Kim Hennigsen, Bill Johnson, Remigius Kintu, Jeff McKaughan, Morgan Norval, Tom Ofcansky, Tom Schaaf, Peter Tsouras, Alex Vines and Roger Winter. These and others were most generous with information, ideas and suggestions – and, especially, their time – for which I am very grateful. Needless to say, however, the analysis and conclusions, and whatever omissions or errors attach to them, are mine alone.

Finally, I want to thank many people for their support and patience, as I have often had to add new material and do rewrites. My family and friends have been especially understanding in this regard. I owe special thanks as well to Arms and Armour Press and its director, Mr Rod Dymott, for the extensions for adding and rewriting sections of the book, which has benefited considerably in the process.

Introduction

Warfare in modern Africa has in many ways become synonymous with the concepts of insurgency or 'low-intensity conflict'. The disturbances that accompanied independence, the struggles between surrogates during the Cold War, and the post-Cold War re-emergence of long-standing ethnic and regional disputes have all ensured that Africa continues to see decade after decade of insurgent conflict.

I have chosen the term 'insurgency' rather than 'low-intensity conflict' to characterise the hostilities that have beset Africa, since 'low-intensity conflict' also includes terrorism, a phenomenon from which Africa has been relatively free to date. I should stress, however, that this by no means excludes acts of terror by insurgents or by government forces against the non-combatant population, which continue to be widespread.

Insurgents have adapted one of two frameworks for their operations and tactics. Ironically, the best-known, that of Mao Zedong, was utilised the least. Its most ardent practitioner, the Angolan guerrilla leader Jonas Savimbi, finally failed when he violated the basic tenets of his own doctrine in the short but extremely destructive war of 1992–1994. Elsewhere, however, the insurgents in Eritrea and Ethiopia adapted the concept to their needs and ousted one of Africa's most brutal dictatorships in 1991. This formula was also used by Robert Mugabe and ZANU against the Rhodesians in the 1970s.

The other model for insurgency is that based on the Soviet partisan forces operating behind Nazi lines in World War II Russia. The Soviets exported some training in guerrilla warfare with the assistance they or their satellites provided. This was the model used by the MPLA in Angola and FRELIMO in Mozambique, as well as by Joshua Nkomo's ZAPU. Its most persistent practitioners, however, were SWAPO and its armed wing, PLAN.

I have been quite cautious in the use of the term 'counterinsurgency' (abbreviated as COIN). In the strictest sense, COIN warfare is based on doctrine and fought with specially-trained troops using a particular set of tactics. COIN can be an over-arching concept used to direct national defence against a perceived all-encompassing threat, as in its use by the South African military to counter the 'total onslaught' in the 1980s. (Note, however, that the South African military had coventional forces, organised, equipped, and trained as such, not only to provide conventional defence but also to back the rest of its military forces in fighting in South-West Africa and Angola. Aside from this portion of its military endeavour, most of the fighting by South African forces in the demanding operational environment of southern Africa was decidedly non-conventional.)

The reader will note that most African government military forces often fought long and hard, with mixed success, against insurgents. However, they normally did this using conventional forces, and normally their only recourse against insurgents 'swimming in the sea of the people' was to make war against the population believed to support the insurgents. I call this type of warfare 'counter-guerrilla warfare', which, put simply, encompasses a range of actions against guerrilla or insurgent forces. The results of such fighting are mixed, but in general the population suffers heavily from government 'counter-guerrilla' operations. Continuing reports of widespread atrocities and abuses that accompany war reporting from Africa suggest that 'counter-guerrilla' operations continue to dominate the operations by most government forces. Much of this is due to lack of resources to field

7

and train a proper force; unfortunately, the cheapest option remains the most brutal. However, I should hasten to add that government forces in no way have retained any sort of monopoly on brutality.

Most of the individual chapters of this book were originally separate overviews of select African conflicts or campaigns written as operational histories. Thanks to the interest of Rod Dymott of Arms and Armour Press in publishing a book on African insurgency warfare, I have assembled these disparate operational studies (and written several additional ones) in this book with several purposes in mind. The first and foremost is to provide an operational history of the major Cold War conflicts on the African continent. The second is to periodise these conflicts in an attempt to better understand the major military developments. Finally, I add my observations on some lessons learned as well as on other aspects of the fighting. In the case of southern Africa, I have felt compelled to provide a separate chapter to detail these issues. The work is still perhaps heavily balanced on the side of narrative overviews of the operational course of the various conflicts, but I hope thereby to ensure that I give the reader a solid account of events wherever possible. As the conflicts described below will inevitably be further detailed and examined by other authors in future publications, some of my analysis will likely be modified or countered by new research and analysis. So be it; however, I am more hopeful that the narrative of events presented here will better stand the test of time.

In writing and editing this book, some trade-offs had to be made so that a one-volume study could remain feasible. My often extensive and detailed operational histories had to be heavily edited to be accommodated in a book of this size. But by doing so I was able to provide discussions of the conflicts continent-wide instead of limiting its scope to southern African conflicts. Regrettably, much of the bibliographic documentation had to be cut back as well. I hope to publish the full corpus in a future annotated bibliography and research guide to African insurgency and counterinsurgency during the Cold War. However, for the time being I have listed references at the end of the book that will lead interested readers to further information about the subject. While the body of work on southern African conflicts is extensive, especially for Rhodesia and Southwest Africa, that for other parts of the continent is not. It is to be hoped that future students of insurgencies and counterinsurgency warfare will find many opportunities for research and publication on conflicts in central and western Africa as well as the Horn.

Most of the detailed discussions of insurgencies end by the early 1990s. At that time many of the old Cold War contests ended in the wake of the collapse of the USSR and the Warsaw Pact. But already a new series of conflicts had erupted, marking a new era in the history of warfare on the continent. Fighting in Somalia, Liberia, Rwanda, Zaire, and a new chapter in the Sudan conflict all indicate new forces at work on the continent. I have broadly, and briefly, discussed the new situation in the final chapter, and merely wish to note here that a more detailed review of these new conflicts, which continue as of writing, will some day require a separate book at least as long as this.

List of Abbreviations

4WD	Four-wheel drive	BATE	Technical Explosives Action Brigade (in Portuguese: Brigada de Accao Technica de Explosivos) (UNITA)
AAMG	Anti-aircraft machine-gun		
AC	Armoured car		
ADA	Air defence artillery		
AFL	Armed Forces of Liberia	BDAA	(Angolan) Air Defence Brigade (Portuguese: Brigada da Defesa Anti-Aerea)
AMU	Area Force Unit		
AID	Islamic Salvation Army (French: Armée Islamic du Salut) (Algeria)		
		Bde	Brigade
AK	General designation for a class of Soviet-manufactured 7.62mm automatic rifles (Russian: Automat Kalashnikova), eg. A-47, AKM	BET	Borkou-Ennedi-Tibesti (Chadian northern region)
		BF	Railway Protection Troops (Batalhoes Ferroviarios),
ALF	Afar Liberation Front	BIL	(Angolan) Light Infantry Brigade (Portuguese: Brigada da Infantaria Ligeira)
ALPS	Saharan Peoples Liberation Army (French: Armée de Libération Popular Saharaoui) (see POLISARIO Front)		
		BIM	(Mozambican/Angolan) Motorised Infantry Brigade (Portuguese: Brigada de Infantaria Motorizada)/Motorised Infantry Battalion (Portuguese: Batalho de Infantaria Motorizada)
AML	General designation for a class of French-manufactured and licensed Panhard wheeled armoured vehicles (French: Automitrailleuse Légère) (Note: produced in South Africa as the Eland series of armoured cars)		
		BIM	(Moroccan) Motorised Infantry Brigade/Battalion (French: Brigade/ Battalion d'Infanterie Motorisé)
AN	Anya Nya (Sudan)		
ANGOP	Angolan government news service	BM	Name for a Soviet/Warsaw Pact-made series of multiple rocket launchers (Russian: Bayevaya Mashina 'Combat Vehicle')
AN-II	Anya Nya II (Sudan)		
ANC	African National Congress		
ANC	Congolese National Army (French: Armée National Congolaise) (Zaire)	BMATT	British Military Advisory and Training Team
ANL	(Chadian) National Liberation Army (French: Armée Nationale de la Libération)	BMD	Soviet-made airborne amphibious troop carrier (Russian: Boyevaya Mashina Desantinka)
ANLM	Afar National Liberation Movement	BMP	Soviet-made infantry fighting vehicle series (Russian: Boyevaya Mashina Pekhotj)
ANT	Chadian National Army (French: Armée Nationale du Tchad)	Bn	Battalion
AOR	Area of responsibility	BPV	(Angolan) People's Vigilance Brigades (Portuguese: Brigadas Populares de Vigiliancia)
APC	Armoured personnel carrier		
APL	Lumumba Patriotic Army (French: Armée Patriotique Lumumba)	BRDM	Soviet-made armoured scout car series (Russian: Bronevannaya Razvedjvtel'naya Dozornaya Mashina)
APR	Rwandan Patriotic Army (French: Armée Patriotique Rwandais)		
ARLA	Revolutionary Army for the Liberation of the Azawad (French: Armée Révolutionnaire de Libération de l'Azaouad)	BRIL	(Angolan) Light Infantry Brigade (see BIL)
		BRIM	(Angolan) Motorised Infantry Brigade (see BIM)
AS	African Serviceman (Rhodesia)		
AT	Anti-tank	BSAP	British South African Police
ATGM	Anti-tank guided missile	BTR	Soviet-made armoured personnel carrier of various versions (Russian: Bronetransporter)
ATOPS	Anti-terrorist operations		
AVLB	Armoured Vehicle Launched Bridge		
		BTT	Territorial Troops Battalion

	(Portuguese: Batalhao das Tropas Territorial)
C3(I)	Command, control, communications (and intelligence)
CANU	Caprivi African National Union (SWA/Namibia)
CAUNC	Comité d'Action de l'Union Nationale des Cabindais
CCFAN	(Chadian) Command Council of the Northern Armed Forces (French: Conseil de commandement des Forces armées du nord)
CDR	(Chadian) Democratic Revolu tionary Council (French: Conseil Democratique Révolutionnaire)
CEMG	Chief of General Staff (French: Chef d'Etat-Major)
CF	Citizen Force (South Africa)
CFB	Benguela Railway (Portuguese: Caminho de Ferra de Benguela)
CIA	(US) Central Intelligence Agency
CIM	(Angolan) Military Counterintelligence (Portuguese: Contra-intelligencia Militar)
CIO	(Rhodesian) Central Intelligence Organisation
CLMC	Comando Militar para a Libertacao de Cabinda
CMP	(Mozambican) Provincial Military Command (Portuguese: Comando Militar Provincial)
CNR	(Chadian) National Reconciliation Committee (French: Comité national de redressement)
CNDD	(Burundi) National Council for the Defence of Democracy (French: Conseil National pour la Défense de la Démocratie); see also FDD
codo	(Chadian) rebel commando unit
COIN	Counterinsurgency
COINOPS	Counterinsurgency operations
COMECON	Council for Mutual Economic Assistance
COMOPS	Combined Operations Headquarters (Rhodesia)
COPE	(UNITA) Strategic Operational Command (Portuguese: Comando Operacional Estrategico)
Coy	Company
CPPA	Corps of Angolan People's Police (Portuguese: Corpo de Policia Popular de Angola)
CRR	Wheeled reconnaissance vehicle including those of the Brazilian Cascaval EE-9 series (Portuguese: Carro de Reconhecimento subre Rodas)
CS	Combat Support
CSD	Defence and Security Council (MPLA)
CSI	Chief of Staff, Intelligence (SADF)
CSS	Combat Service Support

CV	Consolidated Village
DDNST	(Zairian) Department of National Defence and Territorial Security (French: Département de Défense National et Sécurité de Territoire)
DDS	(Chadian) Directorate of Documentation and Security (French: Direction de la Documentation et de la Sécurité)
DISA	Angolan Directorate for Security and Intelligence (Portuguese: Direcao de Informacao e Seguranca de Angola)
DPs	displaced persons
DPOM	(Angolan) Directorate for Protection of Mining Operations (Portuguese: Direcao para e Protecao das Operacoes Mineiras)
DSP	(Zairian) Special Presidential Division (French: Division Special Presidential)
EAF	Ethiopian Air Force
ECOWAS	Economic Community of West African States
EDM	Ethiopian Democratic Movement
EDU	Ethiopian Democratic Union
EGF	Ethiopian Ground Force (Army)
ECOMOG	ECOWAS Monitoring Group (Liberia)
EIF	Eritrean Islamic Front
ELF	Eritrean Liberation Front
EMG	General Staff (various) (French: Etat-Major Général; Portuguese: Estado Maior Geral)
ENLA	National Army for the Liberation of Angola (Portuguese: Frente Nacional de Libertacao de Angola) (FNLA)
EOL	Executive Outcomes Limited
EPA	Popular Army of Angola (Portuguese: Exercito Popular de Angola)
EPDM	Ethiopian People's Democratic Movement
EPLA	Eritrean People's Liberation Army (EPLF)
EPLF	Eritrean People's Liberation Front
EPRDF	Ethiopian People's Revolutionary Democratic Front
EPRP	Ethiopian People's Revolutionary Party
EUNC	Eritrean Unified National Council
FAA	Angolan Armed Forces (Portuguese: Forcas Armadas de Angola)
FALA	Armed Forces for the Liberation of Angola (UNITA) (Portuguese: Forcas Armadas de Libertacao de Angola)
FAM	Mozambican Armed Forces (Portuguese: Forcas Armadas de Mocambique)
FAN	Nigerien Armed Forces (French: Forces Armées Nigeriens)

FAN   (Chadian) Armed Forces of the North (French: Forces Armées du Nord)

FANT   Chadian National Armed Forces (French: Forces Armées Nationales Tchadiennes)

FAO   (Chadian) Western Armed Forces (French: Forces Armées Occidentales)

FAP   (Chadian) People's Armed Forces (French: Forces Armées Populaires)

FAPA-DAA   Popular Air Force of Angola and Anti-Air Defence (Portuguese: Forca Aerea Popular de Angola e Defesa Anti-Aerea)

FAPLA   Popular Armed Forces for the Liberation of Angola (Portuguese: Forcas Armadas Populares de Libertacao de Angola)

FAR   (Cuban) Revolutionary Armed Forces (Spanish: Fuerzas Armadas Revolucionarias)

FAR   (Moroccan) Royal Armed Forces (French: Forces Armées Royales)

FAR   Rwandan Armed Forces (French: Forces Armées Rwandaises)

FAT   Chadian Armed Forces (French: Forces Armées Tchadiennes)

FAZ   Zairian Armed Forces (French: Forces Armées Zairoises)

FAZA   Zairian Air Force

FAZN   Zairian Navy

FDD   (Burundi) Forces for the Defence of Democracy (French: Forces pour la Défense de la Démocratie); see CNDD

FE   (Angolan) Special Forces (Portuguese: Forcas Especiais)

FEDEMU   Federal Democratic Movement of Uganda

FF   Fire Force

FIAA   (Tuareg) Islamic Arab Front of the Azawad (French: Front Islamique Arabe de l'Azaouad)

FIS   Islamic Salvation Front (French: Front Islamique du Salut) (Algeria)

FNLC   National Front for the Liberation of the Congo (French: Front National pour la Libération du Congo)

FNLA   National Front for the Liberation of Angola (Portuguese: Frente Nacional de Libertacao de Angola)

FNT   National Chadian Front (French: Front National Tchadien)

FLAA   (Tuareg) Front for the Liberation of the Air and the Azawad (French: Front pour la Libération de l'Air et de l'Azaouad)

FLEC   Front for the Liberation of the Enclave of Cabinda (Portuguese: Frente de Libertacao do Enclave de Cabinda)

FODELICO   Democratic Force for the Liberation of Congo-Kinshasa (Forces Démocratiques pour la Libération du Congo-Kinshasa)

FP   POLISARIO Front (French: Front POLISARIO or Spanish Frente POLISARIO); see POLISARIO entry

FPLA   (Tuareg) Popular Front for the Liberation of the Azawad (French: Front Populaire de la Libération de l'Azaouad)

FPLM   Popular Forces for the Liberation of Mozambique (Portuguese: Forcas Populars de Libertacao de Mocambique); see also FAM

FPR   Rwandan Patriotic Front (French: Front Patriotique Rwandais)

FRELIMO   Mozambique Liberation Front (Portuguese: Frente de Libertacao de Mocambique)

FRODEBU   Front for Democracy in Burundi (French: Front pour la Démocratie en Burundi)

FROLINA   (Burundi) National Liberation Front (French: Front de Libération Nationale)

FROLINAT   Chadian National Liberation Front (French: Front de Libération Nationale du Tchad)

FRUD   (Djibouti) Front for the Restoration of Unity and Democracy (French: Front pour la Restauration de l'Unité et de la Démocratie)

FT   Ground Forces (Portuguese: Forcas Terrestres) of the Angolan Armed Forces

FT   Ground Force (French: Force Terrestre) of the Zairian Armed Forces

FUNA   Former Ugandan National Army

GHQ   general headquarters

GIA   Armed Islamic Group (French: Groupe Islamique Armée) (Algeria)

GN   National Gendarmerie (various countries; French: Gendarmerie Nationale)

GOC   General Officer Commanding

GPMG   General purpose machine gun (see also PK)

GR   (Moroccan) Royal Gendarmerie (French: Gendarmerie Royale)

GRL   (Angolan) Liaison Reconnaissance Group (Portuguese: Grupo de Reconhecimento de Ligacao)

GSP   Soviet-made self-propelled tracked ferry (Russian: Gusenichnij Samokhodnij Parom, 'tracked self-propelled ferry')

GT   Tactical group (FAPLA) (in Portuguese: grupo tactico)

GUNT	(Chadian) Transitional Government of National Unity (French: Gouvernement d'Union Nationale de Transition)
HMG	Heavy machine gun
HNG	Hayada Nagadgelyada Gaashaandhiga
HPZ	Humanitarian Protection Zone
HQ	Headquarters
HSM	Holy Spirit Movement (Uganda)
IAF	Inter-African Force (Chad)
ICRC	International Committee of the Red Cross
ICV	infantry combat vehicle
IED	improvised explosive device
IFV	infantry fighting vehicle
IGLF	Issa and Gurgura Liberation Front
IGNU	(Liberian) Interim Government of National Unity
ISO	(Ugandan) Internal Security Organisation
INPFL	Independent National Patriotic Front of Liberia
JOC	Joint Operations Centre or Command (Rhodesia)
JMC	Joint Monitoring Commission
KIA	killed in action
LCB	Angolan counterguerrilla forces (Portuguese: Luta Contra Banditos)
LDF	Lofa Defence Force (Liberia)
LDF	Local Defence Force (Rwanda)
LDU	Local Defence Unit
LIG	Libyan Islamic Group
LOC	line of communication
LPC	Liberian Peace Council (aka National Peace Council)
LRA	Lord's Resistance Army (Uganda)
LUDF	Liberian United Defence Force
LWT	light workshop troop
MAG	machine-gun
MARNET	Military Area Radio Net
MDD	(Chadian) Movement for Democracy and Development (French: Mouvement pour la Démocratie et le Développement)
MFDC	Movement of Democratic Forces of Casamance (French: Mouvement des Forces Démocratiques de Casamance)
MG	machine-gun
MGPA	Popular Navy of Angola (Portuguese: Marinha de Guerra Popular de Angola)
MININT	(Angolan) Ministry of Interior (Portuguese: Ministerio de Interior)
MINSE	(Angolan) Ministry of State Security (Portuguese: Ministerio de Seguranca do Estado)
MK	(African National Congress) 'Spear of the Nation' (Xhosa: Umkhonto wa Sizwe)
MNC/L	Congolese National Movement/ Lumumbist (Zaire) (French:

	Mouvement National Congolais-Lumumba)
MNR	Mozambican National Resistance
MNRA	Mozambican National Resistance Army
MNRCS	Mouvement National pour la Révolution Culturelle et Sociale
MNRD	National Revolutionary Movement for Development (Rwanda)
MOSANAT	Movement for the National Salvation of Chad (French: Mouvement pour le Salut National du Tchad)
MPA	(Tuareg) Popular Movement of the Azawad (French: Mouvement Populaire de l'Azaouad)
MPS	Mouvement Patriotique du Salut
MPLA	Popular Movement for the Liberation of Angola (Portuguese: Movimento Popular de Libertacao de Angola)
MPLT	Popular Movement for the Liberation of Chad (French: Mouvement Populaire pour la Libération du Tchad)
MPS	(Chadian) Patriotic Salvation Movement (French:Mouvement Populaire du Salut)
MPV	mine-protected vehicle
MRF	(Chadian) Movement for the Federal Republic (French: Mouvement pour la République Fédérale)
MRL	multiple rocket launcher
MRLM	Movement for the Redemption of the Liberian Muslims
MRM	Mozambican Resistance Movement (see RENAMO)
MRM	Movement for the Redemption of (Liberian) Muslims
NA	Nigerian Army
NALU	National Army for the Liberation of Uganda
NASA	(Ugandan) National Security Agency
NCO	Non-commissioned officer
NDP	National Democratic Party
NGO	non-governmental organisation
NIF	(Sudanese) National Islamic Front
NLC	Northern Logistics Command (SADF)
NPC	National Peace Council (Liberia) (aka Liberian Peace Council)
NPFL	National Patriotic Front of Liberia
NPRAG	National Patriotic Reconstruction Authority Government (i.e., NPFL)
NRA	National Resistance Army (Uganda; see NRM)
NRC	National Resistance Council (Uganda), Nimba Redemption Council Liberia)
NRM	National Resistance Movement

	(Uganda)
NSA	(Liberian) National Security Agency
NS	National Serviceman (Rhodesia)
NSRCC	National Salvation Revolutionary Command Council (Sudan)
NSS	National Security Service (Somali)
NSM	National Service Member (SADF)
NSS	(Somali) National Security Service (Somali: Ciidima Nabadsugida Soomaaliyeed, CNS or NSS)
OA	operational area
ODP	Popular Defence Organisation (Portuguese: Organizacao de Defesa Popular)
OJM	Organisation of Mozambican Youth (Organisacao da Juventude de Mocambique)
OLA	Oromo Liberation Army (OLF)
OLF	Oromo Liberation Front
OPO	Ovambo People's Organisation (SWA/Namibia)
OPS-K	SWAPOLCOIN Operation 'K' Unit ('Koevoet')
OPS	operational sector
OSCA	operations in support of civil authorities
PA	strongpoint on Moroccan Berm (French: Point d'Appui)
PALIPEHUTU	(Burundi) Party for the Liberation of the Hutu People (French: Parti pour la Libération du Peuple Hutu)
PALIR	People in Arms to Liberate Rwanda (French: Le Peuple en Armes pour Libérer le Rwanda)
PAM	(Angolan) riot police (Portuguese: Policia Anti-Motim)
PATU	Police Anti-Terrorist Unit
PC	(Angolan) command post (Portuguese: posta da comando)
PCA	(Angolan) forward command post (Portuguese: posta da comando avancado)
PCL	Congolese Party of Liberation (French: Parti Congolaise de Libération)
PDF	(Sudanese) People's Defence Force
PF	permanent force
PGHQ	Police General Headquarters (Rhodesia)
PK	Soviet MG series (Russian: Pulemyot Kalashnikova) e.g., PKM
PLAN	People's Liberation Army of Namibia (SWAPO)
PLC	Congolese Liberation Party (Parti de Liberation Congolaise)
PLF	Popular Liberation Front (Eritrea)
PMAC	(Ethiopian) Provisional Military Administrative Council
PMN	(Chadian) National Military

	Police (French: Police Militaire Nationale)
PMT	(Chadian) Territorial Military Police (French: Police Militaire Territoriale)
POLISARIO	Popular Movement for the Liberation of Saguia el-Hamra and Rio de Oro (strictly speaking, 'POLISARIO Front'; in Spanish: Frente Popular para la Liberacion de Saguia el-Hamra y Rio de Oro, Frente POLISARIO; in French: Front Popular pour la Libération de Saguia el-Hamra et Rio de Oro, Front POLISARIO); also abbreviated FP
PPA	Angolan People's Police
PPF	(Sudanese) People's Police Force
PPM	Mozambican People's Police (Portuguese: Policia Popular de Mocambique)
PPT	Parti Progressiste Tchadien
PRC	People's Republic of China
PRP	Popular Revolutionary Party (French: Parti de la Révolution Populaire) (Zaire)
PRM	Mozambican Revolutionary Party (Partido Revolucionario de Mocambique)
PSO	(Sudanese) Public Security Organisation
PT	Soviet designator for a model of amphibious tanks (e.g., the PT-76) (Russian: Plyavayushchii Tank-Amfibiya-76)
PTSM	Soviet-made amphibious transport (Russian: Plyavayushchyego Transportera Mekhanizatsiya, 'mechanised amphibious transporter')
PV	Protected Village
QRF	Quick Reaction Force (US/ Somalia)
RAR	Rhodesian Africa Rifles
RANU	Rwandese Alliance for National Unity
RC	Resistance Council (Uganda)
RCC	Revolutionary Command Council (Sudan)
RDR	Rhodesian Defence Regiment
RENAMO	National Resistance Movement/ National Resistance of Mozambique (Portuguese: Resistencia Nacional de Mocambique)
RhACR	Rhodesian Armoured Car Regiment
RhAF	Rhodesian Air Force
RIM	(Moroccan) Motorised Infantry Regiment (French: Regiment d'Infanterie Motorisé)
RLI	Rhodesian Light Infantry
RM	Reaction Force (Afrikaans: Reaksiemag), also known as

13

	'Romeo Mike'		
RM	military region (Portuguese: regaio militar)		Somali: Wadajirka Umadda Soomaliyeed, WUS)
RPA	Rwandan Patriotic Army (see also APR)	SNASP	(Mozambican) Popular National Security Service (Portuguese: Servico Nacional de Seguranca Popular)
RPF	Rwanda Patriotic Front		
RPD	Soviet-made hand-held machine gun of the Dogtyaryov type (Russian: Ruchnoj Pulemyot Degtyaryova)	SNF	Somali National Front
		SNM	Somali National Movement (in Somali: Midnimadda Dhaqdhaqaaqa Soomaliyeed, MDS)
RPG	rocket-propelled grenade series (loose English rendition of the Russian Reaktivniy Protivotankovyi Granatomet, 'rocket, anti-tank grenade (launcher)')	SP	(Chadian) Presidential Guard (French: Sécurité Presidentielle)
		SPAF	Sudan People's Armed Forces (see also SAF)
		SPLA	Sudan People's Liberation Army
RPP	Rassemblement Populaire pour le Progräs (Djibouti)	SPLA-M	Mainstream SPLA (i.e., Garang or Torit Faction)
RPK	Soviet-made hand-held machine gun of the Kalashnikov type (Russian: Ruchnoj Puleymot Kalashnikova)	SPLA-U	United SPLA (.i.e, Anti-Garang, aka Nasir Faction)
		SPLM	Sudan People's Liberation Movement
RPF	Rwandan Patriotic Front (see also FPR)	SPM	Somali Patriotic Movement (in Somali: Dhaqdhaqaaqa Wadaniyinta Soomaliyeed, DWS)
RR	Rhodesia Regiment		
RSLMF	Republic of Sierra Leone Military Force	SRSP	Somali Revolutionary Socialist Party
RUF	Revolutionary United Front (Sierra Leone)	SSB	Special Service Battalion
		SSLF	Southern Sudanese Liberation Front
SA-	NATO designation for Soviet-manufactured surface-to-air missiles	SSC	Special Service Company
		SSDF	Somali Salvation Democratic Front (in Somali: Jabhada Babaadinta Demogratiga Soomaliyeed, JBDS)
SAA	South African Army		
SAAF	South African Air Force		
SADF	South African Defence Force		
SAF	Sudanese Armed Forces	SSIM	Southern Sudan Independence Movement
SALF	Somali-Abo Liberation Front		
SAM	Surface-to-air missile	SSS	(Sudanese) State Security Service
SAM	Somali Alliance Movement	SWA	South-West Africa (Namibia)
SAP	South African Police	SWAPO	South-West Africa People's Organisation
SARM	(Zairian) Service for Military Action and Intelligence (French: Service d'Action Militaire et de Renseignment)	SWAPOL	South-West Africa Police
		SWAPOLCOIN	South-West Africa Police Counter-Insurgency Wing (Afrikaans equivalent: SWAPOLTEIN)
SARP	South African Railways Police		
SAS	(Rhodesian) Special Air Service	SWASPES	South-West African Specialist Units
SASP	South African Security Police		
SB	Special Branch, also Police Special Branch	SWATF	South-West Africa Territory Force
SDM	Somali Democratic Movement (in Somali: Dhaqdhaqaaqa Demogradiyed Soomaliyeed, DDS)	TF	Railway Troops (Tropas Ferroviarios)
		TFAI	Territory of the Afars and Issas
		TGF	(Mozambican) Border Guard Troops (Portuguese: Tropas de Guarda Frontieras)
SFA	Security Force Auxiliaries		
SIMI	(UNITA) Military Intelligence Service (Portuguese: Servico de Intelligencia Militar)	TGFA	Angolan Border Guard Troops (Portuguese: Tropas de Guarda Frontieras Angolanas)
SISE	(Mozambican) State Security Information Service (Portuguese: Servico de Informacao de Seguranca Estatal)	TI	(Angolan) Intervention Troops (Portuguese: Tropas Intervencao)
SLF	Sidamo Liberation Front	TLF	Tigrean Liberation Front
SNA	Somali National Army (in Somali: Ciidanka Soomaaliyeed, CS)	TMM	Soviet-made truck-mounted scissors bridge (Russian: Tyazhyelji Mekhanizirovannji
SNA	Somali National Alliance (in		

	Most, 'heavy mechanised bridge')		UCPDA; see above)
TPDF	Tanzanian People's Defence Force	UPDA	Ugandan People's Democratic
TPLF	Tigrean People's Liberation Front		Army (see UPDM)
TPM	Mine Protection Troops	UPDM	Ugandan People's Democratic
TPOM	(Angolan) Troops for Protection		Movement
	of Mining Operations	UPF	Uganda People's Front
	(Portuguese: Tropas para e	USC	United Somali Congress (in
	Protecao das Operacoes Mineiras)		Somali: Golaha Midnimadda
TT	Territorial Troops (Angola)		Soomaliyeed, GMS)
	(Portuguese: Tropas Territoriais)	USCR	United States Committee for
TTL	Tribal Trust Lands (Rhodesia)		Refugees
UCPDA	Ugandan Christian People's	USF	United Somali Front
	Democratic Alliance (see HSM)	VTT	troop transport vehicle (French:
UDF	United Defence Force (Liberia)		véhicule transport de troup)
UFA	Uganda Freedom Army (see	WIA	wounded in action
	UFM)	WNBF	West Nile Bank Front (Uganda)
UFM	Uganda Freedom Movement	WSLF	Western Somali Liberation Front
ULIMO	United Liberation Movement of	ZAF	Zimbabwe Air Force
	Liberia for Democracy	ZAPU	Zimbabwe African People's
UNAMIR	United Nations Assistance		Union
	Mission in Rwanda	ZANLA	Zimbabwe African Liberation
UNAVEM	United Nations Angola		Army (see ZANU)
	Verification Mission	ZANU	Zimbabwe African National
UNIR	(Chadian) National Union for		Union
	Independence and the Revolution	ZDF	Zimbabwe Defence Force
	(French: Union Nationale pour	ZIPA	Zimbabwe People's Army
	l'Independence et la Révolution)	ZIPRA	Zimbabwe People's
UNITA	National Movement for the Total		Revolutionary Army (see ZAPU)
	Liberation of Angola (Portuguese:	ZM	military zone (Portuguese: zona
	Uniao Nacional para		militar)
	Independenca Total de Angola)	ZNA	Zimbabwe National Army
UNITAF	Unified Task Force (Somalia)	ZPU	Soviet-made anti-aircraft machine
UNLA	Uganda National Liberation Army		gun (Russian: Zenitnaya
UNLF	Uganda National Liberation Front		Pulemyetnaya Ustanovka, 'anti-
UNOMOZ	United Nations Operation in		aircraft machine gun piece')
	Mozambique	ZRP	Zimbabwe Republic Police
UNOSOM	United Nations Operation in	ZRPF	Zimbabwe Republic Police Force
	Somalia	ZSU	Soviet-made self-propelled air
UNRF	Ugandan National Rescue Front		defence artillery (Russian:
UNSYG	United Nations Secretary General		Zenitnaya Samokhodnaya U
UPA	Ugandan People's Army (see UPF)		stanovka, 'independent anti-
UPC	Uganda People's Congress		aircraft piece')
UPCDA	Uganda People's Christian	ZU	Soviet-made air defence artillery
	Democratic Alliance/Army (an		series (Russian: Zenitnaya
	alternative for the acronym		Ustanovka, 'anti-aircraft piece')

Chapter One

The Rhodesian COIN War, 1972—1980

Perhaps one of the best-documented COIN wars in Africa, the Rhodesian war is in many ways more misunderstood than others that have taken place since then. Although a political settlement ended the war and subsequent events swept away the society that had steadfastly maintained the COIN effort with dwindling resources in the face of international sanctions, many lessons of the war were adapted and refined in other southern African conflicts. Ex-Rhodesian personnel were involved in these COIN wars as well. Ideas rooted in a mixture of United States doctrine painfully learned from Vietnam that had been merged with Rhodesian experience in its past conflicts were instrumental in forcing a political settlement, imperfect though it was, that in many ways represented the first crack in the iron cordon that the USSR and its allies were attempting to draw around the area. The COIN doctrine and tactics learned from the Rhodesian war as taken over by the South Africans were put to extremely good use and completed the frustration of Soviet military designs on the southern part of the continent. Ironically, the Zimbabwe military, successor to the Rhodesian, fought a barbarous and costly anti-guerrilla campaign in Matabeleland shortly after the end of the Rhodesian war; few lessons from the latter appear to have been retained by the new security forces.

PHASES OF THE CONFLICT

Much of the history of the Rhodesian conflict, which lasted from 1962 to 1980, lies outside the purview of the present study, which focuses on the period from 1975 onward. This was the period in which the security situation suffered a sharp downward turn due to the insurgents' ability to have free use of newly-independent Mozambique as a base.

■ **Incipient stage of the insurgency, 1962–1965** Minor armed incursions began, 1962. ZANU formed from ZAPU, 1963. First members of ZANU were sent to China for training during this period.

■ **The insurgents begin to receive Soviet/WP and Chinese training and equipment, 1965–1972** This period was initiated by the Unilateral Declaration of Independence (UDI), presided over by Ian Smith's government. Political alignments crystallised, with the UK supporting majority rule. During this period both ZANU and ZAPU external elements began incursions into Rhodesia, marking the beginning of the armed struggle controlled by Soviet and Chinese-trained insurgents.

■ **The insurgency attains strategic proportions, 1972–1975** During this phase insurgent infiltration by ZANU into Rhodesia from Mozambican bases south of the Zambezi began, compounding security problems. The first Operational Zone was established. The period ended with the independence of Mozambique and an actively hostile state thus established on the eastern border of Rhodesia.

■ **Rearguard action against the inevitable, 1975–1979** The penultimate phase of the war. ZANU moved its forces to Mozambique, leaving ZAPU and its armed wing, the Zimbabwe People's Republican Army (ZIPRA), in Zambia to preside over a largely useless conventional force that presented an easy target for Rhodesian security forces. The latter divided the country into Operational Zones, but had already lost large parts of the interior to the insurgents, especially ZANU, whose grassroots organisation provided it with a large internal as well as external power base.

■ **From Rhodesia to Zimbabwe, 1979–1980**, with final peace talks preceded by an intensive episode of violence as Rhodesian security forces conducted increasingly destructive raids against Zambia and Mozambique to thwart ZANU and ZAPU attempts to improve their positions at time of settlement.

Despite the protracted period of guerrilla warfare, the insurgency by ZIPRA and ZANLA never was able to develop into the final stage (Stage III) of a classical insurgency, the 'War of Movement', due to the ability of the Rhodesian forces to locate and engage the enemy. Despite the decision to effectively relinquish certain areas of the country to the insurgents (notably the Tribal Trust Lands, or TTLs), there were never totally 'no go' areas for the security forces, which could and did routinely traverse them or target units or bases in them at will. The Rhodesian border, ever harder to defend, still remained relatively secure in a sense in that insurgents could infiltrate across it but that no 'classical' invasion ever took place. Indeed, the raids of 1979 by the Rhodesian Army against ZANLA in Zambia effectively derailed any such plans.

BACKGROUND TO THE CONFLICT

The Unilateral Declaration of Independence (UDI) on 11 November 1965 ushered in the final era of Rhodesian history. The UDI, engineered by the Rhodesian Front government of Prime Minister Ian Smith, was in effect through 1980. Despite the opposition of the United Kingdom to UDI and the subsequent imposition of sanctions by the United Nations in response to British requests, Rhodesia was able to maintain its independence for 15 years in the face of a large-scale, well-organised, and heavily supported Black African nationalist insurgency. Legislation was passed both before and after UDI by the Rhodesian legislature restricting the political freedom of the African population. Black nationalist opposition to UDI and the Smith government had been suppressed by the mid-1960s, with the two largest parties, the National Democratic Party (NDP) and the Zimbabwe African People's Union (ZAPU), banned in 1961 and 1962 respectively, driven into exile or underground. Despite widespread discontent among Black Africans over restrictions on their political freedom and economic opportunities under UDI, the nationalist movement, led by Joshua Nkomo, Reverend Ndabaningi Sithole, and Robert Mugabe, was riven by leadership disputes and accomplished little through the late 1960s. In 1963 the Zimbabwe African National Union (ZANU) was formed after Nkomo, based at Dar es-Salaam in Tanzania, had ousted Sithole and Mugabe from ZAPU.

By the late 1960s the Black African resistance to the UDI government was dominated by the two largest movements, Nkomo's ZAPU, in Dar es-Salaam, and ZANU, led by Sithole and Mugabe. The latter, a Marxist, gradually gained a dominant role through the early 1970s at the expense of Sithole, a Congregationalist minister. Nkomo, who had started his career in Bulawayo as a labour union leader, was also a professed Marxist. Despite these apparent outward ideological similarities, the Black Nationalists were divided along ethnic lines. Nkomo's ZAPU was dominated by the Ndebele (Matabele) ethnic group, while ZANU was the resistance vehicle for the majority Shona people of Southern Rhodesia. Cold War politics also played a major role in separating the two groups. ZAPU was backed by the Soviet Union and the Warsaw Pact, while ZANU received its support from Communist China. Despite training and other support for both groups by Algeria, China, Tanzania,

Zambia, and (after the mid-1970s) Ethiopia, the two groups remained hostile to one another throughout the conflict.

ZAPU and ZANU differed considerably on the methodology for toppling the UDI regime. ZAPU, with its Soviet backing, emphasised the formation of a conventional force to invade Rhodesia and forcibly establish its rule. Based in Zambia, Tanzania, and Angola, the ZAPU armed wing accomplished little beyond raids into northern Rhodesian border areas. Its concentrations of personnel in conventional military camps and bases made it a repeated target of punishing cross-border raids by Rhodesian security forces. ZANU, on the other hand, established an alliance with the Black Nationalist movement fighting for independence in neighbouring Mozambique. This movement, the Mozambique Liberation Front (FRELIMO), had by the early 1970s, with assistance from various Communist countries and using bases in Tanzania, established territorial control over large areas of northern Mozambique. It soon found a ready ally in ZANU, which it assisted to set up bases north of the Zambezi River in Tete province. ZANU sought to build popular support for a broad-based insurgency inside Rhodesia, a move that ultimately proved the more successful. By the late 1970s most of the insurgents active inside the country's borders were from the Zimbabwe African National Liberation Army (ZANLA), the ZANU military wing.

OVERVIEW OF THE RHODESIAN CONFLICT, 1972–1980

THE CONFLICT IN PERSPECTIVE

The Rhodesian conflict has been documented extensively elsewhere, and our discussion focuses heavily upon the lessons learned from the conflict as a prelude to the large-scale superpower confrontations of the late 1970s and the 1980s. During the incipient stage of the insurgency, 1962-1965, the strategic stage was set for UDI and the ensuing insurgent war. Through the end of the 1960s and into the 1970s the security situation remained relatively under control, although the Smith regime was unable to contain the growth of nationalism among Rhodesia's black population. It was this incipient nationalism that was taken over by ZAPU and later ZANU, both Marxist movements. This stage of the conflict, when the insurgency was taken over by communist-trained guerrillas, 1965-1972, saw ZANU especially reorganise and change its strategy. Agreements were made with FRELIMO insurgents in Mozambique for cooperation and to seek bases for infiltration.

The Zimbabwean nationalist insurgents stepped up their fight against the Rhodesian government from 1972. This was the period in which the insurgency attained strategic proportions (1972-1975). Rearmed and better-trained insurgents, using Soviet and Chinese weaponry, began to establish zones of de facto territorial control inside Rhodesia, despite subsequent efforts to control them with border minefields and cross-border raids to disrupt their base camps and LOCs. The collapse of Portuguese rule in Angola and Mozambique after the April 1974 coup in Lisbon signalled the start of a major power shift in southern Africa. South Africa remained the only ally of the regime, but an uncertain one at that. Many Rhodesians now believed that it was but a matter of time before black majority rule came about. The main purpose of the counterinsurgency was to ensure that the Zimbabwean nationalists would be forced to make concessions to the white minority in any final settlement.

The period from 1975 to 1979 was the rearguard action against the inevitable. During this phase the Rhodesian security forces continued to strike at external targets but also sought greater internal controls on the black population. White manpower at this time was under severe strain, and the government was ultimately forced to increase the recruitment and fielding of security units with blacks in them, with blacks of military age eligible for call-up by 1978. The PRC-backed ZANU emerged as the main threat in this period, as ZAPU and ZIPRA still remained a client of the Soviets. It was ZANU and ZANLA, however, under Robert Mugabe and his supporters, that continued to pose the greatest threat, especially after the independence of Mozambique and the opening of the entire border with Rhodesia to insurgent activity. During this period the military proficiency of the Rhodesian forces was at its peak.

The end of the conflict came in 1980. Negotiating an end to the war, 1979–1980, was in many ways like the previous period in that it was also a rearguard action. The security forces, however, were now kept busy ensuring that Zimbabwean insurgents obtained as little advantage as possible in attempting to pre-empt a settlement. The security forces, now working for the black transitional government (from June 1979) continued their fight to deter insurgents from short-circuiting a settlement, with their efforts especially directed against ZANU conventional forces in Zambia. However, ZAPU bases in Mozambique continued to be attacked as well.

Throughout the conflict the security forces performed superbly at the tactical/operational level. The high quality of personnel and training overcame the disadvantages faced by a force that was required by the arms embargo to use older, often obsolete, weapons and equipment. Improvisation on the use and reuse of such equipment, ingenious modifications to suit local conditions, and innovations to counter the use of mine warfare by insurgents became a hallmark of the Rhodesian security forces. Yet in the end the inability to sustain a conflict that tied up such a large percentage of manpower in the field, combined with the loss of support from Portugal and even South Africa, proved to be the writing on the wall. By the late 1970s most white Rhodesians knew that it was only a matter of time before their political control and thus their way of life was to be swept away by a new order under black African majority rule.

THE EARLY PHASES OF THE INSURGENCY UP TO 1972

The conflict began in 1964 with three acts of terrorism that resulted in one person killed and the apprehension or elimination of three groups of black African nationalists. Of note at this time was the attempted infiltration of a group into Rhodesia from Zambia whose car was found to contain plastic explosive. Investigation revealed that the Soviet-trained team planned to conduct sabotage against targets in Bulawayo.

1964 was also a year marked by infighting within ZAPU, during which Sithole's forces broke away and formed ZANU. Considerable infighting among the black African nationalists took place at this time in the townships in Salisbury and Bulawayo. Eventually both ZAPU and ZANU were banned and the principal leaders apprehended and incarcerated, including Nkomo, Sithole, Mugabe, and Chinamano. The banning of the two black nationalist movements and the imprisonment of its key leadership had the effect of driving the movement underground inside Rhodesia and forcing minor figures abroad to build up an external network. From this date the African National Congress (ANC) of Bishop Abel Muzorewa emerged as an internal spokesman for the insurgents and dissidents who had fled to Zambia, Botswana, and other countries.

The next series of incursions took place in 1966, during which two whites were killed in April. In all, three groups of infiltrators were eliminated. 1967 was marked by further small incursions in the early part of the year. However, in August a major development occurred, with a group of 90 black nationalists crossing from Zambia east of Victoria Falls. This group was made up of ZAPU as well as South African black nationalists of the ANC. The aim of the group was to establish themselves in the Tjolotjo TTL and form an internal base of operations. However, they were detected by the security forces and 47 killed and 20 captured in a three-week period. The remainder fled to Botswana where they were detained and deported to Zambia. The security forces had four killed, the first casualties in hostile action inside Rhodesia since 1897.

The period 1967-1971 was marked by repeated attempts by the insurgents to infiltrate into Rhodesia, mostly from Zambia, and establish themselves in TTLs. However, at first their operations to do so were done in large groups which left an easy trail for trackers. In order to infiltrate with the least chance of detection, they were forced to chose difficult terrain which also degraded their overland movement and tended to isolate them from their intended support base. Security forces were also able, once they did detect the insurgents, to fix and engage them with little concern that the operations would involve local civilians. Two major incursions in March and August 1968 met with disaster for the would-be infiltrators. In the March infiltration the insurgents established bases from the Zambezi River to the Escarpment but were detected by a game ranger. The 123-man group was engaged over a period of several weeks and 69 killed; the rest fled back to Zambia. In August an entire infiltration group of 30 was detected when one insurgent deserted and informed security forces; 25 were killed and the rest captured within a 48-hour period. The March 1968 attempted infiltration, like the August 1967 one, consisted of half ZAPU and half South African ANC. The presence of the latter prompted the South African government to send police (SAP) to assist Rhodesian security forces, as the plan for the joint infiltrations had been for the ANC members to use the ZAPU bases, once established, to infiltrate into the Republic of South Africa (RSA) itself. The SAP was to remain deployed in Rhodesia through 1975.

After 1968 the insurgents began to infiltrate in smaller groups, with ZAPU targeting the Wankie area and ZANU the Zambezi valley. Throughout late 1972 the security forces were able to deal with these attempted incursions. Indeed, a false sense of security began to develop among the Rhodesian white population that they would be able to handily deal with attempts by the black nationalists to infiltrate. As a result, no serious efforts were made to gain the active support of Rhodesia's black population, especially those in the TTLs. It proved to be a fatal error, as the resentment by the black African population remained largely undetected or ignored, and was later (from the early 1970s) to assist Robert Mugabe's ZANU operatives as they built internal support networks for insurgents based in Mozambique.

This early period of the war ended with a major internal development among the insurgents. As the split between ZAPU and ZANU continued, the reaction to the reverses at the hands of the security forces differed markedly. ZAPU remained effectively out of the conflict as an efficient guerrilla organisation. While its members continued to receive training in the USSR, Cuba, and North Korea, and established a large conventional presence in Zambia, they proved no match for Rhodesian security forces, which were constantly developing greater reactive capability to incidents of attempted infiltration. It was left to ZANU to make a major review of both strategy and tactics, and develop a means to counter the increased COIN proficiency of the Rhodesian security forces. This entailed application of the guerrilla warfare theories of Mao Zedong, a major change that was seen from 1971 onwards.

ZANU turned away from operations in remote areas that avoided contact with the black African population. Instead, smaller groups were infiltrated. Most, however, did not have the mission of conducting attacks on government or white targets. Instead, they began to organise internal support networks in the TTLs and other black areas, taking advantage of the continued denial by Rhodesian whites of the black population's political and economic aspirations. Through 1971 and 1972 a series of logistical support networks was established among the Kore Kore in the north-east. Government informers and sympathisers were systematically identified and dealt with as a first step to deny the security forces intelligence about insurgent movements. By 1971 ZANU resumed infiltrations in earnest in the north-east, using small groups that moved in via Mozambican bases. Mozambique itself was the scene of an insurgent war against the Portuguese, and their security forces in areas bordering north-east Rhodesia were hard-pressed by FRELIMO insurgents. In the next two years Tete province would be occupied by FRELIMO, who had ethnic connections with ZANU (both comprised Shona groups) and were sympathetic to their liberation aims. ZANU took advantage of the 1971 rainy season to establish their first internal networks in the Kore Kore area, without any significant notice by local administrators.

THE INSURGENCY ATTAINS STRATEGIC PROPORTIONS, 1972–1975

By 1972 the Portuguese security forces in Mozambique had begun to lose control of Tete province, including the 'pedicle' that bordered Rhodesia, Zambia, and Malawi, to FRELIMO insurgents. The latter were sympathetic to the Rhodesian insurgents, especially ZANU, due to ethnic ties (i.e., Shona and related groups) between the two. ZANU began to receive assistance from FRELIMO to open a new front along the north-eastern border of Rhodesia with Mozambique. The Kore Kore, historically suspicious of outside rule in general and that of the UDI government in particular, were successfully targeted by ZANU in the early 1970s to provide the insurgents with a major internal base as well as a fertile recruiting ground.

The first real insurgent activity on a strategic scale came in December 1972. On the 21st a series of coordinated attacks on white farmsteads in the Centenary district were planned by ZANU. Only one, unsuccessful, attack took place prematurely due to a misunderstanding of instructions, and security force response neutralised the attackers. However, the follow-up investigation to the attacks indicated that a new phase of the conflict had begun, marked by a number of serious developments.

■ First, the local Kore Kore not only had provided no information on impending attacks or movements of insurgents, but remained uncooperative. In many cases informant nworks vanished within weeks as insurgents consolidated their control over local communities through propaganda or coercion.

■ ZANU had prepared its attacks carefully, ensuring passive support from the locals, and had implanted an insurgent network in the north-east which ensured continued local support. This was shown by continued attacks on farms in the area over the next several weeks. More ZANU insurgents infiltrated into the area, reinforcing the first successful ZANU internal base inside Rhodesia.

■ The inability of the security forces to prevent ZANU organising its support networks and infiltrating operatives into Rhodesia was not lost on the local black African population, further eroding with them the authority of the central government and the credibility of the security forces.

■ The security forces themselves faced demoralisation over their inability to locate and engage the ZANU groups responsible for many of the attacks. This included the inability to use local sources to provide intelligence about the insurgents as had been the case up to this time.

It was in this context of increasing security force concern that the first of the joint operational sectors (OPS), Hurricane, was established following the December attacks. It supported an operational strategy that consisted of: 'Large external operations to turn off the tap; a cordon sanitaire with warning devices, patrolled and backed by a 20 km wide no-go area; population control, consisting of Protected Villages, food control, curfews, and (eventually) martial law, and massive psychological action.'[1]

Most of the above COIN elements were already practised to some degree, but Hurricane made them components of a unified strategy for the first time. The strategy was to be directed toward the Mozambique border areas and regions to the north where the Kore Kore dwelt. The initial success of Hurricane was to prompt the central government to pattern new operational sectors after it. Hurricane began operating in earnest almost immediately, with its first HQ at Centenary, then later at Bindura and finally at Salisbury itself as the scope of operations increased. The initial phase of Hurricane was marked with a degree of success.

■ Hurricane was managed by the Rhodesian Army using a joint security committee system similar to that already used in the 1960s and proven successful.
■ OPS Hurricane initially had considerable security force assets–Army, Air Force, and British South African Police (BSAP)–to draw from. This included most regular assets of the Army and Air Force as well as sixteen companies of the BSAP.
■ Available assets allowed the formulation of a COIN programme based on two key requirements. These were to cut off the flow of insurgents (primarily ZANU) from bases in Mozambique and to control local populations among which they had already established support networks.

Hurricane's ambitious agenda was based on the presupposition that initial successes would snowball into a degradation of insurgent capabilities and that stemming ZANU infiltration and attacks as well as continuing massive population control would be successful. However, both of these main goals of Hurricane eventually began to prove impossible to meet. In response to Hurricane, the insurgents began to widen their own scope of operations, with new fronts opened on other border areas. This in turn prompted the security forces to respond in like fashion. However, by 1976 (see below) the security situation had once again become all but unmanageable both in Hurricane and elsewhere, prompting the creation of new operational sectors.

Nevertheless, from early 1973 the response by the security forces in creating Hurricane gave the central government cause for optimism. The ability to establish a joint operational sector with the majority of available security forces in Rhodesia had a definite impact the next two years. This was due primarily to the ability to use most security forces to their maximum effect in part of eastern Rhodesia. The objective of the activates associated with Hurricane was to build a cordon sanitaire at the border and across key infiltration routes, from which the local residents had been removed to resettlement areas. Infiltrating insurgents could thus be more easily tracked and engaged. Meanwhile, the resettled population, located in Protected Villages (PVs) or Consolidated Villages (CVs), would be more easy to control and monitor.

The security forces were able to benefit from a new communications system and new airfields constructed throughout the country. The ability to deploy troops in affected areas in sufficient numbers to effectively counter infiltration as well as to root out insurgent infrastructure put the insurgents on the defensive throughout late 1974. Four new districts were set up to assist in internal control, namely Centenary, Rushinga, Mudzi, and Mutasa. These were primarily aimed at reimposing government rule on rural areas, especially those inhabited by the Kore Kore. The cordon sanitaire protecting the border was begun at this time as well, although insurgents had already become established internally and the exclusion zone proved unable to entirely prevent further border crossings. However, at first the establishment of 'no-go' areas proved a significant help against the insurgents, with the first set up on 17 May 1973 on the Mozambique border. Others were to follow as the population was removed from intended 'free-fire' zones.

The removal of the black African population to government-monitored settlements began in earnest in late 1973, but was earlier imposed (19 January 1973) as a form of collective punishment on local communities some of whose members assisted insurgents.

The forced removal of a community that was generally politically inactive except for the actions of a few ZANU or ZAPU supporters in its midst, however, soon had the effect of turning whole populations against the central government. The methodical consolidation of local populations into PVs/CVs began at the end of 1973 following intensified insurgent activity inside Rhodesia. The PV/CV scheme was ultimately to result in the resettlement of 750,000 rural black Africans in 200 or so PVs. A new branch of the security forces, the Guard Force, was later to be developed to monitor the resettled villagers.

Throughout most of 1973 the security forces attempted to make OPS Hurricane work as effectively as possible. However, in July they were unable to prevent the first of many incidents of the abduction of schoolchildren by ZANU insurgents. The aim of the latter was to take them to Mozambique for training as insurgent cadre. The central problem of the security forces at this time was the firm establishment of ZANU/ZANLA inside Rhodesia itself throughout the north-eastern part of the country and their inability to contain the further spread of insurgent networks or obtain any support from most of the rural population in the region's TTLs. From late 1973 the Kore Kore remained the ethnic group most affected by the insurgents. The inability of the security forces to control the population in the affected area is shown by the statistics: 179 insurgent casualties recorded for 1973 as against 44 security force members and twelve white civilians. At the end of 1973, 145 insurgents still reportedly remained active inside Hurricane. Despite the presence of most of the Rhodesian security forces in the sector, manpower remained a problem. This resulted in the extension of national service for whites from nine months to a full year from December 1973.

Most of the activity associated with Hurricane was designed to counter infiltration from Mozambique by ZANU. However, Zambia and ZIPRA were not forgotten. On 9 January 1973 the border was closed to traffic (except copper), a move which prompted Zambian President Kaunda to utilise other routes for Zambian copper exports rather than send them through Rhodesia and South Africa.

1974 was to prove a decisive year for the conflict in a number of ways. The security forces made significant headway against the insurgents in the north-east after the PV programme was applied to the Chiweshe and Madziwa TTLs during Operations 'Overload' and 'Overload Two' (July–August and August–October respectively). In the former operation alone, 47,000 were removed to 21 PVs in a six-week period. The insurgents, deprived of their support base in the area, were forced north and then attacked with most of Rhodesia's security assets brought to bear against them. By late 1974 the insurgents, mainly ZANU, had incurred very heavy losses, mostly in north-east Rhodesia. This prompted ZIPRA to reopen its Zambia front in north-west Rhodesia, resulting in complaints by the Rhodesian government against that of Zambia in October.

Despite insurgent attempts to counter government operations, however, most of 1974 saw a continued string of government gains against them. Battlefield successes were paired with a number of civil measures. Among these were the inclusion of some district commissioners in security operations, extending to 60 days the length of detention without trial, and allowing the government to impose work requirements on local populations for the maintenance of key infrastructure. The security forces about this time initiated a series of monetary rewards for information supporting COIN efforts, from recovery of weapons used by ZANLA and ZIPRA to the capture of senior insurgent leaders.[2] However, the main gains against the insurgents were made on the battlefield, and were the result of a new combat tactic used by the security forces. This was the Fire Force, which optimised the mobility and firepower assets available to security forces: 'Initially [the Fire Force] consisted of three elements: G-cars, K-cars and members of the Rhodesian Light Infantry as the fighting force on the ground. G-cars were normally helicopters armed with twin Browning machine guns and each carried four troops. K- or kill-cars were Alouette helicopters armed with 20mm cannon to provide fire support. At a later stage Lynx fixed-wing aircraft were included to provide further close support as well as a DC-3 Dakota aircraft which could carry twenty paratroopers to be deployed as stop-groups. Fire Force call-ups normally originated from Security Force operation posts on high ground which then "talked" the aircraft onto the target.[3]

The first Fire Force was formed at Mount Darwin and Centenary in June 1974, and proved quite successful, being based on the successes used in inserting security forces in close proximity to insurgents in previous operations in the Madziwa and Kandeya TTLs.

The end of 1974 saw the acquiescence by the government in demands to negotiate with ZAPU and ZANU, under continuing pressure from the international community but also from South Africa. The latter put the Smith government under pressure to engage actively in talks with nationalist leaders, probably knowing that such talks would be unproductive at best, in order to relieve political pressure and the threat of intensified economic sanctions against the RSA by the international community. As Rhodesia's transport lifelines passed through the RSA, it had little choice but to comply. As a gesture of the Rhodesian government's commitment to negotiations, a ceasefire and security force stand down took effect in December, and senior black nationalist leaders were released. However, this was not to have the intended effect of promoting talks: 'By the 11th December 1974 it was estimated that there were only 70 terrorists left within Rhodesia. These 70 were of course hard-core terrorists and included Rex Nhongo amongst them. On the 11th December 1974 Rhodesia accepted the South African initiated detente exercise or ceasefire. Militarily, this may have been a mistake. With only 70 left it would have been a matter of weeks, possibly months, before they were totally eliminated. However, the ceasefire was accepted which meant that the SAP [police] were confined to their camps and were not to do anything other than patrol the immediate vicinity of those camps for their own protection. The Rhodesian Security Forces were restricted to non-offensive patrolling. What this meant was that the 70 hard-core terrorists were able to move out of Rhodesia with impunity, visiting all kraals en route out, stating that they had won the war and had brought Ian Smith to the negotiating table. It must be added that 11th December 1974 also saw the release of all the Nationalist leaders from detention to engage in talks with the Government. Psychologically, therefore, the Government lost a tremendous amount of face with the Kore Kore people who were influenced by the terrorists and of course with the majority of the law abiding black population of Rhodesia who saw the rabid nationalists being released from detention. It was now known that it is unwise to enter into these sort of negotiations with terrorists unless there are guarantees that they will abide by the rules. For example, on the 16th December 1974, five days after the ceasefire had been accepted, a group of terrorists (under the leadership of one Herbert Shugu, subsequently a "top" terrorist training commander, last heard of at Tembue base camp) sent an emissary to a South African camp with an invitation to them to come and talk surrender terms. The SAP, somewhat naively, accepted the invitation and were ambushed on the Mazoe high level bridge where six of them were killed. So much for the ceasefire.'[4]

The nationalist leaders released included Robert Mugabe, who rapidly consolidated his control over ZANU and its infrastructure in Mozambique by March 1975, forcing out the Reverend Ndabaningi Sithole. Eventually Mugabe was to make his way from Rhodesia to Mozambique, and move the entire ZANU/ZANLA operation there, where under the new FRELIMO government it was to receive refuge and active military assistance. As for the ceasefire and attempts at detente, they collapsed by 10 January 1975. In mid-January a group of 60 ZANU infiltrated from Mozambique, effectively ending any pretence of a ceasefire. The group was speedily neutralised, with the now mature Hurricane operational/tactical COIN apparatus working at its best. By the year's end there were only three groups of ten insurgents still active in eastern Rhodesia.

However, the war for the hearts and minds of Rhodesia's black African population had been lost long before. Any residual attempts at credibility on the government's part had failed in the 1974 ceasefire fiasco. The blacks saw the ceasefire and release of detainees (especially without any substantial concessions by the insurgents) as a sign of weakness. ZANU continued to organise during the ceasefire, and outside Rhodesia large numbers of insurgents continued to be trained and receive Soviet and Chinese weapons and equipment at bases in Zambia and Mozambique. A further blow to white prestige was the collapse of the Portuguese administration in Mozambique after the 1974 coup. FRELIMO's takeover there reinforced ZANU propaganda that an armed insurgent struggle not only could be successful but that it would henceforth be a strong ally for the nationalists.

REARGUARD ACTION AGAINST THE INEVITABLE, 1975-1979

The penultimate phase of the Rhodesian conflict was actually initiated by the coup in Portugal in April 1974. The political fallout from this event was realised the following year as Portugal's African possessions became independent, Mozambique included. Once FRELIMO became established in Maputo, it began to give active assistance to the black nationalists, especially ZANU. From late 1974 Mozambique was used by ZANU as its main base, with Rhodesian blacks who fled across the border being quickly trained and fielded as insurgents for infiltration along the country's eastern border.

The new-found strengths of ZANU in its Mozambican bases were clearly evident by early 1976. On 21 January the first group of a three-pronged infiltration operation was detected near Nyampanda. However, of the 90 insurgents only four were killed and one captured. The information later developed indicated that subsequent attacks were to be directed along the entire Mozambican border. Another, by a group of 130, took place in late February in Melsetter and the remaining infiltration, by the last large group, took place in March in the far south-east. OPS Hurricane, effective for the past three years, had been outflanked. In response, the security forces established OPS Thrasher and OPS Repulse in February and May 1976 respectively.

OPS Thrasher was at first designed to complement Hurricane by covering the border with Mozambique south of the Nyampanda area. Its HQ, JOC Thrasher, was at Umtali, HQ of 3 Brigade, and extended along the border opposite Manica province in Mozambique. However, the use by ZANU of bases in Gaza province in Mozambique forced the security forces to establish OPS Repulse in the south-east, with its HQ, JOC Repulse, at Fort Victoria, the HQ of 4 Brigade. Part of the aim of Repulse was to provide security for the newly-opened Rutenga rail line to South Africa. JOC Hurricane continued to cover northern Rhodesia from Lake Kariba to Nyampanda, with the HQ at Salisbury.

In 1976 the Soviets began to become heavily involved with the effort to support ZANU in its Mozambican bases. They were busily involved in building up the Mozambican military (the FPLM or FAM), and took this opportunity to attempt to woo Mugabe and ZANU from PRC influence by competing with the Chinese to supply equipment and training. This substantially benefited ZANU and ZANLA, although Mugabe, conscious of continued Soviet support to his rival Nkomo and ZAPU/ZIPRA, remained wary of the USSR through the post-independence period. In 1976 the Zimbabwe People's Army (ZIPA) was founded in an attempt to eliminate the ZANU-ZAPU rivalry, but its bases, in Tanzania, were remote from the fighting in Rhodesia and, due to the tribal basis of the rivalry between ZANU and ZAPU, the attempt to combine elements of both in ZIPA merely gave this rivalry a new theatre for play. Interfactional fighting in the Tanzanian camps eventually discredited ZIPA; over 600 recruits died in the internecine conflicts. Though ZIPA did manage to infiltrate groups into Rhodesia, they were rarely effective apart from committing small-scale terrorist-type acts, and the groups rarely held together for long.

Meanwhile, ZAPU resumed activity from its Zambian bases. ZANU and ZIPRA had earlier been threatened by the OAU Liberation Committee with a cut-off of funding if it did not resume action against the white government. Accordingly, in mid-1976 ZIPRA groups resumed infiltration across the Zambezi. These attempts, though not as successful as the ZANU infiltrations, were still a matter of concern as they were led by Soviet-trained operatives and were well-armed and supplied. Many infiltrations crossed the Zambezi and attempted to implant groups among the Ndebele population in south-east Rhodesia, with mixed success. The attempts prompted the security forces in August 1976 to establish a fourth JOC and OPS, Tangent, with its HQ at Bulawayo, location of 1 Brigade HQ. Tangent included the length of the Botswana border and the Zambezi border area to Lake Kariba. The increased COIN infrastructure eventually required a national joint centre. This resulted in the creation of Combined Operations (COMOPS) in March 1977, under Lieutenant General Walls, a former SAS commander.

The security situation, despite continued expansion of the COIN infrastructure, continued on its precarious course. Three new operational sectors had stretched the security forces thin. South Africa, which had earlier shown itself willing to put pressure on Rhodesia in return for a reduction in international pressure to make its own internal reforms, announced on 9 August that it supported majority rule in Rhodesia. This was followed by the subsequent withdrawal of 26 of the 40 helicopters it had on loan to the Rhodesian security forces, further degrading the latter's COIN capabilities. In October 1978 the Rhodesians evaded sanctions to import eleven Bell 205 helicopters, which partly remedied the loss of the Alouette IIIs returned to South Africa. They proved difficult to maintain, however, and by June 1979 only five remained operational, the others falling victim to accidents or being used for spare parts.

Meanwhile, political manoeuvring by the black nationalists continued. With the Geneva Conference of 1976, the UK and US governments decided to engage the Patriotic Front (PF) as the main focus of negotiations. The PF had been created under OAU auspices to unite external ZANU and ZAPU elements into a unified entity to lobby for political support for their cause. The nine-week conference produced little apart from this recognition; however, it was a significant political victory for the nationalists.

The security situation continued to deteriorate in 1977, with an average of one man per day being killed in the security forces. The kill ratio, which had been 1:10 in favour of the security forces, began to drop, and by 1978 was 1:7. At this time Rhodesia's white population began to show its manpower limitations to support the COIN effort. National Service was extended to two years, and whites in the 38–50 age group called up. Defence expenditure now absorbed 44 per cent of Rhodesia's budget.

However, ZANLA and ZIPRA infiltration from Zambia and Mozambique continued to increase. ZAPU had begun to take a leaf from ZANU's book and seek to establish itself in TTLs in the east. ZANU for its part attempted to infiltrate as far west as possible to ensure that its internal influence was as extensive as possible, and to block ZAPU from extending its control outside predominantly Ndebele areas. This manoeuvring for control of the population indicated that both movements realised that it was only a matter of time before the white government would be replaced and that control of TTLs would enhance the electoral prospects of whatever group controlled them at the time. Engagements between bands of ZANLA and ZIPRA took place in the Maranda and Belingwe TTLs, reflecting the deep level of competition that had begun for population control by the two factions.

1977 ended with the first action of a new facet in COIN strategy. This was the November raid by the Rhodesian Special Air Service (SAS), the Rhodesian Light Infantry (RLI), and the Air Force on ZANLA bases in the Chimoio and Tembue areas in Mozambique. The unexpected attack killed at least 1,200 insurgents and possibly as many as 2,000. Most died in the ground attack from the Umtali area against the huge ZANLA base camp complex near Chimoio known as 'New Farm' or Vanduzi in Operation 'Dingo'. The raid, though condemned in the international press, was not only designed to show the insurgents that they were not safe in external bases, but was the first of a number of 'externals' geared to keeping both ZANU and ZAPU off balance and preventing them from continuing the massive infiltrations into Rhodesia's TTLs. The policy was only partly successful, as infiltrations were to continue. ZANU/ZANLA was better able to withstand the onslaught than ZAPU/ZIPRA.

Late 1977 also saw the extension of the war to the Midlands, with a large ZANLA bomb exploding in a store in Salisbury, killing eleven and wounding 76. This incident and the fear of more prompted the establishment of the central OPS, Grapple, which completed the coverage of all of the nation by a COIN territorial structure. The establishment of Grapple could not prevent further terrorist-type attacks, however. In December the fuel storage tanks outside Salisbury were attacked and severely damaged, adversely affecting Rhodesia's fuel storage capabilities. Grapple was not the last of the OPS established. The special OPS Splinter was set up in June 1978 to counter a new tactic used by the insurgents, namely infiltration from Lake Kariba from Zambia to the southern shore, which had a long, indented coastline that favoured such attempts.

September 1978 saw the first successful attack by the insurgents on a Rhodesian commercial aircraft. ZIPRA insurgents brought down an Air Rhodesia Viscount with a Soviet-made SA-7, then killed ten of the eighteen survivors. The attack indicated a new capability possessed by the insurgents, who had hitherto used only anti-aircraft artillery against Rhodesian Air Force planes and helicopters.

FROM RHODESIA TO ZIMBABWE, 1979-1980

The final stage of the war was a holding action by the security forces to allow the transitional government of Bishop Muzorewa to arrange a final settlement to bring an end to the conflict. The government resulting from the Internal Settlement, which seated Muzorewa's government in November 1978, in many ways forced ZANU and ZAPU to redouble their efforts to discredit the new regime. External operations dominated the publicity in this phase of the conflict, but significant internal developments took place as well. Martial law, first introduced in September 1978, was extended in January 1979. Security forces were unable to prevent the infiltration of ZIPRA groups from Zambia despite major cross-border raids. One group used an SA-7 to bring down a second Air Rhodesia Viscount, killing all 59 aboard. On the Mozambican front, ZANU continued its infiltration as well.

The manpower situation for the security forces was now critical. In March whites aged 50 to 59 were made subject to call-up in urban areas. The government had already begun to recruit ever-growing numbers of black Africans for the security forces, but acted too late in this. The previous year it had made black Africans in the 18–25 age group subject to call-up. A major development in recruiting this manpower source had been initiated with the creation of the Security Force Auxiliaries. This was a scheme initiated by the Police Special Branch to raise local village militias; other groups directly supported Bishop Muzorewa and Reverend Sithole. After a pilot project in the Msana TTL proved successful, the auxiliary recruitment proceeded in earnest, with 2,000 being recruited by the end of 1978.

External operations by the security forces were to continue through late 1979, not only targeting ZANLA bases in Mozambique but also ZIPRA bases in Zambia. These operations were well-planned and executed, and generally successful in their immediate objectives, namely the destruction of insurgent base camps and host-country support facilities. However, against ZANU/ZANLA in Mozambique they resulted in further dispersal of the forward insurgent bases and made larger bases, which were relocated further away from the border, more difficult to strike at. The security forces ranged ever further into Mozambique to target the insurgents and by mid- and late-1979 had struck at targets that included facilities at the port of Beira as well as other installations in Gaza and Sofala provinces. Security forces faced an ever-increasing degree of risk in these operations, which met with growing ZANLA resistance and reaction by Mozambique's army and border guards. However, the continuation of such operations was cut short by political developments that ended the conflict.

In the external operations against ZIPRA targets in Zambia, however, Rhodesia's security forces were much more successful. ZIPRA had always maintained a large, well armed and equipped conventional force that it planned to use in a strike against Rhodesia's northern border in an attempt to gain control of territory to influence any political outcome. Although such an attempt would have likely failed and cost ZIPRA heavy casualties, the Rhodesians would also have paid dearly for their victory. Thus it was decided to pre-empt such a possibility. In a series of operations from April through July 1979 the Rhodesian Army and Air Force virtually destroyed ZIPRA's capabilities to conduct a conventional attack against Rhodesia. Operations 'Bastille', 'Carpet', and 'Chicory' neutralised the conventional threat from ZIPRA, destroying its logistical support base, cutting LOCs that could support a conventional attack, and even capturing (in Operation 'Carpet') its intelligence HQ.

Security operations continued throughout 1979 up to the December ceasefire that ended seven years of internal conflict. At the time there were at least 22,000 insurgents inside Rhodesia, an increase of 10,000 from the previous year. The security forces had been able to muster at least 60,000 full-time and part-time personnel to monitor the April 1979 elections won by Muzorewa, but could not sustain such a deployment. At the end, the security forces were stretched to the limit. The cumulative impact of manpower limitations and economic sanctions had begun to set in. Moreover, they had been outmanoeuvred by the insurgents' ability to change their tactics to adapt to those of the security forces. 'Ian Smith and his inflexible colleagues had been entirely circumvented in a revolutionary struggle of classic proportions fought on a total frontage. It could be proudly asserted that Rhodesia had never lost a single battle but had most ignominiously lost the war.'[5]

LESSONS LEARNED FROM RHODESIA

This discussion of the Rhodesian war concludes with a review of the key lessons learned from the conflict. The first four emphasise three strengths of the Rhodesian security forces–joint operations, the role of air support, the importance of maintaining bases and LOCs, and undertaking cross-border strikes at insurgent bases and logistics. Intelligence and its uses had its strengths and weaknesses. The last two, however, are areas in which the Rhodesians showed fatal shortcomings.

The principal beneficiaries of the lessons of the Rhodesian war were the South Africans. The 1974 Lisbon coup spurred them into action, as they saw how unprepared the Rhodesians had been in its aftermath. Faced with a nascent conflict in South-West Africa, they took to heart the lessons of the conflict throughout the late 1970s. Not only did they build on the Rhodesians' strengths, but they avoided making their key mistakes, refusing to abandon areas of the country to the insurgents, and building black South-West African units to fight the counterinsurgency effort. Intelligence operations and analysis were emphasised, and used to develop policy. Border security and territorial control were the keys to ensuring that the insurgents never became established among the rural population to the point where they could indoctrinate and mobilise Namibia's African population. While attempts to interdict LOCs were made, they were restricted to the northern part of the country and the use of land mines in some areas. Most of the rest of Namibia was free from insurgent activity.

In fairness to the Rhodesians, however, it must be said that they were in a much more precarious state than the South Africans. The country was less developed and had a much smaller European population – both in absolute and relative terms – than did South Africa. This impacted on its military manpower reserves. In addition, it had difficult borders to defend along three frontiers with Zambia, Mozambique and Botswana.

THE IMPORTANCE OF JOINT OPERATIONS

The counterinsurgency (COIN) organisations that evolved throughout the 1970s eventually came to dominate the armed forces. These COIN elements, which by the end of the conflict consisted of a central HQ Combined Operations (or COMOPS) and subordinate Operational Sectors, was built around a joint command structure that coordinated operations of regular military forces, special forces, and civilian security bodies within its AOR. The constant interaction of different forces at all levels was essential for ensuring a total effort at countering insurgent operations both within Rhodesian territory as well as planning external operations.

The institution of the Fire Force concept in support of the operations sector was the product of a joint effort between the Army and Special Forces on one hand and the Air Force on the other. The Fire Force combined firepower (ground and air) and mobility to create the main means of locating and engaging insurgents. In area operations, cooperation between the military and civil authorities (i.e., between the services and the police) was extremely productive in ensuring that unnecessary redundancy in operations and protective coverage was avoided but at the same time providing for complete coordinated response by all security forces to incidents. While the system was not without its growing pains, it was driven by manpower shortages and the need to establish definite areas of responsibility within the total effort in order to conserve ever-scarce personnel, material, and financial resources.

The establishment of OPS Hurricane at the end of 1972 resulted in three years of gains by the security forces against the insurgents. This was primarily due, however, to the restricted front at the time. Most of Rhodesia's security assets could be brought to bear against ZIPRA and ZANLA attempts to infiltrate. However, ZANU/ZANLA took advantage of the evolving political and military situation in Mozambique to extend its operations southward to outflank Hurricane, and force the security forces to form first Thrasher and then Repulse between February and May of 1976. While Thrasher and Repulse worked as well as Hurricane, taking advantage of three years of experience in COIN operations, they were working with fewer resources per JOC. Despite this predicament, the expansion of the operational sectors to cover the entire country by March 1977 proved generally effective in limiting insurgent attacks on the white population, and would have been more successful had additional security force personnel been available to deploy against the threat.

It is interesting to compare the Rhodesian joint experience with that of the South Africans in northern South-West Africa in the 1980s. Joint operational sectors there were established in 1980, following the end of the Rhodesian conflict. Many lessons learned by the Rhodesians were applied by the South Africans in their joint structures and operations. That they had more success is probably due to their greater manpower and other resources, however.

USE OF AIR OPERATIONS TO SUPPORT COIN

Rhodesia's small and ageing air force was able to provide a remarkable degree of support to the COIN effort. This support consisted of operations by fixed-wing and helicopter formations. The Fire Force concept illustrates the effective integration of air and ground forces to provide an integrated combat unit that maximised firepower and mobility.

However, helicopters were used for rapid redeployment of support personnel and assets as well (e.g., communications, logistics, engineers) to forward areas in support of both reactive operations and area operations. Fixed-wing aircraft were used for a comprehensive range of air–ground support functions. These included reconnaissance, fire support, protection for external operations, air drops of weapons and equipment, and many other activities. All of these operations were coordinated with ground units. This interaction between ground troops (Army/Special Forces/Police) and Air Force developed as the conflict progressed. The lessons learned from the Rhodesian experience in COIN were taken to heart by the South Africans.

Air operations also figured heavily in external operations. The degree of risk in such operations increased as the war progressed, with the greatest threat (and losses) in Mozambique. Helicopters were used to deliver and retrieve personnel engaged in the externals, while fixed-wing aircraft provided the range of air–ground support. At times the Rhodesian Air Force was used to conduct aerial bombing during externals as well, and proved quite effective against targets in Zambia in 1979. Air support to externals provided valuable lessons learned and was again further developed by the South Africans in Angola.

MINE-RESISTANT VEHICLES AND LOC SECURITY

Early in the conflict the Rhodesian government became aware of its inability to patrol most roads in the country to prevent the implanting of land mines. The need for mine-resistant vehicles was the ultimate product of the need to ensure the survivability of military vehicles and especially their occupants. The evolution of successive generations of mine-resistant vehicles, although limited by the restricted industrial base in Rhodesia, exhibited a rapid ability in problem-solving to produce the best possible means of protecting troops in their vehicles. Such protection naturally improved morale. Mine-resistant engineering also ensured that vehicles would suffer less damage and be easier to repair after mine incidents.

Developing mine-resistant vehicles enabled the security forces to retain their mobility on the ground and their ability to transport troops. The importance of this is seen when we look by way of contrast at the situation in Mozambique and Angola, where the Portuguese security forces suffered heavy casualties due to land mines and consequently were forced to restrict ground operations in some areas.

CROSS-BORDER OPERATIONS

Like the South African external operations against targets in Angola in the 1970s and 1980s, cross-border operations by the Rhodesians garnered considerable international attention (and condemnation). They were carefully planned and executed, and achieved their immediate tactical objectives, but did little to change the growing strategic advantage of the insurgents, especially ZANU/ZANLA. However, it was not until the latter phases of the war that such operations had a wider impact, crippling the ZIPRA ability to launch large-scale attacks and weakening some of ZANLA's capabilities for a short period.

The first major external operation took place in late 1978, and was probably inspired by the SADF raid on Cassinga in Angola in May of that year. From late 1978 to late 1979 the Rhodesians undertook at least 21 externals, seven against Zambia, one (an air raid) against Angola, and the rest against Mozambique. The externals in Mozambique became increasingly costly for the security forces as greater distances, improved ZANLA and FPLM ground and air defence, and logistical difficulties made operations ever more hazardous. By the time the war ended, Rhodesia's external operations had provided a virtual syllabus of what to do and not to do in such efforts. South Africa was able to benefit from the Rhodesian experience not only in the smaller, more limited cross-border operations against the ANC but also in the large-scale externals against SWAPO/PLAN bases in southern Angola.

INTELLIGENCE ANALYSIS IN DECISION-MAKING

Rhodesian intelligence capabilities were very good – perhaps at the time the best in sub-Saharan Africa next to those of South Africa – and provided excellent information to planners at the operational level. This resulted in a high success rate for most COIN operations, as well as external operations. However, the Rhodesian leadership often chose to disregard the advice of their intelligence advisers, or, where there were differing opinions, chose the one that most suited their views of the situation. A good example is that of the early 1970s, in which the restructuring of ZANU and ZANLA was generally ignored. The ZANLA threat soon posed the greatest challenge to the Rhodesian security establishment.

Failure by top decision makers was not the only shortcoming in the Rhodesian government's use of intelligence. The regime also failed to develop contingency plans on the basis of intelligence estimates – they, as well as many others in southern Africa, were caught unprepared by the 1974 Lisbon coup, which soon meant that the duration of the Rhodesian COIN effort became little more than an elaborate means of buying time until a political settlement could be arranged on the least disadvantageous terms.

Overall, the Rhodesians were able to obtain, develop, and act upon tactical intelligence extremely well. This they were able to do from the early days of the conflict, and the high success of COIN operations reflects this. However, they were slower learners in the realm of strategic intelligence, and suffered for it throughout most of the war. It appears, however, that the establishment of Marxist regimes in Maputo and Luanda were an incentive for the Rhodesians to improve their intelligence capabilities. Their appraisal of the situation in southern Africa in the late 1970s was quite competent, and they were able to assess quite correctly the reaction, or lack thereof, of various regional and extra-regional states to their cross-border operations before going ahead with raids into Zambia in 1979 that largely destroyed ZIPRA's offensive capabilities. The record shows that the Rhodesians were also able to correctly assess the situation with regard to ZANLA on the Mozambique front as well; however, constraints on military operations, mostly due to logistics, prevented them from having as high a rate of success.

BORDER SECURITY AND TERRITORIAL CONTROL

Failure to maintain the integrity of Rhodesia's borders, along with the decision to abandon control of some areas of Rhodesia to the insurgents, resulted in the establishment of guerrilla bases and LOCs inside the country by the mid-1970s, primarily by ZANLA. The white population was stretched to breaking point to man security formations, and with few exceptions the need for active support from Rhodesia's black population was neglected until late in the insurgency, when most support had been lost. Proper border controls would have been an excellent preventive measure to ensure that infiltrators would have been more preoccupied with surmounting border controls and survival rather than indoctrinating and organising the local population.

The decision in the mid-1970s to construct a security fence and minefield, mostly on Rhodesia's borders with Mozambique, was in theory a good idea. However, the fence and minefield were to have had watchtowers and active patrols to supplement the static defences but because of manpower and financial restraints these were not provided. As a result, insurgents found it quite easy to infiltrate across mined and fenced areas. Here again was a lesson taken to heart by the South Africans, who were much more successful in the 1980s in their construction of security fences along the Limpopo and on the border with Mozambique.

SUPPORT OF THE LOCAL POPULATION

Rhodesia's African population, properly motivated and mobilised in the early stages of the conflict, could have been a major bulwark against the insurgents, as well as a reservoir of manpower to bolster the security forces. However, this would have ultimately translated into power-sharing and active participation in the political process, and ultimately black African control, an idea which was anathema to most of Rhodesia's European population. While attempts to remedy the long-standing second-class status of blacks in the counterinsurgency effort were eventually made, the changes were effected too late to make a decisive difference. Despite the government's seeming lack of attention in this area, Rhodesian blacks nevertheless enlisted in large numbers in the security forces when the opportunity did present itself, if only for financial reasons.

South Africa's ability to learn from Rhodesia is most marked in this area. From the late 1970s onward the South African administration in northern SWA sought to actively involve the black population there in its own defence. From 1980 it placed an ever-increasing burden of local security on COIN battalions raised and fielded locally from the various ethnic groups in SWA. This effort was highly successful, and indicates what the Rhodesians could have accomplished had they been willing to actively involve the black population from the early days of the conflict.

INSURGENTS IN THE CONFLICT

ZIMBABWE AFRICAN NATIONAL UNION (ZANU)

ZANU was headed by Dr Robert Mugabe. Its active resistance began in 1966. Drawing most of its support from the Shona groups in the central and eastern parts of Rhodesia, ZANU based its operations against the Rhodesian central government in neighbouring Mozambique. Mugabe and his supporters followed a Maoist revolutionary strategy and were supported by the PRC. ZANLA was ZANU's military arm, and after the mid-1970s the main threat to the Rhodesian regime, establishing insurgent zones inside Rhodesia. Following the transition from Rhodesia to Zimbabwe, ZANU became the ruling political party and Mugabe the state president (April 1980).

ZIMBABWE AFRICAN NATIONAL LIBERATION ARMY (ZANLA)

ZANLA was the military wing of Robert Mugabe's Zimbabwe African National Union (ZANU). Through the final period of the war, 1972–1980, ZANLA, commanded by Rex Nhongo (aka Solomon Mujuru), was based in Mozambique, with additional training camps in Tanzania. After 1975 it had the full support of the FRELIMO government in Mozambique and operated in central and eastern Rhodesia. It had approximately 6,000 to 7,500 trained personnel in camps in Mozambique and at least that number in training in Tanzania and Mozambique by the war's end. Upon independence, most of the personnel for the new Zimbabwe National Army (ZNA) were drawn from former ZANLA; Rex Nhongo became the new army commander in 1983.

ZIMBABWE AFRICAN PEOPLE'S UNION (ZAPU)

ZAPU was founded by Joshua Nkomo in 1961; it was a successor of the banned Southern Rhodesia African National Congress. ZAPU too was banned, in 1962, and for the remainder of the insurgent conflict was based at Lusaka in Zambia. It drew much of its strength from the Matabele (Ndebele) population of south-western Rhodesia. Lusaka was also the HQ for ZAPU's military arm, ZIPRA.

ZIMBABWE PEOPLE'S REVOLUTIONARY ARMY (ZIPRA)

ZIPRA was the armed wing of Joshua Nkomo's Zimbabwe African People's Union. It began military operations against the central government in 1966 in alliance with insurgents from the ANC. Throughout the Rhodesian conflict ZIPRA was based for the most part in neighbouring Zambia. It received extensive Soviet and East Bloc training in conventional arms and tactics. Toward the end of the conflict ZIPRA had about 10,000 trained personnel in base camps in Zambia, with ZIPRA HQ at Lusaka and at least 2,000 personnel operating inside Rhodesia. As many as 17,000 additional personnel were in training by the end of the war in Angola, where the MPLA had allowed them facilities near Luena.

OTHER ZIMBABWE NATIONALIST INSURGENT MOVEMENTS
FROLIZI and ZIPA both sought to transcend the increasing ethnic exclusiveness, especially in leadership, of ZAPU (Ndebele) and ZANU (Shona). In October 1971, James Chikerema, a ZAPU/ZIPRA dissident leader, and Nathan Shamuyarira, leader of a breakaway ZANU/ZANLA faction, formed the Front for the Liberation of Zimbabwe (FROLIZI). The aim was to provide a liberation organisation rising above ethnic differences and thus better coordinating the insurgent struggle. However, despite the best efforts of its founders, FROLIZI divided in 1973 - on ethnic lines - and played little subsequent role in the conflict. The Zimbabwe People's Army (ZIPA, aka the 'Third Force'), formed in November 1975, was the product of an effort by the Zimbabwe insurgents' southern African supporters to again come to terms with the ethnic divisions in the war against the Smith government. The force was intended to be the military vehicle of the Patriotic Front after the latter's formation in 1976, but ethnic fighting among its leadership soon resulted in ZIPA following FROLIZI's fate.

NOTES
To provide an exhaustive bibliography or set of references to the Rhodesian conflict would merely be to duplicate much previous work. I therefore refer the reader to two excellent publications on the conflict and the references they contain. These are J. K. Cillers' *Counterinsurgency in Rhodesia* (London, Croom Helm, 1985) and Henrik Ellert's *The Rhodesian Front War* (Harare, Mambo Press, 1989). In addition, the staff study at Headquarters, United States Marine Corps, by Charles D. Melson, 'Counter Revolutionary Warfare in Rhodesia' (Washington, DC, HQMC, October 1986) contains additional valuable documentation. Melson's Rhodesian conflict bibliography (HQMC, November 1991) is the most comprehensive listing to date of sources for the Rhodesian conflict and includes references to a range of documents by the Rhodesian military and security forces on COIN warfare.

1. Cillers, p. 15, quoting the local OPS official in charge of Hurricane planning.
2. Cillers, pp. 18-19.
3. Cillers, p. 22.
4. Lieutenant Colonel R. E. H. Lockley, 'A brief operational history of the campaign in Rhodesia from 1964 to 1976' (Paper, Salisbury, HQ COMOPS, May 1978), pp. 13-14.
5. Cillers, p. 57.

Chapter Two

The COIN War in South-West Africa, 1966–1989

The COIN effort against SWAPO (South-West Africa People's Organisation) in South-West Africa (SWA) or Namibia (1966–1989) is the only case of a clear-cut victory by security forces–in this case the South Africans' – against a communist-backed insurgency with considerable foreign support based in supposedly invulnerable positions across the Angolan border. Ironically, elections following a ceasefire in Namibia resulted in a SWAPO-dominated government being voted in to rule the country after its independence in 1990. However, from 1984 on, the security situation in Namibia was clearly resolved in favour of the security forces, including both military and civil authorities. In many ways the conflict in SWA/Namibia demonstrates the success of classic COIN efforts after the style of Malaya and Kenya. It is unfortunate that many lessons learned by the South Africans in the course of their COIN effort still remain relatively little-known.[1]

STUDYING THE WAR

The documentation for the COIN war in SWA/Namibia is extensive, and already some comprehensive studies of the conflict have appeared.[2] Here we will undertake an overview of the conflict with an eye to discussing the major phases of the conflict, the lessons learned from each, and the interrelationship of some of the key factors. The war in SWA/Namibia may be divided into four main phases. The first runs through 1978, and comprises the attempts to contain the war from its origins in 1966 to the development of a new policy of intervention by means of cross-border raids, the first of which was the raid on Cassinga and other sites in southern Angola in May 1978. The second phase comprises the period of 'externals', i.e., cross-border raids, which culminated with the very successful Operation 'Askari' in December 1983–January 1984. The third phase runs from early 1984 to mid-1988, and represents the period of ascendancy by South African security forces, including the climax of interventions in Angola, Operations 'Modular', 'Hooper', and 'Packer' – ironically, not against SWAPO but against FAPLA and the Cubans. The final phase of the war, which represents the prelude for independence, lasted through Namibia's independence on 20 February 1990.

Although the eventual political settlement permitted SWAPO to win and control the new government of independent Namibia, it was only after a free and fair election of the sort to which it would have never agreed in the heyday of the Cold War. SWAPO was ultimately cornered by its lack of success as an insurgent organisation into accepting the results of a democratic election to determine the fate of Namibia. By the end of the 1980s former East Bloc supporters had new governments unwilling or financially unable to back the insurgents. Cuba had committed itself to leaving Angola. Also, by this time many members of SWAPO and their allies had come to see an armed struggle as not only useless but also irrelevant in the light of new developments in Africa and the world. SWAPO itself had thus changed during the course of the multi-decade struggle, even though the leadership still continued to voice much of their old rhetoric. It is unlikely that even SWAPO's leadership believed it any longer.

The operational history of the COIN war in SWA/Namibia falls into four well-defined phases that are linked not only to major developments in the internal COIN strategy of the security forces, but also to events in neighbouring Angola.

OVERVIEW OF THE CONFLICT IN SWA/NAMIBIA

EARLY STAGES OF THE INSURGENCY, TO 1978

Although the SWA insurgency began in 1966, it was only after the installation of the MPLA government in Angola (1975) that SWAPO and its armed wing, PLAN, began to pose a serious threat. The MPLA regime gave assistance to the insurgents in the form of facilities and logistics support. This first phase (up to 1978) was marked by:

■ Withdrawal of SADF elements from Angola by March 1976;
■ The development of a formal organisation for SWAPO/PLAN inside Angola–regular unit deployments, training sites, regular logistical support, and base camps;
■ Additional communist country support for SWAPO by communist countries in Angola and at SWAPO/PLAN sites in Zambia and Tanzania;
■ Intensification by SWAPO of operations to discourage the development of any South African-supported Ovambo organisations inside Namibia;
■ Continued training and fielding by the SADF of troops raised from the local population, including Ovambo, Kavango, and Bushman units;
■ SADF initiation of covert operations inside Angola against FAPLA, Cuban, and SWAPO elements as well as covert SADF support to UNITA.

The war in SWA/Namibia had begun in earnest in 1972 with a sharp upsurge in the number of landmine incidents in the Caprivi strip. This coincided with the initiation of major operations, again primarily using landmines, by Rhodesian insurgents as well. Both SWAPO/PLAN groups operating in Caprivi and Rhodesian guerrillas were based in Zambia, which provided them refuge, and, from the early/mid-1970s, assistance as well. Zambia served as a conduit for Soviet/Warsaw Pact and Chinese aid to dissident groups acting against South Africa, Rhodesia, and Portuguese colonial authorities. The Soviet embassy in Lusaka was apparently responsible for coordinating these activities; countries such as Algeria and Tanzania also provided training and assistance.

The People's Liberation Army of Namibia (PLAN) was the armed wing of SWAPO responsible for 'military' operations to advance the group's political agenda. In reality PLAN's tactics normally depended on terror and intimidation of the general population – the heritage of Stalinist-era World War Two partisan tactics that had been passed to them by their East German trainers – rather than direct confrontation with the security forces. However, when cornered or when it possessed a superiority of numbers, PLAN could and did engage security forces with a tenacity and skill that reflected on the quality of training provided by its East German instructors. The average PLAN soldier was quite well-trained in comparison to his FAPLA counterpart. One of the reasons for a continuing lack of insurgent effectiveness was the requirement by the Angolan government laid against SWAPO for it to provide at least two brigades' worth of fighters to assist FAPLA against UNITA.

On 1 April 1974 the SADF assumed the responsibility for security in the Operational Area (OA). In many ways this was a pro forma action, as the military was already involved. Since mid-1973 there had been a slow but steady covert buildup of SADF personnel and equipment in the area. The handover from police to military was made without incident and the first inkling the public had of this was in June. During the week of the 22nd of that month the SADF had its first combat KIA in the OA, a lieutenant who was serving at the time with the SADF Reconnaissance Commando. Already by this time the security forces were making limited cross-border raids into Angola against SWAPO bases there.[3]

The involvement of the SADF in the conflict meant that many more resources could be used to fight the insurgents, who at that time were aided to a limited extent by the guerrillas fighting the Portuguese in Angola. The South Africans provided some limited and very low-visibility assistance to Portuguese forces, but the vast, underdeveloped areas of south-eastern Angola provided an ideal refuge for small groups of guerrillas who could plan and execute operations with little risk of detection by the security forces. Still, the South African cooperation with the Portuguese, and the increasing effectiveness of Lisbon's security forces through the early 1970s, meant that Angola was becoming a difficult operating environment for SWAPO. Throughout the mid-1970s Zambia was the main base for SWAPO, despite the general lack of geographical proximity of that country to the Ovambo-inhabited regions of northern SWA. Still, the capability of SWAPO to operate from Angola represented a major security concern for South Africa.

The strategic situation in southern Africa rapidly changed in 1974 and 1975. In 1974 the Portuguese government was overthrown by a junta of leftist military officers who soon divested themselves of Portugal's African colonial empire. In Angola this process was marked by a violent civil war between insurgent forces supported by the USSR and Cuba on one hand and the West on the other. South Africa provided its support, at first covertly, to those insurgent elements fighting the Soviet and Cuban-backed Popular Movement for the Liberation of Angola (MPLA). The two guerrilla movements involved were the National Front for the Liberation of Angola (FNLA), operating in the northern part of Angola, and which was heavily backed by the United States and Zaire, and the Ovimbundu-based National Union for the Total Independence of Angola (UNITA), headed by Dr Jonas Savimbi. Although an advocate of socialism and negritude (both anathema to the apartheid regime), and trained in guerrilla tactics in China, Savimbi was a pragmatist and accepted US and especially South African assistance.

South Africa saw a golden opportunity in the support to Savimbi, as UNITA's success would not only mean a defeat for Soviet and Cuban expansionism, but also would result in the establishment of a sympathetic government in Luanda. Thus SWAPO would be denied access to bases in southern Angola. Although in 1975 the FNLA and UNITA made significant initial gains against the MPLA, the introduction of Cuban combat troops and a massive increase in Soviet weapons and equipment began to turn the tide in favour of the MPLA. It was therefore decided by South Africa to intervene militarily in Angola, using Angolans trained and equipped by the SADF and spearheaded by small groups of regular South African troops. The South African Air Force (SAAF) provided air support to the advancing forces and also targeted MPLA and Cuban logistical columns.

The intervention in Angola was codenamed Operation 'Savannah'. Its operational framework was based on three task forces, each formed of UNITA soldiers with South African advisers, technicians, and some troops. The first liaison with UNITA began in September, with the first engagement on 2 October near Nova Lisboa, now Huambo. This engagement halted the advance of three FAPLA columns toward the city. The subsequent introduction of South African-manufactured Eland-90 armoured cars substantially increased the capabilities of the operation. By October most of southern and south-eastern Angola had fallen to the task forces, which had halted south of Luanda, not, as the MPLA claimed, due to FAPLA and Cuban resistance, but as they awaited a military-political solution to the conflict that was in the making elsewhere – to the north. There, the advancing FNLA forces, backed by several battalions of Zairian troops, advanced to take possession of Luanda. However, the advance was halted near the capital by the MPLA, reinforced with Cuban troops, who routed the FNLA and up to the end of the year pushed it back toward the border with Zaire. By December it was obvious that the South African position was untenable, both strategically and in the face of negative world public opinion, and the forces were gradually withdrawn by 27 March 1976.

The intervention incidents involving SWAPO had continued on the border. They were, however, overshadowed by the other events accompanying the South African withdrawal.

These included the massive flight of refugees from Angola, the southward withdrawal of UNITA and some FNLA forces into remote parts of Angola, and the advance to the border of FAPLA and Cuban troops by April. Security concerns over SWAPO soon surfaced again. In Steenkamp's words: 'Now the worst fears of the military planners – the fears that had led in such large measure to Operation "Savannah" being launched – started coming true. PLAN set up an extensive network of permanent training camps and permanent bases in southern Angola and the insurgency escalated significantly.'[4] It took a little over two years for the security forces to finally conclude that such a situation was intolerable – not only from the standpoint of security south of the Angolan border, but also in the sense that any marked success enjoyed by SWAPO might be seen as an encouragement to other African states to support the insurgents. Already Zambia had done so, allowing PLAN to establish bases north of the Zambezi River opposite SADF positions in Eastern Caprivi. Another concern was that the anti-regime African National Congress (ANC) would be encouraged by SWAPO success and step up attempts by its armed wing, the Umkhontowa Sizwe (MK), to infiltrate into the RSA. Although small, 'hot pursuit' raids after PLAN raiders were still being undertaken, it was clear that more drastic approaches to the problem of SWAPO sanctuaries in Angola were required.

CROSS-BORDER RAIDS, 1978–1984

This period was marked by the external operations which received international attention. The major developments of this phase, which was the most dynamic of the war, include:

■ Major cross-border raids by SADF/SWATF troops against PLAN sites in southern Angola, especially in Cunene province;
■ The establishment in 1980 of the South-West Africa Territory Force (SWATF) and its employment in operations against SWAPO;
■ Formation of an effective SWA Police COIN element and capability;
■ The redeployment of SWAPO/PLAN elements under pressure from South African attacks to sites further north, after unsuccessful attempts to colocate them with FAPLA and Cuban units;
■ Increasing aggressiveness of FAPLA and Cuban units, with deployment of forces in southern Angola, to include armour, to counter SADF/SWATF cross-border raids;
■ Establishment by FAPLA of a line of air defence sites across southern Angola at roughly 15 degrees south (line of the Moçâmedes railway) in an attempt to deter South African aircraft from striking at SWAPO/PLAN bases in southern Namibia.

Following the South African withdrawal from Angola in 1976, local attention focused on the efforts by the international community to secure the independence of SWA/Namibia. Despite the continued anti-democratic stance of SWAPO, the UN, dominated by the East Bloc and its third-world allies, was able to advance an agenda that recognised SWAPO as the sole representative body for the country. Attempts by the USSR and its supporters to use the UN reached a climax in April and May 1978 with the UN General Assembly Ninth Special Session on Namibia, which called, among other things, for economic sanctions against South Africa. The latter, already concerned about SWAPO claims for the strategic Walvis Bay area, felt it had little to lose by rejecting calls to set up a SWAPO regime in Namibia, one that it believed would be supported by the USSR and Cuba, and would constitute another nation on its borders that would harbour ANC and other guerrillas. By 1978, SWAPO armed infiltrations into Namibia had increased to the point where assassinations and land mine incidents were commonplace throughout the northern part of the country.

The period 1978–1984 set the pattern for South African strategy in the war. The basis of this strategy was to deny SWAPO sanctuary in Angola or Zambia, where its camps provided bases for infiltrations into Namibia with the aim of coercing the general popula-tion into supporting further actions, as well as attacks against SADF military installations throughout the Operational Area. While at first the South Africans were reluctant to main-tain a presence in southern Angola, the continued reestablishment of PLAN base camps near the border finally led, in 1981 and after, to virtual South African control of most of Cunene province.

The first cross-border raids, 1978–1981

The SADF cross-border raids into Angola were a lesson of the Rhodesian conflict that was only put into practice after three years of increasingly difficult incidents in northern SWA that included repeated shellings by SWAPO. The international consequences of such a move had to be considered, as South Africa stood to lose much of the remaining support it had in the world community by undertaking cross-border actions. Nor did South Africa wish to provoke the USSR or Cuba by another invasion on the scale of Operation 'Savannah'. However, once it became clear that SWAPO had no intention of sharing power or setting up a democratic system, and that the continued training and equipping of a large force north of the SWA border was intended to back up the insurgents' intentions, the SADF planned a limited strike at SWAPO bases in eastern Cunene and the Cassinga area of Huila. The size of SWAPO forces and the amount of its Soviet–Warsaw Pact arma-ment suggested to the South Africans that mere cross-border strikes similar to those undertaken by the Rhodesians might not be sufficient. Despite this concern, the initial decision was made to go into Angola, destroy as much of SWAPO's capability as possible, and then exit leaving no residual forces.

The first of the celebrated 'externals', Operation 'Reindeer', began on 4 May 1978, when the SADF struck at the PLAN 'Moscow' base near Cassinga and the large 'Vietnam' complex to the south near Chetequera. Cassinga, 250km north of the SWA border, was hit by an airborne battalion that was later airlifted out by helicopter the same day. At the same time, the Chetequera complex, 28km north of the border, was attacked by a mecha-nised force based at Oshivelo backed up by the newly-formed 32 Battalion. Troops of the latter, as well as other SADF units in the Operational Area, provided blocking forces in support of the main operations. The UN response was as predicted, with a Security Council resolution (UNSCR) of 6 May condemning the attack and calling for the withdrawal of South African troops (who had already left on the 5th); SWAPO also called off further nego-tiations on the transition proposal. However, the precedent had been set, and subsequent assessment of the damage caused to the insurgent base system and LOCs clearly indicated Operation 'Reindeer's effectiveness. More 'externals' were to follow.

The second cross-border action, Operation 'Saffron', was in response to a SWAPO rocket attack against the SADF base at Katima Mulilo by insurgents based in Zambia. Nine SADF conscripts died in the attack, and the operation, initiated on 23 August, effectively ended SWAPO presence in the Zambian border area north of the Caprivi Strip. This was apparently due more to Zambian desire not to become involved in supporting SWAPO and thus paying the price for harbouring the insurgents than to the efficacy of the actions, which ended on the 27th netting relatively few insurgents. However, the operation was a success in that SWAPO was for the remainder of the war remained confined to bases in south-western Angola, thus limiting the insurgents' operational range.

Angola, with its strong Soviet and Cuban backing, proved to be of a different mindset than Zambia, and opted to continue support to SWAPO/PLAN, and to have its troops help the Cubans in providing assistance to the insurgents, even colocating its troops in PLAN base camps. This continued support to PLAN incursions prompted yet another strike by the SADF into southern Angola. This was Operation 'Sceptic', launched on 25 May, which targeted the extensive 'Smokeshell' complex and several other base camps in Cunene province just north of the border. The complex, some 62km^2 in size, was a major PLAN centre, and routing insurgents from this and conducting follow-up and related actions required until the end of June. The predictable UN condemnation was disregarded as South Africa reaffirmed its policy of striking at insurgent bases that supported PLAN infiltrations.

Establishment of a SADF presence in Cunene, 1981-1984

Up to mid-1981 the South Africans continued to face problems from SWAPO in Cunene despite continued attempts to disrupt the PLAN bases and logistics there. The presence of the Angolan army in southern Cunene, with an infantry brigade each at Xangongo and Ngiva, also presented a major potential difficulty for any force attempting to linger to conduct follow-up sweeps or mop-up operations. These two brigades in the Angolan Military Region 5 were backed up by the 2nd Motorised Brigade at Cahama, a heavy mechanised formation that counted among its assets a tank battalion, three motorised battalions, and a heavy artillery regiment. Any South African units remaining inside Angola for any length of time would have to face these units as well as others to the north and west, plus Cuban troops deployed there as well. Also, SADF intelligence had received word that continued resupply to PLAN of weapons and equipment had been continuing, and that massive stockpiles were located throughout south-central Cunene province. Accordingly, SADF COIN policy toward southern Angola took another change in course to meet the new circumstances.

By 1981, the South Africans had in place a new security force structure in the Operational Area. This new structure included three Operational Sectors, 10 (Kakoland and Ovamboland, HQ Oshakati), 20 (Kavango and West Caprivi, HQ Rundu), and 70 (East Caprivi, HQ Katima Mulilo). The sectors controlled SADF battalions manned by Army reservists. However, they also controlled elements of a new force. In 1980 South Africa had established an army for SWA/Namibia, the South-West Africa Territory Force (SWATF), which was to include units manned by Namibians. In the fashion of the ethnic battalions of the South African Army, most SWATF battalions were composed of a particular ethnic group. A brigade-sized force at Windhoek formed the strategic reserve. The other elements of the force included Area Defence Units, which were manned by part-time soldiers after the fashion of South African commando units. The commander of SAA units in SWA was also the SWATF commander.

From the start, the security forces had no problem recruiting and retaining soldiers for SWATF, which was primarily a light infantry force organised and deployed to fight a COIN war. Those units in the Operational Area often included a reaction force comprising small, highly mobile teams sent against groups of insurgents once the latter had been detected. Some of the SWATF units, especially those manned by Bushmen, were skilled in bushcraft and tracking, and were constantly used to detect and track down infiltrating PLAN groups. SWATF units in the north, which included two Ovambo battalions, two Bushman battalions, a Kavango battalion, and a Caprivian battalion, were under control of the Operational Area sectors. From the start the units were led by SADF officers and senior NCOs seconded to SWATF, with the aim of gradually replacing them once trained Namibian personnel were available. SWATF was not the only Namibian COIN element. One of the most effective COIN forces, organised in the late 1970s, was the unit commonly known as Koevoet, or 'Crowbar'. This unit was in fact a part of the South-West Africa Police counterinsurgency branch. Organised from scratch by South African police officers, it recruited Ovambos, especially former PLAN fighters. It had a reputation for aggressive tactics and a high success rate in tracking down and wiping out infiltrating PLAN groups.

By 1981 the SADF force structure in the Operational Area was bolstered by two relatively new units that had been organised and fielded to meet the special requirements of the security force mission there. These were 61 Mechanised Battalion Group, which had its origins in one of the battle groups in Operation 'Sceptic', and 32 Battalion. 61 Mechanised Battalion Group provided a mechanised spearhead for larger cross-border incursions and served as a deterrent against attacks by FAPLA and Cuban units. Backing up this unit was a unit HQ, 62 Mechanised Battalion, which was manned as necessary for operations by South African soldiers normally assigned to mechanised infantry forces in the RSA. 32 Battalion, nicknamed 'Buffalo Battalion', established after Operation 'Savannah' from former Angolan FNLA fighters, was a large light infantry force used for special operations in addition to routine COIN tasks. Its very existence had been a secret until the end of the 1970s.

The defence of the Operational Area, as coordinated by the various Sector HQs, required an elaborate security network, both physical and organisational. The former included a line of border posts, watchtowers, and military camps dedicated to monitoring the border and responding to infiltrations as soon as they were detected. They were backed up by SAAF units based in northern SWA/Namibia to provide air support if needed when contact was made with infiltrating PLAN. They also were on hand to respond to any aggressive moves made by FAPLA or Cuban units.

Despite a reinforced security force structure in place, PLAN incursions at this time actually increased as the East Bloc backers of SWAPO, the USSR and East Germany, continued to provide equipment and training to its fighters, especially to make up for losses caused by South African raids. Military assistance provided to SWAPO included training for PLAN fighters by East German instructors not only in Angola but for some handpicked personnel in East Germany itself. The latter were formed into the 'Volcano' unit, which numbered 1,700 or so and which was deployed at the start of the 1980s. This unit would cause considerable problems for SWA/Namibian security management in 1982–1983. PLAN had also relocated bases somewhat northward to avoid being within range of SADF or SWATF forces making quick cross-border incursions in pursuit of infiltrators. In some cases the new bases were near to or even colocated with FAPLA and Cuban installations. PLAN bases were becoming increasingly difficult to detect from the air and were employing increasingly heavier ground defences. In addition, the PLAN HQ at both Xangongo and Ngiva were in close proximity to FAPLA brigade HQs which were receiving massive quantities of conventional arms and ammunition. Clearly the increased PLAN activity and the new FAPLA and Cuban security posture were designed to discourage the South Africans from continuing their policy of cross-border strikes. Into the summer of 1981, PLAN felt confident enough to step up its cross-border incursions, which provoked the normal response from security forces in the Operational Area.

The response of the SADF was to initiate a comprehensive series of interrelated operations to contain PLAN infiltration and to follow these up with a major strike against the SWAPO bases in Cunene. By July these operations had resulted in a 'buffer area' east of Oshikango (just south of the border and the road north through Namacunde to Ngiva). However, the main operation was yet to follow – Operation 'Carnation'. This, as with previous operations, severely disrupted the PLAN infrastructure east of Ngiva.

While Operation 'Carnation' was still in progress, however, the main strike was launched on 23 August. Operation 'Protea' was launched with SADF and SWATF units organised into two large mechanised task forces moving on both sides of the Cunene River. The first task force moved to secure the crossing between Humbe and Xangongo to block FAPLA or Cuban relief forces, as well as to prevent PLAN from retreating westward. On 24 August the second task force moved against Xangongo and took it after some resistance from PLAN and FAPLA forces. It then moved east against Ngiva, breaking through an attempt by FAPLA to block it at Mongua. On 26 Ngiva was attacked and taken after two days of fighting. The South Africans returned south of the border on 1 September, but not before capturing or destroying a vast amount of military equipment comprising the range of conventional ground equipment provided by the Soviet Union and its allies to FAPLA and SWAPO.

The impact of Operation 'Protea' on the conflict was as immense as the captured military materiel. Over 1,000 PLAN and FAPLA were killed and FAPLA had been defeated in three separate engagements. The PLAN base camp and logistical network along the border from the Cunene River east to Ngiva had been completely disrupted. The subsequent international criticism of South Africa's action was more than offset by the reality of the damage inflicted to SWAPO. In many ways 'Protea' was a turning point in the conflict, not least because of the garrisons left behind by the SADF at Xangongo and Ngiva when they withdrew. The stay-behind garrisons, whose presence was denied by the South African government, were to prove extremely useful to the COIN effort by preventing PLAN (and FAPLA) from reestablishing an infrastructure in south-central Cunene. They also provided forward bases for reconnaissance operations and blocking forces intercepting PLAN groups that had been detected after entering SWA/Namibia and who were then trying to flee northward back to Angolan sanctuaries.

A follow-up operation to 'Protea' took place in November, launched on the 1st of that month. This was Operation 'Daisy', which was conducted by a task force built around elements of the 61st, 32 Battalion, and SWATF elements. Many of the SADF personnel were reservists mobilised for the operation. Operation 'Daisy''s target was a complex of PLAN bases 240km inside Angola in the Bambi and Chetequera area of north-east Cunene. The primary objective for the operation was the destruction of the PLAN base complex at Chetequera, where the insurgents had regrouped after being scattered by Operation 'Protea'. This vast base, over 35km^2 in size, was set to become the new PLAN logistics centre, while another complex nearby, Bambi, was the new HQ. Bambi was one of the major surviving regional PLAN HQs.[5]

The SADF/SWATF force, which included elements of 61 Mechanised Battalion Group and SWATF 10 Sector forces, numbering about 1,000, attacked the base on 1 November after moving north for three days along the Ngiva–Anhaca–Nehone axis and then north toward the sources of the Cunene River. The target area was located east-north-east of Cuvelai. Previous to the attack a HAG had been set up at Ionde, about mid-way to the objective. The attack was made from a tactical HQ established at Ionde, an old Portuguese mission site. For almost three weeks the force systematically searched out and destroyed the PLAN infrastructure in the vicinity of the Bambi HQ and the Chetequera base camp. No ground interference came from FAPLA or the Cubans, who had learned their lesson after having been bloodied during 'Protea'.

By 20 November the task force had finished its task of methodically destroying bunkers and supplies, and moved back toward the border. A total of 70 or so insurgents had been killed while the security forces had lost three. While most PLAN elements at the bases had quickly departed as the security forces approached and thus eluded being killed or captured, the extra materiel loss to the insurgents, combined with the fact that even such a seemingly distant complex of bases and HQs was not secure from the South Africans, further disrupted their infrastructure and conduct of operations in southern Angola.

Despite the lack of ground interference in 'Daisy', the Angolan Air Force (FAPA) had nonetheless attempted to confront the SAAF during the operation. Although the toll in the first post-Korea air combat for the SAAF was one FAPA MiG-21 downed, the incident was one more bit of evidence of a larger defence structure gradually being put into place by FAPLA. This was centred around a line of air defence sites roughly following the Moçâmedes Railway inland from Namibe through Lubango (the HQ of FAPLA Military Region 5) and thence east to Menongue (HQ of FAPLA Military Region 6). For FAPLA, this protective network had a dual purpose. First, with its SAMs it was to deter the SAAF from

41

operating too far northward but also it was to allow some backup to FAPA and Cuban pilots who challenged South African air supremacy. Second, the air defence line also protected the main inland route from the coast to Menongue and Cuito Cuanavale, key bases in the struggle against UNITA, which had by this time effective territorial control of most of south-eastern Angola. That the South Africans took the FAPA air defence threat seriously is shown by their first action during Operation 'Protea' – air strikes that disabled the air defence radars that had been put in place by this time.

1981 had been a good year for SADF and SWATF in the continuing COIN war. The security forces had killed over 2,500 PLAN while suffering the loss of 56. However, at least 154 civilians had been killed by PLAN, either directly or by land mines they had laid. But it remained obvious to the security forces that as long as PLAN could infiltrate and intimidate or terrorise the general population, the insurgents would have a claim to success that would be recognised by sympathetic political and media groups. More ominous, however, was the evidence that FAPLA and the Cubans, though checked, were by no means out of the picture. Indeed, FAPLA continued to increase in numbers as it received more Soviet/Warsaw Pact equipment to face the growing UNITA threat in the south-east. This equipment, although already old and redundant for the Soviets and their allies, was still a significant upgrade by local standards. T-34 tanks were replaced with T-54/55 tanks; older APCs were replaced with BTR-60s. Shipments of other, already effective, ground equipment, such as artillery (122mm D-30 howitzers and 122mm BM-21 MRLs), were simply increased. Even more threatening was the gradual replacement by FAPA of the MiG-21 by the vastly more capable MiG-23, and the ultimate introduction of ground attack aircraft such as the Su-22.

To face the growing threat the South Africans had, by way of their own military development programme, an upgrade programme for their forces in the OA. This included the introduction of new or improved weaponry, most of it adapted to fit the rigorous demands of the southern African environment. Most important by the early 1980s was the mine-resistant Ratel infantry fighting vehicle (IFV), one variant of which was fitted with a turret-mounted 90mm cannon capable of shooting out a T-55 tank. Other key innovations included the Buffel armoured personnel carrier (APC), mine-resistant, like the Ratel. In the arena of artillery, the development of the Valkyrie 127mm multiple rocket launcher (MRL) and the remarkable G-5 155mm gun/howitzer (still to be fielded by 1981) represented the SADF answer to the BM-21 and the D-30. Many other examples of equipment adapted to southern African COIN and conventional conflicts that improved South African capabilities could be discussed here. However, in the final analysis most of the reason for SADF and SWATF success against PLAN insurgents and their FAPLA and Cuban allies depended upon superior training, operational skills, communications capabilities, and intelligence collection and analysis.

The two years following Operation 'Protea' saw what was probably the climax of PLAN capabilities, in part due to desperation in the aftermath of the tremendous losses suffered in 1981. In April 1982 a particularly destructive incursion by elements of the PLAN special 'Volcano' unit, though finally contained after six weeks, led to a major response by security forces the following month. PLAN was still forced to move southward across the border from bases in central Cunene, and the activity to neutralise PLAN capabilities consisted of a series of small COIN operations to areas just north of the border. PLAN had earlier suffered a setback in trying to open a new infiltration route into Kakoland when the SADF 32 Battalion hit it in the Cambeno valley in March. Another major operation, 'Mebos', was launched in July and August against PLAN's Central and Eastern Front HQs near Mupa (where they had been relocated from the Ionde and Evale region), which took SADF and SWATF troops 200km north into Angola.

Although 1982 ended with a total of 1,286 insurgents killed and the total number of PLAN active soldiers at around 6,000, SWAPO continued to receive materiel and training assistance from the USSR and East Germany. The following year saw the most ambitious attempt yet by PLAN to strike into the Operational Area. This came in late February when the 'Volcano' unit was infiltrated in groups of 40 to 50 across the border, with one moving southward into the white farming area south of the OA. In the course of containing the insurgents, the security forces launched Operation 'Phoenix', which ran throughout April. This operation was fought on both sides of the border, and focused on actions to pre-empt or blunt the PLAN attacks in the OA, as well as hot pursuit actions into Angola to hit PLAN bases there. The operation required extensive coordination for a large number of separate actions, conducted by a number of military and civilian security forces, occurring simultaneously along some 500km of border. However, the PLAN incursion of 1983 was to raise many questions, as Operation 'Phoenix' ended on 15 April, in the South African government as well as in the security forces as to how it could have happened and whether or not it would happen again.

Despite security force concerns, the 'Volcano' incursions of February 1983 had been PLAN's last gasp. The period 1981-1983 had been a particularly punishing one for the insurgents, and they could not recover from the consequences of the cross-border raids of those years:

■ First, the attrition rate had been considerable. The number of PLAN killed was over 2,500 in 1981, 1,286 during 1982, and 309 by the end of April 1983. The total number of PLAN who had been killed, many of them belonging to the elite 'Volcano' unit, was at least 4,095, a figure that does not include those captured, unable to fight due to combat injuries, or deserters and defectors from PLAN. Recruitment rates could not keep up with such losses.
■ Second, the loss in equipment was crippling. While PLAN continued to have access to small arms, land mines, and some mortars, much had been captured by the South Africans, who in turn gave a considerable amount of it to insurgent groups in southern Africa that they supported.
■ Finally, the disruption of the PLAN base system and logistics network in Cunene by repeated South African cross-border raids forced a relocation north toward the Moçâmedes Railway. This meant that PLAN infiltrators had an additional 200km or so of ground to cover before they reached the border, and that the chances of their detection and/or loss of resupply before they got there were markedly increased.

Other factors degrading FAPLA capabilities included the expansion of UNITA activity westward, and the requirement by the Angolan government that PLAN provide soldiers for at least two brigades to support FAPLA against UNITA; and the continued presence of South African forces at Xangongo and Ngiva, which gave security forces south of the border advance warning of impending PLAN incursions, and which represented forward bases for interdicting insurgents headed to or returning from the OA.

Before 1983 had ended the last of the major 'externals' against PLAN had been initiated by the security forces. This operation was triggered by intelligence that PLAN would undertake a heavy infiltration starting in January, and by November the South Africans began planning for a major operation that would go into Angola to pre-empt PLAN preparations for the offensive–which would involve between 800 and 1,000 insurgents. This was to be done by disrupting PLAN HQs and logistics over north-central Cunene by ground and air attacks. There was no SADF/SWATF plan to deliberately attack FAPLA and Cuban units, however. The main aim was to isolate PLAN from them in order to avoid contact with other forces.

By early December the security forces had sent three mechanised task forces into Angola, initiating Operation 'Askari'. Major contacts were taking place by the third week of the month. While PLAN units were indeed chased down and destroyed, FAPLA and Cuban forces soon moved in to intervene. Fighting near Caiundo in the east and Cahama took place as the security forces continued their mission. The main combat of the operation took place over 3-6 January 1984 as the FAPLA 11 Brigade, reinforced by Cuban units, attacked a South African task force moving north-east of Cuvelai. In the ensuing battle the attackers were badly defeated and driven northward in disarray and resistance collapsed as the South Africans consolidated their gains. A considerable amount of weapons and equipment, though not of the proportions of 'Protea', was captured or destroyed by the security forces. The SADF and SWATF units withdrew south of the border by 15 January.

Operation 'Askari' had a profound effect on the course of the conflict. The PLAN infrastructure in northern Cunene had taken damage from which it would not recover. The South Africans had shown that they could defeat FAPLA and Cuban armour with their mechanised forces – they had destroyed at least 25 tanks during the fighting. The logistics, engineering, and other support for the operation – intended at the start to support COIN and not conventional combat – though strained, had proven up to the task. However, the more aggressive employment of FAPLA and Cuban armour was a harbinger of things to come. Not only was this evidence of the major improvement in quality of FAPLA (which had been expanded in the previous year or two to meet the growing UNITA challenge), but it was an indication that FAPLA would react in a similar fashion to future SADF/SWATF incursions should the forces linger too long inside Angola, or penetrate too far north of the frontier.

As a consequence of 'Askari', a Joint Monitoring Commission (JMC) of FAPLA and SADF representatives was established to monitor the withdrawal of the South Africans by May 1984 from Cunene and at the same time to ensure that PLAN units did not reestablish themselves there. Angolan forces were supposed to have taken control of areas from which the SADF withdrew, but in reality PLAN units soon reestablished themselves, and within months had started infiltrations and raids once more. The JMC, which ultimately located to Ngiva, proved ineffective in its ability to effect any controls on PLAN insurgent activity. However, despite PLAN's resumption of its activities, the toll on the insurgents had finally begun to show. The security forces were able to intercept and contain infiltrators, despite the use of advanced bushcraft and anti-tracking tactics by the small PLAN teams sent southward into SWA/Namibia. By contrast, the security forces continued to develop their skills in detecting, intercepting, and engaging PLAN infiltrators.

South Africa and UNITA: Cooperation up to the mid-1980s

A few words must be said here about the relationship between the South Africans and UNITA during this period of the Angolan conflict. While contacts between the two were denied by both, training of UNITA forces by the South Africans took place during the late 1970s and accompanied a steady covert weapons supply that allowed Savimbi's forces to locate to Jamba, his secure HQ complex in the remote south-eastern Angolan wilderness, in 1979. The reasons for South African support to UNITA are in part closely tied to the policy of the Angolan government toward SWAPO. The South Africans supported UNITA because Angola supported SWAPO. The fight by FAPLA against UNITA required the latter to commit manpower and materiel that could have been used to resist South African cross-border attacks into southern Angola. The Angolan government also, as noted above, required SWAPO to provide PLAN fighters to assist FAPLA's struggle with UNITA. However, by the early 1980s the absolute value of UNITA's insurgent war against the MPLA regime was seen as the insurgents advanced their area of control westward from the Savate area into Cunene. UNITA control of south-western Angola meant that the area east of the Cubango (Kavango) River could not be used by PLAN as a base for its infiltrations.

The South Africans also provided covert operational support to UNITA, with 32 Battalion being tasked with much of this mission. Support to UNITA included assisting it in capturing towns manned by FAPLA garrisons in order that Savimbi could have a more secure area of control. This was probably envisaged as a temporary step, as UNITA was soon able to use its own personnel and resources to capture towns – a case in point is the assault on Cangamba in 1983. However, other towns such as Savate and Mavinga had earlier been taken by 32 Battalion and then turned over to UNITA to garrison. Sometimes a given town would change hands more than once as UNITA troops were still not uniformly capable of resisting FAPLA counterattacks. By 1983-1984, however, UNITA had generally developed its own effective capability to attack and capture FAPLA garrisons. By this time it had begun operating north of the Benguela Railway line into northern and north-western Angola, and by 1985 would reach the far north-west and begin to cooperate with the separatist FLEC movement in Cabinda.

The SADF relationship with UNITA proved beneficial to both sides. UNITA received valuable materiel and training, which it used to good advantage. Most important to UNITA were the bases in the Caprivi used for the transshipment of fuel and other military supplies to Savimbi's centre at Jamba. It would not be until 1985 that actual intervention by SADF forces to assist UNITA would take place. The South Africans, by their cooperation with UNITA, found an energetic and aggressive insurgent force they could work with against a common enemy – the MPLA and the Cubans. UNITA provided the South Africans with valuable intelligence about FAPLA and the Cubans, as well as PLAN activities.

By the early 1980s Savimbi's base at Jamba was protected by a series of towns throughout south-eastern Angola that 32 Battalion had captured and turned over to Savimbi. By this time also UNITA had control of all Cuando Cubango except for the Cuchi-Menongue–Cuito Cuanavale corridor and a few isolated garrisons. The insurgents had even begun to operate in eastern Cunene. Thus UNITA denied PLAN a staging area for operations into Kavango and Caprivi. In addition, UNITA's expansion prompted the MPLA to require SWAPO to give it PLAN units to assist FAPLA in its attempt to contain the insurgents, further degrading the latter's capabilities.

THE STRATEGIC PHASE, 1984-1988

This period was marked by the clear ascendancy of the security forces, and major developments include:

■ The clear link of the resolution of the COIN war to events in Angola, and the active involvement of the superpower supporters on each side;
■ The establishment and later collapse of the Joint Monitoring Commission, an attempt by South African and Angolan forces to work together to monitor a ceasefire in Cunene after Operation 'Askari';
■ Relocation of SWAPO base camps and logistical structures north of Cunene out of reach of South African forces;
■ Abandonment by SWAPO of large-scale infiltration attempts, with the insurgents relying instead upon much smaller-scale operations;
■ Peak of security force effectiveness in responding to SWAPO infiltrations;
■ Initiation by the SADF of large-scale interventions to support UNITA in Cuando Cubango; these operations were not directly connected with the COIN effort against SWAPO, however.[6]

Developments in the COIN war to 1988

The end of Operation 'Askari' did not mean the total disengagement of South African forces from southern Angola. For most of 1984 the SADF remained in effective control of most of Cunene province, this as part of a Joint Monitoring Commission (JMC) that was set up in 1984 as a result of the Lusaka Accords to supervise the disengagement of South

African forces from southern Angola. South African participation in the JMC was contingent on FAPLA containing SWAPO/PLAN operations into Namibia. The SADF had stated that its participation in no way meant that it would not undertake cross-border operations should the JMC fail in its attempt to maintain order in Cunene province.[7]

The JMC consisted of both SADF and FAPLA forces assigned to southern Angola specifically for this purpose. The first meeting of the JMC was held on 26 January at Cuvelai, the scene of the major battle of Operation 'Askari', in response to SADF concerns about the continued infiltration of SWAPO/PLAN operatives into northern Namibia. While SADF began a general withdrawal from Angola on 8 January, many of the same troops eventually returned or remained as part of the South African component of the JMC. Headquartered at Ngiva in the southern part of Cunene province, the JMC was for all practical purposes divided into SADF and FAPLA components, with their areas of influence separated by an east-west line at the latitude of Ngiva. Joint forces patrolled on both sides of the line, but often the military initiative or lack of such on the part of the FAPLA component of the JMC meant that action against SWAPO/PLAN violations rested with the SADF in the southern part of the JMC area. From the start, it became evident that the presence of the JMC in Cunene province was insufficient to prevent some continued low-level SWAPO activity. However, this was capably dealt with by the SADF component of the JMC. The FAPLA component of the JMC, however, was often reluctant to engage in actions to prevent or counter SWAPO violations of the disengagement agreement, in large part due to the reluctance to fight against former allies.

For its part, PLAN, effectively forced northward, shifted its methods of infiltration to smaller groups of insurgents whose purpose would be to enter the Operational Area with the aim of laying land mines or ambushing security force personnel. Many continued to find refuge among some elements of the Ovambo population in the OA. However, other Ovambos remained opposed to SWAPO and PLAN, or tried to remain aloof from the struggle. Refusal to provide aid and comfort to the insurgents often resulted in reprisals against civilians by PLAN guerrillas. Despite this, increasing numbers of local civilians in Ovamboland began to provide information to security forces about PLAN insurgent sightings and other incidents. This was not only due to the gradual success of civil affairs programmes by the security forces but also by the obvious inability of the insurgents to establish themselves among the local population.

In mid/late January 1985, the SADF conducted a conventional military exercise, Operation 'Vuiswys', in the Operational Area of northern Namibia, deploying there for the first time its modernised variant of the British Centurion tank, the Olifant. This use of tanks in the Operational Area was probably in response to FAPLA use of T-54 tanks since 1983. Operation 'Vuiswys' took place in Sector 10 of the Operational Area, 50km south of the Angolan border. A smaller exercise by the SADF 61 Mechanised Battalion Group was conducted in Kavango in the Ruacana area, and used as its scenario a conventional strike into Angola. Such actions inevitably raised the spectre of preparations for a strike into Angola against PLAN bases, and the SADF denied charges by the Angolan government that such an operation was being planned. 'Vuiswys' was a conventional exercise, but the choice of the OA versus the more usual location at the Army Battle School at Lohatlha in the RSA may have been designed to remind FAPLA and the Cubans of the SADF's considerable military strength, only a small part of which was normally ever stationed in northern SWA/Namibia.

With the disbandment on 16 May 1985 of the JMC, FAPLA was left in control of large areas of Cunene province previously occupied or denied to them by the South Africans. SWAPO, which subsequently continued its attempts to penetrate into SWA/Namibia, prompted three successful major responses by the security forces by the end of the year. These included Operation 'Boswilger' on 28-30 June, Operation 'Egret' on 15-22

September, and an unnamed operation or series of operations during the last two weeks of December. While 'Boswilger' was a successful follow-up operation to an initial hot pursuit, 'Egret' and the December operation were carefully planned sweeps of central Cunene, especially the 'shallow area' just north of the border used by PLAN as a final staging point for its infiltrations.

By late summer 1985 South African interest in assisting UNITA against the massive FAPLA military buildup was catalysed by the July–September FAPLA operation 'Congress II' against Savimbi's insurgents, with the Cazombo salient and the town of Mavinga the two major objectives. While UNITA was forced to abandon the Cazombo salient, South African intervention, codenamed 'Wallpaper', especially in the form of air strikes and artillery, assisted UNITA in defeating FAPLA a scant 32km from Mavinga after the Angolan military force had crossed the Lomba River. To counter the offensive against Mavinga, UNITA withdrew troops from the Cazombo salient to move southward. Due to FAPLA synchronising both attacks, South African C-130 and C-160 aircraft were used over a period of about three weeks to airlift UNITA personnel from eastern Moxico province into Mavinga. This rapid move as well as the South African effort to provide limited logistic assistance to UNITA in the Cazombo salient was dubbed by the SADF Operation 'Magneto'.

The following year, on 9 and 10 August, South African forces in Operation 'Alpha Centauri' once again assisted UNITA in destroying the operational capability of the FAPLA base at Cuito Cuanavale by providing artillery support for a UNITA infantry attack, which, though not successful in capturing the town, inflicted substantial damage on it and the ability of FAPLA to launch an offensive against Mavinga that year. South African artillery is by some accounts said to have inflicted most of the damage to the base in a devastating bombardment. However, UNITA apparently proved unequal to the task of capturing the town (which act would have been of marginal benefit anyway), and Cuito Cuanavale remained as a key base which would remain in FAPLA hands through the end of the first Angolan civil war.[8]

Meanwhile, the COIN effort continued unabated in the OA. Ovambo remained the focus of operations by the security forces against infiltrations. However, the little known but apparently effective civil affairs operations in Kavango in the summer of 1985, codenamed 'Opeet' and 'Concert', were geared to maintaining the support of the civilian population for the security forces. The success of both operations effectively denied PLAN the use of Kavango as either a corridor or a base for infiltrations. The insurgents were thus forced to focus upon the area between the Cunene River and the eastern Cunene border north of the SWA/Namibia border – the 'shallow area' – as a staging area for infiltrations. This area was further limited by another major military operation by the security forces in February–March 1986, which targeted PLAN areas north of eastern Ovambo. A series of operations by the security forces in the Onocua-Mucope-Caiundo regions hit yet more insurgent targets north of the border.

For the period 1986-1988, the OA saw relative peace, despite continued attempts by PLAN to infiltrate south through Ovamboland into the white farming areas near Etosha. While actions by security forces in the OA were generally sufficient to contain the infiltrations, a series of operations from 1 to 22 May 1986, mainly targeting the area north of the border in east-central Cunene, apparently disrupted attempts by PLAN to reestablish their base camps and logistics there. 1987 saw continued cross-border raids, starting with one on 24 January which reached the Mongua area and killed 72 PLAN and about 40 FAPLA who tried to come to their assistance from the local garrison. FAPLA once again showed an aggressive posture when it intervened to assist PLAN when the security forces attacked the insurgents near Anhaca. FAPLA was repulsed, and the Angolan government claimed that the SAAF bombed the Ngiva area. On 27-28 July a SWATF force pursuing fleeing PLAN back into the shallow area was ambushed by a combined PLAN-FAPLA force, which then withdrew only to be pursued and defeated by the security forces. On 31 October and 1 November another operation, conducted by a combined SADF and SWATF force, penetrated into central Cunene and killed over 150 insurgents while losing eleven of its own.

Intervention in Angola, 1987-1988

By this time, however, the SADF was involved in the largest of its external operations, namely the series of actions called Operations 'Modular', 'Hooper', and 'Packer', which carried through to the spring of 1988. These three externals comprised the largest commitment of South African forces to Angola to date, and profoundly changed the course of the war. The stalemate over Cuban troop presence was broken, allowing for the South Africans to begin steps to give Namibia its independence. Due to its importance not just in altering the course of the war, but also because of their value as operations worthy of study in their own right, the SADF intervention in Angola is discussed in some detail here.

The fighting in 1987-1988 was the most intensive yet seen in the war, as the conflict took a decisive turn. The USSR and Cuba both thought that they could force a military solution to the conflict, and repeat a two-front strategy similar to that of 1985. The 1987 FAPLA offensive was much better planned and both the forces assembled for the operation as well as the logistical support were impressive. FAPLA was assisted by Soviet and Cuban advisers, and hoped by sheer mass of motorised infantry spearheaded by armour to penetrate UNITA territory. However, the MPLA had miscalculated both the degree of UNITA resistance as well as the willingness of the South Africans to intervene with ground forces. As a result, FAPLA suffered the loss of a fifth of its entire army in casualties as well as at least that percentage of its heavy weaponry and logistics vehicles.

The FAPLA build-up Preparations for the offensive began on 14 May, at which time logistics were built up in the Luena-Lucusse area in MR3 and at Cuito Cuanavale in MR6. Logistical support for the offensive continued through the summer, despite frequent UNITA attempts to sabotage FAPLA and Cuban supply efforts. Airlifted troops and supplies into Luena (MR3) and Menongue and Cuito Cuanavale (MR6) were regarded by most observers as key indicators of an impending offensive. An indicator of the main thrust of the offensive was the stockpiling at FAPLA installations on the east bank of the Cuito River opposite Cuito Cuanavale. Another logistics site was prepared at the crossing of the Lungue-Bungo River south of Lucusse.

Soviet logistical support had actually begun in January 1987, with hundreds of flights from Tashkent and Moscow in the USSR to Luanda. These flights, which lasted for the first six months of 1987, were aboard heavy air transports. Also shipped to Angola was over US$1.5 billion worth of major ground systems and equipment. These included more T-55 tanks, BTR-60 armoured personnel carriers, BRDM-2 armoured cars, and the new BMP-1 infantry fighting vehicle (IFV). Artillery included the range of smaller and medium Soviet systems, as well as BM-14 and BM-21 MRLs. Soviet SAM systems such as SA-8 or SA-13s were present as well, intended for tactical air defence against possible intervening South Africans.[9]

The logistics effort was unprecedented in the history of the war. Each day eight to ten Il-76 transports landed in Menongue from Luanda. Many of these had simply stopped at the capital to refuel after flying from the USSR. The flights carried weapons, spare parts, ammunition, food, and other end items for the MR6 offensive and were offloaded onto trucks to begin the trip to Cuito Cuanavale. The FAPLA resupply convoys, usually as many as 400 trucks, would make the journey every six days. Two brigades had the sole duty of convoy protection during this operation.[10]

South African military planners viewed the impending offensive with concern, as it represented an unprecedented military effort against UNITA. The FAPLA brigade TOEs were filled and in some cases overstrength; there were four motorised brigades operating on the Cuito Cuanavale Front and one on the Lucusse Front. Each motorised brigade had three motorised battalions each with 35 BTR-60 APCs, plus an armoured company of nine to eleven T-54 or T-55 tanks. Total brigade personnel strength was about 1,600 to 1,900. Also operating in support of the brigades on the Cuito Cuanavale Front were two tactical groups, each built around a FAPLA tank battalion.

The strategy remained similar to that of 1985. The Lucusse Front brigades would move south against Gago Coutinho (Lumbala Nguimbo) and then drive on to Mavinga, there to join with the group coming from Cuito Cuanavale. Using Mavinga as a base, FAPLA would then move on against Jamba.[11]

FAPLA was better prepared than in the past for the impending offensive. The operations the previous year had given EPA brigades experience in manoeuvre operations and although only one of the operations, the capture of Munhango, had been successful, FAPLA units had not suffered decisive, large-scale reverses or losses in MR3 or MR6 operations. As a result, FAPLA entered the offensive with a number of strengths. They included better training and support, as well as more foreign advisers. Each brigade had four to seven Soviet advisers as well as Cuban technical support. Mobility was enhanced by improved engineer equipment, including TMMs and AVLBs, and the basing of an engineer command element at Cuito Cuanavale. Morale remained a problem, and large numbers of conscripts that swelled FAPLA's size to over 80,000 remained generally unhappy with their lot.[12]

Concern for South African intervention similar to that which had taken place in 1985 and 1986 prompted FAPLA to augment its air defence, especially in MR6. Both installations and tactical units were provided with a number of Soviet systems; the mobile air defence included SA-7 and SA-14 shoulder-fired SAMs, plus SA-8 and SA-13s attached from FAPA-DAA assets to the operational groups and their manoeuvre brigades. The number of FAPA pilots was augmented with Cubans and other communist country personnel. The intent was to challenge South African air superiority in the area of operations in MR6, and protect convoys travelling between Menongue and Cuito Cuanavale.[13]

However, FAPLA operations were dominated by weak points. Foremost among these was a poor sense of timing. The offensive of 1987 was late, due to a number of factors including UNITA and South African Special Forces raids against key FAPLA installations. Combat units were poorly served by FAPLA artillery, as cannon and MRL fires were not properly targeted. They were thus often vulnerable to UNITA counterbattery fire. Air support was a problem as there was poor air–ground liaison. Despite extensive pre-operational build-ups, logistics continued to be the Achilles' heel of FAPLA. The system was vulnerable to corruption as well as to interdiction by UNITA. Although FAPLA initiated resupply operations as soon as offensives started (a key indicator to UNITA of a FAPLA attack), attrition rates were high and operational units often outran logistics, as supply bases were usually far to the rear of any operations.

UNITA had adequate time to prepare for the onslaught. By the time the offensive was underway, the insurgent forces available to counter the FAPLA offensive in Cuando Cubango included three regular battalions (later increased to five), five semi-regular battalions (later increased to eight), four penetration battalions, and one commando battalion.[14] In Cuando Cubango, already by May UNITA had positioned its 3rd and 5th regular battalions and two semi-regular battalions east of Cuito Cuanavale. Also there were two air defence teams armed with SAMs; four other teams were on the Lomba north of Mavinga.[15] To the north, UNITA forces countering the FAPLA offensive in Moxico included three regular battalions, five semi-regular battalions, and one penetration battalion. UNITA artillery battalions were assigned to support the manoeuvre units on each front.

South African response By the summer it was evident to SADF planners that they would have to commit forces to assist UNITA, although the extent of the projected involvement was still a matter of debate. However, the forces available to the SADF, both in northern Namibia and in South Africa itself, were impressive and could assemble considerable fire-power. In addition to SAAF assets at Oshakati, Grootfontein, and other bases in northern Namibia, the SADF had access to a number of extremely capable ground force units.

SADF Special Forces mentioned in connection with the 1987–1988 fighting include the 4th and 5th Reconnaissance Regiments. These two units of the famed 'Recce Commandos' were responsible for deep reconnaissance and special operations. 5th Reconnaissance Regiment was one of the first units involved in the SADF intervention, and was equipped with Unimog-mounted 106mm recoilless rifles.[16]

The SADF could also draw upon a number of regular South African Army forces in Namibia. The first was 32 Battalion, by this time a large unit based at Rundu with seven infantry companies, a support company with 120mm mortars, and a reconnaissance group. Also attached from 1987 was a battery of Valkyrie 127mm MRLs and a troop (four cannon) of 155mm G-5 artillery. The other major unit in northern Namibia available was 61st Mechanised Battalion Group at Oshakati. This unit was formed around two mecha-nised companies and an artillery battery, with support units. Both 32 Battalion and 61st Mechanised Battalion had taken part in a number of operations in southern Angola, and were experienced, disciplined, and well-trained units.

Other units were available, mostly Citizen Force personnel and units from South Africa. Some had previously been mobilised for operations such as 'Askari' and had performed well. Also directly on hand in the Operational Area were a number of SWATF units. However, the mission of these units was generally full-time counterinsurgency oper-ations against PLAN and most were thus not utilised for conventional action against FAPLA. Ironically, significant clashes between SWATF units and large PLAN/FAPLA forces did take place north of the Operational Area in the summer and autumn of 1987, but were not directly linked to the fighting further east.

The FAPLA advance[17] The main part of the advancing FAPLA units moved in motorised columns. These columns were spearheaded by T-55 tanks and BTR-60 APCs, followed by truck-mounted infantry. Infantry screens went in advance of the force and often flanked it as well. Frontages for the advancing forces were often over 1km wide, flanked by infantry and reinforced with armoured vehicles. The purpose was to keep UNITA anti-tank and mortar teams at a distance.

On 14 September, as a result of an eight-hour attack on the 47th Brigade, 76 FAPLA and two Soviets were killed. UNITA reported a battle on 18 September with FAPLA's 21st Brigade, in which it tried to cross the Lomba River. Five tanks, eight BTR-60s, and a TMM were destroyed by UNITA, and 100 FAPLA killed as government forces attempted to pene-trate south of the Lomba River. FAPLA had been ordered to capture Mavinga by 20 September. UNITA reported further battles on 19 and 20 September. 300 were wounded and fifteen captured from the 47th, 21st, and 59th Brigades. During these engagements, many of the FAPLA casualties were from South African artillery backing up UNITA forces. However, the SADF military planners had determined by this time that actual mechanised attacks would be necessary to contain and then dislodge the FAPLA force.[18]

Meanwhile, fighting on the Lucusse Front had come to a climax. The major battles took place on the Luzi River bridge, where the 43rd Brigade was reduced to half its effective strength. Further battles took place on 21 August, where the 45th Brigade was badly defeated north of the Mulundi River, and on 24 August, when the 54th Brigade was defeated on the Chizilimena Plain. Finally, on 25 October the 3rd Brigade was forced back from Cassamba and withdrew to Calapo on the Lungue-Bungo River. By 1 November FAPLA had withdrawn north of the river and destroyed the bridge behind it.[19]

The Lucusse Front operations were undertaken in total by UNITA, although the South Africans may have provided some assistance in logistical and medical support. The main effect of the collapse of the FAPLA Lucusse Front offensive was the unravelling of the Angolan government's grand plan to use two forces to capture Mavinga.

Operation 'Modular': South African intervention and the defeat of FAPLA[20] By the time the large FAPLA force from Cuito Cuanavale had launched its drive south-eastward, the South African government had decided to intervene on UNITA's behalf by providing artillery and other combat support, and finally ground troops to attack and defeat FAPLA's motorised brigades. The South African intervention to assist UNITA consisted of units of 32 Battalion as well as 61st Mechanised Battalion Group. Earlier delaying attempts by UNITA and SADF artillery bombardments, though devastating to government forces, failed to stop the drive by FAPLA, which advanced on broad, multicolumned fronts reinforced with armour. By the second week of September the two FAPLA operational groups were at the Lomba.

In late September and early October, South African forces now directly intervened to defeat attempts by the first operational group – the EPA 21st and 16th Brigades, with the 1st Tactical Group – to cross the Lomba at two sites west of the Cunzumbia confluence north of Mavinga. The actions saw the extensive use of a battery of G-5 155mm artillery, which performed with devastating effect upon the attacking FAPLA force, which had actually crossed the Lomba but then withdrew after taking massive casualties in fighting from 10 to 19 September. FAPLA's eastern group was unable to continue and the western group was plagued with logistical problems as well as harassing fire from UNITA and SADF units; the 59th Brigade failed to cross the Lomba on 13 September. SADF airstrikes also began to take their toll of FAPLA personnel and equipment. The decision was made by the FAPLA EMG to withdraw after these unsuccessful attempts.

However, UNITA and the SADF felt that a withdrawal would only be for the purposes of giving FAPLA time to regroup and resupply, then renew the attack. They decided to ensure that the returning force would not be combat-capable. The western group – the 47th Brigade with the 2nd Tactical Group south of the Lomba sources, and the 59th Brigade north of the Lomba – were still large, operational units despite significant casualties. The 47th was by now seeking to withdraw to the north of the Lomba, assisted by the 59th on the opposite bank. On 3–4 October 1987, the lagered positions of the 47th Brigade on the south bank of the Lomba were attacked by SADF mechanised forces and UNITA and SADF infantry units. The 47th Brigade, which had started out 1,600 strong from Cuito Cuanavale two months earlier, was destroyed as a fighting force and lost all of its equipment. The 2nd Tactical Group was annihilated as well. A few vehicles and several hundred infantry were able to escape the fighting and join the 59th north of the Lomba.

Throughout October FAPLA withdrew its forces from the Lomba back to the Chambinga area east of Cuito Cuanavale. The withdrawal was done in good order despite harassing ground and air attacks by UNITA and the SADF. However, FAPLA was still considered a threat and on 9 November the SADF attacked and badly mauled the EPA 16th Brigade at the Chambinga River. By this time Cuito Cuanavale had also come under attack from South African artillery. The airfield took considerable damage and FAPLA installations in and around the town suffered from continuous, accurate shelling. By the end of November it was becoming increasingly difficult for FAPLA to maintain a safe headquarters presence there. During November UNITA and the SADF drew their cordon tighter around the Chambinga heights east of Cuito Cuanavale, although FAPLA at times exhibited some skill in avoiding costly engagements during withdrawal. On 13 November the EPA 21st Brigade narrowly averted a trap set by the SADF to destroy it, withdrawing back to the Chambinga and safety. The 1st Tactical Group had not been as lucky, being destroyed in an SADF attack on the 11th. It was evident by this time that FAPLA's combat capability for offensive operations had been seriously reduced by Operation 'Modular'.

On 5 December SADF Operation 'Modular' ended. The South African aim – to assist UNITA in defeating the FAPLA offensive and pursue FAPLA back to Cuito Cuanavale – had been highly successful. An entire FAPLA motorised brigade, the 47th, had been destroyed, along with its supporting 2nd Tactical Group. Major losses had been inflicted on the 59th, 25th, and 21st Brigades, and another, the 16th, was seriously damaged in the fighting of 9 November. Cuito Cuanavale airport was put out of action and FAPLA was forced to move its Headquarters to Nankova, west of the town, to avoid SADF artillery. FAPLA air operations had to be run out of Menongue, far to the west, which limited their efficacy.

Operation 'Hooper': The siege of Cuito Cuanavale[21] Following the series of defeats at the hands of UNITA and the SADF, FAPLA and its Cuban allies retrenched at Cuito Cuanavale. The town was protected by three echelons of defence by six EPA brigades (21st, 59th, 25th, 16th, 66th, and 13th) as well as a strong Cuban contingent reinforced with armour, including T-62 tanks. But for most of December the SADF held off attacking the town's eastern approaches as troops for 'Modular' were replaced by new SADF units for 'Hooper'. In the meantime, South African artillery continued to pound Cuito Cuanavale while ground and air attacks targeted the road to Menongue and the logistics convoys that supported the besieged town.

The aim of Operation 'Hooper' was to dislodge FAPLA from the Chambinga heights on the eastern bank of the Cuito and ensure that the brigades confined there would not break out of the UNITA-SADF cordon. The two largest actions of the fighting were, first, the 14 January attack on the 21st Brigade by UNITA and the SADF. The unit lost most of its equipment and several hundred killed and captured. However, the 21st, reequipped and resupplied, were able to reoccupy their positions two weeks later. Then, on 14–15 February it was the turn of the EPA 59th Brigade, which suffered heavy losses as it was dislodged from its positions east of the Dala River sources; the 21st was also driven from the south bank of the Cuatir again. In the following two months the SADF continued its attempts to dislodge FAPLA, with attacks on the logistics base and dug-in EPA units at Tumpo on 25 and 29 February. Although FAPLA retained its foothold on the east bank of the Cuito River, its defensive line had been contracted to the areas between the Dala and Tumpo Rivers. The South African attacks were spearheaded by elements of 61st Mechanised Battalion Group backed up by the SAA 32 Battalion and SWATF 101 Battalion, plus a number of UNITA regular and semi-regular battalions.

End of the South African involvement: Operations 'Packer' and 'Displace' Operation 'Hooper' ended on 13 March 1988 with the transfer of operations from 20th South African Brigade to 82nd Armoured Brigade, with two squadrons (about 28) of Olifant-1 tanks. 82nd Brigade now controlled Operation 'Packer', the aim of which was to drive FAPLA and Cuban forces west of the Cuito River, or, failing that, to confine them to the bridgehead east of Cuito Cuanavale. Operation 'Hooper' had already driven FAPLA off the Chambinga heights and forced them to retreat to Tumpo logistics base. This latter now became the target of a third attack on 23 March by armoured and mechanised elements of 82nd Brigade and 32 Battalion with UNITA's 5th Regular Battalion, launched in conjunction with an attack by UNITA's 66th, 75th, and 118th Semi-Regular Battalions on FAPLA positions west of the river. The aim was to destroy the entrenched FAPLA forces east of the Cuito River. However, the attack failed after it bogged down in the minefields and defensive works around Tumpo, and the South Africans withdrew, leaving behind two tanks that had become stuck in the deep mud and which could not be towed free (one was later exhibited by FAPLA at Lubango; another was shown to journalists at Cuito Cuanavale after it had been towed free and washed down).[22]

By this time the situation in south-western Angola, with the deployment of Cuban troops there, required that South African forces near Cuito Cuanavale be moved opposite MR5. Operation 'Packer' thus ended on 30 April. After laying a cordon of mines around FAPLA positions at Tumpo, the SADF gradually withdrew its forces from Cuando Cubango and moved them westward to Sector 10 in Namibia to face Cuban troops that had moved south from MR4 to Cunene province. This was Operation 'Displace', which culminated in the battles near Techipa on 26 and 27 June and effectively presaged the end of South African military involvement in Angola.[23]

The fighting at Techipa was the result of continued Cuban probing of South African forward defences in Sector 10, and involved the SADF and SWATF luring a joint Cuban and Angolan force into an ambush where South African armour and artillery caused the advancing force severe casualties. While the conventional threat from the Cubans receded, PLAN took advantage of the announced South African withdrawal from Angola to increase its infiltrations, which were successfully resisted by COIN forces inside SWA/Namibia. Meanwhile, as a result of meetings in July and August, the linkage advocated by the United States since the early 1980s was finally agreed to in principle by all parties to the conflict. The South Africans announced that they would withdraw their forces from Angola by 1 September. At roughly the same time, negotiations at Ruacana on 16 August set up a liaison committee, the Joint Military Monitoring Commission (JMMC), comprising representatives of FAPLA, the FAR, SWATF/SADF, and US mediators. On 22 August a treaty signed at Ruacana ended hostilities.

The strategic situation at the end of 1988 The results of a year of South African involvement in Angola were profound. The armed intervention had decisively changed the course of the war. Despite massive Soviet, Cuban, and MPLA propaganda to the contrary, FAPLA and its supporters had been badly beaten.

■ FAPLA casualties included at least a fifth of its ground force and at least a quarter of its available equipment had been destroyed or captured. Equipment in the latter category wound up in UNITA hands to be fielded against FAPLA.

■ The face-off at Tchipa (late June) with its high Cuban casualties had discouraged the Cubans from a further desire to engage South African forces.

■ Cuban forces agreed to withdraw from Angola, in a linkage with the implementation of UN Resolution 435, which began the independence process for Namibia. This represented a major policy defeat for the MPLA, the Cubans, and the USSR.

■ UNITA remained in control of its south-eastern bastion, stronger than ever despite taking some high casualties in the fighting. UNITA forces had shown themselves highly capable and had successfully conducted joint operations with the SADF in Cuando Cubango (MR6).

■ Most importantly, for the South Africans, the mechanisms had finally been put into motion that would bring its involvement in SWA/Namibia to a successful conclusion under international auspices.

■ The security forces in SWA/Namibia had shown themselves fully capable of maintaining security in the OA simultaneously with the involvement of South African forces in Operation 'Modular' and 'Hooper' north of the border.

The 1 September 1988 withdrawal from Angola, despite being seen by some commentators as evidence of a military setback for the SADF in the fighting of the preceding year, was far from that. The exit from Angola was done in an unhurried, confident manner. By this time international attention was focused to the western part of the Operational Area, where Cuban forces deployed in FAPLA RM 5 faced off against SADF troops south of the border. However, the earlier fighting at Tchipa had taken away the Cubans' enthusiasm for any further confrontations with the South Africans. The security forces in SWA/Namibia itself remained fully capable of maintaining internal security in the OA and in responding to PLAN infiltrations.

CONCLUDING THE WAR, 1988-1990

The last phase of the conflict began on 22 December 1988. On that day, at UN Headquarters in New York, an accord was reached among South Africa, Angola, and Cuba. The accord comprised two separate agreements, the first of which initiated implementation of UNSCR 435 on 1 April 1989, and the second of which was an agreement between Angola and Cuba for a timed and phased withdrawal of the latter's troops from Angola, with the last scheduled to leave by 1 July 1991. The final phase of the COIN war in Namibia saw relatively little activity, with the exception of the fighting that began on 1 April 1989 when SWAPO attempted a massive infiltration across the border to establish bases in northern Namibia.[24]

The debacle suffered by PLAN took place the day after the JMMC was dissolved. This infiltration/invasion, which sent between 1,800 and 1,900 PLAN across the border, had the objective of seizing areas south of the cutline and proclaiming them 'liberated' PLAN bases that they hoped the UN monitors there would recognise. These bases, if under UN recognition/protection, would be safe from security force attacks, and later would then be used to attempt to influence the local population to vote a two-thirds majority in the coming election. PLAN further hoped to take advantage of the demobilisation of SWATF and the confinement of remaining SADF units in Namibia to their bases. However, the SWAPOL units in northern Namibia were able to contain the invasion, and the governmental authorities threatened to abrogate the peace agreement if they were not allowed to remobilise some SWATF units (101 and 102 Battalions). This was agreed to, and at the end of three days the insurgents had been decisively defeated, with as many as 500 casualties, including 200 killed. A rather hastily-developed and ill-advised UN scheme to intern surrendered PLAN members inside Namibia was rejected by the South African authorities, and after considerable international discussion, the insurgents were permitted to return to Angola without fear of attack from the security forces.

SWAPO's last attempt to establish bases south of the cutline had failed, and with it vanished its claim to ever holding any territory as a 'liberated zone' inside SWA/Namibia. Following the events of April 1989, there was little trouble keeping the terms of the peace agreement that also implemented UNSCR 435. South Africa had shown that it would back up the civil and military authorities as they attempted to keep their part of the bargain in the transition to independence for SWA/Namibia. South African rule ended with the installation of the SWAPO government on 21 March 1990. By that time Soviet influence throughout Africa was in retreat. The MPLA had undertaken one last gamble – unwisely – to capture Mavinga, which had stalled by March. In Mozambique the Chissano regime was attempting to put as much distance between itself and Marxism as possible. In Ethiopia, the Mengistu regime was reeling from defeats by the Eritrean and Tigrean guerrillas, and in little over a year would itself be swept away. As for South Africa, the previous month President de Klerk had announced the unbanning of the ANC and the beginning of a transition from the apartheid regime of the National Party to a democratic order that ultimately saw the April 1994 election of Nelson Mandela as RSA president.

Despite the final electoral resolution of Namibia's status in 1989 in SWAPO's favour, it still must be understood that the long military conflict in which the South Africans prevailed made the elections possible. Just as the long conflict moulded and shaped the SADF and SWATF, so did it change SWAPO. The triumph of US diplomacy that emphasised linkage between Namibian independence and Cuban troop withdrawal forced SWAPO into a framework for independence that gave it little leeway but to comply; attempts to disregard this framework and try to disregard the process, as in April 1989, met with disaster. While the outcome of the 1989 elections was largely determined by ethnic politics, with most Ovambos supporting SWAPO, observers noted that it had been 'free and fair', and the new government that took power did so without incident. Although experiencing many expected problems faced by a new government, SWAPO has still managed to steer a course midway between its former benefactor, Luanda, and its former overlord, Pretoria.

NOTES

1. The war has been summarised by Willem Steenkamp in *South Africa's Border War, 1966-1989*, Ashanti Press, Gibraltar, 1989. This work provides a basic chronological overview of the fighting as well as superb photography. Another excellent overview of the war is that of Morgan Norval in his *Death in the Desert: The Namibian Tragedy*, Selous Foundation Press, Washington DC, 1989, which discusses not only the SWAPO insurgency and South African COIN efforts, but also places the conflict in the context of major international issues of the day.
2. See the references in the preceding note. Most of the major incidents in the war have been covered as they occurred by the news media. The dates for the major incidents of the conflict discussed here are based on Steenkamp, *South Africa's Border War*, and on the Foreign Affairs Chronology of World Events, Second Edition, 1978-1991, Council on Foreign Relations Press, New York, 1992.
3. See Steenkamp, pp. 28-9. The Reconnaissance Commando was the precursor of the later Reconnaissance Regiments.
4. Steenkamp, *South Africa's Border War*, p. 61.
5. For Operation 'Daisy', see Norval, pp. 149-50.
6. See Helmoed-Roemer Heitman, *War in Angola: The Final South African Phase*, Ashanti Press, Gibraltar, 1990. See also Michael Hough, 'The Angolan Civil War with Special Reference to the UNITA Movement' in the *Institute of Strategic Studies of the University of Pretoria* [ISSUP] *Strategic Review*, November 1985, pp. 1-12.
7. For the JMC and the reasons for its failure, see the detailed discussion in Norval, pp. 181-94.
8. Breytenbach, p. 234ff; Heitman, pp. 14ff.
9. *The Evidence: Lomba-Kanage 1987*, UNITA, Jamba, Angola, 14 November 1987, p. 1.
10. Fred Bridgeland, *War for Africa* (Ashanti Press, Gibraltar, 1991), pp. 44-5.
11. *The Evidence*, p. 1.
12. *War for Africa*, p. 45.
13. In this FAPLA was only partially successful. South African Air Force (SAAF) tactics neutralised most of this strategy. See Heitman, pp. 310-30 and 346-7. Passive air defence measures played a large part in protecting South African ground forces that intervened against FAPLA. FAPA-DAA defensive measures and intercept tactics were somewhat more successful, but could not prevent most SAAF operations (Heitman, pp. 346-7).
14. *War for Africa*, p. 383. The UNITA regular battalions were the 1st, 2nd, 3rd, and 4th, with the 5th held in reserve. Later the 1st and 3rd regular battalions were teamed up with the SADF 4 SAI Battalion and 61st Mechanised Battalion Group, respectively (ibid., p. 386).
15. Heitman, pp. 27-30.
16. Heitman, p. 35; *War for Africa*, p. 386.
17. Press reporting, 24 August 1987, pp. D1-2
18. Press reports, 11, 14, 16, 22, and 23 September 1987.
19. *The Evidence*, p. 2.
20. See Steenkamp, pp. 150-3 for a detailed overview, as well as Heitman, pp. 109-68.
21. See Steenkamp, pp. 153-60; Heitman, pp. 169-265.
22. Heitman, pp. 266-84.
23. Heitman, pp. 285-307.
24. This fighting was documented in detail by Peter Stiff in his *Nine Days of War: Namibia - Before, During and After*, Galago Books, Alberton, 1989.

Chapter Three

Counterinsurgency Operations in Southern Africa

'The lesson to be learned from counter-insurgency operations is that terrorists fighting a guerrilla-type war can tie up lavishly equipped modern regular forces ten times their number in strength. Moscow and Peking have never underestimated guerrilla power. The money spent arming 'nationalist' and 'neutralist' movements across the world has paid tremendous dividends, for they have enmeshed so many countries in their Communist web. The financial outlay that the Soviets incurred by their systematic arming of the African rebels in the former Portuguese African territories was certainly well spent.'[1]

The above words were commentary on a late 1970s summarisation of military lessons learned in Southern Africa in general and Rhodesia in particular. In the long history of the wars against insurgents in southern Africa, those fought in Rhodesia, SWA/Namibia, Angola, and Mozambique stand out as representative examples of the presence and absence of a counterinsurgency doctrine. Ironically, the two conflicts fought by forces not using a COIN doctrine saw regime survival, but at a terrible economic and social cost. Rhodesia and SWA saw the triumph of the opposition; however, most of the national infrastructure survived and the political culture existing today in Zimbabwe and Namibia is to some degree more democratic than that which has prevailed in Angola and Mozambique. This could not have been without the success of Rhodesian and South African security forces in implementing a total COIN doctrine to prevent the insurgent destruction of political authority and commercial activity. The security forces were less successful in Rhodesia than they were in SWA but, measured by the standards of Angola, or especially Mozambique, they performed extremely well.

Specifically, counterinsurgency, or COIN, consisted of 'all measures, both civil and military, undertaken by a government, independently or with the assistance of friendly nations, to prevent or defeat insurgency.' Counterinsurgency operations, or COINOPS, were 'the military aspects of counter-insurgency. These consist of: a. Anti-terrorist operations (ATOPS); b. Psychological operations (PSYOPS); c. Operations in support of civil authorities (OSCA).' These definitions, used by Rhodesian security forces, apply also to the South African efforts in SWA.

The formula for success in COINOPS was basically fourfold. It included, first, the concept of unified or joint operations, namely: 'Unified operations between the armed forces themselves, between the armed forces and the police, and between the security forces as a whole and the civil administration... Joint operations entail control by a triumvirate–civilian, policeman, soldier–all under the single direction of a military Director of Operations. It is the job of the Director of Operations to make sure the system operates as two blades of a pair of scissors, neither subordinate to the other, but each making it possible for the other to succeed.' The second principle of successful COINOPS consisted of good intelligence, as timely and accurate as possible. Tactical success was a combination of this as well as the third principle, namely 'the speed, mobility, and flexibility of operations, the security of our bases, and the domination of the border and countryside'. The last component of successful COINOPS was one in which the Rhodesians proved deficient but in which the South Africans had much better success: 'The fourth but most important principle is winning the hearts and minds of the people and especially the indigenous people.'[2]

OVERVIEW OF COIN TACTICS IN RHODESIA AND SWA

Rhodesian and South African COIN operations at the tactical level shared many similarities, but it is important to note the differences as well. The strategic as well as the tactical conditions frequently differed to a considerable degree, as the following overview of Army, Police, and Air Force operations shows.[3]

ARMY AND POLICE PARAMILITARY OPERATIONS
Border control

Border control constituted a priority for both Rhodesian and SA/SWA forces. In Rhodesia parts of the border, especially the eastern border with Mozambique, had a protective fence or minefield, or both. However, this posed little difficulty to determined insurgent infiltrators. Active patrols were undertaken wherever possible to police the border, but they proved generally ineffective due to limitations on manpower – absolute numbers of troops and units – as well as the length of the border itself. It was possible to have major border control posts only at major entry points. Elsewhere, the fence, minefields, or other demarcation means were used.

Security forces in SWA had a more favourable set of circumstances working for them. In the first place, only one portion of the long SWA border with Angola posed a problem. Most of the vast border area was thinly populated and some areas, such as Kakoland, quite inhospitable with little cover or concealment for infiltrators. PLAN insurgents attempted to infiltrate into Ovambo, as most were Ovambo themselves. Other areas, such as Kavango and Caprivi, were hostile to them.

Terrain conditions favoured security forces. Flat and featureless, it had vegetation to provide PLAN infiltrators cover in and immediately after the rainy season. The level ground permitted mobile operations by motorised or even mechanised forces in response to incidents. Horse and motorcycle-mounted troops were also used, all with success. Insurgents were mostly on foot and little or no match for security forces rapidly moving down on them with the aid of trackers, primarily local or Angolan Bushmen.

Mobile operations in response to border crossings were only one dimension of control. Ambushes, observation posts, and other static means were used. The border itself was demarcated by the 'cutline', an area cut from the bush and bordered by a fence. The area to a depth of one kilometre south of the 'cutline' was a no-go zone and tracks detected there were immediately investigated.

Patrols

Patrols complemented static defences, and were heavily used in both conflicts. In Rhodesia, most routine patrols were done on foot by members of the RLI, TA, or Police, usually at platoon strength. Their purpose was preventative, to discourage insurgent activity in a given area, or to detect and track or otherwise obtain information about nearby groups of infiltrators. Once such information was developed, it was normally passed to the local JOC for a Fire Force response. The latter would often be guided to contact by the patrol or its forward observers. In addition to patrols in rural areas or areas subject to heavy infiltration, similar operations in urban areas, including black townships, and routine patrols of key points were also conducted by military, paramilitary, and police forces.

Patrols in SWA were normally conducted by motorised or foot units operating at platoon or half-platoon strength, as well as by mounted and motorcycle units. The forces involved could be military, paramilitary, or police. These patrols would be routinely conducted in a random fashion in an area to gather information, show the security force presence, and let insurgents and their supporters know that patrols could come at any time. The flat terrain permitted armoured car patrols as well, with a three- or four-car troop the norm.

Reaction Force operations

These differed markedly, primarily due to differences in terrain and force structure. In Rhodesia, the principal type of unit used to react to insurgent group sightings was the Fire Force (FF), which deployed by paradrop or helicopter. Fire Forces were located at each JOC headquarters and were each responsible for an operational sector. The ground element of the Fire Force company consisted of about 140 men – four troops of 28 men each plus a headquarters troop. Each of the Fire Force troops comprised seven four-man teams (the number that could be carried in an Alouette III). When insurgents were located the force deployed, partly paradropped from a Dakota aircraft (fifteen to twenty men in total), with the rest mounted in helicopters. These included four 'G-cars', light helicopters armed with machine guns each carrying four troops, and one or two 'K-cars', which were Alouette helicopters providing fire and communications support. They had 20mm cannon and circled the target area to suppress hostile fire while the Fire Force teams were air-landed. Often a twin-engine Lynx aircraft would be used for fire support instead. The air-landed troops would attack the insurgents and drive them into the 'stopper' groups formed by the paradropped troops.[4]

In SWA, ground force units were used to respond to insurgent sightings and incidents. The most common type of formation used was the reaction force, or 'Romeo Mike', abbreviated RM. RMs were COIN reaction force teams, normally drawn from the SWATF 101 Battalion (Ovambo). A typical Romeo Mike team included two officers and 20 to 40 enlisted men mounted in four Casspir armoured cars with a logistics vehicle in support. Their mission was rapid response to PLAN sightings with the aim of engaging and neutralising the insurgents. As the conflict progressed other COIN battalions, including 102 Battalion, 201 Battalion, and others also formed RMs. In addition, SWAPOL Ops-K, or Koevoet, used the RM principle to great effect.

Area operations

Area operations included those for cordon and search, sweep, and search and destroy missions. They were either initiated as the result of intelligence on infiltrators or were conducted at random. These were performed by Rhodesian forces in response to sightings of small numbers of insurgents. Due to manpower constraints, however, they were not generally employed at random. South African forces in SWA, however, with their greater numbers of personnel, were able to conduct area operations on a large scale in response to insurgent incidents or sightings. Greater manpower resources also meant that the security forces in SWA could conduct random area operations, including those known as 'Hawk Ops', in which air-landed forces conducted cordon-and-search while helicopters and reconnaissance aircraft provided air–ground support and reconnaissance.

LOC control and protection

Keeping LOCs open was a main priority in both the Rhodesian and SWA conflicts. This not only entailed mine detection and removal operations, but also escort of convoys and civil vehicles. In both conflicts mine-resistant vehicles figured heavily, with the South Africans learning much from the Rhodesian experience. The need to maintain LOCs for rapid movement of security forces as well as to ensure that the civil sector functioned made passage on the roads essential.

In Rhodesia the security forces were responsible for large, sparsely populated areas where unpaved roads presented numerous targets for the insurgent mine-layers. Frequent road patrols, often accompanied by area operations and off-road patrols, were designed to keep the insurgents off balance and on the move, and whenever possible deny them the opportunity to lay mines. In areas where groups of insurgents operated or in areas of heavy insurgent infiltration or transit, security forces provided escorts for civilian vehicles.

Mine detection and removal operations as well as escort operations were also done by the security forces in SWA. In the latter, however, the concentration of infiltration attempts in Ovambo (10 Sector) allowed security forces to concentrate on this region. Insurgents, once detected, were pursued relentlessly to deny them the time to lay mines. Most roads in Ovambo were, as in Rhodesia, not paved. Army engineers attempted to sweep for mines on the major roads on a daily basis, less often on other roads.

Roadblocks were used by security forces in both Rhodesia and SWA. In the latter, they were frequently set up at random, not only with the aim of restricting the use of vehicles by PLAN or its SWAPO supporters, but also to gather intelligence from passers-by. Most roadblocks, however, supplemented larger security force operations, in that they were set up in response to intelligence on nearby insurgent activity.

Operations in aid of the Civil Power

These operations included the protection of key infrastructure as well as government workers and officials. This was done routinely in both Rhodesia and SWA. In the latter, key commercial operations, both rail and road, were protected by armed escorts as well. The aim of such operations was to ensure that the government kept functioning despite the insurgents' attempts to prevent it from doing so.

Civic action

Activity of the military among the civil population was designed not only to show government presence but to do so in a constructive manner, coordinating with the civil authorities in providing services to locals that they would not otherwise receive. In SWA, such presence included the provision of construction teams and equipment by the SADF for local agricultural improvement projects, as well as teachers, medics, and other specialist personnel. Similar attempts were made in Rhodesia, but were limited due to manpower constraints on the security forces, as well as a difference in attitude that saw the black African population as a group to be coerced, not enticed, into supporting the government. Despite this, the Rhodesian Ministry of Internal Affairs (Intaf) continued through the conflict to strive to promote the welfare of the black African population with rural development projects. While from 1973 its African District Commissioner programme was directed heavily toward the refinement and organisation of the Protected Village programme and thus toward a paramilitary role, the establishment of the Guard Force in 1976 relieved Intaf of much of this burden.

MOBILE FORCES OPERATIONS

The critical tactical component of COIN operations involved locating, fixing, and engaging insurgents. The latter had the advantage in mobility and choice of time and place for attack. Thus it was critical for security forces to follow up as quickly and effectively as possible on intelligence about insurgent sightings, evidence of infiltrations, and other incidents. In Rhodesia this task was entrusted to the Fire Force, a combined airborne and heliborne operation. In SWA, the flat terrain of the northern Ovambo area was ideal for motorised and mechanised response, which have been discussed above. However, motorised, mechanised, and air assets were all used to provide the security forces with the maximum mobility possible in order to detect and respond to insurgent incidents. While most of the following types of activities were conducted by both Rhodesian and SWA security forces, it was only with the latter that mobile COIN operations developed to the point where they became a key component of regularly practised military operations.

Area patrols

Area patrols in SWA included those done by SADF, SWATF, and police forces. These included regular patrols of key areas or patrols conducted in response to intelligence of actual or pending infiltrations, as well as random patrols designed as a show of force and to surprise insurgents who may have sought to take advantage of any sort of routine by the security forces. At times the patrols were conducted not just by motorised infantry mounted in Buffel APCs or Casspir ACs, but also by armoured car units using Eland-60s or Eland-90s. Such units took advantage of the flat terrain of Ovamboland to cover large amounts of ground during patrols and, once in contact with insurgents, deliver large amounts of firepower their way. Armoured cars (Elands) were also used by the Rhodesians for patrols, but not to the degree of sophistication or in the numbers used by the South Africans in SWA.

Sweeps

Sweeps were also conducted by mobile motorised, mechanised, or armoured units in Ovamboland. These were designed to engage insurgents or drive them forward along an axis of advance into ambushes set by other units acting as stopper forces.

Convoy escorts

Convoy escorts were one of the most important routine operations by the security forces, and designed to prevent SWAPO/PLAN from denying road transit to either the security forces or the locals. Most convoy escorts were designed to protect commercial cargo and passenger vehicles. Convoys on paved roads and key gravel roads were regularly escorted. However, this was an infrequent service on the smaller, less well-travelled roads.

Support to cordon and search operations

These entailed the use of mobile COIN reaction forces in conjunction with the units conducting the area operations. Larger groups of insurgents, often well-armed, would often seek to break out of security cordons by attempting to slip through security force positions; once sighted, they were hunted down by mobile forces positioned to intercept their escape routes.

Motorcycle and mounted operations

These were conducted by patrols and often used in dense bush where motorised or armoured units were at a disadvantage. SWATF had both mounted and motorcycle units, and used them to great effect in surprising insurgents. Heavy bush often muffled motorcycle engines, which often had sound suppressing mufflers, allowing some patrols to actually surprise insurgents in camp.

POLICE OPERATIONS

The SWA police remained a key part of the security forces throughout the conflict. The police provided not only regular police support (criminal investigations, law enforcement, and traffic patrol), but also provided COIN support through the Southwest Africa Police COIN unit (SWAPOLCOIN) as well as the 'Operations-K' or Koevoet unit, essentially a reaction force. This was also the case in Rhodesia, where the BSAP's paramilitary formation performed COIN functions through the duration of the war.

Police counterinsurgency operations

These operations paralleled those of the military, although the COIN forces involved were generally smaller and did not utilise armoured cars. SWA police, however, did utilise Casspir ACs as well as Buffel APCs provided by SWATF in some of their operations, such as convoy escort and rural patrols. In road patrols the South African Railways Police at times provided the motorised escorts for road convoys in northern SWA.

Protection Force operations

These included VIP protection and guards for key infrastructure throughout SWA (but especially in the OA as well as in the Windhoek area). The force was most prominent in Ovamboland and other areas of the OA, where local political figures were threatened with assassination by SWAPO/PLAN as part of the latter's attempts to discredit the local government as well as the security forces' capability to protect it. In Rhodesia various guard forces were developed in the late 1970s, but were designed to patrol TTLs and other African areas.

Police reaction force operations (Ops-K)

These, discussed at greater length below, were a most effective force against SWAPO/PLAN. Its small units, normally consisting of four or five vehicles, namely Casspir ACs as well as a logistics vehicle or a command vehicle (usually a Casspir as well, although locally-manufactured Wolf Turbos were used from about 1986 onwards), were able to remain out in the bush for extended periods responding to sightings of insurgents and pursuing them.

AIR OPERATIONS

Both the Rhodesian and South African air forces provided heavy support to COIN operations. Our discussion lists a few of the ways in which they provided support. Internal COIN operations were supported by helicopter units in liaison, C3, local logistics support, and medical evacuations (casevac). Fixed-wing assets were used for the above, plus for reconnaissance, local logistics support (air drops), road and power line patrols, spotter patrols in area operations, artillery spotters, forward air control, and night spotter operations.

During external COIN operations the air force provided helicopter liaison, C3, fire support, logistics, and casevac. The fixed-wing assets supported the same, plus lift for paratroops, air strikes, airborne reconnaissance, and even psychological operations (the 'Skyshout' to parallel the Army's 'Groundshout').

SAAF logistics missions in northern SWA included fixed-wing provision of logistics support and troop transport. Helicopter assets were used on a smaller scale for the same purpose, supporting operations in the field by providing food, water, and ammunition and evacuating the wounded.

The role of reservist support to air operations in both conflicts was an important one, providing additional valuable manpower otherwise not available for patrols and other support. In Rhodesia such support was provided by the Police Reserve Air Wing, and was heavily composed of farmers, many of whom had their own aircraft and airstrips. In SWA farmers gave their reserve service to 1 SWA Squadron, under the SWATF. 1 SWA Squadron was responsible for considerable support in helping ground units locate and track insurgents as well as in conducting patrols.

POPULATION CONTROL AND PSYOPS; POPULATION SUPPORT

On and beyond mere military and police measures, however, were operations and programmes designed to maintain and keep the support of local black African populations in both Rhodesian and SWA. The white populations in these countries did not require such measures, but rather organisation to ensure that they could conduct as much self-defence as possible while at the same time playing a role in the counterinsurgency effort as a whole.

Psychological Operations

Psychological Operations were extensively used by the security forces in both the Rhodesian and SWA conflicts and took two basic forms. The first comprised a constant production of various media designed to persuade the population to cease support of the insurgents and to support the government. This included the production of leaflets and posters that attacked the insurgent agenda and urged locals to report them. Often pictures of dead or captured insurgents would be on the leaflets and posters. The broadcast media were also extensively used to voice the government viewpoint and counter broadcasts from countries that supported the insurgencies. A second form of Psychological Operations consisted of support to specific operations, especially externals. This included production of leaflets warning locals away from the scene of the fighting and not to interfere, or using loudspeakers from ground or aerial platforms to broadcast messages aimed at the local population or the insurgents themselves.

Population control

Both the Rhodesian and SWA conflicts saw the imposition of curfews and other restrictions on the population. These included ID checks in public places, checkpoints on roads, random searches of automobiles, and the like, all conducted by the security forces as part of continuing daily operations.

Much more carefully planned, however, were schemes by the Rhodesians designed to separate the insurgent from his population support base. This resulted in the Protected Village (PV) programme, instituted by mid-1974. At that time, 50,000 people were moved from the Chiweshe TTL into 21 PVs during a two-week operation; it was followed by a similar exercise in the Madizwa TTL. The initial result was to deprive the insurgents of their local support, complicating the logistics and affecting their recruiting attempts and access to sources of intelligence. By 1977 the PV programme had spread to all Operational Sectors, monitored by the Guard Force, instituted the year previously.

In SWA, the situation was somewhat different in that the main source of insurgent recruits was the Ovambo population. The key in SWA was to ensure ready detection and neutralisation of any border crossings by SWAPO/PLAN. This was generally successful and the use of protected villages or similar methods was not a feature of the conflict here.

Population support

Support to the civil power as well as civic action were major components of both the Rhodesian and SWA conflicts. In this the South Africans were more successful than the Rhodesians, if only because the efforts of the latter were offset by the extremely difficult security situation. The ability to protect the black African population was a key factor in the conflict, and all the agricultural, commercial, educational, infrastructure, medical, and other improvements proved of little impact in areas of insurgent presence and control. In SWA the situation was quite different as the target area for SWAPO/PLAN was restricted and vigorous security operations kept them from reaching most of the Ovambo population and using it as a base.

Organising the white population in support of the COIN effort was just as important as separating the black population from the insurgents. The whites had a vested interest in seeing the insurgents' aims thwarted and in organising to protect themselves, as rural security was the first to be affected by insurgent activity.

Both the Rhodesians and the South Africans organised rural white farmers into local networks that supported reserve police or army formations. In Rhodesia, farmers' support was coordinated at the local government level by the chairman of the local Civil Defence Committee, who was also normally the Deputy Commissioner of Police. The basic organisation was of a local 'stick' of less than a dozen farmers who provided first-line mutual assistance in the event of incidents and who were connected with the 'Agric Alert' radio system. The latter was used for regular daily communication with the local police office. Such efforts countered, with mixed success, attempts by the insurgents to target farms either for attacks against the owners, or more frequently the black farm labourers, who lived in compounds removed from the owners' residences and who were frequently targeted as sources of food and money.

In SWA the South African system was similar, although the local army reserve formation, the Area Force Unit (AFU), was primarily responsible for providing the coordination. The AFU was the basic military reserve unit, a battalion-level formation that was equivalent to the South African Army Commando, which had specialised companies and platoons that could be dedicated to COIN missions and were staffed primarily by reservists. The Military Area Radio Net (MARNET) system connected farmers to the local AFU headquarters. However, there were differences between SWA and Rhodesia. In SWA, the main white farming area was south of Ovambo, with relatively few farmer targets in the latter. SWAPO/PLAN insurgents were not established south of the border, which meant that local farmers would be able to have advance warning and make necessary preparations whenever a major infiltration was detected. On the other hand, the white farmers remained a symbolic target of the insurgents, who sought to improve their credibility by showing that they could operate outside of Ovambo areas.

RHODESIA

Rhodesia is a case of COIN forces never losing a tactical engagement but nevertheless losing the war for the support of the general population. In many ways this was due to the unwillingness of the white government to completely trust the Africans or relate to them in any way except as ruler and ruled. This attitude lost the war for the UDI government long before the final difficult days of the late 1970s. At that time manpower realities forced the government to recruit more blacks.

Despite its ultimate strategic failure, the Rhodesian effort represents a model for successful operational and tactical level COIN efforts against well-armed and organised insurgents who had the advantage of external bases and wide international support. Rhodesia's lessons were well-learned by the South Africans, who applied them not only to the SWA conflict but in external operations against Angolan targets.

EVOLUTION OF COIN WARFARE

The conflict was marked by the evolution of joint capabilities, built around the triad Army-Air Force-Police. The joint concept had been carried over from earlier experiences by security forces and implemented from the start of the crisis. It evolved through several stages. The first was from the time of the joint local security committees in the late 1960s to the creation of OPS 'Hurricane' in 1972, and was largely informal within the existing security framework. 'Hurricane' formalised the joint concept with the formation of the first Joint Operational Centre (JOC), and was the paradigm for the next stage of joint concepts. Later it utilised an effective joint ground–air COIN reaction force, the Fire Force, to engage insurgents once detected. Eventually each of the operational sectors had a Fire Force. From the mid-1970s, however, the JOC/Operational Centre concept further evolved, adding another leg to the existing triad of security forces by incorporating the Guard Force, and applying the joint security concept to more local levels by establishing sub-JOCs. The final stage in this evolution came on 23 March 1977 with the establishment of Combined Operations Headquarters (COMOPS) under Lieutenant General Peter Walls in Salisbury and the nomination of the senior army officer at each JOC as the commander for COIN operations.

The formation OPS 'Hurricane' was a landmark in the Rhodesian conflict, not only for the template it provided security forces for subsequent JOCs, but also for the changed nature of the threat it was designed to counter. December 1972 saw the intensification of what had been a relatively low-level conflict into a full-fledged insurgency established inside north-eastern Rhodesia. The period 1973–1975 saw limited success by security forces in keeping a tactical ascendancy over the insurgents, primarily ZANU/ZANLA, that were the larger threat. However, the April 1974 coup in Portugal signalled the start of the spread of insurgent operations south along the entire Mozambique border by the end of the year, prompting the creation in February and May 1976 of OPS 'Thrasher' and OPS 'Repulse', with headquarters at Umtali and Fort Victoria, respectively.

Subsequent operational sectors and their JOCs were patterned after OPS 'Hurricane'. The latter had at first been a major success and was thus the model for subsequent operational sector structures set up throughout the rest of the 1970s. The main flaw in the operational sector concept was the tremendous requirement for manpower assets that Rhodesia did not have available. While OPS 'Hurricane' was the only operational sector, it had sufficient forces to throw against infiltrations from the Tete and northern Manica area. But as the conflict progressed and new sectors were established, security forces had to be spread thinner as they were allocated to them. The effectiveness of the security forces in the joint security system resulted in ever greater demands upon them. Indeed, the requirement for joint security intensified in the late 1970s, and as the war progressed the requirement for continued refinement of joint security at more local levels resulted in the formation of sub-JOCs; by the end of the war there were seventeen of them, supported at any one time by 40 to 50 company bases in the bush.

Hand in hand with the operational sector concept went population control measures. The establishment of the protected village (PV) programme began in on 25 July 1974 with Operation 'Overload', and entailed the movement of almost 50,000 residents of the Chiweshe Tribal Trust Lands into 21 PVs in enclaves that could be guarded and monitored. Its initial success prompted Operation 'Overload Two' through August–October with the Madzipa TTL. Subsequent efforts gradually expanded the programme to all Operational Sectors by 1977. However, the PV programme was viewed simply as a population control measure (denial of local support, creation of free-fire zones) and not a preventative measure to deny the insurgents new operational ground. Thus TTLs most affected by infiltration and with insurgent support networks in place were first put in the PV programme, leaving ZANU/ZANLA free to continue to organise support in other TTLs.

However, at first the PV programme served to deny ZANU/ZANLA a population support base and left security forces areas in which to freely operate. But as the conflict progressed the insurgents began to consolidate their recruitment and organisation in the PVs themselves. Thus the programme proved ultimately counter-productive. By the mid-1970s the insurgents had instituted support networks in most of the TTLs, and the PV programme, far from weakening these networks, strengthened them, as security force assets were required for the expanding PV structure. Thus many if not most of the remaining TTLs were progressively neglected and left to the insurgents.

At first the responsibility for security in the PVs was entrusted to the Ministry of Internal Affairs (Intaf), with personnel from its African District Assistant programme deployed in platoon-strength units to guard each village. The PVs were increasingly targeted by the insurgents, and this, plus the growing complexity of the programme and the demands it placed on Intaf, resulted in the recruitment and fielding of the Guard Force in early 1976. The Guard Force, which was a fourth force to join the existing security force triad of Army – Air Force – Police, was integrated into the joint security establishment, with an area Group Headquarters for the force co-located with the local JOC headquarters. The mission of the force evolved through the 1970s to eventually include protection not only of PV complexes and adjacent areas but also infrastructure, such as rail lines, that ran nearby. In some cases local Group headquarters provided personnel for urban operations as well.

External operations have been discussed elsewhere. It should suffice to note that the final phase of the conflict was marked by the externals, which represented a holding action against attempts by the insurgents to pre-empt the political process. The externals proved most successful against ZIPRA bases in Zambia, and were quite limited in their ability to hamper ZANLA and its bases and LOCs in Mozambique. The Rhodesians were able to capitalise on their past joint operational experience to ensure the maximum degree of such endeavour in external operations. This expertise improved as such operations continued for two years.

Psychological operations to win over the population were too little and too late. The security forces never took the insurgents' political campaign seriously, and fought instead a military war. They hoped that by inflicting military defeats on insurgent bands that they could discredit them as a military force and thus demonstrate to the African populace this weakness. However, the latter was a moot issue among the Africans, as the insurgents, especially Mugabe's ZANU, had developed their strategy precisely because of the Rhodesian security forces' tactical advantage. They instead sought to pursue and win a political war, organising the African population to support their cause, acquiring internal bases from which to initiate ever greater numbers of incidents (thus forcing the security forces to disperse over larger areas of operations), and demonstrate by this the inability of the Rhodesian regime and its military to govern the country.

Another, more significant failure of PSYOPS was the unwillingness of the government to work to change white attitudes.

Thus, in the later stages of the war, despite their clear superiority in military tactics, the Rhodesian security forces had already lost the support of the rural population, and with it, the COIN war:

'The real problem is that the Rhodesian military have misunderstood the nature of the war which they are fighting. They have failed to realise that the war is essentially political rather than military and that the guerrillas have no immediate need to be militarily efficient. The guerrilla's aim is to hit soft targets for maximum political impact and keep the Security Forces off balance, spreading them out in the large rural space to allow him freedom to pursue his indoctrination, intimidation and political preparation of his rural base... political control of the countryside has ensured a secure base for the guerrilla enabling him to achieve superior mobility. All the guerrilla needs now is time further to develop these assets and his military proficiency in order to achieve victory.' (Arbuckle 1979: 32)

FIGHTING THE COIN WAR
Mission

The mission of the security forces was:

■ Actively support and participate in joint security management organisations and operations
■ Locate, fix, and engage insurgent groups
■ Protect the civil population from insurgent activity and influence
■ Protect government and commercial institutions and infrastructure, including LOCs and public transport
■ Prevent the spread of insurgent influence in the civil population

The mission to find and engage insurgents later took on a heavily 'external' character as security force strikes against ZIPRA and ZANLA bases in Zambia and Mozambique in the late 1970s became quite common.

COIN institutions

From the start the lack of manpower forced the Rhodesians into working in a joint service mode–Army (regular and special formations), Air Force, and Police. Rhodesian Combined Operations Headquarters was located in Salisbury. This body, which reported directly to the Prime Minister, coordinated all COIN operations in Rhodesia and planned and developed COIN strategies. COMOPS was represented at the cabinet level by its own minister, the Minister of Combined Operations.[5]

Joint Operational Centres Under the Rhodesian security management system, the country was divided into a number of operational sectors, each managed by a Joint Operational Centre. Established during the Rhodesian conflict, the Joint Operational Centres (JOCs) coordinated all security force actions in their areas of control, which corresponded to Operational Sectors (OPS). Local JOCs operated under a main JOC in Salisbury at Defence Headquarters. Sub-JOCs, which totalled seventeen, existed for each of the main JOCs.

Operational Sectors were also known as Joint Operational Commands. They were areas of territorial responsibility for COIN forces. Each Sector was administered by a Joint Operational Centre that coordinated all security force actions in its AOR.

Not all sectors were established at the same time. The first was set up in 1972 and the last in 1978. The sectors, with their responsibilities and dates of creation, were:

- OPS 'Hurricane', in north-eastern Rhodesia, created 1972;
- OPS 'Thrasher', in the eastern highlands, created February 1976;
- OPS 'Repulse', in south-eastern Rhodesia, created May 1976;
- OPS 'Tangent', along the Botswana border, created August 1976;
- OPS 'Grapple', in the Midlands, created in March 1977;
- Salops', covering Salisbury and immediate environs in the centre of the country not covered by 'Grapple';
- OPS 'Splinter', in the Lake Kariba area, created in June 1978.[6]

The first four operational sectors, 'Hurricane', 'Thrasher', 'Repulse' and 'Grapple', were controlled by Rhodesian Army brigadiers. OPS 'Grapple' and 'Salops' were controlled by the Police and were under assistant commissioners.

COIN Forces Counterinsurgency forces in the Rhodesian conflict included the regular Army (a primarily territorial force filled by conscripts), the Special Forces, and the Rhodesian Air Force.

Territorial Army The Territorial Army was the main vehicle for training National Servicemen (NSMs), who served as conscripts in the Rhodesian Army for a tour of eighteen months, as well as retraining former NSMs who had been called up for reserve duty. The principal unit to which these personnel were assigned was the Rhodesian Regiment (RR), in whose territorial battalions the personnel would train and serve when mobilised.

Rhodesian Army Special Forces[7] Rhodesian Army Special Forces constituted a separate headquarters from the regular army and comprised three and later five elements. These included the Rhodesian African Rifles (RAR), the Rhodesian Light Infantry (RLI), the Special Air Service (SAS), the Selous Scouts, and Grey's Scouts. Both the RAR and RLI were originally under Army Headquarters but due to their increasing participation with, and proficiency in, special operations, they were by the late 1970s included among the Rhodesian Army Special Forces, and also were parcelled out to the Joint Operation

Commands (JOCs). After 1977 Special Forces were under the direct control of COMOPS.

The Rhodesian branch of the SAS first achieved prominence in the Malayan conflict in the 1950s. At first used to track insurgents, it became heavily involved in COIN operations by the 1970s and was expanded into a regiment with four squadrons and was heavily used for external operations. An element of the Rhodesian Special Forces, the SAS was an elite unit with rigorous selection standards, and remained all-white to the end of the war, at which time it was disbanded by the Zimbabwe government. The unit was a relatively small formation and at no time did more than 200 or so SAS 'operators' work externally. It was instrumental in establishing the RENAMO insurgency in neighbouring Mozambique in the late 1970s.

The Selous Scouts was formed in 1973 at the start of Operation 'Hurricane'. Its initial mission was one of gathering intelligence on ZIPRA and ZANLA, but the unit became more actively involved in both internal and external operations. The unit employed large numbers of 'turned' insurgents as well as deserters (on the same principle used by the Portuguese colonial authorities with the flechas), which augmented their capabilities considerably. The unit was noted for its 'pseudo' operations as well as training combat tracking personnel. By the end of the war the unit had about 420 personnel; it was dissolved when the Zimbabwe government took power.

Grey's Scouts was a Special Forces mounted unit trained to track insurgents on horseback. Recruiting personnel from the regular Army, it remained relatively small, only adding a second squadron in 1978. The unit did not have more than 250 personnel.

The Rhodesian Air Force (RhAF)[8] The Rhodesian Air Force consisted of the headquarters, eight squadrons under the Operations Directorate based at New Sarum Air Station at Salisbury and Thornhill near Gweru, base defence units, and a Training Directorate. Total personnel by the end of the 1970s numbered about 2,900.

In the late 1970s the Rhodesian Air Force included about 30 older-model fixed-wing combat aircraft–mostly bombers and light attack aircraft–that supported the ground forces in COINOPS, eighteen fixed-wing transports, and 26 fixed-wing training and liaison aircraft.

The RhAF helicopter inventory in the mid-/late 1970s included 27 Aérospatiale Alouette II and IIIs. Rotary-winged assets received a boost in late 1978 when eleven Bell 205 helicopters found their way to Rhodesia via various covert routes. Through accidents and maintenance shortfalls, only five or so were operational by mid-1979.[9]

Rhodesian Police Rhodesian police elements included the British South African Police (BSAP) and subordinate units. The BSAP was the regular Rhodesian police force, operating throughout the conflict in a regular police mission. Its name was a carryover from the colonial period. The force consisted of the Duty Uniform Branch (the regular uniformed force), the Criminal Investigation Department (CID), the Special Branch (CID), the Support Unit, the Police Anti-Terrorist Unit (PATU), and the Police Reserve. Of these, two had a special role in the conflict:

(a) Special Branch (SB). This element of the BSAP (Rhodesian police) was recruited from its CID and under the operational control of the Central Intelligence Organisation (CIO). It was responsible for internal political intelligence.

(b) Support Unit. The BSAP Support Unit was the BSAP paramilitary element. Its structure was similar to that of the Rhodesian African Rifles (RAR), commanded by white police personnel and staffed largely by black African soldiers; Support Unit personnel received extensive paramilitary training. Its most active period of use ran from 1976 to the end of the war in 1980.

COIN units COIN units included Fire Force companies and teams, as well as the Ministry of Internal Affairs (Intaf) and Guard Force and Security Force Auxiliaries.

Fire Forces were located at each JOC headquarters and were each responsible for an operational sector. The ground element of the Fire Force company consisted of about 140 men – four troops of 28 men each plus a headquarters troop. Each of the Fire Force troops comprised seven four-man teams (the number that could be carried in an Alouette III). When insurgents were located the force deployed, partly paradropped from a Dakota aircraft (15–20 men total), with the rest mounted in helicopters. These included four 'G-cars', light helicopters armed with machine guns each carrying four troops, and one or two 'K-cars', which were Alouette helicopters providing fire and communications support. They had 20mm cannon and circled the target area to suppress hostile fire while the Fire Force teams were air-landed. Often a twin-engine Lynx aircraft would be used for fire support instead. The air-landed troops would attack the insurgents and drive them into the 'stopper' groups formed by the paradropped troops.[10]

Rhodesian Ministry of Internal Affairs (Intaf) forces played a significant role in the conflict, though not always a highly visible one. Intaf was responsible for overseeing the affairs of Rhodesia's Black African population, and was thus a valuable source of intelligence and other useful information for security forces in a range of operations. Intaf developed the African District Commissioner programme from 1973 onward to support the Protected Village (PV) programme and also to support operations of the Intaf paramilitary wing, established in the early 1970s to provide protection for Intaf operations in TTLs and other African areas.

The Guard Force and Security Force Auxiliaries figured later in the conflict. The Guard Force was formed to relieve Internal Affairs personnel of the duty of patrolling and monitoring the PV programme, taking over from Intaf in mid-1976. The first elements of this force were fielded in 1976 and eventually deployed throughout the country. It came to number about 20,000, organised in Group Headquarters that were colocated with local JOCs, and while generally restricted to operations in the PVs at times assisted other security force elements in local operations. Eventually it came to be used in other roles as the PV programme peaked. From 1978 the Guard Force was responsible for protection of urban key points as well as railways.[11]

The Security Force Auxiliaries (SFA) was built starting in 1978 from 'returned' insurgents. The force was renamed the Pfumo ve Vanhu ('Spear of the People') in 1979. The SFA was primarily deployed in the TTLs, where it filled the role of local village militias. It was trained by regular Army and some Special Forces personnel. The SFA was at best only partly effective in hampering ZIPRA and ZANLA operations in areas where they were present.[12]

Internal COIN

The primary aim of the internal COIN operations was to prevent cross-border infiltrations by the insurgents as well as to locate, fix, and engage insurgent groups inside Rhodesian territory. To do this a range of operations was conducted. Routine patrols were designed to provide a security force presence in affected areas. Route security comprised road patrols and checkpoints to keep LOCs open, as well as mine-detection operations in areas subject to mining by infiltrators. Once insurgents were detected, reaction was as rapid as possible, normally with the Fire Force assets. However, area operations such as cordon-and-search were used to detect and neutralise small groups of insurgents as well as search for weapons and equipment caches.

External COIN

External operations targetted insurgent bases and LOCs. In doing so the Rhodesian security forces hoped to degrade the guerrillas' capability to launch attacks against targets inside Rhodesia. This facet of COIN strategy was partially successful, although sensationalised by the press. While it deterred ZIPRA from utilising its conventional assets in Zambia, it only prompted ZANLA to be more wary about the positioning of its external bases and support structure, and drew Mozambican security forces into the conflict as well.

SOUTH-WEST AFRICA

During the mid-1970s, many observers believed that it would be a matter of time before SWAPO gained the ascendancy in SWA/Namibia using classic communist insurgent strategy and tactics in the same way that ZANU and ZAPU were using them in Rhodesia. SWAPO was an externally-based insurgency supported to the hilt by the USSR, East Germany, Cuba, and other communist countries (and sympathetic international aid and church organisations), and had the additional benefit of having United Nations approval (engineered by the USSR and other communist countries in conjunction with third-world nations). Historically, such insurgencies in the past proved successful in advancing the influence of the USSR and its allies, generally resulting in the establishment of non-democratic regimes with ties to Moscow. However, the COIN war in Namibia was one of those rare examples where the security forces prevailed. Ironically, SWAPO did in the end gain power, but only as the result of an election pronounced free and fair by international observers. This was, however, a far cry from SWAPO leader Sam Nujoma's famous 1978 statement that his movement was fighting neither for majority rule or the democratic process. SWAPO, said Nujoma, were revolutionaries, with their own ideas of what was best for the people of SWA/Namibia.[13]

Despite this attitude on SWAPO's part, the security forces eventually prevailed, due in large part to the emphasis on aggressively responding to all insurgent incidents inside SWA/Namibia, denying SWAPO/PLAN a secure base in Angola, and working to get and keep the support of the general population. In the end, the only realistic option left to SWAPO/PLAN was the ballot box.

DEVELOPMENTS IN COIN STRATEGY

The evolution of COIN doctrine by the South African security forces in SWA/Namibia progressed through the 1970s but by the early 1980s had matured into a comprehensive doctrine. In many ways it paralleled security practices in the RSA itself, but did not undergo the discredit that the National Security Management System (NSMS) there suffered at the hands of the South African public. The NSMS was a comprehensive doctrine the main aim of which was the maintenance of internal security in the RSA. However, a knowledge of the applications and modifications of certain parts of this doctrine to the SWA/Namibian situation are key to understanding the success of the South Africans there. Perhaps the principal area of endeavour in which the security forces were successful was in the area of civil-military relations. As opposed to the internal security forces in the RSA, those in SWA/Namibia realised early in the conflict that to actively earn the support of the civilian population, and then to keep it, was the key to the conflict.

The key stage in the development of South African COIN doctrine in SWA/Namibia was the mid-1970s. Up to this time the responsibility for border control and internal security rested with the police. The latter, as with all other South African security forces, were heavily preoccupied with the containment of communism in the wake of RSA independence in 1948 and the imposition of apartheid and population control. The turbulent experiences of the following decades as Black African discontent at home coalesced and took inspiration from anti-colonial struggles elsewhere on the continent fuelled the concerns of the security establishment. As a result of this concern with population control and countering communist-inspired revolutionary activity, the security forces in SWA/Namibia were to match increased insurgent activity with their own escalation in the struggle in a fashion generally parallel to security developments in the RSA.

The South African military had been since the beginning of the century the premier fighting force on the continent, and through the experience of the Boer War, two world wars, and the Korean conflict had maintained a considerable experience base and familiarity with modern weaponry and tactics. However, it also had successfully fought on the continent itself, especially in East and North Africa, and had adapted conventional and light forces doctrine and tactics to the African environment. The experience with light forces began to predominate in the 1960s, when it became obvious that most wars in sub-Saharan Africa would be fought in a semi-conventional style at best, and that the typical style that evolved was a Western-style military fighting a communist-backed insurgent force.

Throughout the 1960s a considerable amount of experience had been gained in the struggle against insurgencies worldwide. These included the participation of the Rhodesians in Malaya and in their own COIN struggle; the mercenary experience in the Congo (now Zaire) in the 1960s; the Portuguese fight against insurgencies in their African colonial empire; and the French experience in the long and bitter Algerian civil war of the late 1950s and early 1960s. However, South African military thinkers and planners were especially interested in the French and US experience in Vietnam, where the Viet Minh and later the Viet Cong forced out the armed forces of two nations that vastly outnumbered them in terms of manpower, resources, and firepower. With SWAPO/PLAN, they had an insurgency that used the same philosophy as the Viet Minh/Viet Cong, which harked back to the guerrilla strategy of the Soviet partisans fighting the German army on the Eastern Front in the Second World War. Such an approach to guerrilla warfare emphasised coercion and terror as the main vehicles of population control, and a 'zero-sum' view of loyalties. Anyone not an obvious supporter of the partisans was thus an enemy to be eliminated. Those among the general population who tried to remain neutral had to be coerced – by enforced 'political education' and selective acts of terror – into supporting the guerrillas.

A comprehensive strategy for confronting Marxist revolutionary insurgent movements was developed in the 1960s by a US military officer, John J. McCuen. McCuen, who examined insurgent warfare in Vietnam and Algeria, gave key examples of the application of the concept of revolutionary warfare on society. The latter, the general population of a country, was most at risk from insurgents, especially those of the Marxist-Leninist variety who used coercion and terror against soft targets by an indoctrinated, disciplined cadre of trained guerrilla fighters. The aim of counterrevolutionary warfare was to deny the insurgents the capability to get and maintain the support of the general population through force. Two wars had to be fought at the same time – combat against the insurgent forces as well as a battle to win and retain the support of the population.[14]

McCuen's strategy rested on the 'oilspot' (tache d'huile) concepts of a French military officer and writer, Joseph Gallieni. As developed by McCuen, the struggle for the loyalty and active support of the population was essential, as without it the insurgents could not be defeated, nor could their Marxist-Leninist world view. The latter would only be rejected if the military and civil authorities could guarantee the security of the general population and allow them to enjoy a standard of living and well-being that prevented the guerrillas from recruiting supporters from among it. At the basis of the 'oilspot strategy' was the need for retaining control of military bases. These were of three kinds – those in areas under government control, those in contested areas, and those in areas controlled by the insurgents. It was essential to retain control of bases in areas under government control, and then initiate operations to regain control of bases in contested areas, and finally in insurgent areas. The importance of bases was their use to launch a COIN effort. This latter did not simply consist of military operations. Rather, they were a comprehensive series of actions by military and civil authorities that were designed to protect the local population from attack as well as to allow the government to carry out political, social, and economic measures targeting the surrounding population.

The use of the bases, according to McCuen, was either to retain control of territory for the central government, or to regain control of territory that had been lost. Key priorities for control included major population centres, not only towns and cities but also heavily populated agricultural areas that were key food producing regions, and industrial areas, namely centres for mining, petroleum extraction and refining, and key industries. In the zero-sum strategy of COIN warfare, what was in the firm control of the central government was denied to the insurgent. It was not enough to contest an area with guerrillas. Areas contested by them could still be used for base camps, logistical routes, and staging areas for attacks against government controlled areas. Thus it was essential that the bases possessed by the government be used for aggressive operations by both military and civil authorities to expand areas of control from these centres on the analogy of the oil spot gradually spreading out around its edges.

The South Africans in SWA/Namibia had noted a number of less than successful experiences suffered by others in counterguerrilla warfare. The examples of the French in Algeria and the French and Americans in Vietnam are quite familiar. For Africa, however, the experiences of the Portuguese in Angola and Mozambique, and that of the Rhodesians in their COIN efforts were both sobering and instructive. Sobering, in that the examples revealed the ultimate fate of those others in southern Africa who could or would not pursue the struggle against insurgents with a total commitment to victory. Instructive, in that many weapons, tactics, and concepts were tried with varying degrees of success. Also, by the late 1970s South Africa had its own experience base to draw upon – the participation of South African and Rhodesian mercenaries in the Congo crisis of 1960–1965, the early stages of the conflict in SWA from 1962 to 1975, and the South African intervention in Angola in 1975-1976.

FIGHTING THE COIN WAR

The security forces in the OA as well as in the remainder of SWA/Namibia had specifically defined missions for internal security, based on SAA doctrine. The clearly-defined missions of the various components of the security forces ensured that each had a role in maintaining internal security and was accountable to its chain of command in its responsibilities.

Mission

The general mission of all SADF and SWATF COIN units and Operational Sectors was to carry out the assigned COIN mission within the AOR, specifically:

■ Ensuring the ability of the security forces to operate from secure bases and to ensure the integrity of their own operational planning, execution, and support; this entailed
■ Maintaining an effective mobile reserve force or area reaction capability in the event that normal unit operational capabilities were unable to meet their mission;
■ Supporting and participating in joint security management for the area by means of committees in which representatives of the military, police, and various public services coordinate security responsibilities;
■ Ensuring effective tactical intelligence coverage within the AOR;
■ Protecting the civil administration and infrastructure;
■ Protecting government infrastructure and commercial and industrial installations, LOCs and public transport;
■ Gaining the active support of the local population;
■ Protecting area residents and property from insurgent activity;
■ Promoting civil-military relations.

A secondary mission of the COIN forces was to protect the AOR from conventional attack.

COIN Institutions

Operational Sectors SWA/Namibia was divided into seven Operational Sectors, the northern three of which (Sectors 10, 20, and 70) were under SADF administration. Each Operational Sector was organised and staffed to conduct COIN operations; the northern three also conducted cross-border operations into Angola as required. Directly subordinate to Operational Sectors were Area Force Units (AFUs), COIN battalions, and other operational units.

South of the Operational Area, Operational Sectors were divided into a number of smaller AORs, each of which was the responsibility of an Area Force Unit (AFU). AFU headquarters were staffed mainly by area force personnel (who had fulfilled their Citizen Force reserve obligations), some PF personnel, and sometimes CF personnel. The commander or his deputy would usually be a PF member. The local AFU itself was organised in a fashion similar to a COIN battalion.

In addition to AFUs, the Operational Sector could have a reaction force, employed as a mobile reserve within the unit's area. As opposed to the RSA, where personnel resources were more extensive, in SWA/Namibia the reaction force, if needed, was formed from the AFU itself. Active army units subordinate to the Operational Sector headquarters could include logistical support, engineer and signals units, maintenance units, depots, etc. They supported the AFU and other sector units. They were manned by PF personnel and NSMs in the second half of their tour of duty – 'trained NSMs'.

Each Sector had a headquarters and subordinate infantry and armoured reconnaissance formations, plus CS and CSS units. The infantry formations were either SAA infantry battalion groups or SWATF COIN battalions. Each Sector had an armoured car squadron (company size), with personnel supplied by Special Service Battalions (SSBs, armour training units) in RSA. Normally Sector Headquarters did not control 61, 62, or 32 Battalions, which were directly under the GOC, SAA units in SWA.

10 Sector included Ovamboland as well as Kakoland to the west. It covered the SWA border with Angola for over 700km, a distance roughly equivalent to that from London to Berne. The headquarters was at Oshakati, and the main logistics route supporting it ran northwest from Grootfontein through Tsumeb and Oshivelo. The sector was divided up into territorial AORs, with the border area north of an east–west line through Oshakati covered from west to east by 51, 52, 53, and 54 Infantry Battalion Groups, and the area south by 101 Battalion. The Kakoland area was the AOR of SWATF 102 Battalion.

20 Sector included Kavango and West Caprivi. It covered the Angolan border from the Cubango (Kavango) River east to the Cuando (Kwando) River, about 550km. The headquarters was at Rundu on the Cubango River opposite the Angolan border. Rundu was supplied by a route running north-east from Grootfontein. This route as well as the area west of it was the AOR of SWATF 202 Battalion; east of it was the AOR of SWATF 203 Battalion.

70 Sector encompassed East Caprivi. It covered the Zambian land border from the Cuando to the Zambezi River, and the riverine border with Zambia along the Zambezi to its confluence with the Cuando flowing from the great Okavango Swamp in Botswana, now called the Chobe. Headquarters was at Katima Mulilo. Due to the reduced threat of insurgent activity after 1979, the entire sector was the AOR of only one unit, SWATF 701 Battalion.

COIN forces overview South Africa's long border war in Namibia (1962-1989) saw the involvement of practically every South African military and civilian security organisation in the conflict. From 1975 the threat from SWAPO/PLAN began to crystallise with the latter's support by a sympathetic government in Angola supported by the Soviet Bloc and

Cuba. Earlier, the pursuit of the war shifted to military and paramilitary elements in the security structure coordinated by the South African Defence Force (SADF), almost entirely replacing earlier police efforts in 1972. By the early 1980s, following the creation of the South-West Africa Territory Force (SWATF) and the development of an active COIN wing in the SWA Police, most counterinsurgency efforts against SWAPO were increasingly executed by Namibians themselves.

Following the creation of SWATF in 1980, military forces in SWA/Namibia consisted either of regular SADF units and personnel, or SWATF. The latter was heavily modelled on the SADF, although at a much smaller scale. Although a separate force nominally under the civilian control of the Administrator-General of Namibia in Windhoek, the SWATF remained under command of the General Officer Commanding (GOC), South African Forces in South-West Africa, who also held the post of GOC, SWATF, as well as Minister of Defence in SWA/Namibia.

The South-West Africa Territory Force (SWATF) SWATF was established on 1 August 1980 and disestablished in 1989. It was formed from 65 SADF units in SWA with the purpose of delegating increasing responsibility for SWA/Namibian defence to local forces as well as training those forces. The GOC SWATF was also the GOC, SAA Forces in SWA as well as SWA Secretary for Defence.

The SWATF drew its personnel from full-time (PF) soldiers, most of whom were in the Operational or Standing Forces, from reservists (either CF or AF), and from South African military personnel who were seconded to the force. Often SAA units up to company level were assigned to SWATF battalions during times of peak PLAN infiltration attempts. With the exception of the light aircraft squadron, the 1st SWA Squadron (Windhoek), all SWATF elements were ground forces.

SWATF Organisation SWATF, which had approximately 22,000–25,000 personnel total, comprised the following elements:[15]

■ SWATF Headquarters, Windhoek;
■ The Operational or Standing Forces (mostly PF), eight full-time units altogether, which were built around six ethnic COIN battalions, SWASPES, and a reconnaissance regiment;
■ The Reaction Force (mostly CF), which included a motorised brigade, a parachute battalion, and a light aircraft squadron;
■ Infrastructure units (mostly PF), which provided CS and CSS, plus training, including the Logistics Brigade and the military school at Okahandje that conducted training in both conventional and COIN warfare;
■ The Area Force (which corresponded to the SADF Commando Force), which included 27 local reserve units known as Area Force Units (AFUs) that were organised similar to SAA Commando units.

The SWATF was organised into seven Sectors, which corresponded to the SAA Territorial Commands. Each headquarters was organised to conduct COIN operations either internally or against PLAN elements in Angola. The three northernmost sectors (10, 20, and 70) were under the administration of the SADF. By the late 1980s, 65 per cent on the average of security forces in the OA were SWATF.[16]

SWATF Units. The main SWATF unit types were the motorised battalion and the COIN battalion, described above. Often such units were smaller than those in the SAA, but could be reinforced as required by personnel and units from the latter.

1) Standing Force (ethnic battalions). The force included special units as well as full-time COIN battalions recruited from various ethnic groups throughout SWA/Namibia and stationed in an ethnic area. There were seven such battalions; one (911 Battalion) was multi-ethnic and was part of 91 Brigade. Each battalion had four line companies and head-quarters and support companies staffed mainly by Permanent Force personnel but with augmentations from reservists and conscripts. While the headquarters company provided administrative, intelligence, and logistical support, the support company was equipped with crew-served infantry support weapons (mortars, rocket launchers, and machine guns).[17]

a) 101 Battalion (Ovamboland). Organised in January 1976 as 1 Ovambo Battalion, this unit began training in South Africa (at facilities of 21 Battalion, Lenz) in 1977; in January 1978 it was renamed 35 Battalion and used for training Namibian troops in addition to its COIN role. With the creation of SWATF in 1980 it was renamed 101 Battalion. The 'Romeo Mike' concept, using Buffel APCs, was introduced in 1982 and later that year the unit had its first company outfitted with armoured cars – twelve Casspir Mk 2 MPVs. By April 1984 201 Battalion had four such companies, named Special Services Companies, all equipped with Casspirs (the only SWATF unit to have the vehicles). By the late 1980s the unit had grown to regiment size, with about 2,000 men. It was the principal SWATF field training unit, providing new personnel with operational experience.

101 Battalion comprised a headquarters, a support company and maintenance workshop, a training wing, and four special services companies. The latter were each divided into three (later four) teams of four Casspirs each, called 'Romeo Mikes' (RMs), from the Afrikaans term reaksie maag (reaction force). Each of the latter had 32 to 40 men mounted in four Casspir armoured cars and a Kwevoel-50 (or similar type) logistics vehicle. Distrib-uted among this relatively small team was a considerable amount of firepower, which included two Hispano Suiza HS820 20mm cannon, six .50-calibre heavy machine guns, four MAGs, and four 60mm M4 Mk 1 patrol mortars. In addition, each soldier had his own personal weapons. The purpose of the RMs was to engage PLAN infiltrators by rapidly responding to reports of insurgent activity, and follow up in 'hot pursuit' – often into Angola if necessary.

b) 102 Battalion (Kakoland). This unit, comprising ethnic Ovahimba and Hereros, was based in Opuwo in Kakoland. It was founded in 1978 as 37 Battalion and by the mid-1980s had four companies drawn from the ethnic population of the area, mainly Herero. 102 Battalion's area of responsibility was the western part of 10 Sector, which extended from the western border of Ovamboland to the Atlantic Ocean at Foz do Cunene and areas southward. 102 Battalion personnel were noted for special skills in tracking and operating in the often harsh desert terrain of the area, the Kakoveldt. The inhabitants of Kakoland were traditional rivals of the Ovambos, and the support of many of the latter for SWAPO sealed the animosity of the Herero and Ovahimba toward the insurgents.

c) 201 Battalion (West Caprivi). Founded in 1974 as Alpha Group and in 1975 renamed 31 Battalion (which it was again renamed in 1989 after moving from SWA/Namibia to Schmidtsdrift in South Africa), this unit was composed of ethnic Bushmen. Unit head-quarters was at Omega Base in the Caprivi strip; its organisation reflected the use made of it by the SADF/SWATF for tracking purposes. By 1980, when the unit was renamed the SWATF 201 Battalion, the unit was used for its special tracking skills.

In the late 1980s 201 Battalion comprised a headquarters, a support company and maintenance workshop, a Reconnaissance Wing, and two operational groups of three tracker companies of 100 men each (six in total, an increase from four companies in the early 1980s). Each tracker company had three platoons which could deploy operationally as six teams of trackers (25 to 35 men per team). Each team had three Buffel APCs and a logistics vehicle, and was equipped to operate in the bush for extended periods. The Reconnaissance Wing had six tracker groups of five or six men each. These latter were mixed, with two whites from the SADF or SWATF and four Bushmen. The whites were rotated in and out of these teams so that their acquired tracking skills would be made use of in other units. Teams from the Reconnaissance Wing were used in a similar way to most SAA Reconnaissance Commando personnel – for deployment in internal (SWA) or external (Angola) reconnaissance missions.

201 Battalion grew during the 1980s from about 850 personnel to over 1,000; the number of dependants grew from about 2,700 to 5,000 or so. These latter dwelt with 201 Battalion soldiers at Omega Base, their headquarters, with about 250 South African and Namibian officers, administrators, and training personnel. At any given time about half the unit was at camp training or on leave, with the remainder deployed on operations either in the area or further west in support of 10 Sector.

d) 202 Battalion (Kavango). This large unit, comparable in size to 101 Battalion, was based at Rundu, the location of its principal training base as well. It had been founded in 1975 as 34 Battalion. While not as well-known as 101 Battalion, it performed the important mission of providing the main mobile reserve element for 20 Sector as well as protecting the main supply route to Rundu from Grootfontein. At any given time a company would patrol the route itself while a second would operate to its west as a screen against attempted SWAPO exfiltration out of Ovamboland/20 Sector. At least one company was always at base to provide a reaction force for 20 Sector.

202 Battalion comprised a headquarters and support company, four companies ('A' to 'D') equipped with Buffel APCs, and an armoured reconnaissance wing of two platoons of four Eland-90 armoured cars each. Usually the battalion had an attached SAA infantry company to provide additional patrol and reaction capabilities.

The unit was predominantly ethnic Kavango. By the time SWATF was organised it already had a Kavango majority, which had increased to about 65–70 per cent by 1985. In the late 1980s 202 Battalion had about 2,000 men under arms.

e) 203 Battalion (Bushmanland). 203 Battalion was the second Bushman battalion, with headquarters at Luhebu, near Tsumkwe in Bushmanland. Founded in 1977 as 36 Battalion, it was not as well known as 201 Battalion, but its personnel performed similar functions for the SADF and SWATF. Its unit structure was similar to that of 201 Battalion (see above), but due to its more area-oriented mission, its subordinate units were distributed at a number of bases around the eastern part of 20 Sector, at Mkata, Nhoma, Khanda, Omatebu, Kanum, and Vicks Rus.

Like 201 Battalion, 203 Battalion comprised ethnic Bushmen of the Vasekala and Kung groups.

f) 701 Battalion (East Caprivi). 701 Battalion was the main unit in East Caprivi, based at Mpacha. It was established in August 1977 as 33 Battalion. The unit consisted of a headquarters and administrative element, a support company, and three infantry companies, the last of which was established by the mid-1980s. The unit also had a reconnaissance wing composed of local Bushmen trackers.

Due to the fall-off of SWAPO activity in the area after 1980, elements of 701 Battalion were (since 1981) often used for operations in Sector 10, as Sector 70 had relatively little combat action. While in Sector 10 the unit or its elements occupied one of 54 Battalion's company bases. The unit also took part in several external operations, including 'Sceptic', 'Carnation' and 'Protea'. Training for the unit was done at the SWA Military School, Okahandje.

g) 911 Battalion (Windhoek). 911 Battalion, founded in 1977 as 41 Battalion, included personnel who were ethnic Tswanas, Damaras, Namas, Basters, Hereros, Ovambos, Bushmen, Whites, and Coloureds. It was part of the 91 SWA Brigade, but was also used in a COIN role, especially to reinforce other SWATF units in the OA.

The unit comprised five multi-ethnic line companies. Although the headquarters was in Windhoek, the individual units deployed in Outjosundu, Narubis, Nauaspoort, Drimiopsis, and Houmoed. The first company of the unit began training at Narubis, with the first intake being almost exclusively Nama. The initial training and equipment for the unit were similar to that undertaken by SADF NSMs in the SA Infantry Corps. Since its establishment the unit sought to ensure a mix of personnel from other SWA ethnic groups for its ranks.

2) **Reaction Force.** The Reaction Force, also known as 91 SWA Brigade, had its headquarters at Windhoek. It was a mobile reserve to support SWATF operations in 10 or 20 Sectors in northern Namibia and was modelled on a SADF motorised brigade. It consisted of a headquarters, three infantry battalions (911 Battalion – a PF unit – 912 Battalion or Regiment Erongo, and 913 Battalion or Regiment Namutoni), plus an armoured car regiment (Regiment Windhoek) and an artillery regiment, the 91 Composite Field Regiment. Other units included 91 Maintenance Unit, 91 Field Ambulance Unit, 91 Training Battalion Group, and 91 Mobilization Centre. 911 Battalion, originally known as 41 Battalion (Nama) but by the early 1980s a fully multiethnic unit, was based at Windhoek.

3) **Area Force.** SWATF's Area Force consisted of 26 battalion-sized units that were called commandos before 1980, at which time they were relabelled Area Force Units (AFUs). While some were ethnic units, most were white. By the late 1980s most AFUs had expanded to battalion size and had opened their ranks to all applicants. Their role was one of area security similar to that of South African commandos – light (in some cases motorised) infantry units that could also have mounted, dog, and tracker units. Their personnel were drawn mostly from those who had completed National Service obligations and follow-on reserve CF obligations, and who were thus of the same status as South African 'commando' personnel.

1 SWA Squadron, the SWATF 'Air Wing,' was also technically speaking an AFU, as its members were drawn from personnel with the same service status as commando/AFU personnel. However, 1 SWA Squadron had a much more active role in supporting SWATF and SADF operations in northern SWA/Namibia than ordinary AFUs. Prior to 1980 and the establishment of SWATF, the unit had been named 112 Air Commando Squadron. It was based at Eros Airfield, Windhoek.

4) **Infrastructure.** The SWATF infrastructure included the headquarters and administrative units, the support units, and training elements. Most of these were located in Windhoek or nearby facilities. The headquarters and administrative units included SWATF headquarters and its Headquarters company and 91 SWA Brigade Headquarters. Support units included a signals regiment, a medium workshop, a provost unit, 16 Engineer Squadron, an engineer regiment, a commissariat depot, two transport depots, a composite depot, a specialist unit, and printing, forward postal, and troop information units, plus a band. There was also the HQ Medical Service, SWATF. The training infrastructure included 91 Training Battalion Group, 91 Mobilisation Centre, the Specialist School (part of 1 SWA Specialist Unit), the SWA Military School at Okahandje, and the SWA Services School. There was even a farm for SWATF and SADF units at Bagani Military Base.

A major COIN unit in the SWATF Infrastructure was 1 SWA Specialist Unit (1 SWASPES), which was formed in July 1977 from disparate tracking and specialised units in the SADF. By January 1978 the consolidation was complete and 1 SWASPES was formed, to include units for motorcyclist, mounted and dog handler soldiers. Each constituted a wing of the unit. 1 SWASPES was used for reaction and follow-up actions to infiltration, for high-speed tracking and interdiction of PLAN members. The dog element was also used for explosives detection.[18]

Police Before 1980 all police activity in SWA/Namibia was undertaken by the South African Police (SAP), the South African Railways Police (SARP), or elements of other civilian security services of the South African government. In 1980, however, in accordance with the desire to 'Namibianise' the war, the South-West Africa Police (SWAPOL) were created.

South African Police (SAP) and related services Throughout 1980 the South African Police SWA Division, with its headquarters at Windhoek, was responsible for police functions in Namibia. In 1972 the SAP had the main mission for prosecuting the COIN effort, but in that year the dramatic upsurge in border incidents, especially those involving land-mines, resulted in the SADF being given the mission instead.

Other South African civilian security agencies operating in SWA/Namibia included the South African Railways Police, which had its own Special COIN Section; it continued to maintain liaison with SWAPOL through the mid-1980s, when it was merged with the SAP. The South African Security Police (SASP) were also active in SWA/Namibia through the war; the SASP was a police intelligence service similar to the Special Branch in other former British colonies, and had powers of arrest and detention as well as investigative and intelligence gathering/analysis missions.

1) South-West Africa Police (SWAPOL). SWAPOL was formally established on 1 April 1981, although locally-based police units had already taken charge of police matters on 1 September 1980. Through the end of the war its operations throughout most of Namibia were confined to law-enforcement and public order. However, for the areas north of the 'Red Line' (i.e., the southern boundary of the Operational Area) and the Botswana-SWA border, civilian counterinsurgency police, or SWAPOLCOIN, still had a COIN mission and thus maintained its counterinsurgency force.

SWAPOL headquarters was in Windhoek; it was organised territorially throughout Namibia. It coordinated operations regularly with SWATF and SADF units, and had a liaison relationship with the SAP. In 1985/1986 the force was augmented by the merger with it of the SA Security Police in SWA/Namibia and the SWAPOLCOIN unit. Up to the end of the conflict the structure of the force was:

■ SWAPOL HQ;
■ Directorate of Crime Prevention and Investigations;
■ Directorate of Security Services;
■ Directorate of COIN Services (the former separate SWAPOLCOIN unit);
■ Directorate of Security Police (the former SA Security Police in SWA/Namibia);
■ Directorate of General Services;
■ District commands, totalling ten (1-Windhoek, 2-Gobabis, 3-Karasburg, 4-Keetman-shoep, 5-Mariental, 6-Oshakati, 7-Otjawarongo, 8-Rundu, 9-Swakopmund, 10-Tsumeb), each headed by a District Commissioner. The ten commands controlled 58 police stations throughout SWA/Namibia.[19]

2) SWAPOLCOIN units. SWAPOL Counterinsurgency Wing, or SWAPOLCOIN (in Afrikaans, SWAPOLTEIN) had three operational divisions. These included the SWAPOL Task Force, which patrolled the Botswana-SWA border and the 'Red Line'; the Special Constable Force, which provided VIP protection for Ovambo and other chiefs as well as a guard force for some installations and special functions; and the Ops-K, or Koevoet.

Ops-K ('Koevoet'). This force, the subject of much controversy through the 1980s, was founded in June 1979 using elements of the Special Constable Force as well as South African Security Police personnel. Its mission was and remained a police/paramilitary one, namely of reacting to incidents of SWAPO/PLAN activity in the OA. By the end of the 1980s the unit, extremely successful, had grown to about 2,000, with possibly another 500 personnel who had been trained available as police reservists from volunteers in the Special Constable Force who had had Ops-K training.

Ops-K was organised into three geographical divisions, one each for Kakoland, Ovamboland, and Kavango. The Ovamboland division headquarters at Oshakati, 'Zulu Base,' was also Ops-K GHQ. The unit was quite secretive about many aspects of its operations, but its organisation, as much as is known, reflected its mission of reaction as well as intelligence collection. Headquarters had a large staff organised on military lines to support the unit's operational elements. It maintained regular liaison with SWATF to coordinate COIN operations.

The heart of Koevoet and the key to its success were company-sized units divided into three or four teams of four Casspir or Wolf Turbo armoured cars and a logistics vehicle. These units, acting on intelligence gathered by other Ops-K teams or through intelligence liaison with SWATF or SADF, would react to insurgent sightings and track infiltrators, attempting not to only interdict their penetrations but also to engage in routine hot-pursuit operations across the cutline into Angola.

COIN: Internal dimensions

The three main internal COIN requirements for security forces in SWA were:

- Ensuring the ability of the security forces to operate from secure bases and ensuring the integrity of their own operational planning, execution, and support;
- Gaining the active support of the local population;
- Protection of the civil administration and infrastructure.

The integrity of own forces and military operations. Throughout the SWA/Namibia conflict, this was not an issue for the security forces. Although PLAN infiltrators would target SADF, SWATF, and SWAPOL installations for occasional mortar attacks, these were of a harassment nature and could not be sustained. They virtually ceased after the cross-border operations were initiated in 1978. Military installations were protected by patrols and physical security measures, and PLAN operatives were normally more concerned about their own survival in evading security force detection and tended to avoid incidents that would call attention to themselves. The infiltrators preferred 'soft targets' in the civilian population that minimised the chances for early detection; under such circumstances, the threat to civil and military personnel and installations declined; however, PLAN could and did target family members of ethnic Ovambos that worked for the authorities. As the efficacy of the security forces in responding to such incidents developed through the early 1980s, even these tactics by PLAN ensured rapid response by the 'Romeo Mike' units of the security forces, and PLAN attacks against civilians progressively focused on targets farther and farther from known military installations.

Security forces in the field were more likely to be targeted for attacks and counterattacks by PLAN infiltrators. Forces lagering for the night were sometimes mortared, but defensive measures implemented by the security forces minimised the effect of such attacks whenever they did occur. More common were attempts by PLAN groups fleeing back to Angola to set ambushes to inflict casualties on pursuing security force elements. These were sometimes done with FAPLA assistance. However, when such incidents did occur, they rarely proved effective. Security forces could call on ground reinforcements or air support, and the ambushing force was quickly destroyed.[20] Indeed, the main purpose of ambushes appeared to be to allow part of the force, including the PLAN leadership, to escape. Ambushes took place when fleeing PLAN were unable to 'shotgun' into small groups in an attempt to deter detection, or when the group's leaders believed that they had a good chance of making the border before security forces could close with them. Even in this context the security forces were more than able to deal with their adversaries. In the period between 1984 and 1987, many of the incidents of ambush and confrontation inside Angola resulted in heavy FAPLA casualties as well.

Containing SWAPO/PLAN activities Countering SWAPO/PLAN required a dual strategy of area operations for northern SWA/Namibia, essentially a COIN war, and preventing the insurgents from enjoying effective sanctuary in Angola. Each of these strategies required a different approach. For SWA/Namibia, COIN operations were required, undertaken from secure bases with the aim of controlling the population. For Angola and SWAPO/PLAN refuges there, conventional operations consisting of large, carefully-planned cross-border raids were required, to disrupt the insurgents' base camps and logistics lines, and to impress upon them that they could not use a neighbouring country as a base with impunity.

In many ways the South Africans in Namibia were in a situation similar to that of the Israelis in Lebanon in the early 1980s, as 'the principal elements' determining the shape of the conflict were, to quote Legum: '(i) A guerrilla movement which is offered sanctuary in sovereign state bordering on the contested territory. (ii) The willingness of a major foreign power to provide increasingly sophisticated weapons to the guerrillas, after each hard attack against their positions. (iii) The deep security fears felt by the country under military challenge.'[21]

It should be added that the stated aim of the insurgents was the establishment, by force, of a Marxist regime in SWA/Namibia, and that SWAPO had been recognised by the UN as the sole representative of the Namibian people, in part due to the international machinations of the Soviets and their allies. Soviet supply of arms to SWAPO and its armed wing, PLAN, conformed to its general strategy of undermining South Africa and its sphere of control in southern Africa and implanting sympathetic regimes in the area. However, the continued supply of sophisticated arms to SWAPO/PLAN after repeated debacles for PLAN and their Angolan and Cuban allies in Operations 'Sceptic', 'Protea', 'Daisy', and 'Askari' stopped after it became evident that such armament could not be protected or properly used. After 1984 following the conclusion of Operation 'Askari' PLAN had little conventional armament in Angola except for conventional units supporting FAPLA against UNITA. However, training of PLAN infiltrators by East German instructors continued. The heavy weapons flow from the Soviets was refocused to FAPLA to fight the Angolan government's foe UNITA.

Nevertheless, PLAN still enjoyed sanctuary courtesy of the Angolans, who with their Soviet and Cuban allies made it a major point of policy to host the insurgents who shared their Marxist-Leninist political alignment. The shift in PLAN strategy and tactics after 1984 still left the South Africans with a security challenge, albeit a highly changed one. Henceforth the infiltrations and security incidents were done by small groups of insurgents who were much harder to detect by the security forces, with response shifting to smaller 'Romeo Mike' units geared toward countering these smaller PLAN groups. Individual infiltrators were still often heavily armed to counter the armoured cars of the 'Romeo Mike' units.

The increasing success of the security forces in responding to incidents in terms of time and results through the period 1985–1987 meant that the South African administration in northern SWA/Namibia remained unchallenged and was able to continue its efforts to attract the support of the general population there, one of the critical elements of the South African strategy (see below).

South African security efforts to counter PLAN in the Operational Area included either routine patrols and security measures or responses to insurgent incidents. These efforts must be considered hand-in-hand with civil affairs, as early in the conflict the South Africans realised that COIN operations by the security forces could only serve to isolate infiltrators from the general population, whose support for the security forces was essential. The more efficacious the efforts to gain the confidence and active support of the peoples in the OA, the greater the security force capabilities for detecting and responding to insurgent infiltrations.

Public support and civil affairs By the late 1970s, the Rhodesian security forces had shown themselves totally unable to prevent locals from supporting ZANLA or ZIPRA guerrillas. In the RSA, the townships were seething with discontent and periodic outbreaks of unrest. However, at this same time the security forces in SWA/Namibia were gradually building the confidence of the population there in the administration and the security forces. It could be said that the totally different ethnic and political situation there, coupled with the fair certainty among most Namibians of eventual independence, allowed most to tolerate first South African and then a quasi-autonomous rule. However, such a position cannot explain the continued willingness of Namibians – including Ovambos – to support the administration in Windhoek and even eagerly volunteer to serve in the security forces. South African efforts in Namibia focused on maintaining popular support and on protecting the population.

Throughout the war one low-visibility, but highly successful, component of the COIN effort by the security forces was gaining and keeping the support of the local population in Namibia in general and in the OA in particular. The only area where the civil and military authorities had ongoing difficulties was Ovamboland. Even here the degree of cooperation was surprisingly high despite the ethnic connection to SWAPO and its PLAN fighters. In large part this was due to the continued effort by the civil authorities to run the day-to-day business of government despite the constant presence of PLAN infiltrators. The population clearly benefited from this and the ability of the security forces to protect them more effectively than PLAN could terrorise and intimidate them.

The results of the civil affairs effort are impressive:

■ The only major continuing security problems were in Ovambo and East Caprivi (the latter over by 1980). Elsewhere the civil and military authorities had the ready assistance of the local population in preventing PLAN from avoiding detection and establishing itself inside SWA/Namibia. As noted above, even in Ovamboland a large part of the local population, especially in areas subject to PLAN infiltration, readily assisted security forces with information about sightings and other incidents.

■ South African administration throughout SWA was always firm and unchallenged. As noted above, this allowed government to function without serious interruption. The ability to maintain a system of schools, hospitals, and other social services had obvious benefits. The ability to keep roads open in good repair and relatively safe from insurgent attacks and mining was a result of effective civil-military cooperation.

■ South African media programmes were effective. Despite the vilification of the RSA in world media, the security forces were always able to portray SWAPO and PLAN in the worst possible light. The insurgents, with their training rooted in the tradition of Soviet partisan methods of World War II, did not help themselves in this respect, as their only methods in dealing with the locals were to use terror and intimidation. PLAN deserters, defectors, and prisoners were readily exploited to talk about poor conditions and atrocities against civilians in the camps in Angola.

■ The security forces were effective, and popular (see below). With the formation of the SWA ethnic battalions in the 1970s, and through the transition to SWATF from 1980, the new force never lacked volunteers. Even in an area such as Ovambo, there were always more than enough locals willing to serve in the oversized 101 and 102 Battalions. 101 Battalion proved to be one of the most effective COIN units in the security forces.

The civil authorities in SWA/Namibia took great pains to design and implement a series of development programmes for Namibia in general and the OA in particular. The effort and expense required to maintain a civil development programme while conducting a COIN war were viewed by the authorities as part of a single endeavour.

Development of water resources was a highly visible means of gaining popular support. With the advent of the civil war in Angola and the establishment of a hostile government there in 1975, plans for a joint irrigation project using the Ruacana dam on the Cunene River at the border between the two countries had to be cancelled; as a result, the development of SWA/Namibia's northern area had to suffice with a mere tenth of the planned available water resources. Still, the authorities did well with what they had. The construction of irrigation systems – primarily canals and pipelines, and the digging of wells that could be used for livestock watering points – improved the quality of life for the local Ovambo population in Sector 10. Attempts by PLAN operatives to attack water resources were limited to minor acts of sabotage, as SWAPO was well aware that any permanent damage would have cost them credibility among the general population.[22]

Two key areas of civic action endeavour also included education and medical services. The administration took great pains to ensure that the school system in northern Namibia was available to as many children of school age who desired an education. In this, however, the cultural and security conditions in Ovamboland permitted the employment of one teacher for about 45 students, as opposed to the national average of one for 30 students. PLAN targeted schools as visible symbols of the government, and often abducted school-children, taking them back to Angola in attempts to replenish their ever-sparse ranks. As for access to medical services, the government sought to improve this area through the 1980s; by its end fourteen of 68 hospitals and 31 of 171 medical clinics were located in Ovamboland. However, as just under half the population dwelt in Ovamboland, it is obvious that the area still did not have a proportional amount of medical services.[23]

Protection of public infrastructure was another key area of security force endeavour. In addition to special constables from SWAPOL, personnel from the AFUs augmented hired guards at government offices, banks, schools, hospitals, factories, mines, and utilities sites. Although security incidents did occur, they were relatively rare and almost always confined to Ovamboland.

Other areas of initiative by the public administration to garner support included government. The authorities in SWA/Namibia permitted political parties to participate in elections. Local government was encouraged to ensure that it was representative in its composition of those constituencies it represented. However, in this general area the civil and military authorities in SWA/Namibia, although successful inside Namibia, failed to gain any recognition for their efforts among the international community, who dismissed such efforts as cynical attempts to control the population. Even the political opposition in Namibia and its press attacked the 'Namibianisation' of the conflict from this angle.[24]

One of the cornerstones of security force strategy was the protection of the civilian population as well as civil administration and infrastructure. In this the security forces were highly successful. Such success gave the presence of civil and military authorities a credibility with the local population that SWAPO found almost impossible to counter except in parts of Ovamboland. This credibility formed the basis for either active or passive support for the South African-dominated authorities in Windhoek.

With the exception of Ovambo, the local civilians throughout the Operational Area generally supported the security forces from the start of the conflict. Although the Ovambos straddled the border north into Cunene, SWAPO remained a Namibian organisation. This was due to the one-party requirement for membership in the MPLA of the Angolan government for anyone living north of the cutline. In addition, SWAPO had relatively little use for the local population as their bases and other facilities were provided by the Angolan government by imposition on the population of Cunene. Also, for SWAPO, their village and family ties lay south of the border and not in Angola. SWAPO personnel spoke Afrikaans and English; the local Ovambos of Cunene spoke Portuguese. During the course of the conflict, the local population of Cunene and Huila, regardless of ethnic affiliation, came to resent the SWAPO presence there due to the ill-treatment they received by PLAN. Ironically, the local Ovambos of south Cunene readily appreciated the benefits of South African control there after Operation 'Protea' as it afforded them some much needed security and left them in relative peace compared to the difficult period of the late 1970s.

By the end of the 1970s and especially after the formation of SWATF and SWAPOLCOIN Ops K ('Koevoet'), the security forces had the ready means to respond quickly and in force to sightings of infiltrators. Although PLAN members could still infiltrate into the OA, they could not rely upon the unqualified support of even the local Ovambo population. Many of the latter appreciated the benefits of continued effective government services or wished merely to be left in peace without concern to what they believed to be outside political matters. While some villages or kraals would give aid and comfort to PLAN infiltrators, others resisted and often paid the price for non-cooperation. Due to the continued maintenance of roads and telephone lines, word of insurgent activity was usually quickly brought to the security forces, and an appropriate response rapidly followed. The security forces, for their part, were encouraged if not required to maintain as good relations as possible with the locals when investigating incidents or engaged in pursuits.

■ Again, the only major long-term problem was in Ovambo. The course of the conflict demonstrated that the security forces, with the support of the population in the rest of the OA, were easily able to detect and track down PLAN infiltrators. Even in Ovambo the long-term results of civil affairs programmes coupled with good security force intelligence about PLAN activities meant that PLAN was unable to hide in the population for any length of time.

■ PLAN did little or nothing to help itself in the fight with security forces. The general attitude cultivated among its fighters was that anyone not actively supporting them was a potential enemy. The general population was not to be convinced as much as coerced, often by terror. The latter consisted of making examples of 'sell-outs' and others accused of supporting the government or security forces. In addition, many PLAN activities were directed against the infrastructure. These included mining roads. Those who suffered most, however, were the civilians and not the security forces, who used mine-resistant vehicles.

■ Ethnic factors played heavily outside Ovambo. SWAPO was overwhelmingly Ovambo in composition, and PLAN was almost exclusively Ovambo. The security forces found no lack of PLAN defectors who complained of discrimination and ill-treatment because of their ethnic background. Traditional ethnic animosities between the Ovambos on one hand and the Kavango, Bushman, and Kakolanders also made the latter much less willing to support, much less identify with, a movement that they saw as advancing Ovambo interests.

Protection of civil authorities/infrastructure Hand in hand with the protection of the civilian population went protection of civil authorities. SWAPO/PLAN targeted the local administration for three main reasons. The first was that civil authorities represented the presence of the South African-dominated central government in Windhoek, and thus was a symbolic target, action against which they hoped would demonstrate its weakness and inability to function as a government. The second reason was that even in Ovamboland the civil administration had large numbers of local Namibians working for it; PLAN's insurgent tactics, based on those of World War II Soviet partisan concepts, viewed these people as a group as enemies to be exterminated. Finally, the continuing success of the central government's educational, medical, and social services infrastructure gave the local population a vested interest in the continuation of such services, even if they were present as an obvious means by the civil and military authorities to gain support from the population in the OA.

Security for the administration – its officials and the infrastructure – was generally successful. However, this presence could not be everywhere, and especially in Ovambo PLAN was able to strike at more remote mission centres and schools, and target family members of those serving in the civil and military authorities. Such attacks became the basis for PLAN propaganda wildly distorting such incidents. The tactic used by the security forces to counter this disinformation was to allow as much access by South African and international media as possible to the site of the incident and those directly affected by it. This was only partly successful, however:

■ Most international media were either sympathetic to SWAPO and prepared to overlook its war that continually focused on acts against the civilian population, or follow SWAPO's version of events.

■ Often the world press would present both the SWAPO and security force versions of incidents with attribution but without any attempt at serious analysis to determine which was likely to be correct.

■ In addition, most reported incidents garnered little press outside South Africa. News from SWA/Namibia normally focused on developments in the political process or reports of external operations by security forces.

COIN: External dimensions

The main challenge posed by SWAPO/PLAN was in the insurgents' use of Angola as a base from which to operate against targets in SWA/Namibia. COIN forces thus had to effectively counter the four main advantages SWAPO/PLAN had in using Angolan bases and having the support of the Angolan government:

■ PLAN forward headquarters were deployed to take advantage of the FAPLA support structure, facilitating their infiltration to and exfiltration from Ovamboland, with FAPLA protection;

■ PLAN used FAPLA logistics in order to transport arms and other military equipment to the border;

■ PLAN command and control was expedited because it was able to move closer to the border;

■ The insurgents were able to use the LOCs, medical facilities, and communications system in southern Angola under the government aegis for its own benefit.[25]

PLAN thus posed a threat to the security force infrastructure in northern SWA/Namibia due to its support by the increasingly well-armed FAPLA. It also, with its cross-border tactics, presented a challenge to the security forces as they first sought to contain its activities and then target it for military countermeasures. There was also a pronounced need to ensure that the local population in the Operational Area supported, and received the support of, the security forces. However, in the 1970s the security forces had formulated their own doctrine to counter Marxist insurgencies.

Much of the COIN doctrine used by the South Africans in SWA/Namibia stemmed from McCuen, who stressed the importance of secure bases of operation as the first step in fighting Marxist-Leninist guerrillas. Areas of government control would gradually spread from secure bases that enabled civil and military administration to work successfully. As government control was reestablished, its security forces would increasingly have the capability to fight the insurgents first to a standstill and then to marginalise their agenda with regard to the general population.[26] This was exactly what happened in SWA/Namibia; however, the continued presence of SWAPO in Angola and its bases north of the border meant that security forces were continually concerned with border penetrations and that conventional means were sometimes required to disrupt insurgent bases inside Angola.

Two other powerful influences operated on the South Africans in SWA as they developed their COIN doctrine. The first was the experience of the French in the Algerian war of 1954–1962, and the second was the lessons learned from the Rhodesian conflict. Indeed, a number of professional soldiers from the Rhodesian conflict were subsequently employed by the security forces in Namibia. However, gradually they were persuaded to leave service as their presence became a public relations burden to the South African government.

It should be noted that human and physical geography both set the stage for the fighting in SWA/Namibia. The most populous part of SWA throughout the war was in the north, along the Angolan border, where the Ovambo ethnic group – comprising almost half of the total population of the country – lived as cattle herders and farmers. The savanna and open bush of northern SWA gradually turns to bush the further south one goes, and much of the country, especially along the coast, is desert. Mining and farming areas, where much of the European population dwelt, are found in the interior, well away from the border areas. Thus the brunt of the conflict was borne by the Ovambos and their neighbours in Kakoland to the west and Kavangoland and Caprivi to the east. The Ovambos spanned the border with Angola, and many lived north of the border in Angola's Cunene province. The whole area is remarkably flat and consists of wooded savanna interspersed with large seasonal marshy depressions. Some areas contain dense vegetation rendering visibility almost impossible during parts of the year. Most of the attempted cross-border raids and infiltrations from Angola into Namibia occurred into Ovamboland from bases that SWAPO and its armed wing PLAN established in Cunene. While infiltrations took place throughout the year, they were most frequent in the late winter and early spring. At that time, the rainy season had resulted in extensive vegetation concealment for infiltrators. The latter found it almost impossible to avoid detection other times of the year. PLAN's major incursions always took place in late winter and early spring. On the other hand, many of the South African external operations into Angola took place in late spring, summer, or autumn, partly to take advantage of the minimum amount of concealment for the insurgents in and around their camps.

ANGOLA AND MOZAMBIQUE

Both Angola and Mozambique undertook major counter-guerrilla operations against insurgents and had extensive security structures, Angola's being the more elaborate. The regimes in both countries were able to survive widespread insurgent activity, and, even though neither had any formal COIN doctrine or programme, their security forces and their operations merit a brief overview.

ANGOLA

Angola's elaborate security force structure was set up immediately after independence, with Cuban and Soviet/Warsaw Pact support. By the early 1980s it had achieved the form that it was to more or less keep through the Bicesse Accords and the end of the first civil war in 1991.

MPLA security forces

FAPLA consisted of three main services – an army (EPA), navy (MGPA), and air force (FAPA-DAA) – plus a militia. The service functions at the staff level consisted of separate responsibilities for Army brigades (the EPA or regular Army, centrally controlled), Territorial

Troops and People's Militia (i.e., the Territorial Army), Special Forces, infantry training centres, military schools, the Central Bases for Supply, the Air Force, and the Navy.

Regular military forces The centrally-controlled regular Army (*Exercito Popular de Angola*, EPA) consisted of a headquarters, field units (brigades), schools, and special forces, with the latter three functions separate responsibilities at the FAPLA EMG level. Territorial forces and militia were a separate command at the staff level. In the mid- to late 1980s the EPA included at any given time approximately 80,000–100,000 personnel. Field units were assigned to territorial commanders or the chiefs of centrally-controlled task forces. EPA Special Forces were usually controlled by the FAPLA EMG.

The Air Force (*Forcas Aereas Popular de Angola/Defesa Anti-Aerea*, FAPA/DAA, or simply FAPA) was responsible for air combat operations, air logistics, and air defence. It consisted of approximately 1,500 personnel. Major air bases were at Luanda, Negage, Lubango, Kuito (Bie), Huambo, Menongue, Namibe, Saurimo, and Luena. As with the Navy, most training and equipment was of Soviet or other communist country origin. The Navy (Marinha Guerra Popular de Angola, MGPA) consisted of approximately 2,500 personnel. The main bases were at Luanda, Lobito, and Namibe. Training and equipment was mostly Soviet or other Communist Bloc.

Special Forces' (Forcas Especiais) was the term for a number of elite FAPLA units filling a special forces and reconnaissance role, but their branch also included units responsible for security and troop control; they were collectively called 'Red Berets' (Boinas Vermelhas). Special forces units were used to reinforce regular troops during operations as well as undertake special security and reconnaissance missions. Red Berets served FAPLA well through the end of the civil war. They figured heavily in the major combats in the last year of the war, fighting in the Central Highlands (Kuito and Camacupa) and at the defence of Luena in April and May of 1991. However, while the Special Forces themselves proved a timely bulwark against UNITA forces in specific areas, the bulk of FAPLA was by this time exhausted, limiting their effectiveness.

Territorial Forces (TTs) and the Militia (ODP) Most local security was the responsibility of the MPLA territorial forces, the commander of which was responsible for the local militia force as well. The militia and territorial troops were commanded by the Commander of the *Tropas Territoriais e ODP* (Militia and Territorial Troops) at the General Staff Level. At the local level, however, the military region commander controlled all elements of area-bound forces in his area of responsibility.

Territorial Forces structure The commander of each military region (RM) was responsible for two basic functions. The first was territorial – area security and the maintenance of TT/ODP installations within RM boundaries. The second function was to support major military operations within the area of the RM (directed from FAPLA Headquarters in Luanda) using local resources as well as facilitating special support, especially logistical, for EPA and FAPA forces. In many cases the distinction between the two functions did not exist, especially in the case of RMs 3 (Moxico province) and 6 (Cuando Cubango province), which were the location of continuous large-scale fighting against UNITA forces.

On paper, the Territorial Force was the first line of defence against UNITA and other insurgents (such as remnants of the old FNLA and, in Cabinda, FLEC). A range of forces was at the disposal of territorial commanders; however, most TTs, militia units, and other local forces received considerably less training and other support compared to regular Angolan army forces. Poorly armed and with limited mobility, these forces were often unable to carry out their counterguerrilla role.

Territorial Troops (Tts) Territorial Forces (*Tropas Territoriais*, TTs) units were ground forces responsible for area defence. The TTs, organised into battalions and companies, were subject to the military zone in which their areas of responsibility were located. Thus they were area-bound and were assigned given municipalities or areas of the surrounding countryside to patrol and protect. Their logistical base was limited, and consequently they usually lacked the ability to conduct any but local operations. In addition to other problems, TTs often suffered from manpower shortages, and some areas were secured using 'territorial' battalions made up of TTs, MINSE, and other personnel. TTs could also be used to reinforce or reconstitute regular army units. The standard unit for TTs was the Territorial Troops Battalion (*Batalhao das Tropas Territorial*, BTT), which was a light infantry unit of about 250 personnel.

Militia (ODP) The Militia or Popular Defence Organisation (Organisacao Defesa Popular, ODP) were local militia units assigned to assist regular ground force units (EPA, TT, TGFA units) in area defence and local military operations. ODP formations were area-bound and made up of part-time personnel who staffed units of varying size depending upon the availability of personnel. Their organisation generally paralleled that of the TTs.

Counter-guerrilla Troops (LCBs) The forces known as 'Anti-Bandit' forces, or *Luta Contra Banditos* (LCBs), were assigned to areas of Angola where government forces frequently contested control of the local population with UNITA. These light territorial forces were TTs organised into battalions, and were used to conduct area sweeps and patrols. They were subordinate to local RM or ZM commanders, and operated in coordination with other security forces. Most of these units were deployed in the central and south-western parts of Angola, many operating with SWAPO.

Railway Protection Troops (TFs/BFs) These troops, known as Railway Troops (*Tropas Ferroviarios*, TFs) or Railway Battalions (*Batalhoes Ferroviarios*, BFs), were specially-trained TTs, tasked to guard the Luanda, Benguela, and Moçâmedes Railways. They consisted of company-sized 'battalions' directly subordinate to the military region. The genesis of these units was apparently in the late 1970s as UNITA made Angolan railways a prime target.

Mine Protection Troops (TPM) These troops (*Tropas de Protecao das Mineiras*) were TTs utilised to guard mining installations, especially in the areas north-east of Luanda and in the provinces of Lunda Norte and Lunda Sul. Such operations included providing garrison troops, guarding mining equipment, escorting convoys, and keeping track of morale and political activity by the local population. In their mission they were supplemented by, and often rivals with, the MINSE DPOM units as well as security forces organised by foreign mining companies and contractors. The TPMs as originally established were under the control of the local military region commander but after 1988 were subordinate to a political-military Front through the local ZM commander. Most mines had a company-sized or platoon-sized contingent of TPMs.

Border Guards (TGFA) Border Guards (*Tropas de Guarda Frontieras Angolanas*, TGFA) were a separate force of uniformed ground units responsible for area and border defence and were for the most part, but not exclusively, located in military zones (i.e., provinces) on Angolan borders. The TGFA was commanded by the National Director of the TGFA, a member of the Defence and Security council.

Popular Vigilance Brigades (BPVs) Popular Vigilance Brigades (*Brigadas Populares Vigilancia*, BPV) were organised in 1983 to be a ready area defence to supplement other military and security force operations at the local level. The national-level organisation was controlled by the BPV national committee chairman, a member of the MPLA Politburo and MPLA Central Committee who reported directly to the Angolan president. BPVs were organised along provincial lines, with sub-organisations for localities controlled from a Provincial Support Office.

Military logistics Logistics were controlled by the General Logistics Directorate (*Direccao Geral de Logistica*, DGLog) of the FAPLA EMG, which took delivery of most military supplies from the Ministry of Defence elements who arranged for their shipment to

Angola. The main DGLog warehouses were located at Viana, east of Luanda. Units of the Transport Services (Servicos de Transportes) were responsible for overland delivery of supplies to field units; airlift of supplies from Luanda to interior airfields supporting logistics was also done. At the military region or zone level, resupply was administered by a staff logistics element; major units had their own supply and transport elements.

Logistics, or its failure, was a major problem for FAPLA. Despite its many shortcomings, proper logistical support would have ensured a far greater rate of success in operations against UNITA. However, this never occurred, as inefficiency and corruption were permitted to debilitate this crucial sector of FAPLA's war effort. At each point at which supplies passed from one echelon to another, as much as ten per cent of food and other critical supplies were routinely diverted by the personnel in charge for resale on the black market. Control of logistics was difficult as the flow of supplies was from the national level through the FAPLA EMG to RM or Front Headquarters and then to field units.

Civilian security forces

MININT elements; police The Angolan Ministry of the Interior (Ministerio de Interior, MININT) had a police mission but also had provincial administration oversight, and supported investigations of suspect economic activities and 'economic crimes'. In its security mission the MININT controlled directorates for Police and uniformed MININT troops.

1) Angolan People's Police (PPA). The Angolan People's Police (Policia Popular de Angola, PPA, also known as Corpos de Policia Popular de Angola, CPPA, from its pre-December 1988 name) was organised geographically, with territorial commands the headquarters of which were in each provincial centre. Subordinate to them were local offices in each of the districts into which provinces were divided. The CPPA was under the control of the Ministry of the Interior, and was headed by a commander general (director). The regular police consisted of 8,000 or so members.

2) MININT/MINSE forces. In addition to the regular police, there was a force of special MININT troops at least 10,000 strong under a director for paramilitary and special missions to support the PPA and which could also be used to support military operations. Like the PPA, MININT troops were organised along provincial lines as well.

Like the CPPA, the Ministry of State Security (Ministerio de Segurianca do Estado, MINSE, was organised territorially, with provincial offices the headquarters of which were in each provincial centre. MINSE was created in 1980 from the MININT when the latter's Directorate for Intelligence and Security (Direccao de Informacao e Seguranca de Angola, DISA) was made an independent body. Subordinate to them were local offices in each of the districts into which provinces were divided.

MINSE personnel included plainclothes employees as well as uniformed forces. The latter assisted in the defence of FAPLA areas and installations. Uniformed MINSE personnel served with FAPLA; each unit to at least battalion level and often to company level had a MINSE element to counter subversion and monitor troop morale and other activities. The force was organised along provincial and district lines. MINSE troops could be combined with Army troops to form composite combat units.

3) Special Mine Security Units (DPOM). The DPOM were special mine security units under the control of MINSE. They had the sole mission of mine security and in the late 1980s/early 1990s were provided with military equipment of British, French, South African, and Portuguese make. The DPOM were geographically organised, with a unit per mine; the latter were under the control of the zonal MINSE commander.

Cubans Cuban forces were under the command of the Commanding General of the Cuban Expeditionary Force in Angola, with headquarters at Luanda. This force was directly under the control of the general staff (estado major) of the Cuban Revolutionary Armed Forces

(Fuerzas Armadas Revolucionarias, FAR). Originally sent to keep FAPLA in power and even to be its surrogate military in the late 1970s, the mission of the Cubans evolved into one of protection of oil installations, LOCs, and airfields.

While Cuban troops in Angola were deployed throughout the country, the heaviest concentrations in the mid- to late 1980s were in FAPLA RM 8, with two mechanised infantry regiments at Luanda and one at Caxito; in RM 2, with two regiments at Cabinda and one at Nto, and seven additional battalions deployed around the province; along the Benguela Railway (CFB) line, with regiments at Lobito, Benguela, Caala, Huambo, and Kuito (Bie); and along the Moçâmedes (or Namibe) Railway, with regiments at Namibe, Lubango, Matala, Jamba, and Menongue.

Although the above reflects the distribution of major units, Cuban forces were organised into at least ten groups or task forces, with headquarters at Luanda, Cabinda, Malange, Luena, Lobito, Huambo, Cuito (Bie), Matala, Namibe, and Menongue. The Cuban units were supported by a separate, independent C3 and logistical structure.

The standard Cuban mechanised infantry regiment had about 1,440 personnel. Its main manoeuvre units were two or sometimes three mechanised battalions supported by a tank battalion with 21 medium tanks. Other units organic to the regiment included a mortar or howitzer battery (six guns or mortars), an anti-tank battery (ATGM), and an ADA battery. CS units included reconnaissance, combat engineer, and signals companies; CSS included a maintenance and a service company. There were also headquarters/services and chemical defence platoons. A medical platoon was attached to each regiment.

Mercenary forces The use of foreign forces – including Cubans – by FAPLA to assist it in anti-insurgent operations was as controversial as was the presence of Cuban troops in Angola. Cuban forces, especially in west-central and south-west Angola, provided some military 'backbone' to often timid TT and LCB units. They were also used as a more reliable tactical or reaction force as their armoured vehicles were better maintained and thus usually available for use. Cubans also attempted to promote some method into otherwise disparate and randomly brutal local operations in the earlier phases of the war by encouraging FAPLA troops to refrain from actions that would alienate the population. However, as the war dragged on into the 1980s, reports of atrocities ordered or committed by Cuban troops accompanying FAPLA on their operations became frequent, especially in central and south-west Angola.

Another controversial foreign element used by FAPLA were troops provided by the South-West Africa People's Organisation, or SWAPO. At least half of the members of its military wing, the People's Liberation Army of Namibia (PLAN), were organised into at least one brigade that was normally deployed to central Angola in support of FAPLA operations against UNITA. This unit, the FAPLA 20th Motorised Brigade, also known as the SWAPO 1st Mechanised Brigade, was trained by East German advisers and was regarded as much better trained by UNITA than average FAPLA units. However, the 20th Brigade was used for more conventional operations, while other PLAN troops were used for COIN operations. Most PLAN were trained at Andulo, in northern Bie province. Taught by East Germans and Soviets, the language of instruction was English, and troops were trained in a range of military topics; COIN doctrine was not one of them, however.

Employment of SWAPO and Cubans to support FAPLA local operations was frequent in the northern part of RM5 and adjacent parts of the central highlands. There the territory of the Ovimbundu ethnic group (which provided much of UNITA's leadership) bordered on that of the Ovambo and related groups that supplied PLAN with its personnel. Firm supporters of the government, they also filled a number of aggressive FAPLA and MINSE units. The ethnic and political differences between the Ovambos and others in the south-west and the Ovimbundus were a major motivating factor in the aggressive nature of the counterguerrilla operations undertaken by SWAPO in support of local forces. South-west and south-central Angola were the location of many atrocities claimed by UNITA against non-combatants. The prime purpose appears to have been to force the locals to relocate to more secure areas or to force out members of any ethnic group not deemed reliable by the government.

Two other foreign elements assisted FAPLA against UNITA. These were Katangese ex-Gendarmes from Zaire (Forcas Katangueses, nicknamed 'Tigres') and military personnel of the African National Congress (ANC), nicknamed 'Mabecos.' Both were employed by FAPLA (as special units) in return for their use of facilities in Angola. Neither force was as significant a factor through most of the 1980s as the Cubans or SWAPO, but after 1990, when the Cubans had all but left and when SWAPO/PLAN forces returned to Namibia, the 'Tigres' and the 'Mabecos' were employed in increasingly visible roles by FAPLA. Their mission was varied but included convoy protection, counterguerrilla actions, and security. While their mission provided some support to territorial forces, most was to more centrally-controlled operations by the EPA or MINSE.

FIGHTING THE WAR

Despite the attention given in the media to large-scale FAPLA operations during the Angolan civil war, there existed FAPLA security management efforts at the local level throughout. Security management was the responsibility of the Angolan military, the Ministry of State Security (MINSE), the Ministry of the Interior (MININT), and from 1983 the People's Vigilance Brigades (BPVs). The Angolan president headed a combined military-civilian council, the National Council for Defence and Security, which was formed in April 1984 with the mission of planning and coordinating security management at the national level through weekly meetings. The Angolan president also controlled regional military councils (formed in July 1983) that planned and coordinated local security management efforts, usually at the provincial level, among military, MINSE, MININT, and BPV elements.

Military counter-guerrilla operations were not COINOPS in the sense that they followed a given counterinsurgency doctrine like that used in Rhodesia or SWA/Namibia, but rather in the sense of predominantly military measures to counter the UNITA threat to areas of FAPLA control. This mission was entrusted to those MPLA security forces not part of the centrally-controlled regular Army (EPA). While the latter fought in major operations against UNITA territory in south-east Angola, the territorial forces were responsible for what the MPLA considered basic nationwide security missions – controlling territory, keeping LOCs open, securing critical key points, and tracking down and engaging, wherever possible, UNITA insurgent concentrations. Territorial forces and most of their operations were controlled at the local level – regional (by the RM commander) and, after 1988, zonal (by the ZM commander).

Although FAPLA had no known COIN doctrine, the MPLA still had to devise a strategy to deal with UNITA and the growing security threat it posed through the late 1970s and early 1980s. To do this, it had to address the following major security management problems:

a) The primary requirement for FAPLA was to ensure the integrity of its own military operations, especially that of the regular Army and Air Force. This entailed:

■ Maintaining critical overland LOCs to enable troop movement and resupply;
■ Protection of airfields used for FAPA air missions as well as air resupply, and protection of army posts, training centres, and garrisons;
■ Ensuring the survivability of FAPLA units attacked by insurgents;
■ Preventing South African or other foreign interference with FAPLA counter-guerrilla operations.

In this first area, FAPLA had a poor record. Overland LOCs in operational areas were never under FAPLA control unless troops were transiting them at the time. While most major routes were routinely patrolled and swept for mines, smaller roads had bridges destroyed, were mined, and were subject to constant insurgent interdiction. Large troop contingents or guarded resupply columns even on major routes were routinely attacked. FAPLA units did develop a reaction capability against UNITA's strikes on their units and columns, but could not effectively prevent most ambushes and harassing fire. When attacked, poor morale and training contributed to high personnel and equipment losses for most FAPLA units. As if these were not enough problems, the MPLA provided facilities and logistical support for SWAPO in southern Angola, subjecting Angola to continued destructive cross-border raids by South African forces from Namibia. In return for the MPLA's support of SWAPO, South Africa supported UNITA, providing it with weapons, supplies, training, and even covert combat support using 32 Battalion. From the mid-1980s South Africa thus had a vested interest in UNITA's survival, and constantly acted to thwart massive FAPLA operations against Mavinga.

b) The second major concern was to contain the spread of UNITA operations. This was addressed in two ways, by military means designed to counter UNITA and by population control, to supposedly deny UNITA any benefits from its territorial gains.

■ The establishment of territorial forces and popular defence forces, and the development of a system for their use, was the main strategy to counter the spread of insurgent operations;
■ Ensuring close liaison with MINSE and Police (MININT) elements at the provincial and local level in an attempt to counter UNITA infiltration and report on UNITA movements;
■ Use of foreign forces, especially Cubans, to perform area and static protection duties, which freed more FAPLA local forces for the above missions;
■ Use of other foreign forces, including some Cubans but also SWAPO, ANC, and Katangese ex-gendarmes, to directly support combat operations by FAPLA territorial forces;
■ Population control took the primary form of relocation of those rural populations dwelling in remote areas or in areas suspected of supporting UNITA to secure areas close to urban centres or garrisons;
■ In accessible contested areas, the rural population would be closely monitored, and some relocation and consolidation of population would take place; units would be deployed in key villages and an intelligence network of sympathisers and informers would be put in place to counter UNITA's similar effort.

Here also FAPLA was hard pressed, largely due to factors of its own making. Insufficient resources were allocated to territorial forces. Despite the latter's ability to work with MINSE and Police, security forces at the local level were not able to deal with the UNITA threat. Most money was spent on large counter-guerrilla campaigns. Population control also failed, as the government, unlike UNITA, was unable to offer rural farmers a similar life in more secure areas. In addition, foreign troops such as the Cubans and SWAPO often committed atrocities and other abuses against the civilian populations in attempts to drive them from their homes or in assisting FAPLA in area security operations. As part of its effort to deny areas to UNITA forces, FAPLA laid numerous mines that caused extensive civilian casualties. It also did little to clear mines laid by UNITA and thus avert additional civilian casualties.

c) The third major concern was to attack and engage UNITA forces and conduct other active operations designed to degrade UNITA capabilities.

■ Local (regional and zonal) FAPLA commanders would coordinate with their MINSE and Police counterparts, as well as higher echelons, to determine what UNITA elements could be successfully located and engaged by territorial forces;

■ If territorial forces were not sufficient to counter UNITA, then ad hoc assistance was requested from the regular Army;

■ The regular Army (EPA) at the regional and zonal level routinely planned and executed counterguerrilla operations of a joint nature (EPA, FAPA, TTs, MINSE, Police, and others) coordinated by the local FAPLA commander.

■ The FAPLA staff planned and executed large operations against UNITA-held territory that involved a large degree of troop movement and logistical buildup. These operations were joint efforts by ground, air, and local forces in which local FAPLA commanders coordinated support for the operations but the control of which was normally entrusted to a special operational command directly under FAPLA headquarters.

At best FAPLA efforts in this area diverted UNITA efforts from other parts of Angola by forcing it to defend its areas of control. However, all FAPLA attacks against UNITA's southeastern bastion ultimately failed, usually at great cost. FAPLA losses in the campaigns of 1987 and 1989–1990 both cost the MPLA a billion US dollars or so in weapons and other equipment. If we assume that for each dollar of materiel it cost as much to deliver, maintain, and train personnel in its use, then in just two campaigns FAPLA lost four billion US dollars. While in both cases this was Soviet military assistance, in 1990 the USSR did not replace the losses as it had in 1987–1988. In addition, about 5,000 FAPLA were killed in each of the two campaigns, and at least the same number wounded. While FAPLA saw fit to expend these resources in the south-east, territorial forces throughout the rest of Angola lacked sufficient manpower and materiel to carry out their missions effectively.

Counterguerrilla operations by territorial forces

FAPLA local operations were designed to disrupt local UNITA logistical networks and base camps, as well as to isolate and attack enclaves of insurgent activity. The latter were part of UNITA's military system, and were village complexes several of which comprised a military sector. The military sectors in turn were part of UNITA military regions (subdivisions of UNITA Fronts). The military sectors and their agricultural communities not only provided the insurgents with food but were also virtually self-sufficient pockets of resistance throughout FAPLA-controlled territory. FAPLA, for its part, attempted to contain UNITA influence by relocating rural civilians to areas which could be effectively controlled by the MPLA.

Much if not most of the time territorial forces were caught in a purely reactive mode by pre-emptive insurgent action. UNITA expanded its areas of control by attacking isolated garrisons or by cutting LOCs to surface traffic by destroying bridges or blocking roads. It was the mission of territorial forces to prevent, by aggressive patrols and rapid response, this constant low-level insurgent activity, as well as to react when possible to UNITA troop movements by using the tactical units to spearhead territorial force attacks. The latter apparently did not have a high success rate, even when assisted by Cuban units. All too often UNITA would ambush the reaction force; if the latter was large and commanded too much firepower, UNITA would withdraw and allow the poor logistics that afflicted territorial forces to do the insurgents' work for them.

Territorial forces on the offensive against UNITA forces, on the other hand, enjoyed a higher success rate than those in a simple reactive mode. Raids on UNITA enclaves often met with considerable success in disrupting the insurgents' demographic and economic support base. The raids, which took place twice a year, year at planting and harvest time, were designed to capture or destroy food and cattle, as well as to deport locals in enclave areas to resettlement camps near towns with FAPLA and MINSE garrisons. Often the process was accompanied by considerable brutality and security forces frequently killed any who refused to relocate. Although sometimes yielding considerable 'booty', these operations by FAPLA merely served to further alienate the population and make it seek help from UNITA. Up to the late 1980s the proficiency of most UNITA local forces in enclaves in MPLA territories improved to the point where they could often defeat routine FAPLA territorial force incursions and recover property which was taken.

The fighting between FAPLA and UNITA forces at the local level is responsible for one of the more deplorable aspects of the Angolan civil war, namely the extensive use of mines. The latter were laid by both sides in attempts to control the movements of population. Anti-personnel mines by the tens of thousands were planted to deliberately cause casualties among civilians who sought to use smaller roads and trails, or cultivate their fields. The high numbers of amputees found on both sides fighting the war indicates the efficacy of these mines and that their main effect was on the civilian population and not the military forces of either side. Most of the mines used were of Soviet manufacture, and were employed to the end of the war. Many were also provided to SWAPO/PLAN.

The closest FAPLA came to a true COIN doctrine was its use, starting in 1983/1985, of a strategy designed to contain the progress of UNITA's growing influence in rural areas. The 'Iron Fist' (Punho Ferro) operations of FAPLA were designed to methodically root out UNITA sympathisers in contested areas and replace them with a network of FAPLA and MINSE informers. 'Iron Fist' units were designated special FAPLA units whose operations were coordinated by the FAPLA staff. The area of operations focused on the CFB and adjacent areas in the central plateau and eastern Angola. The process involved the consolidation of villages into enclaves that could be (in theory) controlled by FAPLA security elements through informers. UNITA, however, had its own 'Plan Iron' (Plano Ferro) designed to counter FAPLA's 'Iron Fist.' It disrupted FAPLA operations in contested areas, identified and eliminated informers, and relocated to areas of UNITA control rural populations considered at risk. By 1987–1988 'Iron Fist' operations were largely abandoned.

FAPLA local forces had the assistance of Special Forces (FE) in local counter-guerrilla operations. FE units were used to support reconnaissance and intelligence operations by both territorial and regular Army units. FEs could also be used as intervention forces, as was the case in May-June 1990, when they were used to bolster counterguerrilla operations in the Northern Front and the newly-created Cuanza-Bengo Front. They were also airlifted, in multi-battalion strength, to Huambo and Bie provinces in February 1991 in response to the capture of Cuemba by UNITA.

The FAPLA operations that gave rise to the greatest number of charges of human rights violations by UNITA and its supporters took place in south-western and south-central Angola where Cubans and SWAPO assisted TTs. The main purpose of these operations was to forcibly relocate villagers in certain areas to the vicinity of larger towns that had FAPLA, MINSE, and police units, to deny them contact with UNITA elements, render them dependent upon MPLA authorities, and coopt them into supporting the MPLA. Those targeted for removal or elimination, especially by SWAPO, were members of the Ovimbundu ethnic group, many of whom were supporters of UNITA. Here, as elsewhere, use of anti-personnel mines that targeted local civilians was common.

MOZAMBIQUE

The long civil war in Mozambique was marked by a number of significant developments in the fighting by the FAM against RENAMO. These included the slow evolution of FAM capabilities and the recovery of government forces from their nadir of the early 1980s; the involvement of Zimbabwe's army and air force in the fighting; and finally the settling of the war into a stalemate by the end of the 1980s with little hope for either side of a battle-field resolution. In all of this the performance of the FAM was a critical factor, as FRELIMO's security forces struggled to wrest control of territory and population throughout the country from the insurgents.[27]

FAM security forces
Unlike Angola, the brunt of fighting throughout the long insurgency rested upon the provincial military commanders, who coordinated operations by various military and civilian security services within their geographical areas of responsibility. In fact, the history of the Mozambican conflict is one of mostly small-scale local operations by provincial forces against RENAMO insurgent units and bases, interspersed with a few large-scale operations against the major insurgent bases or RENAMO-held towns. In the late 1980s many of these were joint operations with the Zimbabwean forces deployed in Mozambique.

The forces available for the government anti-insurgent effort included the various FAM services (army, air force, navy, border guards) as well as paramilitary formations (militia, civilian police, and other groups). From 1985 to the end of the insurgency various foreign forces from Zimbabwe, Tanzania, and Malawi were deployed at various times inside Mozambique to assist the FAM in its mission of countering RENAMO and restoring security.

Regular military forces
Throughout the late 1970s and the 1980s the Mozambican military (Forcas Armadas de Mocambique, FAM; also Forcas Populares de Libertacao de Mocambique, or FPLM[28]) kept the FRELIMO regime in power. The principal FAM elements that played a role in the fight against RENAMO included the centrally-controlled Army (Exercito de Mozambique), terri-torial forces and militia, and the Border Guards (Tropas de Guarda Frontiera). Air and naval forces played much less of a role in FAM operations against either RENAMO insur-gents or Rhodesian forces.

The chain of command for ground forces ran from the President through to the Minister of Defence and the CEMG of the FAM. It then went to provincial military comman-ders, who controlled operations in their respective provinces. Main units included brigades, battalions, and companies/squadrons.

The FAM structure was little changed from independence to 1987, at which time it was thoroughly reorganised and a separate army command set up. Changes in the Ministry of Defence resulted in the establishment of new secretaries of state for defence for four new directorates-general: Planning, Logistics, Manpower and Training, and Equipment and Weaponry.[29]

Army It was only in 1987 that the FAM had a separate ground forces commander. Until that time the provincial military commanders, who reported directly to FAM Headquarters, controlled the major army units in their commands. The centrally-controlled elements of the FAM comprised eight motorised infantry brigades, an armoured brigade, and a dozen or so independent battalions, plus special troops. The latter included the Presidential Guard in Maputo plus a number of commando units. The force had 80,000 or so personnel. The actual authorised personnel strength level for the ground force was probably much higher, about 100,000 or so, but the force was usually chronically undermanned, with poor conditions of service contributing to a high desertion rate.

In addition to regular army units under control of FAM headquarters in Maputo, there were regional territorial commands, an Air Defence Command, the Presidential Guard, and the Border Guard. The latter is considered a separate service and is discussed below. Air Defence and Presidential Guard units were primarily deployed in around the capital, Maputo.

The Air Force and Navy The 2,000-man Air Force was responsible for defence of Mozam-bican air space and support to army operations. The air force consisted of eight operational squadrons: four fixed-wing combat (mostly MiG-17s and MiG-21s), one rotary-wing combat (attack helicopters), two transport (one fixed-wing with An-26s and one rotary-wing with Mi-8 and Mi-25), and one training squadron. For the duration of the conflict with RENAMO the Air Force had severe shortcomings in personnel quality and training, maintenance, equip-ment modernisation, and logistics. Training was primarily provided by the USSR and other Warsaw Pact countries. Main bases included Maputo, Beira, Chimoio, Tete, and Nacala. The Mozambican Navy had about 700 personnel and about 20 surface craft, divided between a Coastal Command, with its main bases at Maputo (the headquarters), Beira, Nacala, and Pemba, and a Lake Command, with its headquarters at Metangula on Lake Nyasa. Naval capabilities were very limited, due to lack of resources and training for its personnel.

Territorial Forces and Militia Through the 1980s there were ten FAM provincial military commands. This provincial structure replaced the earlier military organisation of the 1970s, which divided Mozambique into three regions: North, running from the northern border to the Zambezi river; Central, from the Zambezi River to the Save River; and South, from the Save to the southern border. Each regional military command corresponded to a Mozambican province and controlled ten to fifteen local infantry battalions that provided area defence against RENAMO operations.

Border Guards (TGF) Tropas de Guarda Frontiera The border guard had about 6,000 or so personnel, and was divided into four large brigades, each with about 1,500 personnel, deployed from north to south throughout the country. Brigade headquarters were at Lichinga in Niassa province, Moatize in Tete province, Chimoio in Manica province, and at Massingir in Gaza province. The Border Guard formations were organised similarly to those of Army infantry forces.

Military logistics In the mid- and late 1980s the FAM General Staff had two separate direc-torate-generals responsible for military logistics. These were:

■ The Directorate-General (Direcao-Geral) for Logistics, responsible for coordinating general logistics, including rations, clothing, fuel, as well as their transport.
■ The Directorate-General for Equipment and Weapons, responsible for coordinating the provision and maintenance of weapons and equipment, including ordnance.[30]

Paramilitary and civilian security forces

Militia The FAM militia (Milicia Popular), subordinate to the territorial forces, numbered about 30,000 personnel and comprised a number of small, lightly-armed infantry units. The militia was created in 1982 to assist the FAM against RENAMO. Militia units were designated guardians of economic installations (factories and farms), villages, and trans-portation infrastructure. Few of its personnel had modern weapons or even uniforms. The militia augmented the regular army and provided a personnel reserve for it, but also assisted regular military and police units. Military training was haphazard at best, taking second place to political training. The militia was generally not by itself capable of any effective local area defence, and was no match for RENAMO.

Militia organisation was along territorial lines, with territorial military commanders controlling provincial commands. While some units were fairly well organised and inte-grated into provincial or district security structures, other units were less so and were responsible for protecting isolated villages and regions. In most cases these units were only marginally effective in defending villages or other key points unless backed by regular military forces.

Recruitment for the militia was normally the responsibility of a FRELIMO party organ, the Organisation of Mozambican Youth (Organisacao da Juventude de Mocambique, OJM).

Under OJM auspices Mozambican youths were recruited and formed into 'brigades' that assisted the FAM and other security forces as required.

Mozambican national police (PPM) The Mozambique People's Police (Policia Popular de Mocambique, PPM), created in 1979, was a national-level police force that supplemented various municipal and local police forces in maintaining urban security. The PPM, which probably numbered 3,000 or so personnel, was organised along provincial lines and had primarily a law-enforcement function. However, it also investigated suspected RENAMO activity in urban areas and coordinated its operations with other local and provincial security organs.

Popular National Security Service (SNASP) and subordinate security organs Mozambique's secret police, the Servico Nacional de Seguranca Popular, or SNASP, was created in 1975 and disbanded in 1991. Numbering as many as 2,000 personnel, the service was responsible for domestic intelligence, counterintelligence, and the protection of the regime and its officials. The SNASP was controlled by the Ministry for Internal Security and had subordinate directorates for domestic intelligence, counterintelligence, immigration control, VIP protection, and internal security operations. In the latter function SNASP maintained its Counterinsurgency Office (Gabinete de Luta Contra Bandidos), which worked with other security forces in operations against RENAMO. The SNASP Directorate of Counterintelligence controlled the People's Vigilance Brigades (Brigadas Populares de Vigiliancia, BPV), a national network of FRELIMO party workers and informants that numbered as many as 300,000.[31]

Foreign insurgent forces assisting the FAM During the latter part of the 1970s FRELIMO offered refuge to guerrillas operating against the Rhodesian government. Most of these were from the Zimbabwe African National Liberation Army (ZANLA), the armed wing of Robert Mugabe's ZANU. ZANU was distributed in camps in central Mozambique where it could conduct cross-border operations against targets in Rhodesia, but at times assisted the FAM in operations against the Rhodesian-backed RENAMO groups in Sofala province. It is still unclear how effective the ZANLA assistance was, but it remains likely that the impact was minimal, as most ZANU resources continued to be directed against raids into Rhodesia and defence of its bases against Rhodesian military strikes.

Through much of the conflict FRELIMO also offered refuge to armed elements of the African National Congress (ANC), the Umkhonto we Sizwe (MK), or 'Spear of the Nation,' whose HQ was in Maputo. ANC operations, however, were principally against South Africa and their available resources did not allow much if any diversion to directly assist the FAM against RENAMO. Indeed, their presence eventually caused problems for FRELIMO, including the 1983 SAAF raid against suspected ANC targets in Maputo. The ANC left Mozambique (at least officially) as a result of the 1984 Nkomati Accords.

Foreign forces assisting the FAM Through the latter part of the civil war the Mozambican government force were assisted by foreign troops, including those from neighbouring Zimbabwe, Tanzania, Malawi, and Zambia.

Most of the assistance came from Zimbabwe. At independence in 1980 Zimbabwe President Robert Mugabe pledged assistance by Zimbabwe to Mozambican government forces in their struggle against RENAMO. This took the form of Zimbabwe Defence Force (ZDF) ground and air support to the FAM, mainly directed to maintaining civilian transit of the strategic Beira corridor, Zimbabwe's principal outlet to the sea. Elements of the Zimbabwe National Army (ZNA) were deployed in Mozambique throughout most of the 1980s.

It should be noted that during the war, Zimbabwe military forces were supported by two civilian security bodies. The Central Intelligence Organisation (CIO), which was a carryover from Rhodesian times and which continued to function relatively intact under its former management, provided external intelligence in support of ZDF operations and those in Mozambique in particular. The Zimbabwe Republic Police (ZRP) operated in the border areas to prevent wherever possible RENAMO infiltration and attacks into Zimbabwe.

ZDF units were involved in Mozambique through most of the 1980s. The first phase of the deployment was in 1982; in 1983 the first Special Task Force of up to three ZNA battalions in size was deployed to assist the Mozambican Armed Forces in their fight against RENAMO and to help keep vital LOCs open. The key LOCs included the road/rail/pipeline link between Zimbabwe and the Mozambican port of Beira, as well as the Malawi–Zimbabwe road link that ran through part of Mozambique's Tete province.

The second and most important phase of ZDF involvement began in 1985, following the continued deterioration of security despite the March 1994 Nkomati Accords. This second deployment began in summer of 1985 and by July 5,000 ZNA were in central Mozambique. Many of these troops spearheaded a joint ZNA-FAM offensive against the RENAMO headquarters at Gorongosa in that month in Operation 'Grapefruit'. Up to 1987 the force grew to at least 10,000 ZNA deployed inside Mozambique at any given time, plus air force and logistics elements supporting the deployment stationed in Zimbabwe. RENAMO's reaction to ZDF involvement was to avoid direct combat. In 1987 the first cross-border raids into Zimbabwe by RENAMO in retaliation began. Meanwhile, the ZNA expanded its areas of operations to include Zambezia province south of the Zambezi River, and the Chicualacuala Railway line. However, with the progressive decline in military capabilities of both the FAM and RENAMO at the end of the decade, combined with the increased cost of supporting its forces in Mozambique, the Zimbabwe government sought to scale back its role. By late 1990 some ZNA forces began to withdraw from Mozambique, and by early 1991 were ostensibly restricted to sites along the Beira corridor.

FIGHTING THE WAR

Although the FAM had no defined COIN doctrine, it still had to devise a strategy to deal with RENAMO and the growing security threat it posed by its rapid spread from 1981 through 1984. To do this, it had to address the same security management problems as other governments under siege by insurgents:

a) Integrity of own military operations, especially that of the regular Army and Air Force. This entailed:

■ Maintaining critical overland LOCs to enable troop movement and resupply;
■ Protection of airfields used for Air Force missions as well as air resupply, and protection of army posts, training centres, and garrisons;
■ Ensuring the survivability of FAM units and garrisons attacked or threatened by RENAMO;
■ Preventing South African or Rhodesian interference with FAM counter-guerrilla operations.

In this first area, the FAM at first failed on all points with the possible exception of protecting its major air and ground installations. Through the mid-1980s, even these were not free from RENAMO attack. Overland LOCs in operational areas were never under FAM control unless troops were transiting them at the time. Priority was given to the major transit corridors – the Nacala, Beira, and Chicualacuala Railways, and the Nkomati–Maputo road and rail corridor. While most major routes were routinely patrolled and swept for mines, smaller roads had bridges destroyed, were mined, and were subject to constant insurgent interdiction. Large troop contingents or guarded resupply columns even on major routes were routinely attacked. It was only from the mid-1980s, following the deployment of Zimbabwean troops along the Beira and Chicualacuala Railway corridors, that these routes were secured. In the latter half of the 1980s the training and deployment of commando units enabled many garrisons under threat to be reinforced with better trained and led units that reinforced site defence.

b) The second major concern was to contain the spread of RENAMO operations. This was addressed in two ways, by military means designed to counter the insurgents and by population control, to supposedly deny RENAMO any benefits from its territorial gains.

■ The establishment of territorial forces and popular defence forces, and the development of a system for their use was the main strategy to counter the spread of insurgent operations;
■ Ensuring close liaison with SNASP and police elements at the provincial and local level in an attempt to counter RENAMO infiltration and report on insurgent bases and movements;
■ Use of foreign forces, including those from Zimbabwe, Tanzania, and Malawi, to perform LOC and some other protection duties, and to directly support combat operations by the FAM.
■ Population control took the primary form of forming local militia formations under the control of the provincial military commander as well as relocation of those rural populations dwelling in remote areas or in areas suspected of supporting RENAMO to more secure areas close to urban centres or FAM garrisons;
■ In accessible contested areas, the rural population would be closely monitored, and some relocation and consolidation of population would take place; units would be deployed in key villages and an intelligence network of sympathisers and informers would be put in place to counter RENAMO's attempts to build networks and infiltrate personnel.

In this second area, FRELIMO at first also did poorly, largely due to policies that the government put into practice soon after independence, alienating much of the rural population. In addition, a virtually inoperable support system for most military units through the mid- and late 1980s paralysed the FAM's ability to counter RENAMO operations. It was only starting in 1987 that the FRELIMO government began to make major changes in security management and turn away from a conventional force to one more suited to fighting a guerrilla conflict. Population control ultimately failed, as the government was unable to offer rural farmers a similar life in more secure areas. Most militia units formed to support local provincial security structures remained poorly-equipped and led, and were of limited effectiveness. In addition, the government was unable to prevent RENAMO depredations against government, infrastructure, and civilian targets. Displaced persons from fighting in the rural areas swelled Mozambique's cities through the 1980s. By contrast, most RENAMO-controlled areas were, through the late 1980s, generally more secure from FAM attack. Although it is still a subject of some points of controversy, rural populations in many if not most areas of RENAMO control enjoyed a better and more secure life through the 1980s than civilians under FRELIMO rule did. However, this statement has to be carefully qualified and requires a separate discussion due to the debate still raging around it.

c) The third major concern of the FAM was to attack and engage RENAMO forces and conduct other active operations designed to degrade the insurgents' capabilities.

■ Provincial and local FAM commanders would coordinate with their SNASP and Police counterparts, as well as higher echelons, to determine what RENAMO bases and units could be successfully located and engaged;

■ If provincial forces were not sufficient to counter UNITA, then ad hoc assistance was requested from regular Army units or foreign forces (usually ZNA);

■ The regular Army at the provincial and local level routinely planned and executed counter-guerrilla operations of a joint nature (Army, provincial forces, militia, SNASP, police, and others);

■ The FAM general staff planned and directed larger military operations against major RENAMO base areas that involved a large degree of troop movement and logistical buildup. In the latter half of the 1980s these operations were joint efforts by ground, air, and local forces backed by foreign (usually ZNA) units in which provincial commanders coordinated support for the operations but control of which was normally exercised by FAM headquarters.

As was the case in Angola, military counterguerrilla operations were not COINOPS in the sense that they followed a given counterinsurgency doctrine like that used in Rhodesia or SWA/Namibia, but rather in the sense of predominantly military measures to counter the RENAMO threat to areas of FRELIMO control. This mission fell upon most FAM units, but especially those territorial (i.e., area-bound) units under the provincial commands. The territorial forces had the mission of day-to-day work of basic nationwide security missions–controlling territory, keeping LOCs open, securing critical key points, and tracking down and engaging, wherever possible, local insurgent concentrations. Territorial forces and most of their operations were controlled by the provincial military commander, and by subordinate area commands based on the districts into which Mozambican provinces were divided.

NOTES

Although the literature for COIN operations by Rhodesian and South African forces is extensive, discussions on counterguerrilla operations for Angola and Mozambique are quite sparse. For Mozambique, see the discussions by Karl Maier, Kemal Mustafa and Alex Vines in *Conspicuous Destruction: War, Famine & the Reform Process in Mozambique* (New York/Washington/Los Angeles/London: Human Rights Watch, 1992), especially pp. 49ff, 56ff, 64ff, 70ff, 115ff and 128ff. A subsequent book by Human Rights Watch/Africa Watch, *Landmines in Mozambique* (New York/Washington/Los Angeles/London: Human Rights Watch, 1994), pp. 30ff and 37ff as well as pp. 98ff, focuses on landmine use and consequences. As for Angola, a series of Human Rights Watch/Africa Watch publications provides some material. See especially *Angola: Violations of the Laws of War by Both Sides* (1989), especially pp. 59ff, 69ff, 87ff and 96ff; *Landmines in Angola* (1993), especially pp. 13ff, 26ff, 41ff; and *Angola: Arms Trade and Violations of the Laws of War since the 1992 Elections* (1994), especially pp. 25ff and 61ff. The organisation and structure of the post-1993 Angolan army is detailed in my unpublished paper 'The Angolan Army in 1995'.

1. Walker, p. 173.
2. Walker, pp. 167-73; definitions in this and the preceding paragraph are those used by the Rhodesian government in its ATOPS literature.
3. The general format for discussion followed here is that provided by Heitman, *South African Armed Forces*, pp. 194ff.
4. Cillers, p. 22; see also Arbuckle, *RUSI*, December 1979, pp. 29-30.
5. See the excellent overview of military organisation published by the Anti-Apartheid Movement, *Fire Force Exposed* (November 1979; abbreviated hereafter as FFE), pp. 12ff.
6. Cole, pp. 435ff.
7. *FFE*, pp. 13ff and 17ff. for a discussion of the SAS and the Selous Scouts.
8. *ZCS*, pp. 273ff. See also *FFE*, pp. 26ff. However, the discussion of equipment and inventory status throughout the later years of the war must be used with caution. The discussion of aircraft brought down by insurgents in Appendix III (p. 51) and the resulting tally of losses is not supported by other sources.
9. Cole, pp. 438ff.
10. Cillers, p. 22; see also Arbuckle, *RUSI*, December 1979, pp. 29-30.
11. Abbot and Botham, p. 40.

12. Ibid., pp. 40-1.
13. Steenkamp, *Borderstrike!*, p. 9: 'The question of Black majority rule is out. We are not fighting even for majority rule. We are fighting to seize power in Namibia, for the benefit of the Namibian people. We are revolutionaries. We are not counter-revolutionaries...' This statement, by Nujoma on 28 February 1978, in a SABC interview with Cliff Saunders, also saw the SWAPO leader deny – contrary to all evidence – PLAN's role in committing atrocities against the population, and also reaffirmed his plans to take reprisals on any Namibians supporting South African rule.
14. McCuen, John J. *The Art of Counter-revolutionary Warfare*, Stackpole Books, Harrisburg, 1966.
15. Puitz, von Egidj, and Caplan, *Political Who's Who of Namibia*, Magnus Company, Windhoek, 1987, p. 227.
16. Ibid.
17. I am greatly indebted to Mr. Morgan Norval, of the Selous Foundation (Washington, DC), for providing me with invaluable information about SWATF ethnic units. The discussion below is based upon his information, as well as details from his book *Death in the Desert*, Selous Foundation Press, Washington DC, 1989, and from various journal articles, especially in *Paratus*. For an overview of the counterinsurgency aspects of the war in SWA/Namibia, see especially Robert C. Owen, 'Counterrevolution in Namibia' in *Airpower Journal*, Vol. 1, No. 3, Winter 1987/1988, pp. 52-62.
18. *Paratus*, July 1979, pp. 6 ff.
19. Puitz, von Egidj, and Caplan, ibid., p. 242.
20. See, for instance, reports of the operation on 2-28 July 1987, in which a follow-up action by security forces pursuing about 120 insurgents led them into Angola, where they were ambushed by a combined PLAN-FAPLA force. The latter were defeated and pursued, and a second engagement resulted. At the end, 190 PLAN and two FAPLA were reported killed with the loss of no security force personnel (Johannesburg SAPA, 1611 GMT 28 Jul 87). In another operation, PLAN apparently ambushed elements of the security forces undertaking a pre-emptive strike against its Central Front Headquarters on 31 October 1987; SWATF counter-attacks killed about 150 PLAN. The eleven security force casualties apparently resulted from a single mortar attack (Johannesburg SAPA 1433 GMT 3 Dec 87). See also Steenkamp, *Border War*, pp. 150 and 152-3.
21. Legum, p. 178.
22. Norval, pp. 196-7.
23. Norval, pp. 197-201.
24. See 'RSA said to "Namibianize" conflict', in *Southern African Focus* (Windhoek), February 1987, pp. 1-10. The strident anti-regime tone of the article tarnishes an otherwise excellent survey of the institutions and tactics used by civil and military authorities to garner support.
25. *The Namibian* (Windhoek), 19-25 February 1988 issue, p. 4.
26. Stackpole Books, Harrisburg, PA.
27. This account of FAM and ZNA operations is based primarily upon Finnegan, pp. 56-61, as well as information courtesy of Mr Thomas Schaaf. Other information provided by the International Freedom Foundation (Washington DC).
28. In my discussion I prefer, for the sake of convenience, to use the label 'FAM' for the Mozambican military, although use of the label 'FPLM', the name of the old FRELIMO armed wing, persisted through the 1980s. 'FAM' is readily expanded as 'Mozambican Armed Forces' (Forcas Armadas de Mocambique) and is a good general term to include both regular military and paramilitary/militia formations.
29. *ACR*, 1987-1988, pp. B628-9.
30. *Noticias* (Maputo), 22 June 1987, p. 1.
31. *MPC*, p. 149. On 9 July 1991 SNASP was replaced by the State Information Service (SISE).

Chapter Four
The First Angolan Civil War, 1975–1991

In many ways the Angola-SWA/Namibia conflict is *the* African insurgency for study. The range of combat from low-intensity conflict through conventional warfare is found. Both facets of the conflict, the guerrilla war fought throughout most of central and northern Angola, and the larger semi-conventional conflicts which often involved South African forces in southern Angola, deserve careful study for a number of lessons learned. Like Rhodesia, Angola was a proving ground for insurgent warfare. The long sixteen-year civil war (1975–1991), followed by a relatively brief ceasefire, started up once again in late 1992, to continue through late 1994.[1]

INTRODUCTION AND OVERVIEW OF THE ANGOLAN CIVIL WAR, 1975–1991

The overview is designed to stress military developments. As in all other African insurgencies, there are parallel political and socio-economic developments.[2]

THE MPLA AND UNITA, 1975–1979

The military wings of both the MPLA and UNITA originated in the long guerrilla war against Portuguese colonial forces that they fought from 1961 to 1975. However, none of the insurgent movements – MPLA, UNITA, nor FNLA – had the capability to prevail in the evolving superpower struggle over post-1975 Angola without extensive foreign assistance not only in materiel and training, but also manpower. Despite the assistance of elements in Portugal's post-1974 government, the MPLA could not have won on the battlefield without extensive support from Cuban combat forces. Its rivals also had foreign support. UNITA's dramatic 1975 gains were made as the result of South African forces intervening in Operation 'Savannah'. The FNLA had the assistance of the Zairian armed forces. Both the FNLA and UNITA were also assisted by the United States.

However, the backers of UNITA and FNLA were forced to withdraw their support for political reasons. The MPLA's sponsors – the Soviet Bloc and Cuba – helped their client win by providing massive military support. The MPLA's helpers were also adept in manipulating international public opinion against UNITA and the FNLA supporters. For the latter, pursuit of the war became costly both militarily and politically, and the MPLA's rivals lost the direct, overt support of a number of nations, especially South Africa, Zaire, and the United States. Lack of coherence and constancy in the Third World foreign policy of the last in the wake of its Vietnam debacle had global repercussions, hampering American influence in the African continent and elsewhere for the remainder of the decade. The 'Clark Amendment', passed in 1976 and only repealed in 1985, specifically prohibited US government assistance in any form to UNITA.

FAPLA – BUILDING AND FIELDING A FORCE

After independence, FAPLA was rebuilt. Soviet and Cuban assistance transformed it from a guerrilla force to a conventional one along Soviet/Warsaw Pact lines. All but a small part of the surviving force had departed with the defection of Daniel Chipenda, who led the principal pre-1975 MPLA armed faction; many of the original fighters had been casualties of the fighting preceding the MPLA's control of Luanda (November 1975). For at least two years, as Luanda recruited and trained a force, the MPLA's battles were fought by Cuban combat troops, contingents seconded to the MPLA by sympathetic African regimes, and allied units of Namibian and Rhodesian guerrillas.

1976-1979 was marked by intensive recruitment of troops to fill out the ground force, the Angolan People's Army (Exercito Popular de Angola, EPA), with brigades. Most of the force was light infantry. A typical EPA brigade had about 2,100 troops organised into three infantry battalions, artillery and air defence battalions, and various combat support and service support units. Motorised infantry brigades added a tank unit and mounted at least one of the infantry battalions on APCs. From small arms to major ground systems, FAPLA was outfitted with Soviet and Warsaw Pact equipment, much of it older but still serviceable. Doctrine and training followed Soviet lines, and the Soviet Union provided a half dozen or so advisers for each brigade.

Building the MPLA's air force, the Angolan People's Air Force (Forca Aerea Popular de Angola, FAPA) required a different effort. The quality of training required for pilots and support personnel was much higher than that for ground troops, and qualified personnel were almost entirely lacking. Air support for ground operations against UNITA was needed from the start, and Cuban pilots usually filled the gap. Pilots from some Eastern European and other African countries also fought with FAPA. Support services for FAPA were provided by the Soviet Union, which also ran the FAPLA air logistics network from its inception well into the late 1980s.

EVOLUTION OF UNITA CAPABILITIES THROUGH THE LATE 1970S

UNITA adhered more closely than the MPLA to its guerrilla past. This was due not only to its usefulness in this state to its South African backers, but also to its thus being better able to fight better-armed FAPLA and Cuban opponents. After the setbacks of 1976 its guerrilla structure allowed UNITA to elude its enemies and regroup. It also made the organisation and its military arm more amenable to changes later implemented by Savimbi to fight the MPLA and Cubans.

South African support was an essential factor for UNITA from the late 1970s. At first, the SADF relied on 31 and 32 Battalions, plus a few special units, for its forward defence of the Namibian border – in Angola. However, by the late 1970s, with the growth of FAPLA and a consequent increase in SWAPO aggressiveness, the South Africans changed their strategy. Since the MPLA harboured SWAPO and provided camps for the ANC and other anti-regime dissidents, South Africa would henceforth support UNITA. The latter thus ceased to be a light guerrilla force based in the central highlands and parts of the south-east. South African support – logistics and training – meant that UNITA had to secure supply lines to SADF sources of materiel in northern Namibia. Thus the insurgents had to relocate major bases to south-eastern Angola.

South African training of UNITA began in late 1977 or early 1978. The training supplemented but did not replace that for officers provided to UNITA by allies such as Morocco. The SADF trained officers and NCOs, and provided instruction on communications systems, demolitions and other engineer skills, and the use of various crew-served weapons systems. In addition to individual training, SADF teams trained UNITA units, building up a capable light infantry force by the end of the 1970s. The training was done by special teams not only inside Angola but also at facilities in the Caprivi Strip area of northern Namibia.

Despite the benefits gained from the new alliance of convenience, UNITA still faced some disadvantages. Into the early 1980s, its need for trained light infantry units to support and exploit its guerrilla operations often exceeded the number that could be trained. Also, many units, once fielded, lacked sufficient combat experience. Ensuring adequate command and control in operations involving ever greater numbers of units and personnel had to be learned through experience. The need to capture FAPLA garrisons and strongpoints was essential to establishing UNITA territorial control. Skills in siegecraft and assault thus had to be learned. Finally, even insurgent units with sufficient experience and training were often at a marked disadvantage in engagements with motorised FAPLA forces backed by armour, heavy artillery, and air support.

It was at this point that the SADF began a secret programme to assist UNITA by the select use of its forces, especially 32 Battalion, to attack and capture FAPLA garrisons in southern Angola. The towns would then be turned over to UNITA. Elements of 32 Battalion thus captured for UNITA towns throughout eastern Cuando Cubango province, the area dubbed by the Portuguese 'The Land at the End of the Earth'. The principal FAPLA garrisons there were Savate, Mucusso, Rivungo and Mavinga. Mavinga was a key area, controlling access to the south-eastern border area through Cuito Cuanavale from Menongue, and thus critical in protecting territory won from FAPLA along the SWA/Namibian border. Control of the town was thus essential for logistics support to further UNITA penetration of MPLA territory north and north-westward.[3]

Other South African assistance took a similar direct form. SADF demolitions experts were despatched to assist UNITA, although in time the insurgents developed their own capability with a special engineer unit, the Technical Explosives Action Brigade (Brigada de Accao Technica de Explosivos, BATE). The South Africans also trained UNITA maintenance and repair personnel, and until UNITA became self-sufficient in this area, may have also provided direct support as well. The most important contribution was in logistics, with the SADF and South African private firms flying in planeloads of critical supplies to airfields in southern Angola. The use of airlift ensured the timely resupply of UNITA, but also required secure landing strips and support infrastructure.

THE CONFLICT IN STRATEGIC CONTEXT

The strategic interplay between the Soviet- and Cuban-backed MPLA and UNITA and its South African (and other Western) allies in southern Angola from 1975 to the end of the 1980s was no simple contest of superpower surrogates. Angola's civil war reflected a number of complex factors, many of them the epitome of irony. One can cite a few examples:

■ Mulatto and Portuguese Angolans were heavily represented in the MPLA, while UNITA saw itself as a black African nationalist organisation; it was supported by the same South African governments that maintained apartheid in their own country.

■ Indeed, UNITA, originally deriving the conceptual base of its insurgency from Maoist roots, ultimately found its main support in South African and other anti-communists.

■ Many of the latter did so in the belief that they could thereby deny the Soviet Union and East Bloc access to Angolan oil, despite the fact that Western nations were Angola's main customers.

■ The Soviet Union, using its surrogates, especially Cuba, sought by alliance with the MPLA government to counter South African and Western influence in southern Africa, a strategy that was partly successful at best, since most nations in the region, including Angola, sought Western assistance and skills for development wherever possible.

■ East Bloc military assistance and Cuban combat troops were the best the Soviet Union could offer, but were ultimately unsuccessful in countering UNITA or keeping South Africa from conducting cross-border operations against the SWAPO insurgents harboured by the Angolan government.

Many other bizarre examples stemming from the clash of various agendas in the conflict could be cited. Perhaps the most ironic situation of all was in the oil-rich province of Cabinda. Here, communist Cuban troops reinforced Soviet-supported Angolan units that guarded oil installations run by United States and other Western companies from attacks by UNITA – that was supported by United States and other Western military assistance. The latter, however, subscribed to an oil embargo against South Africa, another UNITA supporter.

By the early to mid-1980s the insurgency in Angola had become a major element in the 'Reagan Doctrine' of the United States Government to counter Soviet influence worldwide. The stakes, and the resources involved, increased dramatically. The period 1984-1988 saw a substantial FAPLA military buildup and reorganisation, massive Soviet and Cuban military assistance, and an all-out attempt to destroy UNITA militarily. It was marked by conventional operations against UNITA-controlled territory in the south-east, as UNITA consolidated further territorial gains and extended operations into every province of Angola. In 1987-1988 FAPLA and their Cuban allies suffered crushing defeats at the hands of the South Africans in their intervention to support UNITA, ultimately prompting the New York Accords that began Cuban troop withdrawal from Angola. In 1988 FAPLA was restructured to deal better with UNITA's military threat; the newly configured forces attempted to fill both conventional roles as well as COIN functions. 1989–1990 saw the disastrous 'Final Assault' campaign of FAPLA against Mavinga and the spread of intense fighting first to the north and later to the north-eastern and central part of the country (spring–summer 1990). By the end of the war, UNITA had virtually paralysed FAPLA and prevented major operations anywhere in the country.

EVOLUTION OF THE CONFLICT, 1976–1991

BACKGROUND TO THE ANGOLAN CIVIL WAR

Angola's sixteen-year civil war ended on 15 May 1991 with a ceasefire agreement between the MPLA and UNITA. The war followed an equally long period of struggle against Portuguese colonial rule that had reached a climax in the turbulent events of 1974–1976. At this time the Portuguese left, interfactional fighting led to foreign intervention, and UNITA was driven into remote areas of the centre and south-east.

The 1975 victory of the MPLA in winning was due to Cuban, Soviet, and other communist country assistance. The South African intervention (Operation 'Savannah') in 1975 to assist UNITA, though successful in rolling back the MPLA and Cubans almost to the gates of Luanda, was later abandoned for political reasons. The MPLA and Cubans defeated the other rival faction, the National Front for the Liberation of Angola (FNLA), with a major victory on 11 November at Quifandongo north-east of Luanda. By the end of the year most of northern Angola was secured from the FNLA by the MPLA and Cubans, who then turned their attention to the UNITA-held south.

UNITA, led by Dr Jonas Savimbi, was unable to confront the MPLA and Cubans directly. The South African victories over the communist-backed MPLA allowed UNITA to extend its control over most of the southern half of Angola. The MPLA and Cubans, having learned a painful lesson on the battlefield, were unwilling to risk further battles with the South Africans. But when the latter began to pull out from Angola, Cuban and MPLA columns supported by Cuban aircraft began to attack, driving UNITA southward in a series of operations starting in February 1976. By May Savimbi regrouped his forces on the Cuanza River, and began a new strategy of guerrilla war against the MPLA. One key facet of this strategy was to attack the infrastructure, a tactic reflected in destructive hit-and-run attacks to shut down economically-important targets such as the Benguela Railroad (CFB), which remained for the most part closed for the rest of the civil war.

FIRST PHASE OF THE CIVIL WAR, 1976-1978

During 1976-1978 both the MPLA and UNITA both formed the basic political and military structures that carried them through the civil war. For the MPLA, this period was marked by military operations to secure territorial control of most of Angola, undertaken by elements of FAPLA supported by Cuban ground and air forces. Although FAPLA and the Cubans pushed to the southern and eastern borders of Angola, they could not control most of the territory they occupied in central and south-eastern Angola. Angola east of a line south from Kuito (Bie) to the border with Namibia and south of the CFB remained subject to UNITA operations through this period. UNITA's main base of operations remained in southern Bie province. UNITA, on the other hand, successfully resisted conventional, Cuban-backed MPLA attacks by breaking into small, localised commands.

The first phase of the civil war was characterised by:

■ The assumption of much if not most of the MPLA combat responsibilities and practically all of the combat support/combat service support responsibilities by Cuban, SWAPO, and other forces;
■ Organisation of FAPLA into a conventional force based on the brigade system;
■ Attempts by the MPLA and Cubans to promote a 'hearts-and-minds' campaign that failed in the face of UNITA counter-activities;
■ The establishment by SWAPO of bases and a logistical network in south-western Angola with FAPLA and Cuban assistance;
■ The elimination of the FNLA as a fighting force;
■ The initial regrouping of UNITA in the central highlands;
■ UNITA's decision to form a largely insurgent force;
■ The gradual extension of UNITA control into Cuando Cubango province, with South African assistance.

FAPLA required extensive reorganisation and training by its East Bloc allies, but its immediate needs also included Cuban combat support in operations against UNITA. Despite its effectiveness against Portuguese colonial forces, FAPLA was totally inadequate fighting the South Africans and their UNITA allies during Operation 'Savannah'. The largely insurgent force lacked the numbers, training, and equipment to deal with the rapidly moving South African Defence Force (SADF) columns as they advanced northward. South African armoured cars and artillery, with air support, were able to make quick work of FAPLA and allow SADF motorised infantry and UNITA irregulars to move rapidly in to exploit the breakthroughs. Devastating South African Air Force (SAAF) strikes against FAPLA combat and logistical columns went uncontested as FAPLA air defence proved totally inadequate. In the end, the South African withdrawal was made for political, not military reasons, a fact not lost upon FAPLA and its supporters despite propaganda to the contrary that claimed tactical success as the reason.

Another reason FAPLA required Cuban combat support was the almost total loss of its force during the civil war due to mass defections to FNLA breakaway leader Daniel Chipenda and his military forces. This left the MPLA with less than 600 experienced fighters as well as a number of recruits from the musseques of Luanda. Rebuilding FAPLA took time, and even though FAPLA attracted many former FNLA fighters from northern Angola, the MPLA leadership was concerned about their loyalty and sought to raise troops from other areas of the country. Many FAPLA brigades date from this period; while many commanders and personnel were from the north and thus mainly former FNLA, their loyalties had yet to be tested. Other FAPLA units drew heavily upon Cabinda and the areas east and south-east of Luanda, as well as the capital region (Luanda and Bengo provinces).[4]

While FAPLA retrained, Cubans took the offensive against UNITA in the south-east. Cuban and Soviet pilots of the newly formed FAPLA air force (FAPA) and elements of the Cuban air force hit suspected UNITA bases to support ground operations. The aim of the attacks was to inflict as many casualties as possible, demoralising UNITA and its civilian supporters. Air attacks were followed by ground operations in which Cuban units spearheaded FAPLA assaults against UNITA strongholds. Cubans were not the only foreign troops assisting FAPLA. Units from Congo-Brazzaville, Nigeria, Guinea-Conakry, and São Tomé and Principe assisted as well, as did elements of the former Katangese gendarmerie who had fled Zaire (then Congo) in the late 1960s.[5]

FAPLA's battlefield effort was accompanied by the MPLA's propaganda campaign, conducted principally by ANGOP, the Angolan government news service, and the government-controlled radio station, as well as by allies in the international media. The MPLA carefully regulated journalists' access to the country in an attempt to ensure news stories of the war favourable to it were published. UNITA countered this by bringing journalists through neighbouring states to visit its encampments and observe its operations. However, during the late 1970s world media coverage of Angola remained heavily influenced by the MPLA and its allies. It was only with the establishment of UNITA's own radio station later in the war that MPLA and surrogate propaganda was routinely challenged.[6]

Meanwhile the MPLA and Cubans occupied the central plateau and pushed southward in an offensive starting on 13 March 1976. On 1 April they reached the southern border with SWA/Namibia. By the end of 1976 all but a part of the remote south-eastern province of Cuando Cubango was claimed as captured for the MPLA. This area, known to Portuguese as 'The Land at the End of the Earth,' was remote and undeveloped, with few towns and a poor road network. Savimbi later moved his Headquarters there near an old colonial-era hunting camp and named it Jamba. But during this period it was a sparsely populated area with a few FAPLA bases, including Mavinga and garrisons along the SWA-Namibian and Zambian borders, where low-level fighting continued that involved FAPLA and the Cubans, UNITA, former Chipenda fighters, and South African security forces battling SWAPO insurgents.

Immediately after the start of the MPLA-Cuban offensive Savimbi and his forces left his remaining large base, Gago Coutinho, heading on 14 March in a generally westerly direction, ultimately linking up with other UNITA elements at a base camp near Cuelei (Bie province) by 28 August. Savimbi organised the resistance there, establishing an insurgent network of UNITA-controlled areas in the central Angolan highlands; mid-November this network was extended southward into Cuando-Cubango south of Menongue. UNITA's strategy had been established in the 'Cuanza Manifesto.'[7] The document established a meticulous guerrilla programme for UNITA to fight the MPLA and its communist country backers. UNITA was reorganised. Its army, the Armed Forces for the Liberation of Angola (FALA), was divided into Fronts and Military Regions. Training camps for UNITA regular and insurgent personnel intakes were established. FALA structure was at first completely guerrilla in nature, with the first units trained and fielded being the compact guerrilla columns. In the meantime, training of regular forces began, reportedly with external assistance from South Africa and other countries.

During May and November 1976 the MPLA-Cubans conducted four operations in eastern, southern, and central Angola against UNITA and its supporting population base. UNITA's response was to avoid engagement with the attackers, interfere with resupply and communications, and attack isolated units in the field whenever they were vulnerable. MPLA forces in the field were joined by SWAPO. The latter were granted bases in southern Angola in return for fighting alongside the MPLA against UNITA. Although the Cubans were concerned about a high casualty rate and began to withdraw their forces into the larger urban centres, SWAPO units were ever more committed against UNITA. By the mid-

1980s there were at least two brigades of SWAPO operating against UNITA in the field; SWAPO troops were frequently cited by UNITA as perpetrators of atrocities against the civilian population. This was not the desired policy of the MPLA or especially the Cubans, who often tried to emphasise a 'hearts-and-minds' programme, even though such attempts later broke down (see below).[8]

By this time Savimbi's guerrilla strategy was set, and UNITA planning was based upon a few simple tenets recalling Mao Zedong's principles of guerrilla warfare:

'*Engage government troops only when you have massed twice the number of soldiers or more, to kill as many as possible and demoralise the army by never giving them a victory;*

Destroy all means of communications, make road transportation unsafe with numerous ambushes and destroy all railroads;

Sabotage the economy and create psychological instability among the civilian population that supports the government through acts of urban terrorism;

Disperse when attacked by large government forces, causing frustrated government soldiers to retaliate against the civilian population and thereby cement the ties between peasant supporter and guerrilla.[9]

Established in south-eastern Bie province, UNITA began local operations designed to deny rural areas to the MPLA. Populations of villages in central Bie were persuaded or coerced into leaving and joining UNITA. At the same time, some strategically located villages were destroyed to prevent FAPLA and Cubans from using them as garrisons. Often simple actions such as the destruction of house roofs was enough to deny use of villages during the rainy season. UNITA's actions forced FAPLA garrisons back toward the CFB corridor. UNITA was thus left with control over much of the countryside.

Despite success in challenging MPLA control of parts of central and south-east Angola, in 1977 UNITA had no secure territorial control. Insurgent operations extended southward into Cuando Cubango and westward into Huambo. However, at that time UNITA had little foreign support. Some South African support was claimed by the MPLA for the remnants of Daniel Chipenda's forces south of Menongue. These, however, not only did not work with UNITA but were hostile to it as well. South African covert support for UNITA against the MPLA took place only when doing so clearly benefited security in Namibia.[10]

At this time UNITA was dominated by members of Savimbi's Ovimbundu ethnic group, but key alliances existed with other Angolan peoples as well, including Kwanyama in Cunene, Ganguela, Chokwe, and Lunda (in eastern Angola). UNITA strove to eliminate the appearance of tribalism and seek support from all Angolan ethnic groups. But support from Ovimbundus, the largest ethnic group in Angola, remained key. To stress such popular support in the Angolan central plateau, UNITA held its Fourth Party Congress at a forest site a mere 80km from Huambo. There UNITA resolved, among other items, to establish semi-regular units to counter conventional threats but still continue to conduct guerrilla operations. 'Tribal' tendencies were to be countered by transfers of military and administrative personnel from their home regions.[11]

These events took place as Morocco and other pro-Western countries began to support UNITA with training and equipment to counter what they saw as an attempt by the Soviet Union and its allies to extend control over the African continent. As for FAPLA, by 1978 it was finally transformed into a conventional fighting force of 30 or so brigades, mostly light infantry but with about half a dozen motorised infantry brigades as well. Organised along Soviet and Cuban lines, the new force lacked effective COIN capability. Despite this, 1978 marked the beginning of a Cuban shift in military policy to have FAPLA do the fighting. To avoid politically costly casualties, the Cubans moved their units into garrison and only assisted FAPLA with various support functions including logistics and intelligence.[12]

UNITA's military revival coincided with the final collapse of FNLA resistance in Cuando Cubango. The SADF rehabilitated part of this force, formerly under the command of Daniel Chipenda, forming it into a special Portuguese-speaking unit first known as Bravo Group and later as 32 or Buffalo Battalion. However, the immediate result of the collapse of the FNLA was a contest between UNITA and FAPLA for control of much of Cuando Cubango. In late 1977 UNITA moved first, claiming the capture of Mucusso, Calai, and Dirico. Reacting to this, FAPLA attempted to occupy the area in a March–April 1978 offensive, and reoccupied Calai and Dirico. This followed an operation by FAPLA (November 1977 to March 1978), in which it sought to regain control over areas south of the CFB with a three-part campaign directed against Bie and Moxico provinces. Although somewhat successful, FAPLA's control remained tenuous, with isolated garrisons resupplied by air controlling little outside their fields of fire. These garrisons were later to fall to the combined attacks of UNITA and South African forces.[13]

The two events of 1978 that helped shape the later course of the war did not directly involve the MPLA-UNITA conflict, but instead took place further west and north. The first of these events was the SADF raid on a SWAPO base complex at Cassinga (7 May). The other was the second invasion of Zaire's mineral-rich Shaba province by Katangese ex-gendarmes (11 May). The Katangese were apparently assisted by the MPLA, who provided bases and support, and by Cubans and other communist allies of the MPLA. The invasion, which devastated much of the mining infrastructure in Shaba, led Zaire to increase assistance to UNITA and serve as a conduit for Western aid to the insurgents. As for the SADF attack on Cassinga, Operation 'Reindeer', it was the first of many cross-border raids against SWAPO bases in Angola. The net result of South African policy was the FAPLA deployment of additional forces to Cunene province in a vain attempt to prevent further incursions.[14]

SECOND PHASE OF THE CIVIL WAR, 1978-1983

In the second phase of the Angolan civil war:

■ The Cubans withdrew from most combat operations, providing instead garrison and other support activities;
■ For political purposes, Cuban troop strength increased;
■ FAPLA assumed combat responsibilities for which it was not ready; poor COIN capabilities allowed UNITA operations to spread;
■ South African intervention against SWAPO bases in south-west Angola continued;
■ The Soviet Union increased its military assistance to the MPLA as the latter faced a continuously deteriorating security situation;
■ UNITA established territorial control in south-eastern Angola and began to extend operations north and west;
■ UNITA began to receive substantial support from South Africa and other nations through Namibia.

In this period FAPLA assumed most combat operations, but was unprepared for this role as it did not have a set COIN doctrine. Instead it tried to adapt conventional doctrine to an insurgent situation, with disastrous results. MPLA reprisals against suspected local supporters of UNITA continued to alienate the population, as did continued use of SWAPO troops, who were responsible for many atrocities committed by security forces against the rural population in the south-west and central part of Angola. Use of SWAPO troops was FAPLA's price for continuing to allow SWAPO bases and a logistical support network in south-west Angola. Often such facilities were near to or colocated with FAPLA and Cuban installations in the mistaken belief that they would be safe from South African reprisals. This illusion was shattered by the Cassinga raid of May 1978; further South African operations through this period–'Sceptic', 'Protea', 'Daisy', and 'Askari' were the main ones – later persuaded the MPLA to briefly bar SWAPO from the SWA border area (1984-1985).

FAPLA's poor battlefield performance was cause for concern not only in Luanda but also in Moscow, where it reflected poorly on Soviet efforts to organise and train an effective client force. MPLA and Soviet efforts to analyse and correct the situation remained inadequate for the rest of the war. They answered UNITA's continued expansion north and west at FAPLA's expense in the most basic way – more firepower and personnel. The poor state of FAPLA logistics, beset by infrastructure problems and corruption, was never successfully addressed. Training, usually inadequate, was not improved as personnel were hurried through military instruction and into field units, which had perpetual personnel shortfalls due to desertions and high casualty rates. Morale was poor, and continued so in most units through this phase of the war. FAPLA's conventional battlefield performance also left much to be desired. When FAPLA engaged South African forces to assist SWAPO, it always lost, usually badly beaten with high casualty rates and equipment losses, and eventually began to avoid the SADF.

To help FAPLA, the Soviet Union increased training and resupply. In the early 1980s a major reorganisation and re-equipping of FAPLA was undertaken after losses to less well armed and smaller UNITA forces in central and eastern Angola. Ten military regions were created; each controlled territorial and militia units as well as some regular army units. The military region (RM) performed military administration and maintenance of routine logistical duties for these units. Brigades of the regular army (EPA) were controlled from Luanda through operational commands determined by the tactical situation. The standard manoeuvre unit continued to be the infantry brigade. Through this second phase of the civil war FAPLA continued its evolution toward the huge military force of the 1980s. The Cubans still maintained a separate logistical and support system for their growing presence.[15]

UNITA also grew during 1978-1983/4. By 1980-1981 it had 22 military regions and control over most of Cuando Cubango. UNITA's army, the Armed Forces for the Liberation of Angola (Forcas Armadas de Libertacao de Angola, or FALA), was organised into military fronts (three existed in 1979 – Northern, Eastern, and Western), each responsible for territorial administration and local insurgent operations. In 1979 UNITA formed its first three semi-regular battalions, each with about 600 personnel. Independent battalions remained the main manoeuvre units. Specialised training began in South Africa.[16]

UNITA force structure was slightly modified in 1982 after its Fifth Congress, when unit types were standardised and each front was allocated a mix of units to accomplish its tasks. The augmentation of 150-man compact guerrilla companies to military regions was important as it provided reinforcement capabilities to the operations of the dispersed guerrilla formations, which operated with 15 to 50 personnel per group. UNITA's command and control for operations was thus improved. This was necessary as Savimbi had observed too many casualties – ten per cent in some cases – in attacks; the new structure ensured better top-down planning for operations. UNITA also began using at a minimum 500-man semi-regular infantry battalions, reinforced with artillery (mortars, rocket launchers, or small-calibre field guns) for attacking fixed FAPLA positions.[17]

In December 1979 Savimbi established UNITA Headquarters at Jamba, a site in the far south-eastern part of Angola near the hunting camp of Bambangando, thus announcing to the world his territorial control of part of the country. Jamba grew into a complex of dwellings, training centres, administrative buildings, and other facilities; a nearby village, Likuwa, became the centre for UNITA's logistics and repair. The area was accessible by air and ground from nearby SWA/Namibia. By the early 1980s Jamba was the hub of a logistical network that drew from South African bases in the Caprivi strip in SWA/Namibia as well as from nearby airfields where supplies were regularly flown in from more distant points. Supply routes radiated west, north-west, and north from the Jamba area. The principal south-east/north-west trunk route, dubbed the 'Savimbi Trail,' went north-west along the Cuando River before one branch cut west to Jamba with the other running along the river into the eastern part of the central highlands. Another key route ran from Jamba north-west to Mavinga and from there through Lupire to Tempue. The network followed established routes through areas of UNITA territorial control, but branched out into smaller, less detectable routes once it entered the zone of UNITA's guerrilla operations. By 1984 the 'Savimbi Trail' was heavily travelled by truck traffic; in forward areas and in operations in contested areas the insurgents relied on porters.[18]

At Jamba UNITA set up propaganda machine to counter that of the MPLA. Radio VORGAN (Voza da Radio Gallo Negro) began to counter MPLA claims of victories with UNITA accounts that were usually completely to the contrary. Names of FAPLA soldiers killed or captured were broadcast, as well as charges of inadequate medical care, lack of rations, and other poor conditions of FAPLA military service. Such broadcasts, coupled with the placing of representatives in Europe and the United States, countered the MPLA's attempt to impose a media monopoly on developments inside Angola.[19]

Much of UNITA's improved military capability was due to South Africa. From 1977-1978 South Africa realised that without a military defeat the government in Luanda would neither stop its support to SWAPO or ask Cuban forces to leave. These two issues were critical to South African policies in the region and for independence plans for SWA/Namibia in particular. South Africa's response to the MPLA's intransigence was to train UNITA personnel and provide logistic support. However, military intervention to support UNITA did not occur at this stage except where such assistance would also help to counter SWAPO. South African operations were confined to south-western Angola, well away from UNITA's operations. The MPLA tried hard to contain the spread of UNITA's influence during the late 1970s, without much success. In mid-June and later in October 1978 it launched campaigns to seal off the SWA/Namibia border; none was successful.[20]

UNITA, on the other hand, enjoyed a number of successes in 1979 and 1980 throughout eastern and southern Angola. UNITA forces increased to about 20,000, with new units constantly trained and fielded. Savimbi's goal was a force about 60 per cent irregular (guerrilla) and 40 per cent regular and combat support (field artillery, air defence, and anti-tank units). Savimbi had by this time decided upon retaining the towns UNITA took in certain areas. This new policy of territorial control was necessary before UNITA headquarters was secured at Jamba. Thus Cuangar, Luengue, and Rivungo were captured (May–July) to control the south-eastern part of Cuando Cubango. To the west, Savate was captured on 21 May and successfully defended from a FAPLA counterattack on 20 August. The taking of Savate was to become a matter of some controversy in the early 1980s after a later defector from the South African 32 Battalion claimed that the SADF unit actually captured the town and then turned it over to the insurgents. Similar claims have been made with regard to UNITA's ostensible capture of other towns along the Namibian border.[21]

Although there may have been decisions by the SADF to assist UNITA in cases that would affect directly or indirectly the COIN effort in Namibia, most routine guerrilla operations continued to be carried out by UNITA alone. Still others involved covert SADF cooperation. One such example was the 3 October 1979 capture of Mavinga. The town was abandoned, but in September 1980 UNITA, with SADF help, took the town again, determined to hold it. Two attempts were subsequently made by FAPLA to recapture it, both of which (March and May 1981) were repulsed.[22]

FAPLA's response to the repulse at Mavinga (as well as to South African incursions in Cunene) was to attempt to outflank UNITA defences from the north-west with a task force with Cuban support in July–August 1981, based on Cuito Cuanavale and moving south through Longa toward Rito on the Cuito River. The offensive, built around a motorised brigade, failed, as no supporting infrastructure existed to carry the offensive or retain any areas captured in this remote area of Cuando Cubango. Through the end of 1981 UNITA continued to chip away at FAPLA garrisons in the south-east and secure more UNITA logistical routes and expanded its territorial control. FAPLA's response (through late spring 1982) was in the form of a number of little-publicised operations against UNITA territory, all largely unsuccessful.[23]

UNITA operations from August 1982 through January 1983 drove Cuban and FAPLA garrisons from as much of the area south of the CFB and east of the central highlands as possible, doubling UNITA's area of territorial control in the process. Part of the reason for UNITA's new aggressiveness was the decision by Cuban forces in July 1982 once again to take the field. UNITA's forces, now almost 30,000, were bolstered by a new type of unit, its special forces or commandos, organised in units of 45 men. By this time UNITA's logistical system had established truck transport in all areas it controlled, bringing weapons and equipment to forward points for transshipment by porters into areas to the north and west. Captured Soviet Ural trucks constituted the most common type of vehicle. The network was protected at river crossings by anti-aircraft sites manned by UNITA's growing anti-aircraft artillery corps.

In 1982-1983 UNITA gained significant territory in southern Moxico province. In the most important of these actions, the insurgents used siege techniques characteristic of many subsequent such operations. UNITA gains north of the Cuando River culminated in the capture of Gago Coutinho (Lumbala) on 7 November 1982. FAPLA and Cuban units guarding the town were overwhelmed by a UNITA force twice their size. UNITA operations of late 1982 and early 1983 pushed territorial control north to the Lungue-Bungo River, placing its forward operating area in Moxico not far south of the important city of Luena–headquarters of the 3rd FAPLA Military Region, a major air base, and the capital of Moxico province. In western Moxico, UNITA overran Cangonga on the CFB, about 120km west of Luena, on 11 February. The Cangonga attack was an important indicator of Savimbi's strategy. UNITA was well on its way to controlling most of the eastern CFB corridor as well as the central watershed running north to south through Angola. The latter was a major logistical route, and to secure it it was necessary to cross the CFB to areas north.[25]

UNITA scored a major publicity victory on 12 March 1983 with the capture of Alto Catumbela on the CFB, annihilating the garrison and capturing expatriate Czechoslovak and Portuguese workers. Despite the deployment of 6,000 Cuban and FAPLA troops to rescue the hostages, the government attempt failed (Cubans were withdrawn at the request of the Czechoslovak government because the latter feared harm to the hostages if a rescue were attempted). The Czechoslovak hostages were eventually released after considerable publicity that showed UNITA's skill in exploiting the situation. Beyond the public relations aspect, the operation, the capture of Alto Catumbela, was important as it demonstrated UNITA's capability to capture fortified FAPLA positions.[26]

Throughout 1983, UNITA claimed more victories including those at Tempue (Alto Cuito), Munhango, the penetration of the diamond areas of Lunda, and, in July, the capture of towns in eastern Malange. Most of the towns captured were soon abandoned, but the breaking of the barrier formed by the CFB allowed UNITA to move to the north and north-east of Angola with little difficulty. The military actions of 1983 virtually ensured UNITA's territorial control of the entire area south of the eastern half of the CFB, with the exception of Cuito Cuanavale and Cangamba, which latter UNITA finally captured on 14 August. The capture of Tempue and Cangamba ensured UNITA control of the resupply route from the Namibian border to eastern Bie province, the jumping-off point for troop and supply movements into the north and north-west as UNITA expanded operations. Illustrative of

UNITA's ability to strike near Luanda was the July–September campaign in northern Cuanza Sul province. The MPLA responded with a ten-brigade offensive from 5 September to 10 October, reinforced with air and armour, that reoccupied towns taken by UNITA.

UNITA's operations pressed ever northward and north-eastward, taking Alto Chicapa in Lunda on 29 November. To the east, UNITA took Cazombo in eastern Moxico on 13 November and with it control over the entire Angolan border with Zambia. UNITA also moved as far north as the Zaire border by March–April 1984. FAPLA recouped some earlier losses in northern Bie and eastern Cuanza Sul, but UNITA still operated freely there. Nevertheless, FAPLA claimed in early November to have inflicted a series of severe defeats on 'the second strategic front' of UNITA in Huambo and Bie and in eastern Cuanza Sul; COIN operations were reportedly still in progress around UNITA's Headquarters near Quibala. FAPLA's next objective, Luanda claimed, would be the 'first strategic front' in southern Moxico and Cuando Cubango provinces.

At the end of 1983 Savimbi and UNITA could look at the map of Angola and see their strategy succeeding. The area south of the CFB and east of a line south from Bie (Cuito) to the Namibian border was under UNITA territorial control. FALA had grown to 35,000 combat effectives in almost two dozen military regions throughout Angola. Bie, Huambo, Benguela, and southern Cuanza Sul were areas of increased insurgent activity. South-western Angola as well as areas immediately north of the CFB were also areas of UNITA guerrilla activity. UNITA's near-term plans were to expand into north-western Angola as well as into northern Lunda; this began in November 1983 with a campaign lasting through April 1984.[27]

UNITA's dramatic expansion was cause for grave concern by the MPLA. By late 1983 FAPLA was expanding, restructuring, and rearming. Its ground forces lacked the firepower, mobility, and numbers necessary to conduct successful offensives against UNITA, despite FAPLA (and the Cuban) control of the air. By November 1983 a full-scale reorganisation of FAPLA was under way, with a new Minister of Defence, Colonel Pedro Maria Tonha 'Pedale' and FAPLA chief of staff, Colonel Antonio Franca 'Ndalu.' The principal architect of the FAPLA restructuring was Colonel Iko Carreira, the Air Force chief. The latter claimed that combat operations for the October–November Bie–Huambo–Cuanza Sul operations were Angolan, with Cubans only assisting in technical areas and providing radio jamming. FAPLA was programmed to grow to at least 70 brigades, equipped with Soviet and Warsaw Pact equipment, and supported by an air force also fitted with East Bloc airframes.[28]

The reorganisation of FAPLA was now critical to ensure the hoped-for military victory in the civil war. Up to this time FAPLA had proven unable to stem UNITA's advance northward and westward, and had even failed to root out Savimbi's guerrilla infrastructure on the central plateau that supported the spread of UNITA's network westward along the CFB and into northern Huila province. To the south, FAPLA and the Cubans were unable to keep out South African incursions directed against SWAPO base camps and logistics in Cunene province. In this area FAPLA, the Cubans, and SWAPO were to receive one last punishing blow as the year ended.

1983 closed with a large-scale South African move into Cunene to forestall a SWAPO offensive – Operation 'Askari'. SADF mechanised and motorised units penetrated north as far as Cuvelai and Techamutete and east to Ngiva, Caiundo, and beyond. During these engagements FAPLA, albeit assisted by the Cubans as well as Soviet advisers, performed better than expected where it offered battle to the SADF. Although the South Africans prevailed in the engagements and occupied Cunene, the lesson was not lost upon the SADF that FAPLA had improved its military capabilities and exhibited more aggressiveness. Despite this, FAPLA and Cuban losses were high in terms of both men and materiel, and made them more amenable to a ceasefire. The outcome of the truce that followed Operation 'Askari', however, was of benefit to both the SADF (see the chapter dealing with SWA/Namibia, especially pp. 43ff) and FAPLA. FAPLA was able to devote additional resources from Cunene against UNITA.[29]

FIGHTING TAKES A CONVENTIONAL TURN, 1984-1988

The third phase of the Angolan civil war was the most critical in terms of involvement by outside parties, marked by:

- Massive outside military assistance to both FAPLA and UNITA by their backers;
- Buildup of FAPLA ground forces to about 100,000 personnel in 70 or so brigades;
- Large FAPLA conventional operations against UNITA territory in different regions of eastern, central, and south-eastern Angola;
- Extensive use of air support that attempted to adapt Soviet doctrine and tactics to FAPLA needs;
- Peaking of Cuban troop strength at about 65,000 in 1988;
- Expansion by UNITA to a force of about 65,000 in 1987-1988;
- Extension of regular UNITA operations into all provinces of Angola;
- Development by UNITA of improved anti-aircraft and anti-armour units;
- South African direct military intervention to support UNITA.

In 1983-1984 the MPLA had begun to appreciate the gravity of the security situation, and understood that both reorganisation of its internal security management and appeals for increased Soviet military assistance were its only hope if it wanted to continue to press for a military solution to the conflict. MPLA security concerns were underscored by the spectacular UNITA capture of Sumbe in Cuanza Sul on 25 March 1984. Sumbe, on the Atlantic coast on the north-west corner of Ovimbundu territory, was well within reach of the UNITA command centre near Quibala and thus reached through the many UNITA enclaves throughout Benguela, Huambo, and Bie provinces. The attack was carried out by two reinforced UNITA regular battalions (5,000 men total), who overran the city after a six-hour battle on 25 March. After inflicting high casualties on FAPLA and Cuban forces, and causing considerable damage to government infrastructure, UNITA withdrew in the face of a FAPLA counterattack which inflicted high casualties on the insurgents. Despite the costs, Sumbe was proof that UNITA could conduct conventional operations against FAPLA far from its territorial base in the south-east.

FAPLA REORGANISATION

The MPLA created the Defence and Security Council (CSD) in May 1984, the better to manage and coordinate operations against UNITA and the South Africans, so coordinating security management with civil administration, propaganda, and national-level logistical support. This followed the creation of regional military councils in July 1983, which had begun this task but on a smaller scale. FAPLA also underwent a major expansion and rearming. In the early 1980s FAPLA had an army of 40,000 organised into 30 or so brigades. Of these, at least five were motorised infantry brigades and the remainder light infantry brigades. Backing up the army (EPA) were territorial troops and a large militia force (ODP). The latter was claimed by the MPLA to number about 100,000 but was probably less than half of that.

The reorganisation changed the face of FAPLA entirely. By 1984 FAPLA had expanded to over 70 brigades a number of independent battalions for armour, artillery, and air defence. Upgrading of weapons and equipment and implementation of task-organisation in major military operations was underway. Specific points of the upgrade included:

- Better regional command and control. Military region (RM) commanders were given better control over territorial forces and militia in their AORs. Greater emphasis was placed on coordinating action among the RM assets, regular EPA units, and civilian authorities (MINSE and police), as well as with border guard units (TGFA).

■ Greater emphasis on local COIN operations by territorial forces, entailing use of special counterguerrilla (Lutta Contra Banditos, LCB) units working in conjunction with TTs, militia (ODP), MINSE troops, and police against UNITA. Other units were formed to protect railway operations (TFs). Most LCB and TF units, however, were merely redesignated TTs. The People's Vigilance Brigades (BPV) were created in August 1983 as a part-time force to support security. Most auxiliary forces continued to be poorly trained part-time soldiers, and no specific COIN doctrine was evident in local FAPLA operations. Territorial forces did, however, work with Cuban units and advisers at times.

■ Expansion of the regular Army. The EPA had proven inadequate for both the effort against UNITA and the defence against South African forces. Thus the EPA sought to standardise unit structure for their motorised (motorizada) and light (ligeira) infantry brigades and expand the number of such units. By 1987-1988 there were at least 72 brigades and as many as 120,000 personnel. At least twelve of these were motorised brigades, and FAPLA had begun to take delivery of the BMP-1 IFV to equip them and replace the older BTR-60 APCs.

■ Improved weapons and equipment. Courtesy of the Soviet Union, a major effort was made to up-gun motorised infantry brigades and provide each with at least a company of T-54 or T-55 tanks and three or more battalions of BTR-60 APCs. Emphasis was also placed on unit command and control, organisation, and doctrine. For example, light infantry brigades that regularly worked with motorised units were given a company of tanks as well as other armoured vehicles to improve offensive capability. Each EPA manoeuvre brigade was assigned an artillery battalion that included a mix of heavy mortars, howitzers (usually 122mm D-30s), and MRLs (122mm BM-21s or BM-14s). The EPA also augmented its transport capabilities, importing thousands of trucks and other logistics vehicles from the Soviet Union, Brazil, and other countries.

■ FAPLA deployment addressed security needs better. This entailed placing at least four motorised infantry brigades in eastern and south-eastern Angola (one in RM 3 and three in RM 6) as well as assigning more light infantry brigades into the interior of Angola. Defences in south-west Angola sought to counter South African incursions, with major bases at Cahama, Lubango, and Caiundo, as well as along the Moçâmedes Railway to the north. The air force (FAPA) began construction of a series of air defence sites (SA-2 and SA-6) along the Moçâmedes Railway to challenge South African control of the air.

■ Improved air-ground support. This continued to be a weak link in FAPLA operations, as it took time to build an effective air force. The Cubans continued to provide much-needed air support for FAPLA operations, but FAPLA gradually assumed more of the burden as circumstances allowed. Air support efforts received a setback after 1986 when UNITA began to acquire improved SAM capability.

■ Task organisation. Past FAPLA operations against UNITA were often inadequate due to the limitations of unit command and control. Starting in the mid-1980s, however, task organisation became common, used with most large operations. It was intended to facilitate combat support and combat service support, both of which had been weak in the past.[30]

CONVENTIONAL FIGHTING, 1984-1988

The years 1984-1988 were marked by four major attempts to penetrate and occupy UNITA's 'Terra Libre' in Cuando Cubango and Moxico provinces:

1984 FAPLA launched two major offensives against UNITA. The first, committing a total of thirteen FAPLA brigades, was initiated on 7 April and lasted to 27 July. The principal aim of the offensive was the recapture of the Cazombo salient. To this end FAPLA attacked on a broad front in Moxico, with a separate force sent forward from Luena through

Lucusse toward Lumbala Kaquengue. Other forces deployed to attack in Cuando Cubango province against Mavinga, Savate, and Cuangar. However, a combination of determined resistance by UNITA and an apparent breakdown of FAPLA logistics caused the FAPLA attack to collapse by early July. Despite the failure of the Cazombo salient offensive, FAPLA was able to regroup and resupply, launching a second offensive with twelve brigades totalling 15,000 troops, against UNITA territory in eastern Angola. The main focus of the attack was eastern and south-eastern Angola (western Moxico/eastern Bie as well as the Mavinga area in Cuando Cubango). This second offensive, which began in mid-August, also collapsed; by the end of October FAPLA had returned to garrison. UNITA had lost no ground, while government forces had suffered a series of humiliating defeats aggravated in great part by poor command and control as well as logistics failure.

1985 FAPLA launched Operation 'Second Congress' the primary aim of which was the capture of Mavinga and the disruption of the UNITA logistics network in south-eastern Angola. The secondary objective was the capture of the Cazombo salient (eastern Moxico province). The offensive had a political aim as well, in that FAPLA hoped to capture Mavinga and drive southward toward Jamba as the MPLA Second Party Congress was in session in October 1985 – hence its name. Although FAPLA with Cuban assistance was able to recapture the Cazombo salient by the end of September, its attack against Mavinga was a disaster. South African assistance to UNITA permitted the insurgents to deploy against the invaders, who penetrated to within 12-15km of Mavinga before being forced to retreat on 30 September. South African air strikes subsequently decimated the invading force that had paused to regroup north of the Lomba River. Despite the debacle at the Lomba, FAPLA initiated further operations in December 1985 that lasted into January 1986. The offensive was launched on three fronts. The first was south from Lucusse across the Lungue Bungo River into UNITA territory; the second was from Cuito Cuanavale against Mavinga; and the third was from Caiundo against Savate. This particular FAPLA offensive was beset with major support and morale problems and was as unproductive as the previous year's operations, which had been derisively called by military observers 'the 1984 Winter Games.' The Lucusse front operation, apparently the main FAPLA endeavour, failed after UNITA destroyed a critical logistical column between Canage and Lucusse on 26 December.

1986 By this year FAPLA had begun to receive extensive Soviet assistance, both in materiel and training. The latter included the services of Soviet General Konstantin Shagnovich, who made in 1986 his first attempt at planning an offensive for FAPLA. However, the elaborate, multi-pronged offensive that resulted, could not be effectively executed by FAPLA troops whose logistics repeatedly failed and who were defeated by a skilled combination of UNITA and South African strategy. FAPLA attacked on three main axes: Cuito Cuanavale to Mavinga (MR 6), Lucusse to the regions south of the Lungue-Bungo (MR 3), and from Luena and Cuito (Bie) against Munhango (MRs 3 and 4). Only the latter was successful, with Munhango falling on 28 August. Shagnovich attempted to time the operation so that support assets could be shifted to successive theatres for attacks there. However, operational delays and inadequate training, combined with UNITA resistance, wrought havoc with Shagnovich's elaborate plan, and by the end of the year FAPLA paid the price of violating the principles of mass and economy of force against a more compact and better-supplied foe. Perhaps FAPLA's worst moment came on 9-10 August, when UNITA, backed by South African artillery (the SADF Operation 'Alpha Centauri') and other units, attacked and overran the key FAPLA base at Cuito Cuanavale; before withdrawing they wrought extensive damage to the infrastructure and the logistics stockpiles there. This, coupled with damage to Namibe harbour and the disruption of logistics that resulted after a South African raid, prevented FAPLA from attacking Mavinga from Cuito Cuanavale that year (see page 47).

1987–1988 The fighting from August of 1987 to July of 1988 in many ways was the climax of the superpower involvement in the war. It was marked by extensive South African ground and air intervention to assist UNITA in repelling the most ambitious FAPLA offensive yet to be launched against insurgent-held areas of Cuando Cubango and Moxico provinces. During the course of the fighting FAPLA suffered one of the worst defeats to befall an army since the Second World War. The SADF (Operation 'Modular') intervention began modestly, as UNITA attempted to stiffen its resistance to the invaders in Cuando Cubango in August, and picked up through September as South African artillery repelled two attempts by FAPLA to cross the Lomba River. Finally, South African mechanised forces intervened to annihilate one of the FAPLA task forces in battles on 3–4 October. This defeat was followed by the FAPLA withdrawal toward Cuito Cuanavale, which was put under siege by UNITA and bombarded by the South Africans (Operations 'Hooper' and 'Packer'). At the same time UNITA made considerable gains in the central plateau area and on the CFB, most of which were later regained by FAPLA at great cost. Frustrated in attempts to remedy the situation in the centre and east, FAPLA and the Cubans redeployed forces in south-western Angola to the Namibian border, where they sparred with the SADF until being decisively checked on 26–27 June at Techipa in Cunene province. Following this battle, the Cubans were convinced that further military confrontation with the SADF would not succeed, but launched a propaganda and diplomatic campaign to cover their setbacks and cover their losses. They also apparently decided to leave the MPLA to its fate, accepting shortly thereafter the linkage proposed by the United States that led to Namibian independence in return for Cuban troop withdrawal from Angola (see pp. 48ff).

The situation in mid-1988 The results of a year of South African involvement in Angola were profound. The armed intervention had decisively changed the course of the war. Despite massive Soviet, Cuban, and MPLA propaganda to the contrary, FAPLA and its supporters had been badly beaten.

■ FAPLA casualties included at least a fifth of its ground force KIA/WIA and at least a quarter of its available equipment had been destroyed or captured. Much equipment in the latter category wound up in UNITA hands to be fielded against FAPLA.
■ The battle at Tchipa (late June) with its high Cuban casualties had discouraged the Cubans from a further desire to engage South African forces.
■ Cuban forces agreed to withdraw from Angola, in a linkage with the implementation of UN Resolution 435, which began the independence process for Namibia. This represented a major policy defeat for the MPLA, the Cubans, and the Soviet Union.

The Soviet Union, however, still maintained that it could support FAPLA's military solution to the conflict. To this end, it undertook a massive resupply campaign in late 1987 and into 1988 to replace FAPLA losses with newer equipment. BMP-1s, for instance, which were a relative rarity in 1987, were by 1989 to become the standard fighting vehicle for the FAPLA BRIM. The 130mm M-46 cannon replaced older artillery systems for general support. More and better combat helicopters and ground support fighters were shipped to Angola by Moscow. Nevertheless, most informed observers saw this attempted resuscitation of FAPLA by its patrons as a stopgap measure that put off the inevitable, final, military collapse.

UNITA gains in northern Angola Meanwhile, the guerrilla war continued as UNITA pushed north and west. 1984 marked the year UNITA began to establish its presence in northwestern Angola (Malange, Uige, and Zaire provinces, as well as in Bengo). UNITA initiated its first operations in Cabinda on 12 July. On 25 November it destroyed power line pylons and other infrastructure, cutting off the capital's electrical supply. UNITA began to organise an infrastructure near Luanda itself.[31]

Although UNITA operations there at this stage were generally little more than small-unit military actions, the insurgents began to establish good relations with the local population, which allowed them to build a support network. UNITA was thus able increasingly to retaliate against FAPLA attacks in the south-east with attacks on government infrastructure near the capital; it also resisted FAPLA attempts to drive them out of their new enclaves. UNITA's operations in Zaire and Uige provinces were a source of concern to the MPLA. The insurgents, though briefly occupying some towns, in general avoided the larger centres and focused on rural guerrilla operations.[32]

UNITA insurgent operations throughout Angola, 1987-1988 Good relations with the local population established by UNITA during 1983-1985 paid off in 1987. In response to the FAPLA thrust against Mavinga, UNITA initiated operations throughout northern Angola, including the destruction of the water system supplying Luanda in the Quifandongo region and attacks against FAPLA in the coffee-growing regions in the Ucua-Pango Aluquem-Zala areas. The largest operation of all was carefully planned: UNITA launched Operation 'Chendovava' in September 1987, designed to destabilise FAPLA throughout the country, especially in northern Angola. This proved extremely successful, tying down FAPLA units that would otherwise have been deployed at Cuito Cuanavale.

Elsewhere in 1987-9, UNITA showed its strength in the central plateau. On 22 December 1987 a UNITA task force reinforced with a platoon of captured T-54/55 tanks took Munhango, driving two EPA brigades from the town and capturing or destroying most of their equipment. This success was followed by the destruction of the Cuanza River bridge near Camacupa, which cut off Cuemba from western Bie province and possible relief forces. On 10 January UNITA captured Camacupa and laid siege to Cuemba. Insurgent gains in this quarter were held through early autumn before they withdrew their forces.[33]

FAPLA's conventional challenge to UNITA The improvement of FAPLA ground and air equipment in the early 1980s greatly concerned UNITA. Increased numbers of armoured vehicles provided by the Soviet Union, mostly T-54 or T-55 tanks, BTR-60s, and BRDM-2s, filled out FAPLA brigade TO&Es and the actual increase in the number of brigades meant that a considerable amount of armoured firepower could be thrown against UNITA. FAPLA tactics and doctrine evolved to use this new armoured capability effectively. While RPG-7s could cripple or destroy T-54/55 tanks and APCs, FAPLA began to mix them with infantry screens in operations, a tactic which often prevented UNITA bazuqueiros from getting close enough to effectively target hostile armour.

The FAPLA air threat to UNITA lay with more and better fixed-wing aircraft and combat helicopters to support ground operations. Increased use of helicopter resupply and reinforcement to isolated garrisons and forward units diminished UNITA's effectiveness in interdicting overland routes. By the early 1980s FAPA was commonly using the MiG-21MF multi-role fighter, especially in the fighter-bomber role, and was phasing out the older MiG-17. The older Mi-8/17 transport and assault helicopters were augmented by the newer Mi-24/25/35. Although the latter had a more limited range (160km) than the Mi-8 or 17 (480km), it could carry more weaponry as well as eight soldiers. FAPA's combat helicopters provided fire support to ground operations as well as playing a major logistical role. They were also used to insert special forces and teams for deep reconnaissance behind UNITA lines. Finally, FAPA helicopters were used for medical evacuation.

UNITA had some limited countermeasures available to cope with this formidable new ground and air threat. The first was to increase the number of anti-tank and anti-aircraft weapons and units. Anti-aircraft units were outfitted with captured FAPLA weaponry of Soviet make. Anti-tank capabilities were increased by providing more captured RPG-7s and anti-tank guns to field units. Heavy anti-tank units were made more mobile; by 1985 and probably earlier UNITA had South African-provided anti-tank weapons as well as captured 82mm B-10 recoilless rifles mounted on Unimog trucks. These were only stopgap measures. UNITA began to seek new anti-tank and anti-aircraft weapons from its allies, especially the United States. The repeal of the Clark Amendment in the United States Congress opened the way for a successful trip to Washington by Savimbi to negotiate for improved anti-tank and anti-aircraft weapons. The most effective of the latter was the Stinger shoulder-fired SAM, an effective state-of-the-art weapon that began to arrive in Angola in 1986. For anti-armour use, United States-made 106mm recoilless rifles were an improvement over the B-10.[34]

FAPLA counter-guerrilla capabilities and UNITA countermeasures, mid-1980s In the mid-1980s FAPLA's counter-guerrilla capability improved due not to doctrinal development as much as to more resources and better operational planning for its territorial forces. FAPLA's capabilities were targeted primarily against UNITA enclaves in central and west-central Angola. UNITA enclaves were groups of villages clustered by the insurgents to allow pockets of regional control. Enclaves in turn were part of military sectors that comprised military regions. FAPLA strategy in the 1980s was realised by raids against these areas to disrupt autumn planting and spring harvesting, take cattle, and detain and remove villagers to areas of MPLA control (generally near large urban centres or FAPLA garrisons). There were usually a dozen or so such minor local operations undertaken by FAPLA each month, more during the planting and harvest seasons.

UNITA operations to counter FAPLA area sweeps took several forms. The first was the establishment of local militia units who served as the first line of defence until UNITA Territorial Troops could respond to the incursions. The second was to force FAPLA units away from the countryside by gradually capturing isolated smaller garrisons. FAPLA assembly of troops and equipment for any campaigns above battalion level would thus require extensive supply movement and troop deployment that would not go unnoticed by UNITA's intelligence network. Finally, UNITA used all possible means–including coercion–to get local villagers to put themselves under insurgent control as opposed to permitting continued FAPLA domination. FAPLA, Cuban, and SWAPO units often took reprisals upon populations believed to support the insurgents. In contested areas it was not possible for locals to remain neutral. FAPLA's areas of controlled population were often in areas of poor or no farmland, making uprooted peasants dependent upon local authorities for food and thus more amenable to government control. UNITA often targeted the large garrisons and urban areas for military operations, making them unsafe and undesirable living areas.[35]

FAPLA counter-guerrilla operations were usually battalion-size or smaller in scope, entrusted to local units with occasional help from the regular army or SWAPO. Most operations consisted of area sweeps by light infantry to force suspected UNITA supporters from villages and to search for insurgent base camps. A determined UNITA counterattack often foiled such operations and at times caused FAPLA considerable losses. However, such operations placed a limit on UNITA force development. The insurgents needed an extensive local system of militia and territorial troops to tie down FAPLA units and counter small local operations. For this reason UNITA could not drastically enlarge the number of personnel in FAPLA without equal attention to its local forces to ensure adequate control of newly acquired territory and village enclaves. To fail to do so would leave them open to FAPLA raids and thus cost UNITA support from the villagers who relied upon the insurgents for protection.

FINAL PHASE OF THE CIVIL WAR, 1988-1991

The final phase of the civil war opened with a rough strategic balance between the two sides, which by mid-1990 shifted to UNITA. This phase was characterised by:

■ The withdrawal of South Africa, Cuba, and ultimately the Soviet Union and Warsaw Pact nations from the conflict;
■ The reorganisation of FAPLA to maximise mobility and firepower in its motorised units;
■ Increase in EPA personnel to about 120,000;
■ Attempts to improve FAPA air–ground support;
■ Task organisation in FAPLA operations;
■ General decline in the quality of FAPLA logistical capabilities despite an increase in the quantities involved in supporting field operations;
■ Intensification of UNITA operations in all provinces of Angola;
■ Expansion of UNITA's forces to maximum strength;
■ Extension of UNITA territorial control north of the CFB and establishment of territorial control in north-western Angola;
■ Continued development of UNITA anti-aircraft and anti-tank capabilities.

Another FAPLA reorganisation (1988)

The EPA took advantage of the lull in the fighting to undertake a major reorganisation and restructuring during 1988–1989. This involved the modernisation of existing combat units as well as major TOE changes that gave ground forces much more mobility and firepower. The Angolan military also consolidated its ten military regions into four (from May 1990, five) large Political-Military Fronts, each made up of a number of military zones corresponding to provinces. Task organisation was institutionalised with the deployment of task forces, highly mobile units that consisted of a large (brigade equivalent) headquarters to which were attached two or more tactical groups. Both task forces and motorised brigades were now equipped with the Soviet-made BMP-1 infantry fighting vehicle (IFV) as standard equipment.

The number of brigades continued to grow, reaching about 80 in early 1989. As the fighting with UNITA progressed, however, brigades declined to only about 50 or so by late 1990, distributed over the five Political-Military Fronts. The brigades were assisted by about 20 military task forces, most formed during the preceding year from regular brigades. These units, with independent tactical groups and battalions, comprised some 120,000 personnel. About 15,000 Cubans were left in Angola, but all were due for departure soon. Soviet advisers remained, as did the ANC, some SWAPO, and some Katangese ex-gendarmes. If anything, the reorganisation did prepare FAPLA to fight almost alone by late 1990.

1989-1990: Operation 'Final Assault'[36]

In August 1989 FAPLA began to demonstrate its newly-felt strength in campaigns against UNITA in Cunene (Ionde Front), Cuando Cubango (Cuito Cuanavale Front), and in Bie and Moxico (Bie and Munhango Fronts). All the attacks, which lasted from early August through early November, failed to effectively penetrate or occupy UNITA territory. However, FAPLA was to make one more massive attempt to crush UNITA and take Mavinga.

By late November 1989 preparations for a massive attack on UNITA were evident. Five reinforced motorised infantry brigades, two mechanised battalions, an artillery brigade, and support units had gathered at Cuito Cuanavale. This gave FAPLA 12,000 combat troops plus support for the coming operation. Other preparations included the deployment of six tactical groups (1,800 personnel) equipped with BMP-1s to lead the offensive and the deployment of additional artillery brigades. Final logistical preparations and personnel plus-ups began in mid-December.

The expected offensive, codenamed Operation 'Final Assault' (*Ultimo Assalta*), was launched on 19 December from the high ground east of Cuito Cuanavale, and by 22 December split into three axes of advance. Rapidly moving tactical groups reinforced with tanks spearheaded the offensive and broke UNITA defensive lines, allowing regular infantry to exploit the breakthroughs. FAPLA ground operations at this stage were well coordinated with artillery and air support. UNITA opposed FAPLA with much lighter forces consisting of infantry backed by 4WD-mounted recoilless rifles and heavy machine guns, plus artillery. UNITA even had a few mechanised and armoured units using captured FAPLA vehicles. UNITA tried to contain the attackers east of Cuito Cuanavale at the Cunzumbia River, but FAPLA broke through on 5 January. By 2 February FAPLA units penetrated to Mavinga, but were unable to advance further. The offensive stalled due to increased UNITA resistance, resupply difficulties, and high attrition rates experienced by FAPLA.

For the next three months FAPLA forces were besieged at Mavinga by UNITA in 'The War of the Trenches.' Resupply became increasingly difficult. FAPLA, despite good offensive capabilities, proved poor at defence. Angolan air support failed. Maintenance suffered; tanks and BMP-1s not lost to UNITA often broke down due to lack of repairs. UNITA's trump card was hunger and thirst among the besieged. FAPLA had planned to use the airfield at Mavinga for air resupply but was unable to capture and secure it.

UNITA also undertook a crucial strategic move to force FAPLA from Mavinga, launching a massive campaign in north-western Angola, near the capital, Luanda. This offensive was directed at capturing government garrisons there and establishing zones of UNITA control. Insurgent operations repeatedly cut water and electricity supplies to Luanda. Wherever possible, any infrastructure allowing MPLA government control or military operations was destroyed. By late April the security situation in north-western Angola around the capital was very grave, and additional forces were unavailable with the commitment on the Mavinga front. In the end, lacking the means or the reason to continue at the Mavinga front, FAPLA withdrew on 7 and 8 May. The retreat to Cuito Cuanavale became a panicked rout as vehicles ran out of fuel and were abandoned. By 15 May all units withdrawing from Mavinga had reached Cuito Cuanavale.

Summer 1990: War in the North[37]

Summer of 1990 saw a dramatic realignment in the military balance of power in Angola following FAPLA's forced withdrawal from Mavinga. Continued Cuban troop withdrawals and the inability of FAPLA to recapture territory in northern and eastern Angola taken earlier by UNITA ensured that the latter's position was more secure than ever, and that the MPLA had to change its strategy. In order to implement its new three-fold design to protect the capital, recapture lost territories in Uige and Zaire provinces, and regain control of the border with Zaire (claimed by the MPLA to be the main transshipment point for covert Western assistance to UNITA), FAPLA moved the bulk of its army across the country during the month of May.

Preparations for FAPLA attacks on UNITA developed rapidly. By early June task forces began to deploy in the north from Viana east of Luanda. By July FAPLA task forces and tactical groups began a series of attempts to move from Sanza Pombo in Uige province north-eastward through Macocola toward the UNITA base at Quimbele. On 19 June FAPLA took Macocola, north of Sanza Pombo, and attempted to advance north of the town toward Quimbele. On 28 June a coordinated attack was launched from Sanza Pombo and Macocola against Quimbele. Despite air support, FAPLA was engaged by UNITA 9km north of Macocola and forced back to the town. In the meantime logistics collapsed, prompting a general breakdown of discipline among some units, which began pillaging the local population in the region south-west of Sanza Pombo. Other task force units were engaged in local operations elsewhere in Uige province and thus unable to be committed to stabilise the situation at Sanza Pombo. As a result, UNITA was able to regain much of the territory FAPLA had taken, even though the latter retained Macocola.

Throughout early July UNITA continued to harass FAPLA units in Uige, which continued to be plagued with food shortages and low morale; toward the end of the month FAPLA planned for elements of a task force in Malange to move into the Macocola area to assist the Uige Task Force. Despite extensive air strikes, FAPLA remained confined to the Macocola–Sanza Pombo corridor and a few other bases and could not break out of the UNITA cordon. The most ambitious FAPLA campaign northern Angola had yet seen had failed.

With the collapse of the Northern Front campaign, FAPLA withdrew to bases in early July for regrouping and resupply. That this was not immediately adequate was indicated by the poor morale exhibited by some of its tactical groups. The Uige task force's ability to control its sub-units had become difficult. Desertions were rampant, especially among those units that were composed of local recruits. The impact of these desertions upon the units was significant, as tactical groups usually had about 300 or so personnel, and for such relatively small units losses were quickly felt in terms of degraded operational capability.

Elsewhere in northern Angola FAPLA operations garnered few real gains. Task forces in Zaire and Malange provinces, despite some offensive capability, were on the whole unable to compete with local UNITA forces. FAPLA tactical groups were constantly outmanoeuvred and their logistics repeatedly broke down. Despite the introduction of two more task forces in the north by early autumn, large parts of Zaire, Uige, and Malange provinces remained in UNITA hands.

Closer to the capital FAPLA enjoyed more success. An elite task force was able to disrupt many UNITA base areas in Bengo and Cuanza Norte, but still could not confront and engage UNITA forces nor could it prevent raids on the power and water lines supplying Luanda. By late October another task force was deployed to assist the first; each worked closely with a light infantry brigade in respective AORs north and south of the capital. They also utilised ANC and Katangese units as well.

FAPLA's lack of success in northern Angola; UNITA gains in Bie

FAPLA's singular lack of success against UNITA in northern Angola in summer 1990 puzzled many observers. That the planned operations were to take place relatively close to the capital appeared to make things easier. While most units moved overland from Cuando Cubango, some were airlifted to Luanda to deploy almost immediately. Other units were recruited locally. New units were quickly outfitted from the vast stocks of tanks, APCs, and logistical vehicles shipped from the Soviet Union to Luanda. Air support for the Northern Front was coordinated from the FAPA base at Negage near Uige.

FAPLA operations in the north were initially conducted from Viana, just east of Luanda. There on 1 June the Cuanza-Bengo Front, consisting of Luanda, Bengo, Cuanza Norte and Cuanza Sul provinces, was activated to protect the capital and its supply lines (including electrical and water). To counter UNITA, troops airlifted into Luanda were assembled into a task force at an Advanced Command Post (PCA) at Viana, later moved to Uige after being augmented by elements of two other task forces that had moved overland from the Southern Front. It was from these troops that the ill-fated FAPLA task force sent against Quimbele was drawn.[38]

The subsequent fate of FAPLA operations in the Northern Front, discussed above, illustrates limits on the use of tactical groups. While tactical groups were employed with some success during the fighting at Mavinga, the extremely difficult terrain in north-western Angola is unsuitable for armoured and mechanised operations by heavy armour such as tanks. FAPLA units were often forced by the roads and the terrain to advance in column and were unable to disperse easily during UNITA attacks. The proximity to Luanda allowed ready equipping of FAPLA with Soviet-made tanks, BMPs, and trucks. However, the pervasive corruption and ineptitude within the FAPLA logistics structure was not addressed, and breakdowns of logistics, manifested in food and fuel shortages, became increasingly frequent during June and July. Discipline also suffered as hungry FAPLA troops preyed upon local villagers. Ethnic and regional affiliations posed increasing problems for FAPLA as well. To discourage both desertions to home villages and connections with the local population, new recruits were transported into localities distant from their homes. Control of the civilian population was attempted as well, with deportations from Uige province rural areas to 'concentration centres' in the north-east.

UNITA's record in the north is exactly the opposite. Insurgent military formations, consisting for the most part of semi-regular battalions and compact guerrilla columns, were since 1985 well-established in the area. Establishment of training camps for military personnel in the north allowed more rapid recruitment and training of local UNITA personnel. The difficult terrain allowed relatively safe insurgent movement, and afforded good cover if not ideal concealment. The locals were sympathetic to UNITA and the depredations of poorly-controlled FAPLA units added to the number who opposed the MPLA. FAPLA deserters found service with UNITA attractive; about 60 per cent of all FAPLA deserters in the Northern Front joined UNITA. The MPLA, on its part, claimed that the main reason for UNITA successes in the region was its proximity to Zaire, and repeatedly claimed Zairian collusion in resupplying and training the insurgents. Some of the most hard-fought engagements in the closing days of the war were fought in late 1990 in Zaire province.

1991 began with a significant UNITA victory, the 1 January capture of Munhango, Jonas Savimbi's birthplace. FAPLA was not able to recapture the town, and UNITA was able to exploit its victory further by the 29 January capture of Cuemba to the west. Despite FAPLA's attempts to recapture them, these towns remained in UNITA's hands as of the 15 May ceasefire. FAPLA's Third Task Force advanced from Luena in early February against the UNITA positions near Munhango but was driven back. FAPLA units in Bie province that tried to advance against Cuemba from the west were also unsuccessful.

Fighting continued in early 1991 in the Northern Front as well. The most spectacular military action was that undertaken by UNITA on Sunday, 10 February 1991. It attacked Ambriz in Bengo province, destroying a power station and an oil rig storage area. The town was briefly occupied but UNITA left before elements of a FAPLA reaction force could respond. The attack itself was based in Zaire province immediately north of Bengo. Other UNITA attacks were reported near Soyo. Elsewhere in Zaire province fighting reportedly continued as UNITA consolidated its hold upon the areas north-east of Tomboco and south of Noqui. Mbanza Congo, Cuimba, and a few other sites in the eastern part of the province were still under FAPLA control. Similar intense fighting took place in Uige province. In Malange province, January to March 1991 was marked by the fight by FAPLA to keep UNITA from closing the rail line west to Luanda, and keeping open the road through the central part of the province. After the fall of Munhango this road was the only overland route from Luanda to the Lunda provinces. UNITA's strategy was now focusing on picking off FAPLA garrisons almost at will and causing the MPLA to divert significant military resources to keep transport routes open.

The battle for Luena

The last major round of military activity began on 1 April 1991, six weeks before the cease-fire was to take effect (16 May 1991). According to UNITA, FAPLA had been reinforcing Luena in Moxico province, headquarters of its Eastern Front, since mid-February with the aim of using it as the base for another attack against Munhango. UNITA attempted to disrupt this logistical buildup and hoped that Luena, a provincial capital, would also fall into its hands. FAPLA, for its part, claimed that UNITA wanted to capture Luena so that it would possess a major Angolan urban centre at the time of ceasefire. Regardless of motives, the fighting was intense as Luena was bitterly contested for six weeks. In battles that continued through April up to the ceasefire, FAPLA forces at Luena, commanded by Moxico ZM commander Colonel Neco, managed a skilful defence against determined UNITA attacks. In late April UNITA managed to close the airport at Luena and forced over-land resupply from Saurimo to the north. Despite UNITA attacks on ground convoys, FAPLA relief columns were able to reach Luena in early May, allowing FAPLA to retain the town. In the fighting, the local population ultimately sided with FAPLA. The effective defence of Luena was a victory FAPLA could claim.

Despite FAPLA's retention of Luena, elsewhere its overall position suffered. Late 1990 and early 1991 had been a time during which the Angolan military lost the initiative against UNITA. The key turning point was the capture of Munhango and Cuemba and the shift of the brunt of conventional fighting to the central plateau. This occurred while UNITA continued to expand and consolidate its hold over large parts of FAPLA's Northern and Cuanza-Bengo Fronts. At the local level, UNITA gains continued to spread. FAPLA's manpower problem resulted in tenuous control by the MPLA in most areas, as isolated garrisons with limited mobility and offensive capability due to logistical breakdowns sought to retain area control. UNITA, on the other hand, was able to strike at targets of choice throughout most of Angola. In mid-May 1991, FAPLA fought hard to stabilise the situation, with little conventional progress against UNITA in Bie and Huambo provinces and little COIN success in the Northern Front. By the 15th UNITA had overrun many FAPLA garrisons throughout the country as the ceasefire drew near.

CABINDA, FLEC, AND OIL

The fighting between UNITA and the MPLA government often overshadowed a second conflict that had plagued Angola since before independence, namely that of the seces-sionists in Cabinda and their struggle for autonomy from the Luanda government. The roots of the insurgency are quite different from those of UNITA's fight against the MPLA.

CABINDA AND THE POLITICS OF OIL

Originally a Portuguese colonial enclave on the coast of Africa north of the Zaire (Congo) River, Cabinda was a backwater until the discovery of oil made it a crucial prize in any future political dispensation. It was incorporated into Angola in 1958. During 1975–1976, several overt attempts were made by Zaire to occupy the area, but the MPLA, with Cuban assistance, was able to prevent this. What the MPLA and its allies were not able to do, however, was quash the local independence movement, a secessionist group called the Front for the Liberation of the Enclave of Cabinda (in Portuguese: Frente de Libertacao do Enclave de Cabinda, FLEC).

Cabinda's oil has made it Angola's richest province. Separated from Angola, the enclave comprises 7,270 square kilometres and had in the early 1990s about 120,000 people. Practically all of these were members of the BaKongo ethnic group, speaking the

Fiote dialect of the Kongo language; at least 85 per cent were Roman Catholics. Divided into four districts–Cabinda, Luanda, Buco Zau, and Belize – the enclave lies a short distance from the Equator, and has a hot, humid climate. Inland, dense forests are interspersed with some cultivation. In the north-east the enclave abuts the Massabi Mountains where it borders with Congo. The combination of terrain and vegetation makes the area ideal for insurgent hit-and-run tactics, and difficult for counterinsurgency operations.[39]

ORIGIN AND EARLY HISTORY OF FLEC[40]

FLEC was founded by Luis Ranque Franque in 1959 in Brazzaville. From its start the movement was separatist in nature, but soon lost any voice amid infighting that was to constantly mark Cabindan separatist politics. Ranque Franque, despite setbacks to rivals (especially Telo Gerard), was finally successful in organising an umbrella coalition in alliance with Nzita Henrique Tiago, leader of the Comité d'Action de l'Union Nationale des Cabindais, CAUNC, which was based in Leopoldville, the Congo (now Kinshasa, Zaire).

Cabinda's neighbours, Congo-Brazzaville and Congo-Leopoldville (later Zaire), had a vested interest in promoting Cabindan separatism. First, for both countries Cabinda was a potentially valuable prize, if it could be detached and then annexed or controlled; the country could gravitate to Kongo regions of either of its neighbours. Second, neighbouring governments, caught up in the temper of the times, supported African nationalist insurgencies against the Portuguese colonial government. Indeed, the first FLEC government-in-exile was founded on 10 January 1967 in Tshela, Congo-Leopoldville (Zaire), in a fashion similar to the FNLA (also supported by Leopoldville).

FLEC, despite its attempt to galvanise the Cabindan population, remained a largely expatriate movement through the rest of the 1960s and even into the 1970s. The discovery of oil in Cabinda in 1966 ended any doubts as to the desire of Luanda to control the enclave, even though FLEC's claims became more strident than ever. Indeed, with oil Cabinda could easily have become a self-supporting country free of the financial problems that beset many African countries. Despite the widespread conflict throughout Angola accompanying the end of Portuguese rule, FLEC played little part, even though Zairian troops entered Cabinda to attempt to take over the area. The FAZ units and their allies were defeated militarily by Cuban troops sent to Cabinda to assist the MPLA in retaining control of the strategic enclave.

In part due to the stresses accompanying the turbulent events of 1975, FLEC split into two factions, led by Ranque Franque and Nzita Tiago. Many of the differences settled around personalities and agenda, although both factions were externally-based and not run from inside Cabinda. Later even the Ranque Franque faction suffered defections, with splinter groups led by Marcelino Luemba Tubi and Luis Matos Fernandes. In 1977 these formed a military group, the Comando Militar para a Libertacao de Cabinda (CLMC).

FLEC IN THE 1980S; WORKING WITH UNITA

Despite its disunity, FLEC and its factions cooperated with UNITA throughout the 1980s, working toward a common goal of defeating FAPLA and the Cubans. Both sides undoubtedly planned to settle their differences, by whatever means possible, following their triumph over the common enemy.

FLEC's disunity in the 1980s remained its fatal flaw. After the middle of the decade, UNITA began to operate in Cabinda, and attract much support there from Cabindans who were dissatisfied with FLEC and its preoccupation with internal squabbles over the struggle against the central government. UNITA forged alliances with some local FLEC leaders, but appears in general to have operated independently against the MPLA without coming into conflict with the various factions.

The MPLA remained unable to come to terms with FLEC through the 1980s. At first, the MPLA continued to reject Cabindan demands for better treatment as serving the regime's enemies. The MPLA's main desire in Cabinda was to maintain control of the oilfields there; this included ensuring their security against FLEC attack. As long as FLEC was weak and divided, the secessionists could do little.

The situation changed in the mid-1980s when UNITA began operating in Cabinda. Savimbi's forces were able to come to an understanding with various FLEC leaders, at least local commanders. They provided the additional military support that FLEC groups needed to intensify their war against the central government in the interior. Faced with a rapidly deteriorating security situation in the interior of Cabinda, the MPLA sought to negotiate with various FLEC factions in the late 1980s. However, a major problem that had developed was determining precisely which faction could be negotiated with. In addition, UNITA remained present, always able to undermine any local efforts toward negotiations by undertaking military action. Under such circumstances little could be accomplished toward resolving Cabindan secessionists' complaints against the regime. This situation continued throughout 1991.

FLEC FACTIONS SINCE THE BICESSE ACCORDS[41]

Despite the May 1991 Bicesse Accords, fighting continued in Cabinda. No FLEC group was a signatory to the accords, and continued activity against FAPLA troops; most UNITA forces, although adhering to the ceasefire, remained neutral. A very few UNITA fighters, however, who had Cabindan ethnic affiliation and connections, apparently did desert UNITA and join one of the FLEC factions. Despite this, there is little evidence that FLEC factional ranks increased much.

By October and November of 1991 FLEC activities increased remarkably, and FAPLA was forced to transfer at least one task force from Bengo to reinforce Cabinda. By November at least 15,000 FAPLA troops were present in Cabinda, but they had by all accounts lost control of the Cabindan hinterland. FAPLA could move only in convoys and its garrisons were virtually all it controlled at any one time. FLEC groups, however, were unable to threaten offshore oil installations and the insurgency, although an embarrassment to the MPLA, did not present any imminent threat.

NOTES

1. See the separate chapter, 'The Second Angolan Civil War', below.
2. For the political developments, see the portions pertinent to Angola and regional political issues in Colin Legum, *The Battlefronts of Southern Africa*, Africana Publishing Company, New York and London, 1988. The political overview of the war is covered most recently by W. Martin James III, *A Political History of the Civil War in Angola, 1974-1990*, Transaction Publishers, New Brunswick and London, 1992. While no comprehensive discussion of the social or economic impact of the conflict has been published as yet, the reader should consult two publications by Human Rights Watch/Africa Watch that provide case studies on the human costs of the fighting, especially on the civilian population. These are *Angola: Violations of the Laws of War by Both Sides*, Human Rights Watch, New York-Washington-London, 1988, and *Land Mines in Angola, Human Rights Watch*, New York-Washington-Los Angeles-London, 1993.
3. Information courtesy of Mr Antonio Figuera, a former member of 32 Battalion.
4. Information courtesy of the International Freedom Foundation (IFF) (Washington, DC).
5. UNITA: *Identity of a Free Angola*, Jomba, Angola; UNITA, 1985, pp. 29-30.
6. One exception was was the publicity UNITA received from the visit of Leon de Costa Dash, Jr, in 1977. See *Munger Africana Library Notes*, pp. 40-1.
7. Bridgland, *Jonas Savimbi*, pp. 194-218, 231-3.
8. Bridgland, pp. 236-7, 276-8.
9. Bridgland, pp. 236-7.
10. Bridgland, p. 253.
11. Bridgland, pp. 249-54.
12. Bridgland, pp. 256-8, 270.
13. Bridgland, pp. 266-70.

14. Bridgland, pp. 267-72.
15. Information courtesy of International Freedom Foundation (IFF) (Washington, DC).
16. UNITA, p. 29.
17. UNITA, pp. 29-30; Bridgland, pp. 268-9, 285.
18. Information courtesy of IFF (Washington, DC).
19. Information courtesy of IFF (Washington, DC).
20. Information courtesy of IFF (Washington, DC).
21. UNITA, p. 30; Bridgland, pp. 293-6, 300.
22. Bridgland, pp. 300, 330-3.
23. UNITA, p. 30.
24. Bridgland, pp. 360-8.
25. Bridgland, pp. 378-9.
26. Bridgland, pp. 396-400.
27. *Africa Defence Journal* (Paris), December 1983, p. 25; January 1984, p. 21.
28. *Africa Defence Journal* (Paris), December 1983, pp. 24-5.
29. Bridgland, pp. 424-6. A good overview of the Angolan situation as of mid-1984 is found in Hough, *ISSUP Strategic Review*, November 1985. See above, p.55.
30. Information courtesy of IFF (Washington, DC).
31. Bridgland, pp. 432-7.
32. Information courtesy of FAIS (Washington, DC).
33. Steenkamp, p. 153; UNITA communiqués 22 and 30 December 1987.
34. Information courtesy of IFF and Free Angola Information SErvice (FAIS) (Washington, DC).
35. See Nicholas Rowe, 'The Village of the Living Dead', *American Spectator*, August 1986, pp. 14-15.
36. See FAIS briefings No. 1 (16 December 1989), No. 2 (20 December 1989), No. 3 (3 January 1990), No. 4 (18 January 1990), No. 5 (29 January 1990), No. 6 (15 February 1990), No. 7 (22 February 1990) and No. 8 (22 February 1990); see also 'MPLA's Military Offensive against Mavinga' (Synopsis), 8 May 1990. For the course of the conflict in 1989-1990, see the author's discussion of the attack by FAPLA against Mavinga and its failure in 'Battle of Mavinga' in *Museum Ordnance*, May 1992, pp. 16-19. Subsequent events are discussed in 'Angola: War in the North' in *African Armed Forces*, October 1994, pp. 28-31 (part I) and January/December 1995, pp. 29-33 (part II).
37. See UNITA communiqué 28/90, 19 June 1990; UNITA military updates 6/10/90, 6/20/90; UNITA HQs communiqué 28/90, 2 July 1990; see also *Africa Defence Journal*, August 1990, p. 27.
38. See UNITA communiqué 27/90, 12 June 1990; UNITA military update 6/10/90.
39. See the statistics given in FBIS *AFR-93-142*, pp. 22-4.
40. Material for this section based on 'Angola' in Janke, Peter, and Sim, Richard, *Guerrilla and Terrorist Organizations: A World Directory and Bibliography*, Macmillan, New York, 1983, pp. 130-1; see also Kaplan, Irving ed., *Angola: A Country Study*, DA Pam 550-59, Washington DC, 1979, pp. 130-1, 200.
41. Information for this section courtesy of the International Freedom Foundation (Washington DC) and the Georgetown University Center for Strategic and International Studies (Washington DC).

Chapter Five

The Mozambican Insurgency, 1975–1992

BACKGROUND TO THE MOZAMBICAN INSURGENCY

Of all Africa's insurgent wars, few have been as bitterly controversial and marked by disinformation as the one which raged in Mozambique from 1976 to 1992. The war, which pitted the central government of the Front for the Liberation of Mozambique (FRELIMO) against the guerrillas of the National Mozambican Resistance (MNR, or RENAMO), killed between 350,000 and 600,000 people, displaced another two million (of a population of about fifteen million total), and virtually destroyed most of the country's rural infrastructure. However, by mid-August 1992 the long war neared its end with the 7 August agreement signed in Rome between the opposing factions, which called for a ceasefire and peace settlement by 1 October. It took two years before elections which, though confirming the continued rule of the central government of President Joaquin Chissano, also revealed that a significant portion of the Mozambican population still supported RENAMO.[1]

Even in the wake of the long-hoped peace, partisans of both factions, both inside Mozambique and internationally, continue to vehemently disagree over two controversial issues surrounding the RENAMO insurgency and their local and regional implications. These issues also bear directly upon matters of interest to students of insurgent warfare and counterguerrilla techniques. The first issue concerns the origins and early support for RENAMO while the second issue is over the nature and degree of internal support and external assistance received by RENAMO. By the mid-1980s the movement had won the effective control of the Mozambican countryside despite efforts by the then-Marxist government and its security forces to contain it. A main area of controversy, however, remains over how this situation came to be. RENAMO's chief, Mr Afonso Dhlakama, claimed in late 1992 that the insurgents controlled 85 per cent of Mozambique's population. This figure, however, best applies to the mid- and late 1980s; the impact of government reforms (including the abandonment of Marxism), improved effectiveness of the security forces, and the impact of a severe drought on the rural areas from which RENAMO drew its strength sharply changed the situation by 1992. The recent (1994) elections strongly suggest that the government regained much of the ground it had lost in the 1980s, although voter patterns indicated a rather complex picture of support for both sides. Few would deny, however, the fact of RENAMO's control over most of rural Mozambique in the mid- and late 1980s, or that the FRELIMO government was reduced to dire straits during the period 1984–1988.[2]

RENAMO has, since its foundation in 1976, built upon a major split between the urban and rural segments of Mozambican society. In the late 1980s the central government controlled the cities while RENAMO held sway over the countryside and enjoyed the allegiance, either voluntary or coerced, of the population there. Although RENAMO had adherents from all Mozambican ethnic groups and from all regions, its power was strongest in the central part of the country in the lower Zambezi River valley and the adjacent highlands of the Gorongosa Massif, the site of RENAMO headquarters for most of the guerrilla war. Dhlakama's loose style of administration, based on his cultural background (he is the son of a traditional chief) even led many to believe that there was actually more than one movement that called itself RENAMO. In reality, the far-flung elements of the insurgent movement, though disparate, were part of a loose-knit unity. Such a structure gave local RENAMO commanders considerable autonomy that allowed wide latitude in recruitment of personnel, conduct of operations, and treatment of the civilian population. This situation resulted in the guerrillas enjoying real popular support in some areas; in others they terrorised the population through forced recruitment, abductions, and massacres of the civilian population, flooding neighbouring Zimbabwe, Malawi, and South Africa with refugees.[3]

INDEPENDENCE AND AFTER: SETTING THE STAGE FOR CONFLICT

RENAMO's roots are to be found in the aftermath of the end of Portuguese colonial rule. The insurgent movement, the Front for the Liberation of Mozambique, or FRELIMO, had fought a long insurgent war against colonial forces, but it was only with the death of the Portuguese strongman Salazar and the subsequent leftist military coup of 1974 that real steps toward independence were undertaken. By that time the Soviet Union had become a firm backer of FRELIMO, supplying it with arms and training, often through surrogates, based in neighbouring Zambia and Tanzania. The Portuguese colonial administration, in its turn, received assistance from the government of neighbouring Rhodesia, whose anti-government insurgents were also supported by the Soviet Union.

Mozambique became officially independent in 1975. By that time FRELIMO's relations with the Soviet Union and other East Bloc countries were quite close. The original founder of FRELIMO, Eduardo Mondlane, had been murdered in 1969 and his place later taken by the FRELIMO military commander Samora Machel, who claimed himself to be a communist and strove to establish close relations between Mozambique and the USSR/Warsaw Pact. Despite FRELIMO's official assertions at the time that Mondlane was murdered by the Portuguese secret intelligence service, PIDE, subsequent discussions claimed that Machel, operating with the support of the Soviets and with the active collusion of the pro-Soviet faction within FRELIMO, killed Mondlane (indeed, Machel became FRELIMO military commander after apparently also killing the incumbent, Filipe Magaia, in 1966). Machel soon began to receive military assistance from China and other sympathetic nations, to include military aid, training and fielding a new army, first known as the Popular Forces for the Liberation of Mozambique (FPLM) and later as the Mozambican Armed Forces (Forcas Armadas Mocambicanas, or FAM).[4]

However, by this time serious disaffection had set in among many FRELIMO members. Originally attracted by Mondlane's leadership style and strong nationalist sentiments, by independence they were increasingly concerned about Machel's autocratic ruling style and his ever-increasing communist connections. After independence such dissent within FRELIMO was brutally crushed. Machel and his supporters within FRELIMO also began to undertake steps to turn Mozambique into a 'communist' society by purging it of traditional leadership down to the local village level. Here again any resistance was cruelly suppressed. Mozambican nationalists and traditionalists who had earlier fought against what many considered an aberrant manifestation of Western political and economic ideology – colonialism – now found themselves mortally threatened by an even greater perversion of Western thought, Marxism-Leninism, albeit distorted by an African adaptation. FRELIMO's policies soon alienated many non-Marxist party members as well as the rural dwellers and the traditional leaders, and many began to return to the bush soon after independence. Much of the discontent among the bulk of the Mozambican population, however, ultimately boiled down to unfulfilled expectations, and their alienation evolved over a much longer period following independence. In the immediate post-independence period many rural Mozambicans continued to support the government and its agenda.

However, through FRELIMO's attempts at Marxist-inspired social engineering, the stage was set ultimately for widespread popular discontent that generated internal support for any movement that would give the rural population hope of relief from the depredations of the central government, as well as allow alienated FRELIMO members a refuge from persecution by the new government's agents, including FAM counterintelligence and the secret police, or SNASP. Many of the FRELIMO insurgents that had fought the Portuguese colonial regime and were thus already skilled in bush warfare were among the disaffected. Another source of armed dissent came from former Mozambican members of the colonial anti-insurgent forces, the flechas ('arrows'). Many had fled into the bush and others had settled in Rhodesia and South Africa. From late 1976, they were joined by defecting members of FRELIMO as well. By this time the regimes in Salisbury and Pretoria had grave concerns about the new FRELIMO government and its support to both Rhodesian insurgents and the African National Congress (ANC).[5]

Internationally, Machel and FRELIMO steered Mozambique into the communist camp, formalising a number of economic and military agreements with the Soviet Union and its allies in hopes of receiving badly-needed economic assistance. Regionally, FRELIMO joined with its supporters in Zambia and Tanzania and the newly-independent Angola to work against the white-dominated regimes of Rhodesia and South Africa. It continued to actively assist guerrillas working against Rhodesia (which it had done before Mozambique's independence), providing them bases and logistical support in the border areas of Manica and Sofala provinces. As noted above, FRELIMO also continued its ties with the ANC, providing its operatives with bases and other facilities in Mozambique from which they conducted operations against the South African government. Machel and his FRELIMO supporters thus helped set the stage for Rhodesian and South African support for internal dissent by supporting anti-regime dissidents of both of these neighbours. Mozambique also (following United Nations guidance) cut economic ties with Rhodesia and South Africa, thus giving those countries little to lose by supporting destabilisation of the FRELIMO government in reprisal for the latter's support of insurgents working against the white regimes.

PHASES OF THE CONFLICT
The following discussion divides the conflict into the following phases:

■ The origin of RENAMO and its early operations, during which period it was supported by the Rhodesians, up to 1979;
■ A transition phase, during which RENAMO almost collapsed before being taken over and rebuilt by the South Africans, 1979-1981;
■ The period of South African support and RENAMO expansion to most of Mozambique, 1981-1984, a period ending with the March 1984 Nkomati Accords;
■ The period of continued RENAMO growth and FRELIMO decline, marked by the first major involvement by Zimbabwean forces, 1984-1986/7;
■ The revival of the FAM and the decline of RENAMO, leading to a stalemate by the early 1990s and the 1992 ceasefire.

OVERVIEW OF THE MOZAMBICAN INSURGENCY

RENAMO'S ORIGINS
RENAMO dates from early 1977, although it claims Christmas Day, 1976, as its actual foundation date.[6] Even before that time there was armed resistance to the FRELIMO government. Armed dissent from alienated FRELIMO fighters who had fled into the bush began earlier in the year in Manica province. Many of RENAMO's detractors claim that the insurgency was a complete invention of the Rhodesian security forces. In this assertion they follow the official FRELIMO claims, contrary to evidence from former Rhodesian security personnel who note that they at first helped to train and arm fugitive flechas and ex-

Above: SAAF Alouette-III in use in northern SWA/Namibia. This versatile helicopter was used for a range of tasks that chiefly included reconnaissance, fire support, medical evacuation, and troop transport and resupply. Alouette-IIIs figured most importantly in the earlier Rhodesian bush war, where they formed an integral part of the 'Fire Force' units.

Below: Ohatopi base, typical of many smaller SADF/SWATF fortified posts along the SWA border with Angola. Note the heavy earth revetments; outside are double barbed wire/concertina fences and a minefield.

Above: SWA Specialist (SWASPES) motorcycle forces. The flat terrain of northern SWA/Namibia made the use of motorcycles specifically equipped with silencers an ideal means for rapid, silent approach against insurgent encampments.

Below: SWASPES mounted forces in northern SWA taking a break from patrol to water their horses. The 'mounties' were used for tracking and patrols, due to their ability to cover wider areas more quickly than units on foot; they also were much quieter than armoured cars or APCs.

Above: SAAF C-47/DC-3 Dakota, one of the mainstays for troop and cargo transport throughout the war. Its capability to land on airstrips throughout northern SWA not usable by the larger C-130 Hercules meant that smaller garrisons and units in the field could be resupplied quickly and efficiently.

Right: Troops of the SWATF 202 Battalion mounted on a Buffel APC. The Buffel was a highly versatile troop carrier that could be fitted with additional weaponry. The sides of the Buffel were hinged to allow rapid debussing of troops in the event of an engagement. This photo was taken during the SADF/SWATF withdrawal from Angola in September 1990 as forces crossed the Kavango River into SWA.

Right: The Casspir armoured car. This vehicle was used by the SWATF 101 Battalion (shown here) as well as by the SWA Police, including the famous COIN unit known as OPS-K or 'Koevoet'. Like the Buffel, the Casspir could be fitted with additional firepower. Each Casspir carried a squad of eight to ten men.

Above: The Ratel IFV. While developed to support SADF mechanised warfare, the various types of the Ratel were often used in COIN operations due to their mobility, manoeuvrability, versatility, and varied firepower. Depicted here is a Ratel-90, which is fitted with a turret-mounted 90mm cannon. The Ratel was used from 1978 in SADF mechanised operations in Angola.

Below: SADF 32 ('Buffalo') Battalion troops on patrol in thick bush. Note the distinctive uniform, based on the Portuguese colonial model. 32 Battalion, composed mostly of Portuguese-speaking black Angolans, was generally used for operations inside Angola.

Above: 201 Battalion soldiers debus from their Buffel as they are fired upon during a patrol in northern SWA 20 Sector near the Angolan border.

Below: The soldiers, having debussed, move against the insurgents to their front. One soldier remains in the Buffel to provide fire support with a heavy machine gun mounted behind the cab while another soldier fires a 60mm patrol mortar at the insurgents.

Above: Method of advance by security forces in line with mixed infantry and APCs, useful in the thick bush of northern SWA to flush out insurgents. This method would also be used when approaching PLAN encampments in Angola; in such cases sappers would precede the advancing forces to clear mines.

Left: 101 Battalion troops on patrol talking with one of the PBs (locals). Security forces not only practised good relations with the local Namibian population, but also strove to develop a rapport with them that often proved invaluable in gathering intelligence on the movements of PLAN infiltrators.

Left: SADF troops take a break by their Buffel APC. Most South African troops in the Operational Area of northern SWA were reservists or conscripts. SADF personnel were used to staff sector headquarters and support elements as well as the five 'modular' battalions in 10 and 20 sector.

Below: 101 Battalion hot pursuit operations into Angola by a 'Romeo Mike' company. Depicted here and overleaf are some of the vehicles of the company headquarters and support section, which consisted of a command vehicle (Casspir armoured car with communications equipment), a mine-protected recovery vehicle, and a mine-protected supply truck. The command section controlled three Romeo Mike teams of four Casspirs each. **Top:** Mine protected recovery vehicle (right) and Casspir, side by side. **Bottom:** Interior of the command Casspir, showing the communications equipment.

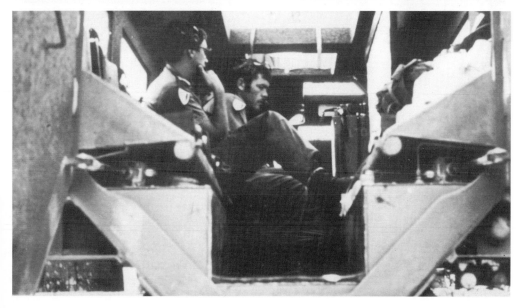

Above: 101 Battalion hot pursuit operations into Angola by a 'Romeo Mike' company. The headquarters section taking a break with members of one of the Romeo Mike teams.

Below: SADF forces withdraw from Angola in September 1988. Here, a G-5 155mm gun moves across a temporary bridge built by SADF engineers across the Kavango River.

Above: Joint Military Monitoring Commission (JMMC) meeting at Ruacana in July 1988, not long after the SADF inflicted a major setback against a combined FAPLA and Cuban force at Techipa.

Below: Patrol boats of the South African Navy (SAN) Marines, a detachment of which was stationed at Mpacha and Katima Mulilo in 70 Sector. The marines provided routine riverine patrols in eastern Caprivi.

Above: Wreckage of Soviet-made Mi-8 helicopter shot down by UNITA near Cuemba, March 1986.

Below: UNITA soldiers pick through the remains of a convoy of the FAPLA 54th Brigade, destroyed in May 1986 at the Lufucasse River in Angola's Moxico province, affixing pictures of Jonas Savimbi to one of the trucks as their 'signature'.

Above: Captured Brazilian-made Engesa truck. Next to the USSR, Brazil furnished FAPLA with the greatest number of logistic vehicles.

Below: FAPLA convoy ambushed by UNITA in Moxico province in 1985 being stripped by the insurgents.

Above: Captured FAPLA vehicles at the Mavinga battlefield, May 1990.

Left: UNITA maintenance facility at Likuwa, near Jamba. Here small arms are being repaired.

Left: André Matsangaisse, first leader of RENAMO.

Above: RENAMO base camp with captured FAM anti-aircraft weapons.

Below: Afonso Dhlakama, RENAMO leader who succeeded Matsangaisse, reviewing some of his fighters.

Above: SPLA commanders prepare an operation using a large-scale model. This allows all involved to work through the planning.

Below: SPLA forces crossing a river in southern Sudan's Equatoria province. In the foreground is a Mercedes truck captured from the Sudanese military.

Above: SPLA troops in bivouac, showing an assortment of vehicles, including wheeled APCs captured from the Sudanese military.

Right: Chadian fighters from Habré's FANT, 1987.

Right: A casualty of the Toyota Wars. A BMP-1 destroyed by the FANT at Fada, January 1987.

Above: A casualty of the Toyota Wars. A jeep mounted with an MRL destroyed by the FANT at Fada, January 1987.

Below: Habré's commanders, including Hassan Djamous (right).

FRELIMO fighters who had already made their way across the Rhodesian border. At this time perhaps one cannot yet speak of any formal organisation calling itself 'RENAMO' but rather of a number of loosely-organised bands of resistance fighters many of whom had the active support of the Rhodesian military. Formal support came later, as Rhodesians sought to capitalise on their psychological warfare broadcasts and clandestine cross-border operations designed to create the impression that there was a sophisticated, highly organised Mozambican resistance. Assistance from the Rhodesians, however, can only in part explain the rapid growth of armed insurgent activity in Mozambique (by 1979 insurgents operated throughout the central parts of the country). The widespread support the Mozambican resistance enjoyed in most regions of Mozambique was due in large part to the repressive policies of the FRELIMO government in its attempt to remake the society and economy of the country, as well as the savage reprisals taken against actual or suspected dissidents. These actions, it should be stressed, were often done by RENAMO as well, either in response to government acts, or to make an example of government supporters to the population.

RENAMO was originally conceived by the Rhodesian Central Intelligence Organisation (CIO) in 1976 as a means to counter the Machel government's support to insurgents of the Zimbabwe African National Union (ZANU) and its armed wing, the Zimbabwe African National Liberation Army (ZANLA). ZANLA was established in bases in Mozambique along the Rhodesian border, and allowed to proceed with its 'rolling infiltration' of eastern Rhodesia from February 1976 onward. Thus the genesis of the proposal: Dissuade the Mozambican government from supporting Rhodesian insurgents by fostering one in Mozambique itself. Anti-regime feeling was steadily rising there as the newly-established government attempted to implement by force a series of ill-advised and unworkable social and political innovations that were creating economic chaos and major social dislocations in the countryside. However, from early 1976 the CIO felt that this anti-regime sentiment was still too weak to find expression in a popular insurgency against the Machel regime.

Hence the need by the Rhodesians to aggravate the anti-regime sentiment by propaganda means. CIO psychological operations personnel had begun transmitting anti-government propaganda from the clandestine Voz da Africa Libre, or 'Voice of Free Africa', in Portuguese, from a transmitter in Gwelo. The station used 'a huge old-fashioned 400 kilowatt transmitter nicknamed *Big Bertha*' for its task, which initially consisted of commentaries on Mozambican Radio Maputo. The staff would monitor the latter's broadcasts and rewrite them, countering the Mozambican government's propaganda efforts with their own commentaries. The new radio station soon became so popular with Mozambicans that the Machel government sought the assistance of East German technicians to jam it. However, the powerful transmitter defied such efforts.

The clandestine Voz da Africa Libre, which claimed to be the radio for the Mozambican National Resistance, was successful in focusing anti-regime sentiment and persuading disgruntled FRELIMO to desert. However, the organisation that they sought to join did not exist, so the Rhodesians created one, beginning training for anti-regime operatives at Odzi near Umtali and furnishing them with arms and supplies. Rhodesian Special Air Service (SAS) personnel eventually took over the training as part of a top secret project beginning in 1977.

The first leader of RENAMO was André Matsangaisse, an ex-FRELIMO platoon commander who had become alienated from Machel's leadership of the party. The Mozambican government later stressed that Matsangaisse had been punished for theft and expelled from the armed forces and placed in a re-education camp at Gorongosa, although RENAMO asserts that the actual reason for his punishment, which included imprisonment, was objection to government policies. Like his successor, Afonso Dhlakama, Matsangaisse, or 'Commander André,' as his subordinates called him, joined FRELIMO out of nationalist motives, but became increasingly disillusioned with Machel's leadership of the movement and then abandoned FRELIMO after it began to destroy Mozambican society in an attempt to remake it as a 'Marxist' entity.

Matsangaisse, on escaping from detention, made his way to Umtali and the Rhodesians, and was immediately recognised as a strong potential leader for the new resistance movement. One of his first acts in this capacity was to lead a raid against the detention camp at Gorongosa from which he had escaped, freeing over 500 prisoners, most of them ex-FRELIMO fighters. At least 300 decided to follow Matsangaisse back to Rhodesia. This group, along with the cadre already trained, were the first RENAMO fighters. The raid on Gorongosa also established Matsangaisse as the movement's leader. Personally popular, and with continued assistance from the Rhodesians, Matsangaisse rapidly gained support for the armed resistance he began to conduct in Sofala province. The term for the RENAMO insurgents, the 'Matsangas', used throughout much of the country, was a continuing term of respect for Matsangaisse's memory.

By 1978 armed conflict was prevalent throughout the central part of the country, and only part of it due to the Rhodesian-backed insurgents. Unrest was caused by a number of groups. In the provinces of Niassa and Tete, for example, the Mozambican Revolutionary Party (Partido Revolucionario de Mocambique, PRM), was active from May of that year, while at the same time elements of the Makonde ethnic group in northern Mozambique were also in open rebellion against the government. Much of the resistance was apparently inspired by traditional leaders under attack by the government. However, by the end of the 1970s the surviving resistance elements inside Mozambique were increasingly dominated by RENAMO.[7]

RENAMO'S RELATIONSHIP WITH RHODESIAN SECURITY FORCES[8]

RENAMO, organised and supported by Rhodesian military intelligence, has been labelled a 'created insurgency,' and to a great extent this sobriquet is justified. However, it began to enjoy considerable independent success due to widespread resistance by the Mozambican population to government policy, especially that in rural areas. It should be stressed, however, that antipathy to FRELIMO and its programmes, as well as support, often varied from one locality to another, and was influenced by a number of factors ranging from ethnic affiliation to local economic structures. Where it did occur, support for RENAMO often stemmed from reaction to FRELIMO's social engineering policies and to the economic ruin brought about by the government's gross mismanagement of industry and commerce. Without widespread popular discontent with FRELIMO to exploit, RENAMO could not have developed a firm support base among Mozambicans. On the other hand, it has been repeatedly and convincingly documented that the Rhodesian security forces actively created and promoted organised armed dissidence against the FRELIMO government to serve their own interests.

There were two obvious benefits for the Rhodesians in their support for anti-regime insurgents in Mozambique, both connected with the fact that the MNR would have to maintain contact in order to keep receiving weapons and supplies. The first benefit was realised in intelligence about ZANLA insurgents' base camps and logistic networks in Mozambique, especially in Manica province, also the focus of most early MNR activity. Such information as was provided by anti-regime insurgents in Mozambique was used both in estimates of insurgent capabilities and in planning Rhodesian military operations. The second benefit was in the area of Rhodesian COIN operations. These took the form either of 'pseudo-operations,' in which special units masquerading as guerrillas operated on the Mozambican side of the border, or of pursuit operations in reaction to ZANLA activity in the Rhodesian border region. In these operations the assistance of MNR cadres as guides and in providing tactical intelligence was valuable. Finally, an indirect benefit to the Rhodesians was the destabilisation to Mozambican government control of areas in which the MNR operated, and the potential political leverage that existed considering the obvious, but unspoken, linkage between Maputo's support of ZANLA and Salisbury's support to the MNR. However, by the late 1970s FRELIMO was of the belief that continued support to ZANLA, despite the problems posed by the MNR, would be of more long-term benefit than curbing it to accommodate Rhodesia. Maputo rightly figured that the Rhodesian government's days were numbered, and that a change of regime would end support for the MNR from that quarter. However, it made a fatal error in assuming that this would result in the collapse of the insurgents.

From the start the MNR also benefited from their contact with the Rhodesians, utilising the latter's expertise and infrastructure in training and organising their force in the late 1970s. The first major operations by combined MNR and Rhodesian forces began in January 1979 with attacks on the Mavuzi hydroelectric station near the Chicamba Real Dam in Manica province. From this time on SAS personnel continued operations with the MNR and frequently would be attached in small groups with the insurgents to assist them in training and operational matters.[9]

OVERVIEW OF THE INSURGENCY FROM 1979 THROUGH EARLY 1981

This stage of the Mozambican insurgency was still dominated by Rhodesian interests, although subsequent events indicate that negotiations were underway between the Rhodesian military and CIO with South Africa to transfer control of the insurgents in the event of a change of government (and policy) in Salisbury. Main developments in 1979–1980 included:

■ Increased efforts by government security forces to counter the spread of the MNR outside Manica and Sofala.
■ The first major operations by the MNR against targets outside the Rhodesian border region.
■ Development of a major base complex by the MNR in northern Sofala in the Gorongosa national park area.
■ The major subsequent developments in this phase of the conflict were the change of government in Rhodesia-Zimbabwe and the decision of the newly-independent regime there to support FRELIMO in its struggle with RENAMO.

By early 1979 the FRELIMO government was forced to admit that it had a serious security problem throughout the country caused by armed dissidents. At this time various media reports call it the Mozambican Resistance Movement (MRM) or the Mozambican National Resistance (MNR), and even the Mozambican National Resistance Army (MNRA).[10]

FRELIMO attempted to counter internal security threats by increasing the size of its armed forces as well as forming a police force (the People's Police of Mozambique, or PPM).[11]

However, increased security measures by the government proved ineffective. The insurgents operated throughout Mozambique,with the centre of their power in Manica, Sofala, Zambezia, and Tete provinces. Early accounts of fighting in the border areas are often difficult to sort out, as much of it was due to cross-border raids by Rhodesian security forces in pursuit of anti-regime insurgents based in Mozambique.

The first major RENAMO action to attract world media attention was the 23 March 1979 attack on the outskirts of Beira. In reality the critical part of the operation was done by Rhodesian security personnel. However, the following month FRELIMO identified the insurgents as the Mozambican National Resistance, or MNR, and claimed that it was formed from black dissidents and white Portuguese who were supported by Rhodesia. Its headquarters was located in the Gorongosa Massif south of the lower Zambezi River, and was the target of a 10 April FAM operation (apparently unsuccessful). At this time the MNR's actions began to become known through broadcasts from the Voice of Free Africa radio station, located in Salisbury, Rhodesia. FRELIMO claimed that the MNR was headed by one Domingos Arouca and six former FRELIMO commanders. Before 1978, FRELIMO claimed, the insurgents had called themselves the United Democratic Front (UDF) of Mozambique.[12]

The Beira attack was soon followed by other insurgent actions, including the April 1979 sabotage of the Tete–Mutarara rail line, apparently the action that prompted the FAM attack against suspected MNR camps in the Gorongosa. By July news accounts began to identify 'Commander André Matade Matsangaisse' as RENAMO leader. Interviews from this time record his claims that the movement, called the Mozambican Resistance Movement, was an anti-communist, all-black insurgency. Matsangaisse claimed operations in the regions of Beira, Tete, Chimoio, and Maputo. He also admitted to unspecified foreign support.[13]

By September 1979 fighting had begun to centre in the area north of the Gorongosa Massif, 100km east of the Rhodesian border, around the town of Macossa. which later fell to the MNR. These and other local insurgent successes prompted a series of operations against the MNR in October and November, including a second FAM attack against the Gorongosa Massif and MNR camps there on 3 November. Despite such actions by the FAM, the insurgents continued to claim widespread successes against the government.[14]

By this time the FAM was well aware of its inadequacies in dealing with the ever-spreading insurgency. It had earlier established 'resettlement camps' in Niassa province for suspected insurgents and their families released from 're-education facilities,' but this policy was unworkable due to the deteriorating security situation. The FAM was at this time a relatively small (20,000–24,000) force trained along conventional lines and armed with Soviet-made equipment. It was not trained or equipped to fight a COIN war. Machel and his supporters had even refused to implement a formal rank structure for the new force until the need for such became overwhelmingly necessary in 1980. Rank structures were announced on 25 September. At that time an officer corps was created as well. Such changes, though more than cosmetic, were still inadequate to deal with the deteriorating security situation created by the MNR.[15]

In late 1979–early 1980 the MNR was claimed by the government to have 4,000 effective troops. News media began to increasingly report its activities throughout the country; it was also known as the MRM (Mozambican Resistance Movement) or the 'André Group,' from its leader. FRELIMO admitted that the insurgency, which it claimed to have been founded in 1975, was the main internal security threat. The ferocity of the conflict was already apparent as reports of atrocities by the insurgents were publicised by the Mozambican government.[16]

By this time RENAMO had recruited many who had suffered greatly at the hands of the Machel regime, and their antipathy was evident in their actions. Just as Rhodesia used to attract anti-regime fugitives, the newly-independent Zimbabwe began to see FRELIMO refugees, who told of increasing control by the insurgents of the opposite border areas of Mozambique. Much insurgent hatred was focused upon FRELIMO, evident in the attack on Espungabera (on the border with Zimbabwe, about 150km south-south-east of Chimoio) on 1 December 1979. FRELIMO officials and sympathisers who were caught were decapitated and their heads impaled on stakes. All government facilities and infrastructure were destroyed wherever possible.[17]

In the late 1970s insurgent strategy and tactics were taking the shape they would have for the rest of the war. Infrastructure such as railways, bridges, and power stations and lines were targeted. The centre of RENAMO's operations was that area extending from the

Mozambique-Zimbabwe border north in a large arc through the Manica highlands and the Gorongosa Massif across the Zambezi River to the southern tip of Malawi. Here the number of incidents reported, especially those contacts initiated by RENAMO, was greatest. Rail lines and other communications were repeatedly hit by RENAMO and FAM made little or no attempt to effectively protect known targets. For instance, in September 1979 the Umtali (Mutare)–Beira rail line was cut and a train derailed; the insurgents were able to repeat this operation in almost the same manner in October with no interference from the FAM. Another tempting target proved to be the power lines serving Mozambique from the Cabora Bassa dam. Through mid-1980 Manica and Sofala took the brunt of MNR attacks, despite a joint Mozambique-Zimbabwe agreement to patrol their common border.[18]

This latter presaged another feature of the Mozambican insurgency that persisted to the end of the war: the involvement of Zimbabwe's armed forces. Newly independent in 1980, the Zimbabwean government was determined to use the Mutare–Beira railway as well as the road and pipeline in the 'Beira corridor' to reduce its dependence upon South African ports. It thus began to coordinate patrols, then soon to conduct joint operations, with the FAM to attempt to control the 1,250km common border and deny MNR insurgents, who targeted Beira corridor facilities, refuge inside Zimbabwe, where many former Rhodesian supporters remained. Insurgent operatives were already familiar with the Rhodesian border regions, as many of them had been trained at camps opposite the main points of entry into Mozambique.[19]

Zimbabwe's involvement followed a major blow to the MNR. The Espungabera attack discussed above (1 December 1979) was to be the last successful MNR operation for some time. From late 1979 to the end of 1980 the insurgency almost collapsed. This was in part due to the loss of Rhodesian support when Rhodesia became Zimbabwe; the new government, which took power in early 1980, was friendly to FRELIMO, which had assisted Zimbabwean insurgents. In February 1980 most of the support infrastructure including the MNR radio was clandestinely removed to South Africa. This shift no doubt caused a hiatus in support, both moral and material. The immediate cause of the insurgents' problems, however, was the death of Matsangaisse on 18 October 1979 in the course of a FAM attack on the main MNR base at the Gorongosa Massif. The base, which fell on 22 October, had been under attack since the start of the month and the operation required a massive commitment of FAM resources. Despite substantial covert aid from Rhodesia, the base had to be abandoned. All non-Mozambicans were airlifted out by helicopter the same day as Matsangaisse was mortally wounded in the base's defence.[20]

1980 was to be a fateful year for all parties in the insurgency – FRELIMO, the MNR insurgents, Zimbabwe, and the South Africans, who were now the main external supporters of the MNR. FRELIMO had apparently thought that the insurgents would collapse due to their loss of Rhodesian support and the assistance to the FAM of Zimbabwe's armed forces. However, the fighting continued. In May Espungabera was again occupied by the insurgents. The MNR had apparently far more than the 4,000 effectives claimed by the government, but an exact estimate of insurgent strength at this time is not possible. In the wake of Matsangaisse's death the movement had fragmented, and the extent of groups affiliated with the MNR is hard to determine, as is overall insurgent strength. Government successes against insurgent bases continue to take their toll, however. In July the FAM attacked the Sitatonga Mountain camp of the MNR, which had become the main MNR base, overrunning it on the 9th and claiming 272 insurgents killed and 300 captured–a major defeat for the guerrillas. This FAM operation was one of number of coordinated anti-insurgent moves along the border against the MNR, and certainly one of the most successful.[21]

Under South African tutelage the insurgents once again took the offensive by mid-1981. Until this time, however, FRELIMO enjoyed some success in regaining the initiative in the fighting with the MNR. While the impact of Matsangaisse's death was undoubtedly a major shock to the MNR's structure and capabilities, accounts which claim only several hundred active operatives remaining inside Mozambique are probably exaggerated. Some MNR groups had remained capable enough, occupying Espungabera in May of 1980, for instance. Others doubtless turned to banditry, as some accounts claimed. Documentation for this period is poor and often contradictory, but what is evident is the temporary ascendancy of the FAM in the conflict. FRELIMO's armed forces were able to actively prosecute the war against the insurgents in the wake of the shift of power from Rhodesia to Zimbabwe, and also took advantage of military cooperation with their now-friendly neighbour to the west. South Africa had apparently at this time not yet developed a coherent programme to support the MNR, although it had assumed the take-over responsibilities from the Rhodesians. During the period following Matsangaisse's death, the South Africans appear to have remained aloof from the secession struggles, but finally decided to support Afonso Dhlakama, deputy to Matsangaisse, in his bid to lead RENAMO. In the meantime, subsequent developments suggest that FRELIMO and the FAM became somewhat complacent in the wake of their successes at Gorongosa, Sitatonga, and elsewhere, believing that RENAMO had been decisively beaten.[22]

SOUTH AFRICAN SUPPORT AND RENAMO EXPANSION, 1980–1984

The South African phase of direct support to RENAMO lasted from 1980 to early 1984. This period can be characterised by several key developments:

■ Cessation of any organised support from former Rhodesia (see above);
■ The assumption of RENAMO's external basing by South Africa, with its training and external support facilities provided by the South African Defence Force (SADF) at bases in the eastern Transvaal region of South Africa;
■ The rapid rehabilitation of RENAMO by the end of 1980 and reinsertion of insurgents into southern Manica province first through the Garagua area and later other bases;
■ The development of an extensive logistical network in southern Manica that later spread north and east to the Zambezi to support a growing number of base camps;
■ Spread of the insurgency to southern Mozambique from bases in northern Gaza;
■ Spread of the insurgency northward into Zambezia and Tete from bases in northern Manica and Sofala, with additional support attributed by FRELIMO to bases in Malawi operated by South African military intelligence;
■ The continued inability of the FAM to prevent the spread of the insurgency and the emergence of major differences within FRELIMO and the FAM as to how to address the problem;
■ The tactical initiative passed to RENAMO by late 1983–early 1984, with the insurgents initiating well over half of the number of contacts with FAM.

With the transfer of support from Rhodesia to South Africa, the revitalisation of the MNR (now increasingly called RENAMO) went hand in hand with its direction toward a new end. This latter was the desire of South Africa's government to gain the upper hand in regional affairs and thereby counter what it perceived to be Soviet-backed efforts to dominate southern Africa. The ascendancy in the RSA of the NP government of Pieter Willem Botha, the former Minister of Defence, and a number of like-minded military men, including Minister of Defence Magnus Malan, promoted the development of an elaborate internal security management system designed to counter Soviet-backed efforts to destabilise South Africa. The Soviet (and surrogate) challenge to South Africa's regional role was matched by a policy developed by the South African government to destabilise neighbouring regimes that harboured black nationalist groups such as SWAPO and the ANC. The latter, prominently supported by FRELIMO, were regarded as a particular threat in the form of terrorist attacks within the Republic. Despite FRELIMO's ostensible agreement not to support active anti-regime groups by giving them sanctuary and facilities, by the early 1980s the ANC and other opposition groups were established in Mozambique. They were well-supplied by the Soviets with FRELIMO benefiting from its role as a surrogate. Doubtless this consideration was foremost in South Africa's decision to support RENAMO - to match destabilisation with destabilisation.[23]

However, amid the outward hardening of attitudes between the RSA and the black governments of other southern African states that characterised this period, the beginnings of change were afoot for Mozambique's political orientation. Machel and FRELIMO had, from 1980, attempted to make Mozambique a member of the Communist bloc's Council for Mutual Economic Assistance (better known by its acronym, COMECON) in the hope of realising economic benefits for development assistance from this action. However, the Soviet Union and its allies rejected Mozambique's application for COMECON membership, and relegated Machel's government to observer status only. As Mozambique's economic position continued its decline, and as RENAMO activity continued to increase, Machel sought ways to attract foreign capital by beginning to shift his political alignment away from the East Bloc and toward a 'nonaligned' posture. In reality, this change signified a willingness of Mozambique to accept Western capital and investment. However, by the early 1980s the security situation continued to deteriorate and Western investors remained reluctant. It was obvious to all inside FRELIMO that steps ultimately had to be taken to improve the security of foreign business and investment.

Meanwhile, RENAMO continued to make gains against the central government. South African support for the insurgents was quite beneficial to them, and went far beyond simply preventing their collapse into bands of bandits. An initial period, marked by a general loss of momentum, followed the transfer of RENAMO from Rhodesian to South African tutelage as the insurgents reorganised and relocated many of their bases. South African military intelligence also provided training for RENAMO at bases in the eastern Transvaal. From mid-1981 onward RENAMO began a revival, acquiring victory after victory over the FAM, despite increasing levels of Zimbabwean military assistance and the introduction of ZNA troops into Mozambique in 1982. By mid-June 1981 there was fighting along the border east of the Zimbabwe town of Chipinge; 3,000 RENAMO fighters were estimated by the FAM to be in the vicinity of Espungabera alone. Refugees from the fighting in border areas were fleeing into Zimbabwe, and doubtless among these were RENAMO infiltrators gathering intelligence and building informant networks among expatriate Mozambicans. By August–September 1981 the insurgents (probably with considerable expatriate assistance) distributed a political programme espousing a multiparty democratic Mozambique with a free market economy. Fighting by that time had expanded, with the zone of the most intense combat taking place in a 150km square bounded in the west by the Zimbabwe border, in the south by the Save River, in the east by the Indian Ocean, and in the north by the Beira corridor.[24]

Indeed, the rapid regeneration of the Mozambican resistance had been phenomenal, even in light of the massive external assistance the movement had been receiving. By the end of 1980 the South Africans had established a large-scale effort to train insurgents in the eastern Transvaal and elsewhere, and had put into place a supply network to sustain the growing numbers of Mozambican insurgents who were cycled through their training camps. The initial focal point of insurgent activity was based on Garagua, in southern Manica province. This large base, well east of the mountains, was an entrepot for resupply from South Africa, and in turn supported a spreading network of insurgent base camps. By the following year, some estimates of RENAMO strength ran as high as 6,000 to 7,000.[25] But for this revival the insurgents paid a price, namely that of subordination to the South African security structure, in particular that of the South African Army (SAA) and its 5th

Reconnaissance Regiment (Special Forces) at Phalaborwa in the eastern Transvaal. South African plans for RENAMO required close management of the insurgent external structure, especially in the areas of training, logistics, and the RENAMO propaganda machine.[26]

Some continuing connections with, and support from ex-Rhodesian security force members for, RENAMO apparently persisted into the early 1980s. One example of support to RENAMO was the 29 October 1981 destruction of bridges on the railway and road in the Beira corridor that blocked a shipment of equipment for the ZNA. This shipment was destined for the North Korean-trained 5th Brigade operating against insurgents in the Matabeleland region of Zimbabwe, and RENAMO's action seriously disrupted ZNA operations there. On the Zimbabwean side, the Umtali (Mutare) Special Branch regional chief, who had held the post since the late 1970s, was subsequently claimed to have been implicated in this action.[27]

1981 closed with the FAM capture of Garagua base in Manica province. Following a week-long operation, Garagua was overrun on 7 December. Of particular value to the FAM were documents that had been hastily discarded in a latrine. These, claimed the FAM, indicated extensive support by the South Africans to RENAMO. Despite the Garagua action, RENAMO activity continued to spread and intensify throughout Mozambique.[28]

South African support from late 1981 gave RENAMO the impetus it needed to spread its operations rapidly. The early operations through 1981 had been largely in Manica and Sofala provinces, which were sparsely populated. The move by RENAMO into northern and eastern Inhambane took advantage of the largely undeveloped nature of the province. The insurgents were able to establish a well-defined network of base camps and logistical routes, but were not able to expand their activities to more populated areas. This situation changed with South African support. RENAMO made several attempts to cut off the Maputo area from the rest of Mozambique in early and mid-1982, but enjoyed only limited success (see below).[29]

In March 1982 FRELIMO, ever more aware of the insurgent threat, reorganised the FAM, creating the post of FAM Deputy Chief of Staff and ten provincial military commanders. Efforts to improve the morale and conditions of service of FAM soldiers, even including the publication of a magazine, *Combat*, were also implemented. The FAM restructuring and other steps were undertaken with the aim of improving command and control of local operations and combat effectiveness. Also part of the programme was the recall of at least 1,500 former FRELIMO fighters to the military, and the formation of a militia under provincial command. This was the first big military reorganisation since independence; the next would take place in 1987. FAM was attempting to respond to RENAMO's increasingly frequent attacks on large towns and the garrisons based there; previously the insurgents had mostly targeted rural villages. The pattern of attacks was ruthlessly effective. Government and party officials were killed, sometimes quite cruelly; health workers and teachers were also not spared. All physical infrastructure representing the central government's presence was destroyed or damaged beyond repair. FRELIMO by this time admitted to RENAMO activity in six of the ten provinces of Mozambique, although the insurgents themselves claimed to operate freely throughout the country. Despite the central government's efforts to counter the growing RENAMO threat, the insurgents in 1983 were able to establish bases in the key provinces of Zambezia and Nampula.[30]

The military reorganisation came amid bitter political infighting within FRELIMO. The Fourth Congress of the party, held from 26 to 30 April 1983, resulted in the demotion of a number of top leaders who had dominated the party hierarchy since before independence and had been blamed for much of the crisis in defence and economic issues. At the same time, FRELIMO attempted to broaden its popular base by expanding its Central Committee membership from 65 to 130, most of whom were from Mozambique's rural regions and thus directly in contact with constituents who suffered from the spread of

RENAMO activities. Despite these changes, the Congress reaffirmed Marxism-Leninism as its guiding philosophy.[31]

Through all of this, the debate between opposing factions within the FRELIMO government and the FAM as to the best approach to RENAMO continued to rage. The hardliners in FRELIMO desired no compromise with the insurgents or their demands, and in the end the only major concession the government was able to make to RENAMO fighters was the promise of an amnesty. Although many in the FAM argued for countering RENAMO with a COIN doctrine, through the early and mid-1980s the emphasis in training the FAM, especially at the main military academy at Nampula, was on conventional Warsaw Pact doctrine. This general unwillingness to adopt a flexible approach in countering RENAMO was also manifested in continued attempts to 'villagise' elements of the rural population for security or other reasons, and to continue FRELIMO's social programmes. As a result, large portions of the general population remained alienated from the government, often fleeing into the bush to avoid forced relocation, and thus often predisposed to support the insurgents.[32]

This is not to imply, however, that the insurgents were welcomed with open arms everywhere. Ethnic and regional differences, as well as political factors, between the insurgents and the populations of target areas often resulted in actions by RENAMO against civilians that frequently exceeded acts of brutality by FAM troops (see below). Already by the early 1980s the conduct of the war, especially with respect to the widely-publicised incidents of RENAMO atrocities, had become a major issue in international public opinion. Dhlakama's delegation of considerable discretionary authority to his regional and provincial commanders continued to act against any efforts to improve guerrilla troop control and conduct. Still, atrocities against the civilian population continued, with many of the worst excesses being conscious acts to terrorise the local population.

The human rights aspect aside, however, RENAMO's modus operandi proved quite effective in helping to establish its control, often garnering it support out of fear if for no other reason. However, its defenders emphasised those aspects of RENAMO activity among sympathetic elements of the Mozambican population that the insurgents wanted the rest of the world to see. By the early 1980s RENAMO was beginning to receive outside attention. Reports began to surface from sympathetic visitors as well as Europeans who had been captured by RENAMO during operations. Most noted that the insurgents were well-armed and fed (often producing their own food), armed for the most part with captured light infantry weapons, especially Soviet-made AK-47s or other communist country copies, plus land mines, light machine guns, and mortars. A system of base camps each supporting a local RENAMO force dotted the countryside of central Mozambique, forming a loose but interlocking network of territorial control in the rural areas. FRELIMO was left with control of the towns and cities. Much of Mozambique, however, was not effectively controlled by either side, and from these areas increasing numbers of the local population were fleeing to towns and cities, or to neighbouring countries, to escape the continuing fighting and man-made famine resulting from the disruption of agriculture over wide areas.[33]

By 1982 the effects of improved training and support, reportedly in great part from South Africa, was having a telling effect against Mozambican government security forces. The Beira Corridor was increasingly threatened by RENAMO, prompting a ZNA-aided FAM operation announced on 31 May, in which at least 3,000 FAM troops were sent to Beira to assist local forces to keep the route to Zimbabwe open. Facing them were at least 2,000 RENAMO in northern Manica province alone. Increasingly stymied by RENAMO, the FAM leadership took the unusual step later that summer of recalling 1,500 demobilised FRELIMO guerrillas to bolster its forces. By that time RENAMO, now at least 12,000 strong, controlled much of Gaza and Zambezia provinces in addition to its original core area in

Sofala and Manica, and had begun to probe southward into Inhambane and initiate operations near Maputo. As noted above, however, these insurgent operations, directed primarily at the lower Limpopo River valley, had limited success, despite their proximity to South African-supported logistical networks further west.[34]

Further north, however, RENAMO began to expand operations dramatically in Tete and Zambezia provinces. South African-supported base camps had been established in southern Malawi, and RENAMO used these to launch a series of operations against central Mozambican sites in September and October 1982. The tea and cotton producing areas around Gurue in northern Zambezia were hit, as well as the coastal areas around Quelimane. However, the RENAMO offensive collapsed in mid-November after the base camps were closed by Malawi after negotiations with FRELIMO. This followed an operation by the FAM near the Malawi border that overran the main RENAMO base camp in western Zambezia on 2 November.[35]

FAM operations, however, were not able to contain RENAMO's spread, nor the insurgents' successes in the field. In January 1983 the RENAMO self-styled Department of Defence claimed that in 1982 its forces had fought in 1,582 actions and had initiated 123 acts of railway sabotage and destroyed 57 trains. It further claimed that it had killed 1,521 FAM. In his New Year's address RENAMO President Dhlakama stated that RENAMO had consolidated its gains in Sofala and Gaza provinces, and had established itself in Maputo, Tete, and Zambezia provinces. The crisis of the FRELIMO government was underscored by a study by the Pretoria-based Institute of Strategic Studies that noted that FRELIMO had more trained fighters at the end of 1982–11,000 to 13,000–than FRELIMO had had at the height of its insurgency against the Portuguese.[36]

Despite the slight downturn in RENAMO fortunes by late 1982, the spread of the insurgency continued throughout the country. In Zambezia and neighbouring regions this was apparently due in large part to the Machel regime's inability at this stage to remedy the effects of earlier Marxist-style social programmes or to curb often savage reprisals by security forces against rural communities suspected of supporting the insurgents in areas of RENAMO activity. Much of Mozambique, especially the central part of the country, was at any rate by now beyond the effective reach of central government control and administration. Many rural dwellers continued to be alienated by FRELIMO and provided ready recruits for the insurgents. For this reason the above-mentioned insurgent expansion in northern Zambezia was only temporarily halted by the November closure of RENAMO's Malawi base camps. The presence of RENAMO operatives who had infiltrated into the area continued to support insurgent activity there. The penetration of some RENAMO units to the coast north of Quelimane facilitated resupply by sea. By the end of the year RENAMO units were firmly emplaced in the Gurue area, and had begun destroying the cotton and tea industrial infrastructure there. Air resupply, reportedly from Malawi and South Africa, continued. By mid-1983 RENAMO had begun operations in Nampula province, threatening the Nacala railway.[37]

By 1983 RENAMO had at least 5,000 to 6,000 trained personnel in Mozambique, based in a network of hundreds of camps. These latter spanned the country from the Zimbabwe border east to the Indian Ocean and the mid-section of Mozambique as far as the three northern provinces of Cabo Delgado, Nampula, and Niassa. In the south, the insurgents had begun to probe into Inhambane and parts of Gaza provinces, although in many areas here support for the government remained strong. Central Mozambique, however, remained RENAMO's stronghold. But, even here, there were no 'liberated zones' as such (as in Angola with UNITA), namely areas where RENAMO had not only expelled FRELIMO garrisons and administration and installed their own infrastructure, but was able to prevent invasion and reoccupation by government forces. South Africa continued to be RENAMO's main foreign supplier. With South African training and logistical support, the insurgents were moving their areas of control ever southward into Inhambane. Even staunch supporters of FRELIMO admitted that RENAMO, to do this, enjoyed considerable local support or took advantage of dissatisfaction with government policies.[38]

In August 1983 a major offensive was announced by the FAM in Zambezia. Although the reporting was in routine format and government security forces were predictably noted as conducting a successful operation, the action was indicative of a major strategic shift in the fighting. RENAMO had by this time broken out of the earlier area of fighting bounded on the west by the Zimbabwe border, and had begun to operate in the lower Zambezi valley and inflict significant damage to the economic infrastructure there. Its overt military actions there and elsewhere were preceded by a series of infiltrations by RENAMO cadres, organisation of local resistance, and development of base camps and logistics networks, all of which took months.[39]

Continuing FAM activity in August and September against RENAMO also focused upon another new crisis area, northern Inhambane province, where base camps south of the Save River had been established at Mabote, Vilanculos, and Nova Mambone; smaller RENAMO camps were also reported throughout the province, including to the south near Jangamo, in the vicinity of the provincial capital itself, Inhambane city. However, despite impressive initial gains in southern Mozambique, the RENAMO offensive was hampered by poor weather that degraded or delayed operations, in addition to frequent lack of support by the local populations. Also damaging to RENAMO was the FAM capture of the Tome base camp in August 1983; Tome had been a major centre for controlling operations in southern Inhambane, southern Gaza, and Maputo provinces. FAM provincial and local commanders in southern Mozambique also had the added benefit of support from the generally pro-FRELIMO local population, which prevented RENAMO from establishing itself there.[40]

In retrospect the FAM offensives of 1983 in central and southern Mozambique can be seen as desperate steps in countering an insurgency that was rapidly spreading and well-nigh impossible for government security forces to control. An ambitious offensive, called 'The 50th Birthday of President Samora Machel,' was launched in October in Gaza, Inhambane, Sofala, and Manica provinces, but was only able to claim 318 insurgents killed, 102 captured, and 222 weapons captured for its efforts in the vast area south of the Zambezi and north of the Limpopo. Base camps in the vicinity of Ati and Mongoro (Gaza), Chinhica (Manica), Muanza (Sofala), and Tome (Inhambane) were listed as captured.[41] At the capture of Tome base camp, on 23 August, the FAM apprehended seventeen-year old Alexandre Zaqueu, who claimed that he had been kidnapped and forcibly impressed into RENAMO. His statements, as reported in the government press, indicate frequent air resupply, usually by parachute, to RENAMO bases. In addition, Zaqueu also said that whites, probably South Africans, instructed RENAMO in the use of radio equipment; sophisticated British Racal radios began to be recovered by the FAM during operations from this period.[42]

By early 1984 RENAMO had clearly bested the FAM in central Mozambique, not only in promoting the South Africans' agenda of destabilising the FRELIMO government, but in its own members' desire to rid themselves of any traces of central government rule. FRELIMO's inability to moderate its programmes for restructuring Mozambique's social and economic life continued to arouse considerable antipathy among the population, especially that in rural areas. Despite the increasing cooperation of Zimbabwe's security forces the insurgents continued to operate freely in Manica, and even began to operate across the border into Zimbabwe.[43]

The FAM, armed and trained for conventional war, was increasingly unable to protect RENAMO targets. Security forces were tied down guarding priority towns and facilities, while the insurgents were free to roam the countryside and strike at will. Apart from FRELIMO's labelling of RENAMO as the kizimba, or 'hyaena,' bandits, in the propaganda war, little effective action could be undertaken. The insurgents continued their now-typical pattern of terror in their operations. One example was in the capture of Maringue, Sofala province, on Christmas Eve 1983, where suspected FRELIMO sympathisers and military trainees were decapitated and the heads impaled on stakes while other civilians were forced to watch. In the south, RENAMO continued to expand, but at a slower pace than further north. In December FAM provincial forces operated against base camps near Malaissa, in the vicinity of Inhambane city itself.[44]

The continued inability of the FAM to stop RENAMO's spread was paralleled by the unwillingness of Zimbabwe to actively assist its neighbour by committing troops in a combat role, despite the deployment in 1982 of troops to guard key points along the Beira corridor. The compelling evidence of South African support to RENAMO doubtless led Zimbabwe to consider its own position–Zimbabwe itself was facing a low-level insurgency in Matabeleland, on the border with South Africa. The latter could have caused this security problem to intensify markedly should it have wished. Thus Zimbabwe focused upon its own security problems first and abstained from extensive involvement with Mozambique. The latter was unable, despite increased levels of military assistance from the Soviet Union and its allies, and even from Portugal, to train and field troops capable of containing the South African-supported RENAMO troops. South Africa, for its part, desired Mozambique to cease harbouring operatives of the African National Congress (ANC) on its territory. Thus, by late winter 1984, FRELIMO decided to open serious negotiations with the South African government designed to ensure that each government would cease support for the other's dissidents. On 16 March 1984, Mozambique and South Africa signed the Nkomati Accords, designed to normalise relations between the two governments under the conditions noted above. Many thought that this would signify the subsequent collapse of RENAMO, but events proved just the opposite.[45]

HISTORY OF THE INSURGENCY FROM THE NKOMATI ACCORDS TO LATE 1986/EARLY 1987

The insurgency from the Nkomati Accords to the late 1980s was marked by a number of important developments:

■ South Africa withdrew formal government support to RENAMO, but some elements within the government, especially Military Intelligence, continued to support the insurgents.
■ RENAMO, bereft of South African help, remained a viable insurgent organisation, but with redirected strategic goals.
■ RENAMO also began to receive outside assistance to replace that lost with the Nkomati Accords, and struggled to build an external lobby independent of South African control. The external RENAMO support community was often riven with internal disputes as a result.
■ Zimbabwe intervened militarily in the war, occupying the Beira corridor and assisting the FAM in large-scale offensives against RENAMO targets.
■ In October 1986 President Machel was killed in an aeroplane crash; his successor, Joaquim Chissano, began to attempt a restructuring of the FAM the better to counter RENAMO; at the same time Chissano and the FRELIMO leadership began to implement reforms to reverse many of the programmes of the Machel era.
■ In addition to Zimbabwe, Zambia, Malawi, and Tanzania all provided help to Mozambique in the form of troops and military assistance.
■ British and Portuguese military training assistance was provided to the FAM.

As the summer of 1984 progressed it became obvious to most observers that RENAMO would not collapse, despite the ostensible removal of South African aid. Although convincing claims were made by the Mozambican government that much of this assistance still was provided by the South African government, only more covertly,[46] it was also quite evident that RENAMO had become to a large degree self-sustaining. It captured most of its weapons from the FAM and either produced its own food staples or received them as taxes from the rural population. FRELIMO, however, was practically exhausted, unable to defend its rural infrastructure from the depredations of RENAMO nor able to recapture lost rural areas. By early 1985 RENAMO was initiating 85 per cent of the contacts with FAM units.[47]

Any claims of continued South African support aside, RENAMO had been given a 'golden handshake' by South African military intelligence immediately before the signing of the Nkomati Accords–two years' worth of weapons, ammunition and other supplies. By the end of 1984 RENAMO was active in all but the extreme north of Mozambique. It controlled over 85 per cent of the rural population and confined FRELIMO to the towns in most areas. The far-flung guerrilla units were controlled from the Gorongosa Massif in the old game park in northern Sofala province. The Gorongosa Mountains there rose sharply from the surrounding forest; covered with dense jungle, the rugged terrain was a natural haven for the insurgents. By the early 1980s at least four major RENAMO base camps had become established there, all ranged around an airfield capable of accommo-dating small transport planes. (It was believed that South Africa continued to resupply the insurgents after Nkomati via this airfield by flights from the Comoros.) The Goron-gosa base complex itself consisted of administrative, medical, logistics, and training centres. The central base, Casa Banana, also nicknamed Casa Branca, or 'The White House,' accommodated RENAMO headquarters and at least 1,000 insurgents. From this central post Dhlakama and his staff could contact other provincial commanders as well as RENAMO personnel abroad via radio. The base even printed its own propaganda leaflets, which were distributed over most of the northern two-thirds of Manica-Sofala and parts of neighbouring Zambezia and Tete.[48]

Of grave concern also to the Mozambican government as well as others who wished to see the Nkomati Accords work was the progressive uncovering and documentation by the South African government of an extensive international network providing support for RENAMO. This organisation, which used counterfeit US dollars and South African rands to purchase arms and other equipment for the insurgents, involved businessmen not only in Africa but in Latin America and Europe as well. Much of it continued to involve the large South African Portuguese community. More problematic for the South African government was increasing evidence that elements of the SADF, in particular within its military intelli-gence organisation (CSI), continued to supply the Mozambican insurgents. Despite calls by Mozambique and other regional states to South Africa to enforce its part in the Nkomati Accords, little apart from the announcement of border controls and closer monitoring of Mozambican nationals inside South Africa and its security forces was promised by Pretoria. The latter was unwilling to take any further action that would imply that it did not have full control of its security services. From the first anniversary of the accords into 1985 the attitude on all sides was one of pessimism; Pretoria abandoned further efforts to bring the Mozambican government and insurgents together.[49]

The FAM was saved from total military collapse at this stage of the conflict by the intervention of Zimbabwe, which by mid-1985 decided to commit troops to combat oper-ations in support of the FAM, and also to unilaterally undertake operations against RENAMO targets. To this end the Zimbabwe National Army (ZNA) despatched three battal-ions–about 2,000 troops in total – to guard the Beira corridor and ensure the safe passage of traffic from Beira inland to the border.[50]

From mid-1985 the ZNA had between 7,000 and 8,000 troops in Mozambique (at one time peaking in early 1986 to 12,000), most guarding the Beira corridor but others involved in fighting to the south. This represented about 17 per cent of its total force.[51]

The most significant development resulting from increased ZNA involvement came in the late summer of 1985, when Zimbabwean forces acting with FAM units mounted a large-scale campaign against RENAMO bases in the Gorongosa area. In a series of coordinated area operations beginning on 1 July, the joint forces closed in on RENAMO headquarters at the base of the Gorongosa Massif. 2,000 or so ZNA troops, led by those of the 1st Parachute Group and supported by helicopters, were parachuted and airlifted near the site, while FAM units moved north from Vila Paiva de Andrada. On 28 August the assault began, and on 6 September the FRELIMO government announced its success. Casa Banana, the central RENAMO base at Gorongosa, as well as other nearby base camps, fell in two successive phases of the assault, launched on 28 August and 2 September. The first was directed against the Casa Banana area (with its 800m airfield) to the immediate south of the Gorongosa Massif itself, while the second concentrated on attacking the smaller camps in the vicinity.[52]

The fall of Casa Banana was a serious setback for RENAMO. Although the insurgents were able to evacuate their camps in the Gorongosa area, they had short warning and had to leave behind significant quantities of weapons, equipment, and records. As RENAMO units withdrew, they broke into small groups and began to harass the ZNA and FAM attackers, inflicting a number of casualties.[53]

Despite this, RENAMO took heavy casualties (several hundred at least, but probably not the 1,000 or so claimed by FRELIMO) as it withdrew its forces deeper into the Gorongosa Massif or dispersed them into surrounding areas. Many weapons and other military supplies were captured by the joint FAM-ZNA force as well, later being displayed on the occasion of the visit of President Machel to the site a week later. Machel's claim that 'we have broken the back of the snake' was soon disproved.[54]

Some RENAMO forces from the Gorongosa area moved southward into Inhambane, north and east into Zambezia, or south-west toward the mountainous border region with Zimbabwe. However, as subsequent events demonstrated, many insurgents never left the Gorongosa area, as the ZNA and FAM were able to retain possession only of the airstrip and the base camps in the immediate vicinity, despite attempts to secure the surrounding countryside and its inhabitants. As late as 16 October fighting continued in the Gorongosa region.[55]

The increased ZNA involvement forced RENAMO to change its style of operations. Before this time, insurgent camps had been large, relatively accessible installations geared to support military operations by large groups. However, increased ZNA ground and air involvement forced the insurgents to relocate and reconfigure their camps. Many of the latter were now built in remote areas and constructed in such a manner as to avoid ready detection from the air by the ZAF. RENAMO also took greater care in moving its troops, often operating at night to avoid aerial detection. RENAMO still found it easy to avoid detection of most of its operations, which were for the most part conducted by small groups of company size or less, by the FAM or ZNA. The defence of the Beira Corridor and other stationary targets by the latter was done only at great cost and by the use of methods often reminiscent of the Vietnam War milieu.

Subsequent to the capture of Gorongosa the FAM captured the RENAMO base at Indoro in northern Sofala on 13 September. Indoro had been used by elements of the withdrawing insurgents as a gathering point. The same day the RENAMO camp at Nhamatanda, also in northern Sofala, was captured as well.[56]

These operations were complemented by others undertaken by the FAM in Maputo and Zambezia provinces. In the latter, the large RENAMO base camp complex near Vuruca, on the border between Namacurra and Mocuba districts, was occupied on 20 September. The most important of these secondary actions, however, was the FAM capture of Xichocoxa camp in Inhambane, about 60km north-east of Panda. This camp had been sited by RENAMO to replace the Tome base camp, captured by the FAM in August 1983. The loss of Xichocoxa was to RENAMO operations in southern Mozambique comparable to the capture of Casa Banana for operations in central Mozambique. The camp had been used to control RENAMO forces in Gaza, Inhambane, and Maputo provinces. Another serious loss for RENAMO was the capture of Malungame base, about 50km from Maputo itself, in operations in southern Mozambique that lasted until the end of September. These secondary operations were all part of a major country-wide COIN effort as the FAM, assisted by the ZNA, sought to regain the initiative by disrupting as many RENAMO base camps as possible. At the least, the RENAMO base camp network in the Gorongosa area as well as its logistics for northern Manica province had been disrupted.[57]

Meanwhile, RENAMO continued its offensive operations elsewhere, building up for further operations in northern Sofala and in adjacent parts of Zambezia. In the latter province Caia fell to RENAMO on 18 December and the following month Marromeu, a major sugar refining centre, was captured and its infrastructure destroyed. The ZNA, with FAM support, attempted to recapture the town two weeks later and lost two senior ZNA officers, including Colonel Flint Magama, the deputy commander of the ZNA 1st Brigade, when the helicopter carrying them was downed by RENAMO on 24 January in northern Sofala province.[58]

Soon afterward the main focus of activity shifted back to Gorongosa. Although Gorongosa had fallen to the ZNA, it could not be held by the FAM. After its capture, a ZNA contingent briefly held the Casa Banana area before turning it over to a battalion-sized FAM contingent. On the night of 14–15 February 1986 this FAM unit was overrun by a 400-man RENAMO force and routed, fleeing toward Cavallo and Vila Paiva de Andrada. The attack had been expected for some time, and the government forces' morale was low; RENAMO's attack was made with an infantry force supported with B-10 RCLs and 82mm mortars. The much better armed FAM garrison, on the other hand, lost all of its equipment, including a range of crew-served weapons, two BTR-60PB armoured cars, several trucks, and a large quantity of ammunition. By the end of March RENAMO forces attacked the main FAM garrison in the region, but were repulsed.[59]

Almost immediately RENAMO began to consolidate and reinforce its positions in and around the Gorongosa Massif, expecting the FAM and its ZNA allies to attempt to recapture Gorongosa once again. This was not long in coming, for in early April ZNA units positioned themselves to move against Casa Banana once more. 3,000 ZNA troops supported by 24 helicopters and seventeen FAM and ZAF combat aircraft moved against Gorongosa on 13 April. RENAMO had been forewarned, however, and withdrew 1,500 or so troops from the four bases at Gorongosa that were the focus of the ZNA attack. The latter found deserted camps and faced a series of vicious counterattacks by RENAMO. The ZNA reoccupation of Gorongosa, although a necessary reaction to counter the propaganda victory of the RENAMO recapture of the base in February, accomplished little. The main centre for subsequent ZNA activity was to the south, at Vila Paiva de Andrada and the airfield there, giving the ZNA the option to move northward against the Gorongosa area at will and still maintain land LOCs with the Beira corridor. RENAMO, for its part, reacted to the increased ZNA operations by 'declaring war' on Zimbabwe and increasing cross-border raids against the mountainous border area of that country with Mozambique, causing damage to the tea industry; insurgent operations peaked there in 1987. It also relocated its headquarters base to Zambezia.[60]

By this time the Nkomati Accords had virtually become a dead letter, although throughout 1986 elements of the South African government continued to support them. However, the continued inability or unwillingness of Pretoria to control either rogue security service support or financing and supply by private interests inside the RSA meant that the insurgents still enjoyed much outside logistical support. Available evidence strongly suggests that few inside the South African government were ever committed to giving the accords a real chance of success. Explicit data from the 'Gorongosa Diaries' captured in 1985 at RENAMO's base camps there indicated continuing support from the highest levels of the SADF. At the least, the continuing lack of enforcement of the accords by South Africa suggested a major policy rift within the government itself.[61]

Regardless of the circumstances of RSA non-compliance with the Nkomati Accords, they continued to have the most negative impact on the government effort to contain RENAMO. Coupled with the continued success of RENAMO and its effective expansion of operations through most of the country, the pattern of the insurgency throughout Mozambique had put FRELIMO in a very critical state by late 1986. The subsequent recovery of momentum by the government took years to effect, but starting in 1987 major social and economic policy changes, continued foreign assistance, and reforms and reorganisation of the military and security services began to result in a stemming of the RENAMO tide.

FRELIMO began to seek greater regional cooperation in combating the insurgents. Tanzania committed troops for operations in northern Mozambique. Zimbabwe's commitment increased, not just in terms of troop numbers but also in the involvement. The Zimbabwe armed forces attempted to utilise their version of state-of-the art COIN tactics. ZAF aircraft bombed suspected RENAMO camps, then hit them with helicopter gunship strafing. Such attacks would sometimes be followed by ground attacks against the base area, but usually the ZNA and the FAM would find abandoned facilities; after the allies' withdrawal, RENAMO would usually move back into the area, sometimes into the same camp, and resume operations once more. The main obstacle in 1986 to a regional effort to combat RENAMO was Malawi, whose president, Hastings Banda, had long-standing ties to South Africa, and who was repeatedly accused of encouraging the latter's attempt to support the insurgents from Malawi territory. In October 1986 President Machel issued an ultimatum to Malawi to cooperate, or unspecified reprisals would be undertaken. In the end, Malawi finally agreed to commit a limited presence – one battalion or so – to ensuring the security of the Nacala Railroad.[62]

Winning the acquiescence of Malawi in order to forge a unified policy against RENAMO among Mozambique's neighbours was Machel's last accomplishment. In October 1986 he was killed when returning to Mozambique, in a plane crash near Komatipoort in South Africa. A major shift in government policy occurred in October 1986 with the death of President Machel. Machel's successor, Joaquin Chissano, formerly FRELIMO's foreign minister, was to be much more the pragmatist than his predecessor, and accelerated ties to South Africa and the West begun under Machel. His presidency also saw an end to many of the social and political excesses of the Machel area, as Chissano and the FRELIMO leadership saw the writing on the wall for Soviet support to African 'Marxist' regimes. Chissano's military leadership was to undertake serious attempts to reconfigure the FAM into a COIN force and try to develop new strategies to counter RENAMO's influence with the rural population.[63]

Machel's death came amid a new major offensive by RENAMO, launched from bases in the Malawi-Mozambique border area. Three groups of insurgents, each numbering about 8,000 to 10,000 (far less than the 12,000 for each column claimed by some media reports), moved into Mozambique. One invaded Tete province, heading west along the north bank of the Zambezi. A second drove south from southern Malawi toward the Zambezi. A third moved from bases west of Milange into central Zambezia province. At the same time, RENAMO also declared war against Zimbabwe for its military intervention in Mozambique. The ZNA had by this time approximately 8,000 troops in the Beira corridor, down from a high of 12,000 for the offensives of late 1985 and early 1986. Zimbabwe, for its part, maintained its intent to keep troops in Mozambique and prevent the FRELIMO government from falling, despite increasingly severe budget problems due to the military involvement. The offensive had apparently been well-planned, and was to be undertaken in three successive stages. The first began with the invasion of Tete and the capture of as much territory there as possible, followed by similar general attacks against Zambezia and Sofala. This phase, which was scheduled to end in February 1987, was to be followed by a second, devoted to the consolidation and defence of captured territory. Finally, with this done, the third phase planned by RENAMO was to be a drive southward against Maputo.[64]

RENAMO's initial phase of the operation swept all before it, threatening the Beira corridor and pouring into the lower Zambezi River valley. By the end of November RENAMO forces had captured Sena, Mutara, Vilanova, Bane, and Vilacaia. The loss of Sena, with its strategic bridge, was of particular concern to FRELIMO. Elsewhere in Zambezia the situation was grave, with all district capitals falling to RENAMO; even Quelimane, the capital of the province, was threatened. The ZNA did not operate north of the Zambezi, and FAM units there, without backing from their allies, fared poorly in countering RENAMO. Elsewhere, in Tete province, RENAMO made significant territorial gains even when it could not hold all the territory it initially captured. Ulongwe, the capital for Angonia district on the Malawi border, was overrun on 8 November, but reoccupied by the FAM on the 13th. However, all of rural Angonia remained under RENAMO domination.[65]

PROGRESSION TO STALEMATE, 1986/7-1992

The final phase of the long civil war in Mozambique was marked by the following developments:

■ The progressive improvement in military capabilities of the FAM following the 1987 reorganisation;
■ A major series of offensives by the FAM in central Mozambique from late 1986/early 1987 that succeeded in reversing RENAMO gains;
■ The failure of RENAMO to establish itself in southern Mozambique and launch an attack to capture Maputo;
■ Increasing involvement by Zimbabwean and other foreign forces in the fighting, and expansion of the ZNA areas of operation in support of the FAM;
■ A peaking of RENAMO's control of both population and territory, and an increase in acts of violence against the population;
■ A gradual decline of RENAMO capabilities at the end of the 1980s due to a severe drought that affected the rural population base;
■ A stalemate between RENAMO and the government, marked by a decline in military capabilities on both sides.

By early 1987 the fortunes of war in central Mozambique had begun to once more swing back to FRELIMO's favour. The involvement of allied troops, plus the reorganisation of the FAM in late spring, signalled a new commitment by the Chissano government to deal with RENAMO militarily. However, matters did not get off to an easy start. A joint January offensive by the FAM and ZNA was able to recapture the lower Zambezi towns lost to RENAMO the previous autumn; other operations in Gorongosa and in the Magude area were apparently less successful. RENAMO's offensive in Zambezia was not yet over, however. In early February it penetrated the tea-growing areas of northern Zambezia, capturing Socone and Gurue in operations the first two weeks of February, and doing extensive damage to the tea-processing infrastructure there.[66]

The main FRELIMO actions, apart from more aggressive fighting, were in the areas of military reform and civil affairs. In the latter, an effort was made to repudiate many policies of the Machel era and liberalise the government's relations with the civilian population. In the military arena, Chissano replaced Colonel-General Mabote with Lieutenant General Hama Thai, Air Force Commander, as well as cleaning house elsewhere. All provincial military commanders, as well as the heads of the three armed services and the major FAM headquarters directorates, were replaced. The debate in the military between the proponents of a conventional force and those who favoured a much lighter COIN force began to swing toward the latter. Emphasis was put upon training and improving logistics. In addition, Mozambique entered into military training agreements with a number of countries, most importantly Great Britain and Portugal, who both provided COIN training for FAM members. The success of the new programmes can be measured by looking at the FAM Zambezia offensive of spring and early summer 1987, the first of many interrelated operations that lasted into the following year, in which all the provincial capitals were recaptured by FAM infantry assisted by 'Red Beret' commandos (see below).[67]

Faced with the combined ZNA and FAM offensive in Zambezia, RENAMO launched new attacks further south. Starting in April 1987, the insurgents moved large numbers of well-armed units across the Mozambican border from South Africa. Although the latter repeatedly claimed that it had ceased support to RENAMO, private funding for the insurgents continued. In addition, elements of South African military intelligence continued to support RENAMO despite the official ban on doing so. The new RENAMO attacks targeted the southern provinces of Gaza and Inhambane, which had remained basically pro-FRELIMO through the war. The campaign was marked by a series of attacks against the civilian population, including massacres, ambushes of civilian transport, and other acts of terror. The campaigns by RENAMO, designed to establish bases from which to attack Maputo, continued through the end of 1987 and into 1988. By December civilian road and rail traffic north of the Maputo area had come under attack, and RENAMO's attacks in January and February in the area targeted sites around Maputo itself. The FAM fought hard to counter RENAMO's drive southward, despite being stretched very thin across most of the country.[68]

Internationally, the renewed attempts by FRELIMO to stem the RENAMO tide were assisted by extensive publicity surrounding the series of massacres attributed to RENAMO. From July through October 1987, the mass killings of civilians at Homoine (18 July), Manjacaze (10 August), and Taninga (16 October) captured the attention of the outside world and fixed international public opinion against RENAMO. Although some of the evidence linking RENAMO to these actions is problematic, most supports the theory that these were terror killings designed to be an example to the local population in southern Mozambique. Furthermore, they apparently took place in the context of military operations by RENAMO in the southern Mozambican provinces of Gaza, Inhambane, and Maputo. Far from its traditional bases and support population, RENAMO by its actions was apparently trying to coerce at least part of the local populations in southern Mozambique to support it and reject government authority.[69]

Meanwhile, the FAM's campaigns against RENAMO continued. Perhaps the most important major operation of late 1987 was that undertaken in Maputo province, 75km west of the capital itself. On 20 November government troops began an operation that culminated four days later with the storming of Matsenquenha base (Mamacaaga District), just 3km from the South African border. The operation further disrupted RENAMO operations in the area, but continued insurgent activity kept very much alive the debate as to whether South Africa continued to support anti-regime guerrillas. The presence of bases so close to the South African border appeared to many to confirm this support, attributed by some to rogue elements of South African military intelligence as well as to private businessmen, including former Mozambican Portuguese who had been forced to leave the country after 1975.[70]

By the end of 1987 it appeared that the FAM had succeeded in taking the initiative against RENAMO in some parts of the country. More effective military measures were combined with offers of amnesty by FRELIMO for RENAMO personnel who surrendered to the authorities, as well as pardons and parole for those who had already been imprisoned for supporting the insurgents. The questionable success of the much-publicised programme was indicated by its extension for another year after it was scheduled to have expired in December 1988; it had resulted in the rallying of only 3,000 or so former insurgents, including two members of RENAMO's external support organisation, who charged continuing South African support. This latter continued, despite disclaimers by the South African government; private sources of assistance, as well as dissident sources of funding and supply from within the SADF, continued to flow into Mozambique, and a base camp network existed to channel this aid into the southern part of the country, with many bases within 15km of the border between the two nations. The ZNA continued operations against RENAMO in support of the FAM. The most notable of these was the July–August 1989 attack against RENAMO's Gorongosa base in an attempt to capture or kill Dhlakama as he was leaving for negotiations in Nairobi. A ZNA brigade-sized task force supported by FAM combat helicopters attacked the Gorongosa area, but RENAMO forces there were able to evade the attackers. Dhlakama was able to reach Nairobi on 3 August, where he condemned the attack.[71]

By the end of the 1980s much of RENAMO's original raison d'être had been overtaken by events. The liberalisation by the government of economic and political structures begun earlier continued, designed to eliminate much of the domestic disaffection with FRELIMO. These measures culminated in the Mozambican government's June 1989 programme to completely liberalise political and economic activity, and seek international mediation of the civil war. Contacts between RENAMO and the government, once initiated, continued. Despite initial complications, these contacts, once under way, reached their climax in negotiations in Rome in July and August 1990. These meetings led first to the retrenchment of ZNA troops to the Beira corridor and other sites and later to their significant reduction pending their final withdrawal. Zimbabwe, a party to the mediation, had specific interests in Mozambique, namely the security of the strategic Beira corridor and its commercial traffic. South Africa also made major efforts to take action against aid to RENAMO from dissident elements in the military and intelligence organisations. This was in great part due to the perceived economic benefits of cooperation between South Africa and Mozambique, including improvements to the Maputo transportation corridor and electrical power from the Cabora Bassa dam in Tete province.[72]

As the Cold War came to an end, the shrinking aid programmes of Mozambique's former communist country allies ended. By the end of the 1980s, this was a pronounced trend. In the case of the Soviet Union, it was by design, as continuing aid to a country regarded as not a communist state could be ill-spared due to problems at home.[73]

The Soviets had between 700 and 800 advisers in Mozambique to train and otherwise support the FAM, in addition to the extensive conventional aid programme it provided. But in June 1989, plans were announced to drastically reorient Soviet aid to the FAM. Advisers were to be withdrawn over the next two years. This announcement followed upon another the previous month in which plans were divulged to completely change FAM structure (reorganised only two years previously) and reorient the Soviet aid programme. Assistance in the form of conventional training and heavy weapons was to end, to be replaced by new training programmes that emphasised support operations. Priority was put on combat support and combat service support equipment such as helicopters, trucks, and communications equipment. Lighter weapons more appropriate for an anti-guerrilla force were to be employed. In fact, the announced aim of the FAM was to restructure itself to a 30,000-man highly mobile COIN force over the coming years.[74]

In the meantime, RENAMO's rural support base had been seriously eroded. In the past, insurgents could easily abandon captured towns (they really had little use for them) and major bases in the face of FAM attacks. Their real strength lay with their control of the rural population and its agricultural base. However, since 1986 the country had been in the throes of a major drought, which was aggravated by the subsequent shifting of the war into important agricultural areas as the conflict expanded northward and southward.[75]

For RENAMO, the drought meant a disruption of the farming that had helped their base camps to be self-sufficient in the production of food. Relations with the local population suffered as the insurgents began to demand food from rural villagers each day where before they had come to collect it as a once-weekly 'tax.' Elsewhere, large elements of the rural population were forced to move away from their farms and villages to the larger cities, thus literally eliminating RENAMO's rural support base.[76]

To add to RENAMO's problems, it lost the propaganda war in the international arena. The end of the Cold War, combined with a shift by South Africa from confrontational politics with its neighbours, led many backers to question the continuing need to support RENAMO against a government that had committed itself to internal economic reforms and political liberalisation. FRELIMO's continuing support base among its international backers remained firm, while RENAMO made few efforts to represent its position in the world media forum. Even the US Government went on public record with a report that accused RENAMO of extensive atrocities against the civilian population, through interviews with refugees in neighbouring countries, in the publication of the 'Gersony Report' in April 1988. Throughout the early 1990s, charges of guerrilla brutality and atrocities against the civil population continued unabated in the world press; RENAMO made no convincing public statements to answer such charges.[77]

With these setbacks, RENAMO declined as a viable insurgent force, maintaining often precarious control of a drought-ravaged countryside which was increasingly unable to support it. It continued desultory operations despite its diminished military capabilities due to the famine, but was at best able to maintain a stalemate in areas of its former strength, losing ground in other regions. But by mid-1992 hope was widespread throughout Mozambique that a peace agreement was near. By the early 1990s, government security forces, following their victories of the late 1980s, were again facing a crisis due to increased RENAMO aggressiveness as well as declining morale in the army. One of the tentative conditions for the 1992 peace settlement was a new army made up of both former FAM and RENAMO; many government soldiers feared for their future employment in such a post-settlement dispensation.[78]

NOTES

1. For a summary of the 7 August agreements and their implications, see 'Renamo leader surfaces', an AP story carried by the *Washington Times*, 11 August 1992, p. A8. For the number of people killed in the war, see the same article. RENAMO claims the lower figure, the Mozambican government the higher one.

2. Ibid. The 85 per cent figure was claimed by Dhlakama as of August 1992.

3. I am indebted for this analysis to Mr Tom Schaaf who was, in the mid-1980s, a United States representative for RENAMO and who has repeatedly travelled inside Mozambique's insurgent-controlled zones and has met Mr Dhlakama personally.

4. For Mondlane's death, see the discussions in Vines, pp. 12–13, and Hoile, 17–20. In the following discussion, 'FAM' is the collective term used for Mozambique's security forces, even though the FPLM was the official name of the military through the 1979 reorganisation (see below). Extensive controversy remains around the leadership struggles within FRELIMO in the late 1960s, and assassinations in 1969–1970 have been variously attributed to interfactional disputes, Portuguese security forces, or even private vendettas by members of the European community in Portugal. See *Mozambique/Country Study*, pp. 50ff.

5. For more specifics on Rhodesian policy toward Mozambican support of insurgents, see the chapter on Rhodesia. The actual policy of Machel toward former African members of the Portuguese COIN forces was exactly opposite to the official propaganda line of FRELIMO, which claimed that the government attempted to attract as many former flechas as possible to form the new army. This policy was part of a greater attempt to eliminate (i.e., imprison and/or kill) as

many Mozambicans as possible who had been connected with the former colonial administration. Many in the new regime, including the security forces, strongly dissented from this policy and were forced to flee. By late 1976 ever-increasing numbers of such personnel were appearing in the Rhodesian border areas as refugees. Information courtesy of Mr Robert McKenzie.

6. Although some supporters of RENAMO place its foundation as Christmas Day 1976, there is no evidence for this. The earliest mention of anti-regime activity by dissident Mozambicans calling themselves the National Resistance Movement is from February 1977. This is considerably later than the first broadcasts of the Rhodesian government-supported clandestine radio station, Voz da Africa Livre, which was on the air by 5 July 1976 (*Chronology*, pp. 30-1).

7. For early resistance movements (non-RENAMO), see *ARB*, 4428b-c.

8. For the role of the Rhodesian security forces in setting up RENAMO, see Cole, Barbara, *The Elite: The Story of the Rhodesian Special Air Service*, Three Knights Publishing, Amanzimtoti, 1984, pp. 242ff. For a discussion of RENAMO's origins with Robert McKenzie, who was involved in the process, the account given here is perhaps the most accurate that I have found to date. A more recent, but much less sympathetic, account is found in William Minter's *Apartheid's Contras*, pp. 32ff. See also the excellent discussion by Herbert Howe in *Mozambique: A Country Study*, Headquarters, Washington DC, Department of the Army Area Handbooks Series; DA Pam 550-64, 1985, pp. 245ff.

9. *Elite*, p. 246.

10. *ARB*, 5236b-c (for MNR and MNRA, events of April 1979); 5344b (for MRM, events of June 1979).

11. The formation of the PPM was announced in June 1979 (*ARB*, 5310b).

12. *ARB*, 5236b-c. Other press accounts imply that the UDF was a separate movement from the MNR.

13. *ARB*, 5301.

14. *ARB*, 5445b-5446a; 5474c-5475a.

15. For 'resettlement camps,' see ARB, 5445c-5446a; for FAM military changes, see *ARB*, 5807a-b.

16. See ARB, 5673b-c; 5908c-5909b (period from December 1979 through July 1980).

17. For the Espungabera attack, see ARB, 5908c-5909b; for fighting in other areas in 1980, see *ARB*, 5673b-c.

18. *ARB*, 5673b-c; 5909b-c.

19. See *ARB*, 5909c. As of December 1980, Zimbabwean troops were already operating to control the border with Mozambique.

20. See Hanlon, pp. 220-1. Some accounts indicate a major falling-out between Matsangaisse and some of his subordinates over the leadership and direction of the movement, and that disaffected RENAMO members assisted the Mozambican security forces in their attack on Gorongosa.

21. See Hanlon, p. 221. The operation is described in *ARB*, 5908c-5909b. For MNR strength, see *ARB*, 5909b-c, which lists a total of 4,000 effectives at the time of the Sitatonga attack. This figure is apparently a FRELIMO or ZNA estimate and is probably much too small. Almost a year later (mid-June 1981), there were 3,000 insurgents in the Espungabera area alone (*ARB*, 6083c-6084a).

22. See Hanlon, pp. 221-4. For the succession struggle, see Vines, pp. 16-19.

23. See the discussion in Vines, pp. 17-18.

24. *ARB*, 6083c-6084a.

25. See Legum, *Battlefronts*, p. 245, where the personnel strength in 1983 is given as 5-6,000.

26. Vines, pp. 18-20.

27. Hanlon, p. 224. Despite the argument presented there, it is unlikely that the Umtali Special Branch was the only office that knew of the arms shipment; ZNA headquarters had to know as well. It may have been that the Zimbabwe security forces were looking for a scapegoat as well as a pretext for replacing an entrenched security operative in a sensitive post with another official of their choice.

28. For the capture of Garagua, see *ARB*, 6285b-c. See also Hanlon, p. 222, for the significance of the Garagua documents.

29. Hanlon, pp. 224-6.

30. *ARB*, 6392a-b.

31. See *MPC*, p. 50.

32. See 'Mozambique: Machel's dilemmas,' in *AC*, 25/19, 19 August 1984, pp. 4-6.

33. *ARB*, 6463c-6464b.

34. *ARB*, 6464a-b; 6497b-c; 6532c-6533a.

35. Hanlon, pp. 226-7. The Malawi government's closing of the camps was in return for allowing oil for Malawi to travel over the Nacala railway (see the discussion, ibid.).

36. *MPC*, pp. 47-8.

37. See Hanlon, pp. 226-7. *ADJ*, January 1984, p. 23, reports RENAMO activity near Nampula city by late 1983.

38. Legum, pp. 245-6.

39. *ARB*, 6954a.
40. *ADJ*, October 1983, p. 33; see also *ARB*, 6954a. For the failed RENAMO offensive, see *AR*, January/February 1986, p. 73.
41. *ADJ*, November 1983, p. 30.
42. Hanlon, pp. 223-4.
43. See *ADJ*, November 1983, p. 28.
44. See *ADJ*, February 1984, pp. 38-9.
45. See *ADJ*, May 1984, pp. 64-6, for the text of the accords. Note also the discussion in Legum, pp. 294-301.
46. See Legum, pp. 358-62 and references, which review most of the Mozambican government data, published during the last two months of 1984.
47. *ARB*, 8011a.
48. *ARB*, 7780a-7781a.
49. See Legum, pp. 361-3.
50. *ARB*, 7779c-7780a.
51. *ADJ*, October 1985, p. 31; *ARB*, 7779c-7781a.
52. *ADJ*, October 1985, p. 34. According to RENAMO representatives in Lisbon, 2,500 ZNA troops and 20,000 FAM participated in these operations in northern Manica province (ibid.). See also *ARB*, 7779c-7781a.
53. In an announcement on 11 September admitting the fall of Casa Banana, RENAMO said that 366 FAM and 102 ZNA were killed, plus one East German and two Soviet advisers (*ADJ*, November 1985, p. 31).
54. *ACR/1985-1986*, p. B678.
55. *ADJ*, December 1985, p. 26. The number of civilians living under RENAMO rule in the Gorongosa area who were 'liberated' by the FAM-ZNA operations is variously given as 1,074 and 7,000 (ibid.); I suspect the latter figure.
56. *ADJ*, November 1985, p. 31.
57. *ADJ*, November 1985, p. 32. On 18, 19, and 23 September three other major base camps in the Milange and Alto Molocue districts were also taken (ibid.). For the capture of Xichocoxa, see *ARB*, 7753c-7754a. For the capture of Malungame, see *Africa Report*, January/February 1986, p. 68.
58. *ACR/1985-1986*, p. B678; *ZPC*, p. 75.
59. For the recapture of Gorongosa, see *Africa*, 176 (April 1986), p. 35; also *ARB*, 7981a-7982a. Both of these sources claim 400 RENAMO troops routed the FAM garrison there. See also *ACR/1985-1986*, p. B678.
60. *New African*, November 1987, p. 23. See also Vines, pp. 61-5.
61. See Legum, pp. 395-400, and references. The 'Gorongosa Diaries' are also called the 'Vaz Diaries.'
62. *ARB*, 8218b-8220a.
63. For Machel's death, see *ARB*, 8256a-8261c.
64. *ARB*, 8260a-c; see map, p. 8256.
65. *ARB*, 8292b-8293c.
66. *ARB*, 8405c-8406a; 8406a-b.
67. *ARB*, 8540b-c; see also 'The Battle for Zambezia,' *Africa Report*, March/April 1989, pp. 13-16. For foreign COIN training, see below.
68. *ACR/1987/1988*, pp. B625-B627.
69. For the massacres, see *ARB*, 8561a-b; 8601a-b; 8474b-c.
70. See Vines, pp. 26-31. For the attack on Matsenquenha base, see *ARB*, 8733b-c.
71. *Europa Yearbook/Africa South of the Sahara, 1991*, p. 721; see also *ARB*, 9206c-9207c. For the Gorongosa attack, see *MPC*, pp. 131-4.
72. Ibid., pp. 721-2. For South African cooperation, see especially *ARB*, 9065c-9066b.
73. Of note is the way that the East German intelligence services regarded Mozambique. Dealings with the latter are in the section of their files for 'non-communist countries' and not 'communist countries' (which, however, did include Angola). Information courtesy HRW.
74. *ARB*, 9323b-c.
75. Ibid., p. 722.
76. See 'Mozambique: A hunger that kills,' *AC*, 33/12, 19 June 1992, pp. 5-6. As of the time of writing, 1992 had been the worst famine year yet.
77. Information courtesy of Mr Thomas Schaaf. For the Gersony Report, see *ARB*, 8857a-b. The report itself was released by the US Department of State's Bureau for Refugee Programs on 20 April 1988.
78. See *AC*, 33/12, 19 June 1992, pp. 5-6.

Chapter Six

The Second Angolan Civil War, 1992–1995

With the renewal of fighting at the beginning of November 1992 in Angola, a second civil war, much more destructive and bitterly fought than the first, broke out. The inexpert and maladroit monitoring by the United Nations of the September 1992 elections, the arbitrary decision that the vote was 'free and fair' despite extensive evidence of fraud on the part of the government, and the vengeful attitude of the government following its declaration of victory all contributed to the feeling by UNITA that it had little if nothing to lose by resorting to arms and resisting the MPLA's winner-take-all policy.

The result has been a human tragedy of enormous proportions, with at least 100,000 killed between November 1992 and November 1994, many more displaced or forced as refugees into neighbouring lands, and massive damage to the country's economic infrastructure of proportions far beyond that of the previous conflict. UNITA's sieges of major cities – Huambo, Kuito, Malange, and Menongue – were marked by immense human suffering. Throughout Angola, the dispensation of food and medical assistance became increasingly influenced by political decisions by one side or another.

As a result of the war, the Angolan government has mortgaged its future through arms purchases on a scale that even exceeds the massive buildups of the mid- to late 1980s. The new Angolan Armed Forces (Forcas Armadas Angolanas, FAA) are now more numerous and better trained than the old FAPLA ever was. The conventional war of the 1980s, once fought in remote parts of the country far from populated regions, shifted into areas such as the Bengo-Cuanza Norte border, Soyo, Cuanza Sul, the Benguela–Huambo– Kuito axis, and northern Huila, compounding human suffering.

OPERATIONAL HISTORY OF THE RECENT ANGOLAN CONFLICT, 1992–1995

INTRODUCTION

The recent conflict in Angola has been the most violent and destructive episode in the country's history since independence. Following the outbreak of fighting in late October 1992, the National Union for the Total Independence of Angola (UNITA) took over most of the country, leaving the government of Jose dos Santos' Popular Movement for the Liberation of Angola (MPLA) with the capital, the oilfields, and a few key cities and ports. The subsequent history of the conflict is one in which the central government rebuilt its military, the Angolan Armed Forces (FAA), and by a difficult but persistent two-year effort gradually regained the initiative and re-established its authority over the areas taken from it by UNITA.

The operational style of the Angolan security forces evolved significantly during the period November 1992–November 1994. There were five main phases of the fighting:

■ The first phase, from November 1992 to January 1993, in which UNITA gained control of as much as three-quarters of the country from the central government;
■ The second phase, from February 1993 to May/June 1993, in which the government, rebuilding its army, attempted a few counterattacks against UNITA, most ending in failure;

■ The third phase, from May/June 1993 to January 1994, in which government forces began systematic attacks to regain lost territory, the process being temporarily side-tracked by a truce with UNITA in early December;

■ The fourth phase, from January 1994 to November 1994, in which government forces regained most of the key areas and administrative centres lost to UNITA since 1992, forcing the latter to accept a ceasefire;

■ A post-ceasefire phase, from November 1994 to February 1995, also saw fighting, but at a much reduced level, both sides manoeuvring at the local level to ensure the best possible last-minute advantage before United Nations Verification Mission (UNAVEM III) forces deployed to enforce the ceasefire.

EVOLUTION OF THE TACTICAL SITUATION
First phase (November 1992–January 1993)

The violence in Luanda that ended on 3 November resulted in a significant part of UNITA's national leadership and their key supporters in the capital being eliminated. During the fighting, UNITA commanders throughout Angola began attacks to gain control of key military installations and arms depots. In the process they also took over most of the country's interior. Despite a December GOA (Government of Angola) counteroffensive using a mix of new FAA troops and Riot Police, UNITA managed to recoup most of its losses and by late January 1993 controlled 105 of 164 Angolan municipalities.[1]

UNITA gains and the GOA response The most immediate threat to the government at this time were the armed thrusts against the capital by UNITA commanders attempting to rescue their compatriots. Repulsed near Viana by a hastily-organised defence consisting of Riot Police and elements of the Angolan military, the UNITA forces subsequently occupied Caxito, the capital of Bengo province, on 4 November. Elsewhere, Ndalatando and most of Cuanza Norte province were in UNITA hands, as were central and northern Bengo and the Quibaxe district and adjacent parts of Uige province. UNITA was also consolidating its control in much of Zaire and Malange provinces by the end of the first week in November. Further east, in the Lundas, UNITA's forces had taken control of many diamond-mining sites in the Cuango River valley, including Cafunfo with its airfield. To the south, Quibala in Cuanza Sul had fallen to UNITA, and the latter had massed its forces to move against Huambo and Kuito. By the last week of the month the MPLA had retained a few key cities in the interior – Malange, Luena, Saurimo, Huambo, Kuito, and Menongue – as well as large parts of the coastal area and south-western Angola where UNITA had traditionally lacked support from the local population.[2]

The central government's forces at this time were unable to defend all areas under UNITA attack, and were incapable of conducting any major offensive operations, having only the shell of an armed force. The MPLA thus maintained the defensive, and attempted to retain control of the large cities of the interior with their airfields that could be later used to support military operations. From the start of the conflict, however, the FAA worked closely with the paramilitary riot police (Policia Anti-Motim) and the Civil Defence Forces to defend the cities from UNITA. The concept of joint operations in urban defence served GOA forces well for the duration of the war and freed many FAA that would have otherwise been relegated to garrison duty.[3]

Finally, although the GOA's forces were not able to launch any but the most local and limited offensive operations against UNITA, operational priorities were apparently being set by the end of November and plans put in place to begin counterattacks against FALA. The FAA began to move troops into central Bengo and Cuanza Norte by mid-December and slightly later into northern Huila. Bengo and Cuanza Norte were the main exceptions in this stage of the conflict to the general GOA policy of avoiding offensive operations until it had a better-trained force. The occupation of Caxito by UNITA threatened Luanda's north-eastern defences and also blocked the FAA from moving against UNITA-occupied areas in northern and central Bengo. UNITA-occupied Ndalatando lay astride the main overland LOC from the capital to Malange. UNITA forces based there threatened the small part of Cuanza Norte still held by the GOA. Any GOA gains here, however small, would benefit the regime's strategic position in the capital area. Thus the FAA from late December 1992 began attempts to regain Caxito and Ndalatando. However, it would take four more months to regain the former and an additional year to recapture parts of Cuanza Norte.[4]

SECOND PHASE (FEBRUARY 1993–MAY/JUNE 1993)

During this phase the Angolan government began to implement its strategy: defend key areas to prevent further UNITA gains, undertake selected offensives, and rebuild the army. The latter was a long process and to do it a South African firm, Executive Outcomes Limited (EOL) was hired for the purpose. For training the FAA, EOL hired former members of South African Army military and paramilitary formations, most of whom had fought in the 1980s in the SWA/Namibian conflict, and who had often operated inside Angola. EOL was also engaged to provide technical support, for instance, piloting aircraft and support for technical systems, until Angolan personnel could be trained to take their place. In addition, a battalion-sized unit of South African mercenary troops was formed to provide backing to FAA troops at critical stages of key operations. Even this was not enough, as the GOA required troops immediately. It turned to a ready source: neighbouring Zaire. Through 1993 at least three brigade-size units of mercenaries were formed. Details are sparse, but it is likely that many of them had seen service in the Zairian Armed Forces (FAZ). The poor conditions of service and pay in the FAZ no doubt led many of its personnel to offer service to the GOA, which provided better support and pay, albeit for much more hazardous work. Throughout the conflict 'tropas Katangueses' often augmented regular FAA troops in operations throughout northern Angola, usually fighting well and at times taking heavy casualties.

Attempted relief of Huambo; fall of Huambo Central Angola presented the FAA with its biggest strategic challenge, as its control by UNITA cut or threatened Luanda's overland LOCs to government forces in southern and eastern Angola. By early 1993 the FAA had established fairly good control of the coastal regions of Benguela province, and consolidated its control over the port cities of Lobito and Benguela. It also had possession of Catumbela air base, which soon became one of the two major air logistics points for government forces for the duration of the conflict.

On 30 January UNITA began a full-scale assault on Huambo with the intent of capturing the city and making it Savimbi's seat of government. The subsequent FAA attempt to relieve Huambo was unsuccessful and provided lessons in what not to do. Air reinforcement of the garrison was not possible due to the denial of the airfield, forcing the relief forces to come overland from the coast. A motorised force moving inland from Benguela attempted to break UNITA's siege of the city, but was delayed by FALA blocking forces. Huambo fell on 8 March while the relief column was still at Ganda. While the FAA force was able to disengage and move back in relatively good order toward the coast, the flight of remaining FAA military personnel and MPLA sympathisers from Huambo itself was a rout marked by a bloody UNITA pursuit. As many as 15,000 of the fugitives met their deaths while trying to reach GOA-controlled areas.[5]

Recapture of Soyo and Caxito; Soyo lost again Soyo was recaptured on 13 March by an FAA force bolstered by foreign mercenaries attacking from Cabinda. A garrison of two 1,000-man brigades with South African mercenaries was then left to guard the installation.

Meanwhile, to the south, fighting raged in central Bengo north-east of Caxito as the FAA unsuccessfully attempted to penetrate UNITA lines and move northward toward Ambriz.[6]

Although events at Soyo overshadowed those in Bengo, the fighting in the latter was much more intense as UNITA attempted to halt government attacks north-eastward from the Luanda and Funda areas. Amid fierce fighting, GOA forces augmented by mercenaries retook Caxito on 22 March. The FAA subsequently then consolidated its gains in central Bengo and formed new defensive lines, bolstered by two regiments at Caxito.[7]

UNITA soon regrouped in northern Zaire province, deploying south of Soyo. The FAA there had little offensive capability, and relied on the mercenaries to organise the town's defences. However, UNITA soon began shelling Soyo, and repulsed several FAA probes by late April.[8] UNITA was content to invest the town as most of its efforts were devoted to containing the FAA in central Bengo and repelling an attack on Ndalatando. It was only after the FAA collapse in the latter operation that UNITA moved and assembled a force to recapture Soyo.[9]

The recapture of Soyo took no more than five days. On 20 May UNITA attacked, with elite 'Red Beret' special units spearheading the main force. The town fell on the 24th and the GOA forces and their mercenary allies were withdrawn from the town by air and sea to Cabinda. Little resistance was encountered by FALA in the final push, and it appears that FAA commanders were among the first to flee, despite the availability of naval fire support. FAA equipment and personnel losses were heavy. On 30 May the FAA commander at Soyo at the time of the UNITA attack was reportedly executed for dereliction of duty.[10]

UNITA siege of Kuito Kuito remained under siege from early 1993 through mid-summer 1994. The FAA force there managed to retain parts of central Kuito and a few of the suburbs, as well as the Kunje region immediately south of the city. Kuito was the only remaining GOA-held site on the central plateau, and its fall would have allowed UNITA to consolidate its hold in central Angola. The airfield, UNITA rightly reasoned, could be used to airlift men and materiel to reinforce the FAA and even allow it to go on the offensive. Thus UNITA sought to deny its use to the FAA at all costs. For over a year Kuito was subjected to UNITA artillery bombardments and the citizens of the city to the most extreme privations. However, the value of Kuito was also clearly evident to the GOA, and justified holding it at all costs with a determined defence. Ground attacks being unsuccessful and very costly in men and equipment, UNITA soon decided to attempt to shell Kuito into submission, a technique that was later refined by Savimbi's forces to ensure intensified bombardments whenever Huambo suffered air attacks by the FAN.[11]

Other military activity The FAA Northern Front was preoccupied with recapturing Ndalatando, and the attempts (see above) in December were the prelude to a series of probes and campaigns to regain the city and with it much of Cuanza Norte, thus relieving the threat to the route south-east via Dondo. As long as Ndalatando remained in UNITA hands Dondo remained under threat and the Lucala River crossings were not secure. The route south-west into Cuanza Sul was liable to interdiction by FALA troops based in Cuanza Norte, who could also strike westward against the power lines and Luanda's defensive perimeter.

After a number of abortive attempts to advance north of the Lucala River toward Ndalatando from Dondo and other bases in Cambambe, the GOA decided to initiate a large-scale offensive in late April 1993 under the command of Lieutenant General Paulo Amaral, Cuanza Norte military commander, with a PCA at Dange-ia-Menha, about halfway between Dondo and Ndalatando. The operation was initiated on 22 April, when a column of about 2,000 that included motorised elements from the Luanda garrison, and which was reinforced with Zairian ('Katanguese') mercenaries, crossed the Lucala. The operation also included secondary attacks in central Bengo eastward on the Caxito–Ucua axis and north along the coast toward Ambriz from Caxito. The Bengo attacks accomplished little in the face of determined FALA Northern Front resistance, not even preventing UNITA from moving against the FAA to isolate Dondo on the road to Luanda near Maria Teresa. A third GOA attack opened an axis of attack westward from Malange.[12]

However, strong UNITA resistance combined with command ineptitude and the short-comings of the inexperienced troops first to slow up the attack by 28 April and then halt it short of its goal on 2 May. Two days later UNITA's counterattack forced the FAA column back and cut its logistics. By 31 May the operation was called off by the GOA, as FAA troops and equipment were needed to support operations elsewhere.[13]

GOA endeavours elsewhere also had no success. On 11 May the GOA claimed that FAA airborne (i.e., air-landed) commandos recaptured the Cuango Valley mining centres of Cafunfo, Lussamba, and Cuango. The GOA had long considered the reoccupation of the area one of its top priorities. Not only did FALA use the Cafunfo airfield as a major logis-tics hub for the region, but the Cuango Valley mining sites used Cafunfo and Lussamba airfields to smuggle diamonds to Zaire and other African countries and thence to Europe. Recapture of the Cuango Valley would not only deny UNITA a portion of its lucrative diamond traffic but also end the use of Cafunfo airfield by UNITA.[14]

The FAA effort to reoccupy the Cuango Valley was the first documented large-scale use of air-landed forces. Despite initial success, the force could not be sustained, apparently due to the failure to ensure secure air resupply. The FAA held the area for a week before UNITA successfully counterattacked, forcing GOA forces to withdraw after heavy casual-ties. UNITA subsequently claimed (probably rightly) that throughout the operation it had never lost control of the mines.[15]

Following FAA's failed attacks against the Cuango valley, the second loss of Soyo, and the collapse of the Ndalatando offensive, UNITA in response launched a general offensive in northern Angola in June to isolate Luanda by forcing the FAA from areas it had gained in central and northern Bengo, dislodging the GOA from the remainder of Cuanza Norte, and attempting to capture Malange.

However, the UNITA offensive was only partly successful. While the FAA was driven back in Bengo, the GOA still held Caxito. In Cuanza Norte, UNITA captured the Lucala FAA base, and later even pushed forward to Dange-ia-Menha and captured it on 27 June, putting to flight four FAA battalions and forcing the GOA civil administration for Cuanza Norte to abandon Dondo. However, Dondo held, thus preserving GOA control over the route south-east from Luanda into Cambambe and from there into Cuanza Sul. The inability of UNITA to capture Malange was perhaps the single major failure of the offensive, as it would have meant the destruction of the FAA North-Eastern Front. However, with the exception of Caxito, the GOA lost virtually all of its 1993 gains by late summer in the north. By late August the FAA nevertheless claimed that it had stabilised the military situation.[16]

THIRD PHASE (MAY/JUNE 1993–JANUARY 1994)

Advance on Huambo The main campaign of 1993 was the FAA attempt to recapture Huambo from UNITA. The main force, which consisted of two operational groups of 5,000 men each, was based on the Benguela coast (the 8th Group, at Lobito, and the 5th Group, at Benguela). The force based at Lobito moved along the northern road inland through Bocoio and Monte Belo toward Balombo, while the Benguela-based force moved inland via Cubal, Ganda, and Alto Catumbela toward Tchindjendje. Two subsidiary operational groups designed to disrupt UNITA flanking operations were based at Lubango in Huila (1st Group) and Quibala in Cuanza Sul.[17]

The operation began in mid-July following FAA sweeps in western Benguela to secure the coastal areas. FAN bombing campaigns hit Huambo and other UNITA targets at deployments and base camps along the routes from the coast inland. The main bombing campaign, however, only began in earnest during the first week of August, with the FAN showing improved capabilities at hitting UNITA targets in Huambo and elsewhere.[18]

The two FAA groups used to cover the flanks of the main advancing forces began to deploy somewhat before the start of the main offensive in an attempt to keep UNITA off-balance in Cuanza Sul and in Huila. In the latter, FAA operations began early, with a task force, the FAA 1st Group, making an attempt to recapture Toco in mid-July as the first step in recovering eight northern Huila districts that had been in UNITA's hands since late 1992. By the end of the month the town was in FAA hands as the FAA 1st Group began to consolidate control in northern Huila and advance on the Lubango–Cacula–Caluquembe axis.[19]

The situation was difficult for GOA Southern Front forces as at first they also had to fight to secure their rear. Two major victories that allowed them some respite were the 20 July recapture of Camucuio in northern Namibe and the destruction of the main UNITA logistics base for west-central Huila near Quipungo in the first week of August.[20]

In Cuanza Sul the GOA had a much more difficult task as the whole of the interior had fallen to UNITA and the population in general supported Savimbi. The FAA 18th Group advancing through the province, reinforced by heliborne air-assault troops, regained the Quibala area by the third week of July and engaged the main FALA blocking force between there and Catofe. UNITA forces gave way and by 9 August the group advanced to the Waku Kungo/Cela area, where it was forced to halt after FALA destroyed the bridges over the Cuiva (Queve) River and positioned artillery to shell crossing areas. The advance as far as Waku Kungo had been made possible by employing FAA units advancing from Seles toward Waku Kungo and from Sumbe toward Quilenda, Gabela, and Conde that denied UNITA secure staging areas from which to flank the column on the west once it had moved south of Quibala.[21]

Meanwhile, the FAA 8th Group, moving along the northern axis of advance east from the coast, scored its first major successes on 26 July with the capture of Bocoio and a defeat of FALA at Serra do Pondo. Despite this victory the advance then slowed and Monte Belo was only reoccupied on 26 August. UNITA had begun to regroup and attempted to cut the 8th Group's resupply lines and block FAA efforts to drive UNITA from the three remaining communes in Bocoio district (Chila, Pafe and Cubal de Lumbo) that dominated the mountains on both sides of the road from the coast. It took another two months to reach Balombo and then move on toward Alto Hama in an attempt to link up with the Cuanza Sul axis.[22]

The fortunes of the FAA group advancing on the southern axis, built around the FAA 5th Armoured Regiment, were somewhat better, the force capturing Cubal by 26 July and advancing to Ganda, which fell on 15 August. Alto Catumbela's fall was reported two days later. After consolidating the gains with area operations against UNITA infrastructure lasting a week or so, the 5th Group moved onward toward Huambo, engaging FALA forces on the 27th near Tchindjendje, which was in Huambo province itself. UNITA withdrew its main operational headquarters to Caala, west of Huambo, in the face of the FAA advance, which by the 30th had reached Ukuma (Cuma), 120km from Huambo.[23]

By 20 October the FAA was 10km inside Huambo province following the capture of Tchindjendje. By mid-November the FAA had Kalenga, 40km inside Huambo province, east of Ukuma. The advancing FAA column had still not linked up with that coming south from Waku Kungo. UNITA activity near Chongoroi was aimed at attacking FAA logistics in the Benguela–Ganda corridor. By early December the FAA advance had slowed, although units remained in place and held territory that they had captured, following a ceasefire agreement.[24]

Cabinda operations and security concerns Despite UNITA claims to the contrary, GOA control in Cabinda at the beginning of the conflict was fairly firm and the province was even used as the base for the temporary reoccupation of Cabinda from March to May. Through mid-1993 insurgent activity against GOA forces in Cabinda was low-level. Much of this was small-unit action not by UNITA but by the splinter factions of the Front for the Liberation of the Enclave of Cabinda (FLEC). FLEC factions had refused to accept the May 1991 ceasefire and had kept on fighting; their numbers were estimated to be in the hundreds. The two largest factions were FLEC-Renovada (FLEC-R), led by Jose Pimbursion; and FLEC-Armed Forces of Cabinda (FLEC-FAC), led by the Kinshasa-based Nzita Tiago.[25]

UNITA, for its part, had more important priorities in the early stages of the conflict, and let Cabinda wait. The GOA retained the coastal area and the critical oil installations, which were heavily defended and judged by UNITA as not worth the manpower and political damage to attack. The Cabinda interior, however, was important as UNITA planned to later use it as a staging area from which to threaten the oilfields if this was needed to put pressure on Western oil companies at the facilities. Also, UNITA rightly figured, any cooperation they could effect with FLEC factions would tie down government forces and thus indirectly serve UNITA operations elsewhere. This was a strategy that had worked in the first civil war from 1985 to 1991.[26]

It was not until late in the year that UNITA made its move. In October the GOA claimed that UNITA was preparing for an attack on southern and eastern regions of Cabinda, basing a battalion in neighbouring Zaire. UNITA countered that the GOA planned the accusation as a pretext to build up troops in the province to counterattack Soyo. Already Soyo had been bombed in October, apparently by aircraft based at Cabinda. However, the late 1993 fighting on the Northern Front apparently prevented UNITA from turning its full attention to Cabinda until December. At that time, UNITA forces infiltrated northern Cabinda from bases in Zaire and established a major presence there.[27]

Late 1993–early 1994 fighting in Bengo and Benguela Late 1993 and early 1994 were used by the FAA to secure base areas in Bengo and Benguela provinces. The Bengo operations lasted to early 1994, and their result was to disrupt FALA bases and staging areas that supported the cordon thrown by UNITA around the capital. The FAA could thus launch further operations without fear of UNITA strikes directed at its rear area. In addition, LOCs taken by the GOA were thus denied to UNITA. Similar operations took place in January and February of 1994 in Benguela and adjacent parts of Huila, though they are less well-documented than the Bengo ones.

FOURTH PHASE (JANUARY 1994–NOVEMBER 1994), NORTHERN ANGOLA

For the FAA, 1993 ended much better than it had begun, and it could count some concrete successes. These included the recapture and successful defence of Caxito, the key to control of central Bengo; the defeat of the general UNITA offensive in mid- and late summer; and a successful drive from the coastal plain of Benguela province almost to Huambo. Disasters of the magnitude of the loss of Huambo and Soyo were unlikely to be repeated, as the FAA had by the end of 1993 probably grown to 85,000 or more troops, with more in training. Many new troops saw combat by the end of the year. Improvements in command and control as well as logistics were implemented as the result of the past year's experiences, and had already yielded impressive results in the advance against Huambo. The FAA was much better armed due to the GOA's ongoing acquisition of armoured vehicles and aircraft.

While the GOA was certainly no longer losing ground to UNITA, it remained to be seen how well it could not only defend its 1993 gains but recapture and hold territory the coming year. UNITA still effectively controlled most of the interior of Angola. However, in the wake of its summer offensive and the GOA's ability to prevent further losses of its territory, it was evident that UNITA's offensive capabilities were on the wane and that its future strategy would be to defend territory from GOA reconquest. Even the GOA urban enclaves such as Malange, Menongue, and Kuito appeared as of early 1994 unlikely to fall to future UNITA attacks. By early 1994 it was clearly evident that the war's future would be the GOA's to win or lose.

Bengo-based offensives against Soyo and Uige (January–November 1994) The FAA fought a bitter series of battles to ensure the security of Caxito and the capital from late 1993 into January 1994. By the new year, however, FAA moves to go on the offensive were evident. Units in Bengo were reinforced with two additional regiments, the 1st Motorised Regiment and the 60th Infantry Regiment, and augmented with tank and motorised units. While the former was deployed to Cambambe district in Cuanza Norte and the FAA operational command at Dondo there, the 60th was sent to Caxito to spearhead a new offensive northward along the coast.

The new FAA offensive that took shape in the first week of January 1994 laid the groundwork for the subsequent GOA reconquest of Bengo, Zaire, and Cuanza Norte provinces. Operational groups were formed for each of these provinces. Forces in central Bengo in early January began an assault with the 49th Infantry Regiment, spearheaded by motorised formations and supported by a full range of air assets, against Nambuangongo and nearby parts of Uige province. This was a precursor to the wider attack that included the advance of the 60th Regiment-based Operational Group north along the coast. FAA forces involved in the Bengo operations included existing army assets earlier deployed to protect Luanda, the newly-deployed regiments, plus additional mechanised elements and fixed-wing and combat helicopter support.[28]

Through the end of January the FAA groups, with considerable air–ground support, moved forward on two axes. The group on the first, or eastern axis (Bengo Province Operational Command), penetrated north-east from the Caxito and Mabubas area to Ucua and beyond to Nambuangongo and neighbouring areas of Uige province. The group on the second, western axis (Zaire Province Operational Command), with mechanised reinforcements and Zairian and South African mercenary support, moved north along the coast toward Ambriz.[29]

The Bengo group, although it captured Nambuangongo by 30 January, lost its momentum and withdrew to the Ucua area by mid-February. However, bitter fighting was reported as late as early March on the Quibaxe–Vista Alegre axis in western Uige.[30]

The western or coastal axis of the attack, under the Zaire Province Operational Command, was successful during late February. The progress of the FAA advance was quite rapid, with a final drive on 24 January engaging UNITA forces defending the southern approaches of Ambriz and taking the city at the end of January. The FAA immediately began to use it as a base from which to attack Nzeto, the next major town to the north. However, the offensive by now began to lose momentum as UNITA's Northern Front forces blocked the Zaire Operational Group on the north side of the Loge River between Ambriz and Mussera. There the FAA group was to remain stalled for the next eight months, despite periods of heavy fighting on the Ambriz–Nzeto axis through early March. To the south, the Bengo Operational Group remained blocked as well by UNITA forces in Nambuangongo and neighbouring areas of Uige. Fighting in other areas left the Zaire and Bengo task forces sitting in advanced positions until additional forces could be sent their way. This was not to happen until the following autumn.[31]

September 1994 finally saw the restarting of the offensive, designed to drive UNITA from Soyo. From 18 September the FAA began to build up forces north of Caxito to push north along the coast from Ambriz toward Soyo; two subsidiary axes of advance covered the main column from flanking attack by UNITA forces further inland. A second axis in north-east Bengo was opened as well, and FAA commandos were deployed from Caxito to Mabubas and thence to Ucua, where FAA units subordinate to the Bengo Group were to push east into Uige and then northward, paralleling the FAA coastal push. This axis of attack was not successful and GOA forces remained stalled on the Bengo-Uige border through mid-November.[32] On 30 September the attack toward Soyo was initiated, with the motorised column south of Nzeto moving northward from Ambriz. This was but one of the attacks conducted in northern and north-eastern Bengo by 5,000 men and 20 tanks reinforced with commando troops and air units. UNITA managed to hold back for two weeks the FAA advance, and the FAA column remained stalled north of Ambriz while it reinforced.[33]

On 14 October the FAA column stalled north of the Loge River finally began to move forward from Ambriz toward Nzeto, which was reached on 26 October and occupied.[34] After Nzeto, the FAA moved rapidly toward Soyo. By 27 October the FAA fought UNITA on the outskirts of Soyo and the town was occupied by the FAA by 4 November.[35]

The Ndalatando campaigns (April–May 1994) The recapture of Ndalatando from UNITA had become by early 1994 a point of honour for the FAA. Stung by the abysmal failure of previous attempts, the FAA committed a large group under the Cuanza Norte Operational Command to reoccupy Ndalatando. The group was composed of units from the 1st Motorised Regiment and 45th Infantry Regiment in Cambambe (Dondo) district, reinforced with some elements of the 16th Regiment. Throughout February the FAA conducted a series of operations designed to secure control of the Lucala River crossings.[36]

The FAA attack to recapture Ndalatando was launched on 3 March as a column consisting of 2,000 troops, reinforced with a tank company, two motorised companies, and a composite artillery regiment moved forward from Dondo across the Lucala River. Combat helicopters and fighter-bomber aircraft based at Dondo and Luanda respectively were dedicated to supporting the attack. The objective of the FAA was to reoccupy Ndalatando and then push forward toward Lucala to the east, then move northward toward Camabatela and thence into Uige province, bypassing the strong UNITA defences on the Bengo border.[37]

By the end of March the Cuanza Norte Operational Group received its first check at FALA hands. This occurred on 26 March east of Dange-ia-Menha, where the force took heavy casualties and was compelled to withdraw to the town of Dange-ia-Menha itself. Although temporarily checked, however, the FAA effort was by no means over, and the PCA in the town held out against a further UNITA counterattack.[38]

The FAA remained near Dange-ia-Menha for about a week, regrouping and resupplying before moving forward against Ndalatando once again on 4 April. After three weeks or so of see-saw battles, the FAA was able to make its first assault against the city, reinforced with armour and motorised units and preceded by air strikes. After another week of fierce fighting Ndalatando finally fell on 4 May.[39]

With the occupation of Ndalatando the FAA still had to contend with UNITA control of the hills to the north and east, which it used to shell FAA units occupying the city. The FAA aim was to secure the town as much as possible and turn it over to civil authorities before again moving east to the strategic Lucala crossroads, with the aim of then moving north into Uige province. Already on 3 May FAA units from the North-Eastern Front moving west from Malange had taken Cacuso. It took the FAA the better part of two weeks to consolidate its control over Ndalatando and then push toward Lucala, 50km to the east. As of 18 May UNITA claimed it still controlled the crossroads. FAA strategy was to occupy Lucala, link up with forces advancing west from Malange, and drive northward via Camabatela into UNITA-occupied Uige. Despite holding fast in the face of the FAA attacks, UNITA's Northern Front forces in Zaire, Uige, and northern

Bengo and Cuanza Norte were by late summer all but cut off by GOA forces from those in the Central Plateau. Also cut was the major UNITA overland supply route running south from Zaire and Uige through Cuanza Norte and Malange into Cuanza Sul and Huambo provinces.[40]

Reoccupation of the Cuango Valley diamond areas (March–July 1994) UNITA's continued control of the strategic Cuango valley mining area was the target of the second major FAA northern Angolan campaign by the FAA. Savimbi's control over the diamond mines in Cafunfo, Cuango, and Lussamba denied the GOA revenues while providing UNITA with a considerable amount of revenue from diamonds smuggled through Zaire and sold on the world market. Cafunfo airfield was a major UNITA logistics hub, and its recapture would possibly give the FAA another airfield from which to stage air support for ground operations in the western Lundas and eastern Malange. At the least, it would deny UNITA its major air centre. Following an FAA buildup at Saurimo, the operation to recapture the Cuango River valley diamond mining area was launched by the first week of March, under the command of the new FAA Eastern Front, and included motorised elements of several regiments, including the 16th Motorised. These were augmented with units of Zairian and South African mercenaries, commandos, and dedicated helicopter and fixed-wing air assets.[41]

The FAA advance was slow and accompanied by area operations designed to disrupt UNITA base camps elsewhere in the Lundas that could be used to stage attacks on FAA LOCs or rear areas. By mid-March Mona Quimbondo had been retaken and the FAA task force continued west toward Alto Cuilo and Cacolo. Bombing accompanied the FAA advance.[42] By the end of the third week of July, parts of Cafunfo had been occupied by the FAA, which went on to retake Lussamba. GOA troops, however, remained unable to expand their perimeter of control around the airfield and allow regular aerial resupply. UNITA's continued targeting of the airfield thus presented severe resupply problems to the FAA in the Cuango valley, and the lack of security for the overland route back to Saurimo compounded the problems, forcing it to rely upon supplies air-landed by helicopter.[43]

UNITA did not officially admit to the loss of Cafunfo until mid-August, a month after the FAA occupied the town. By that time the insurgents had begun a major counteroffensive against the FAA in the Lundas. This was not only designed to recapture the Cuango valley, but was also aimed at the Saurimo region with the apparent objective of denying the use of the airfield there. While recapturing some towns from the FAA, the UNITA effort was ultimately unsuccessful as Cafunfo and the other Cuango Valley sites remained in FAA hands, and attempts to attack Saurimo itself failed.[44]

Cabinda operations UNITA remained well-established in Cabinda throughout 1994, often operating with FLEC factions. Despite a 1 January mortar attack against Malongo, the oil installations remained secure. Continuing UNITA activity in northern Cabinda eventually prompted operations by the FAA that temporarily cleared that part of the province. In late March fighting continued in the Subantando area, but by the end of the month the FAA commander in Cabinda claimed the province was stable despite sporadic UNITA and FLEC activity in the northern and south-eastern part, especially along the Zaire border. The Chimbuande border area remained a problem, being vulnerable to continued UNITA attacks from Zaire. Continued FAA efforts against UNITA and FLEC-Renovada, which attacked near Cabinda city and Tando Zince in late April, appear to have been successful. In late June, the GOA reported that 700 FLEC/FAC and FLEC-Renovada fighters surrendered on 24 June. By this time negotiations between the GOA and FLEC-Renovada had begun, and continued FLEC-FAC activity was analysed as being part of an attempt to derail the talks.[45]

The stable security situation in Cabinda ended in early July as UNITA, beset by FAA operations throughout northern Angola, began major operations in Cabinda in attempts to drive the FAA from the hinterland, tie down FAA units badly needed elsewhere, and pose a possible threat to oil installations. UNITA forces based in Zaire began a series of actions in early July, attacking inland areas. By 14 July UNITA, assisted by FLEC-FAC, had captured Belize and threatened Buco Zau, Chimbuande, and Inhoca. By 10 July the FAA had begun a counter-offensive, regaining Belize by 29 August following battles in Ngandacango and Mondocongue.[46]

In response to the FAA recapture of Belize, another wave of UNITA attacks began in mid-September designed to establish permanent UNITA bases near northern and eastern Cabinda's borders with Zaire. In northern Cabinda UNITA attacked toward Conde, Cavunga, Viete, and Caio Guembo, while in the east Chiobo and Chimbuande were attacked. Chimbuande fell on 11 October, from attacks by UNITA from its regional operational base nearby.[47]

The FAA response to the new UNITA attacks was fairly rapid, and included ground operations backed by aerial bombardments of suspected UNITA or FLEC camps. In one such incident on 25 October FAA aircraft bombed, apparently by mistake, the Zairian military base at Kitona in neighbouring Bas-Zaire. It is likely, however, that this was a thinly-veiled warning to Zaire to stop allowing UNITA and FLEC to use its territory as a base to attack Angolan targets. Whether or not Zairian support ceased is not known; however, the FAA counteroffensive continued into November, with the main UNITA base near Chimbuande finally being captured and destroyed on 28 October. This effectively ended the UNITA threat in Cabinda up to late 1994.[48]

FOURTH PHASE (JANUARY 1994–NOVEMBER 1994), CENTRAL AND SOUTHERN ANGOLA

The culmination of the FAA's 1994 military operations was to come on the Central Front, with the main objective the recapture of Huambo. Huambo had taken on a symbolic status for both sides on and beyond its key military role. In the latter it dominated the Angolan Central Highlands and access from the coast, its airfield was a critical resupply point for whatever side had control of it, and its loss was an equally severe blow to the other side's logistics. The symbolic significance was just as important. For UNITA, retaining control of Huambo meant having the second-largest city in the country as its seat of government. For the government, UNITA's control of the city was a stinging reminder of the military debacle of March 1993.

As of late June 1994 UNITA's hold on Huambo and the Central Plateau still appeared firm. The FAA remained at Ukuma and other positions to which it had withdrawn the previous year. Huambo was the central UNITA administrative centre and a major logistics base, despite air attacks by the Angolan air force. Further east, the siege of Kuito, despite repeated failed attacks by Savimbi's forces, remained in effect and relief flights into the airport were still threatened by UNITA artillery. FALA units on UNITA's Central Front probably numbered as much as 20,000–certainly equal in numbers to the FAA task forces being assembled to push eastward from Benguela.

Siege of Kuito broken The end of the UNITA siege of Kuito came quickly, following an early July attack that attempted to wrest back parts of the city lost to the GOA earlier. By 5 July GOA forces controlled all the wards of the city, and had pushed out to a 12km defensive radius around Kuito. They also raided and destroyed the main UNITA base at Calupanda, 20km from Kuito, the following day. The airport was now relatively secure, and flights of FAA troops and equipment began to reinforce the Kuito operational command. By 3 August the FAA had enlarged its perimeter of control to Cunhinga, 30km to the west, and troops were still being airlifted into the city. The possibility of Kuito providing one of the staging areas for an attack on Huambo to the west became a reality in September.[49]

The recapture of Huambo Through late summer 1994 the pattern of operations in northern Huila was one of counterguerrilla activity by light infantry units, followed by operations designed to retain FAA gains until mid-September. At that time the FAA began a series of major operations, backed by air and motorised units, to open a new axis of advance against UNITA-held Huambo and break through UNITA defensive lines north of Negola. By doing so, the FAA also intended to prevent UNITA from using northern Huila as a base from which to outflank the FAA force advancing from Benguela toward Huambo.[50]

For almost a year FAA units had remained along an essentially static line in central Angola running roughly from Balombo south through Ukuma, west to Ganda, south-west to Chongoroi and thence south-east into Huila to Quilengues, Cacula, and Matala. The two FAA Groups that had advanced into the Central Plateau in August and September remained deployed in forward positions on the Balombo and Ukuma axes. The overall PC for the operation was at Catumbela air base, which saw a continuous buildup of weapons and other logistics materials. What the FAA lacked, however, were sufficient troops to initiate an operation not only to move forward against Huambo but also to ensure that UNITA remained unable to mount a flank attack from bases in northern Huila. To that end it was important to duplicate the 1993 operational plan (see above), but with more troops and greater emphasis on ensuring that northern Huila remained under GOA control. Thus operations on the Central Front had to wait until the conclusion of some of the larger northern Angolan operations freed troops, especially commandos, for the attack.

The grand FAA push to recapture Huambo began on 15 September; it had been preceded by air attacks against UNITA targets in Benguela, Huila, and Huambo provinces, as well as the city of Huambo itself, from late August onward. The FAA ground advance was on three axes by the 5th, 8th, and 1st Groups–in all, at least 25,000 troops–moving from forward bases at Balombo, Ukuma, and Catengue (south-east of Benguela city). The 5th and 8th Groups advanced directly toward Huambo while the 1st drove south-east from Catengue toward Chongoroi to dislodge UNITA from this key site on the main Benguela–Huila LOC. The main advance from the west toward Huambo was supported by operations in Huila province by the 31st, 17th, and 20th Groups in attacks launched on 24 September; the main purpose of the Huila attacks was to open another axis of advance from the south against Huambo as well as to prevent UNITA from outflanking the advancing FAA units. Two subsidiary axes, one from Kuito and one from Waku Kungo, also were opened by the FAA in late summer.[51]

Although the FAA advance met with very stiff UNITA resistance at several points, the groups moved rapidly toward their objective. By 29 October the main FAA group, the 5th, had advanced to Longonjo and pushed onward toward Londuimbali on 1 November, despite heavy UNITA minefields planted to delay their advance. By this time the FAA had captured practically all of northern Huila from UNITA, freeing the 1st and 5th Groups from the threat of any major outflanking by UNITA, and had managed to recapture all sites in southern and south-eastern Benguela province that UNITA had taken in an abortive mid-October counteroffensive against the FAA operations there. On 4 November the FAA occupied Caala in preparation for its final push on Huambo.[52]

The conclusion of the operation came quickly after the fall of Caala. The FAA entered Huambo on 5 and 6 November, and by the 7th UNITA withdrew from Huambo toward Bailundo, leaving the FAA to complete its occupation of the city and consolidate its gains in the immediate area. However, some areas of the city offered considerable resistance to the FAA, and it was not until 9 November that GOA control of the city was confirmed by the foreign press.[53]

Post-ceasefire phase (November 1994–February 1995)

The November ceasefire and the fall of Huambo did not end FAA operations against UNITA. FALA Northern Front forces were still in a position to attack government-held areas in central and northern Bengo as well as neighbouring Cuanza Norte. Thus the first major northern operation by the FAA against UNITA began in late November with the positioning of the 49th, 66th, and 75th Regiments in preparation for an attack against Quibaxe and Pango Aluquem in Cuanza Norte and against Nambuangongo district in Bengo. The 49th Regiment was to be supported from Uige, the airport of which was being used by FAA Mi-17 and Mi-18 helicopters to lift in troops, including commandos, and supplies to support the offensive.[54]

NOTES

The primary sources for the second Angolan civil war are numerous government and UNITA broadcasts. The latter consist of VORGAN news programmes. Angolan government broadcasts include both radio and television. Owing to the relative scarcity of discussions on the fighting, I have provided extensive documentation below for what is a preliminary overview only of the fighting between November 1992 and November 1994. The transcripts of both Angolan government and UNITA broadcasts are contained in FBIS and BBC daily reporting.

1. HRW/Angola, pp. 18–21.
2. See Reuters reports DS-12-02-92 1036, 'Rebels take second town and base, continue advance', 2 December 1992; DS-12-02-92 1716, 'Government threatens rebels with major attack', 2 December 1992; J. Matloff, 'Peace Prospects Dim in Angola', Reuters 00:36 12-02, 2 December 1992; J. Matloff, 'UNITA attacks another Angolan provincial capital', Reuters 11:10 12-03, 3 December 1992.
3. HRW/Angola, pp. 20–1.
4. See RN 1200GMT 921226 (UNITA operations from Ndalatando, destruction of the bridge between Dondo and Ndalatando); VORGAN 1900GMT 921229 (GOA offensive being launched); BBCWS 151GMT 921230 (2,000 GOA troops move on Caxito and Ndalatando); Johannesburg Channel Africa Radio 1600GMT 921230 (UNITA moving troops into Malange and Cuanza Norte; GOA offensive in NW Cuanza Norte; fighting around Ndalatando); VORGAN 1900GMT 921230 (GOA attack on Ndalatando and Caxito); VORGAN 1200GMT 921231 (axes of attack from Funda and Dange-ia-Menha given); VORGAN 1200GMT 930101 and 1900GMT 930103 (GOA withdrawal). The GOA denied, then admitted, and finally denied a second time, that it was conducting an offensive (RN 0600GMT 921231, Johannesburg Channel Africa Radio 1100GMT 921231; RN 1900GMT 921231).
5. The siege and fall of Huambo is reviewed in a long Associated Press article by Christopher McDougall (a0458, DS-04-24-93 1217EDT, 24 April 1993). UNITA's forces numbered about 10,000 and laid siege to the town defended by about 3,000 GOA forces.
6. See VORGAN 0600GMT 930316; on the same day UNITA took Cubal in Benguela (Lisbon RDP Antena 1 Radio 2200GMT 930313; VORGAN 0600GMT 930313).
7. VORGAN 0600GMT 930321; RN 1900GMT 930322 (report of Caxito recapture).
8. VORGAN 1200GMT 930320, 0600GMT 930328; also Johannesburg SAPA 2303GMT 930328.
9. VORGAN 0600GMT 930331, 0600GMT 930426.
10. For the UNITA recapture of Soyo, see VORGAN 1900GMT 930524. Two eyewitness accounts of the fighting were subsequently published in an American magazine, *Soldier of Fortune*. These were 'Improvise or die: SOF debriefs Angola merc', edited by Robert K. Brown, December 1993, pp. 56–87, and 'Merc work: Angola – Hired guns fight on both sides in endless civil war', August 1993, pp. 34–7.
11. For the siege of Kuito during the summer of 1993, see Luanda RN, 1900GMT 930721, 1900GMT 930810, 1900GMT 930811, 1900GMT 930815, 1900GMT 930821, 1900GMT930826, 1900GMT 930830, and 1900GMT 930831. The government broadcasts cited were on the nightly news and designed to give the Angolan public the widest exposure to the events of the siege.
12. VORGAN 0600GMT 930422; 0600GMT 930525; 0600GMT 930428.
13. VORGAN 0600GMT 930428; 1900GMT 930429; 0600GMT 930502.

14. BBCWS 1705GMT 930511.
15. See VORGAN 1200GMT 930523, 1900GMT 930519, and 1200GMT 930516.
16. See BBCWS/Portuguese 2030GMT 930824; RN 1900GMT 930817, 1900GMT 930825, 1900GMT 930830.
17. Lisbon, RDP Antenna 1 Radio Nacional, 2200GMT 930821. See also FBIS-AFR-93-173, 9 Sep 93, p. 13: FAA column advancing on Huambo numbers about 10,000.
18. See FBIS-AFR-93-149, 5 Aug 93, p. 22: FAN bombing campaign starts 3 Aug against Huambo area to support offensive, destroying 2 UNITA columns–between Alto Uama and Bailundo and between Huambo and Cachingues, with other targets in Huambo city hit; 30 raids so far (as of 5 Aug). FBIS-AFR-93-150, 6 Aug 93, p. 8: FAN attacks in support of ground operations directed at areas in Bailundo, Cachiumbo, Ngove, Andulo, and Chinguar. 'Well-defined' targets at Huambo attacked, with UNITA antiair capabilities 'systematically destroyed'.
19. For the UNITA version of the battle for Toco, see VORGAN 1930GMT 930721; FAA possession of the town: RN 1900GMT 930728.
20. Recapture of Camucuio, TPA 1930GMT 930728; capture of the UNITA 'Red Zone' and its logistics complex near Quipungo, RN 1900GMT 930809. Camucuio was again taken briefly by UNITA in late August (VORGAN 1200GMT 930825).
21. For the Cuanza Sul operations, see FBIS-AFR-93-141, 26 July 93, p. 23: Two-pronged attack in Cuanza Sul: Luanda–Quibala and Ebo–Waku Kungo. Air-assault forces supported the former axis between Catofe and Quibala. UNITA claimed forces defeated. See also FBIS-AFR-93-141, 9 Aug 93, p. 21: Despite UNITA's negative spin, the main FAA forces, built around the 18th Regiment, advanced in Cuanza Sul to the Waku Kungo area, at the same time attempting to cover their flanks with operations in Quilenda and elsewhere; secondary FAA attacks from Sumbe to Gabela and Conde attempted to disrupt UNITA blocking forces and prevent the enemy from concentrating forces. Note also VORGAN 1200GMT 930728 and 0600GMT 930809.
22. For the advance on Huambo, see BBCWS 1830GMT 940804; BBCWS 1515GMT 930806; campaigns in Benguela leading to the recapture of Ganda and Algo Catumbela, Johannesburg Radio South, 1500GMT 930817; Central Front operations, including an interview with General Armando da Cruz Neto, Luanda TPA 1930GMT 930819; see also Johannesburg Channel Africa Radio, 1600GMT 930831.
23. For the 5th Armoured Regiment/Group's advance toward Huambo, see Maputo RM, 930908 1400GMT.
24. See in general the overview of Central/Southern Front operations in Luanda RN, 1900GMT 930825, which appraises the situation to that date. For operations in Huila supporting the advance on Huambo, see Luanda RN 1900GMT 930806 and 1900GMT 930809; for the FAA recapture of Quilengues, see Luanda RN 930821.
25. Information courtesy of Center for International and Strategic Studies (CSIS), Washington, DC. For the FLEC factions, see TPA 1930GMT 940319 and RN 1200GMT 940625.
26. Information courtesy CSIS. See also VORGAN 1200GMT 930621, 1900GMT 930704 (GOA PSYOP plan to counter insurgent influence in Cabinda), and 1200GMT 930625 (UNITA denial of plans to attack Cabinda from Zaire).
27. For operations in Cabinda from June 1993, see VORGAN 1200GMT 930625; RN 0600GMT 931023; VORGAN 1200GMT 931023; and TPA 1930GMT 931206.
28. Ibid.; see also VORGAN 0600GMT 940106, which notes that the ground assault was preceded by air bombardments of central Bengo targets 5-7 January.
29. For an overview of the January operations, see the references in the following note. For the identity of the major units in the offensives, see VORGAN, 0600GMT 940926, which reviews the operations to date. It was only by late September that FAA successes elsewhere were to allow the groups stalled north of Ambriz and in the Ucua–Nambuangongo area to move forward once again.
30. RN 0600GMT 940111; VORGAN 0600GMT 940120, 0600GMT 940121, 0600GMT 940124, 0600GMT 940125 (late January offensive by GOA); VORGAN 1900GMT 940125, 1900GMT 940126, 1200GMT 940128, 1200GMT 940129 (Ucua region fighting); VORGAN 1200GMT 940130 (Nambuangongo and Usu fighting). For subsequent fighting, see Johannesburg Channel Africa Radio, 1100GMT 940224 and VORGAN 0600GMT 940307.
31. VORGAN 0600GMT 940307.
32. VORGAN 0600GMT 940912, 1200GMT 940909, 0600GMT 940928.
33. VORGAN 0600GMT 941004, 0600GMT 941005.
34. VORGAN 0600GMT 941015.
35. TPA 1930GMT 941101 (Soyo in GOA hands); BBCWS/Portuguese, 2030GMT 941101 (FAA 'close' to Soyo town); Lisbon RDP Antena 1 Radio Technik 2300GMT 941106 (Soyo taken by FAA); RN 0600GMT 941107 (Soyo in GOA hands since 4 November).

36. For the identity of the units in the group, see VORGAN 0600GMT 940326 and 0600GMT 940926.
37. VORGAN 0600GMT 940307. The composite artillery regiment consisted of four each of 122mm D-30 and 130mm M-46 cannons, and six BM-17 multiple rocket launchers.
38. See VORGAN 0600GMT 940326, 1200GMT 940326, and 1900GMT 940327.
39. VORGAN 1900GMT 940413, 1900GMT 940414, 1900GMT 940415, 1900GMT 940416, 1200GMT 940419, 1900GMT 940420, 1200GMT 940425, 1200GMT 940503 (Ndalatando shelled by Group M-46 artillery from Lukala-2), RN 1900GMT 940507 (Ndalatando capture reported).
40. VORGAN 1200GMT 940524, 1200GMT 940621; RN 1200GMT 940619, 1200GMT 940621, 1200GMT 940627.
41. VORGAN 1900GMT 940309; the headquarters of the Eastern Military Front was at Saurimo (RN 1200GMT 940919). For mercenary support, see VORGAN 0600GMT 940325.
42. See Maputo RM 0500GMT 940321 (Mona Quimbondo retaken), VORGAN 0600GMT 940325, 0600GMT 940327, 1200GMT 940328, 0600GMT 940331. See also RN 1215GMT 940329 and 0600GMT 940328.
43. VORGAN 1200GMT 940723.
44. Maputo RM 1730GMT 940818.
45. For the Malongo attack, see TPA, 1430GMT 940103; for subsequent fighting in Cabinda see TPA 1930GMT 940305; RN 1215GMT 940324; RN 0600GMT 940328 (Gen. Jose Pedro interview). For GOA-FLEC, see TPA 1930GMT 940425 and RN 1200GMT 940625.
46. For the renewed UNITA attacks, see RN 1900GMT 940708; for UNITA's capture of Belize and the FAA counterattacks, see RN 0600GMT 940714; VORGAN 0600GMT 940715; TPA 1840GMT 940716, 1930GMT 940729; RN 1900GMT 940816, 1900GMT 940830; see also BBCWS/Portuguese 2030GMT 940913.
47. See TPA 1930GMT 941017, for details of the attacks.
48. For the bombing of Kitona, see RN 0600GMT 941025. See also TPA 1930GMT 941101 (Chimbuande base captured).
49. See RN 1200GMT 940705 (5 July consolidation of FAA control over Kuito); RN 1900GMT 940706 (6 July FAA raid on Calupanda base); RN 1200GMT 940710, 1200GMT 940718 (expansion of FAA perimeter); VORGAN 0600GMT 940719 (FAA attack on Calupanda); RN 1900GMT 940803 (Cunhinga in FAA hands); see also overview comments in BBCWS/English 1705GMT 940908 and BBCWS/Portuguese 2030GMT 940913 (Kuito as a staging area for an attack west against Huambo).
50. For preparations for the Huila offensive, see VORGAN 0600GMT 940916; RN 1200GMT 940919.
51. For the bombing campaign against UNITA-held areas see VORGAN 0600GMT 940901, 0600GMT 940907; routes were already being cleared in late July (RN 0600GMT 940723). For the main ground attack launched on 15 September and the force size of about 20,000, see BBCWS 1515GMT 4 November 1994. On the 16th the FAA increased operations in Huila province, having first set up a major logistics base at Lubango (VORGAN 0600GMT 940916); the Huila ground campaign was launched on 24 September (VORGAN 0600GMT 940928). From 25 to 27 September FAA Chief of Staff de Matos held meetings with his Central and Southern Front commanders on the status of operations (VORGAN 1200GMT 940924). By mid-October the advance was by three groups, each under a brigadier (VORGAN 0600GMT 13 October 1994); for their identities as the 8th, 5th, and 1st Groups, see VORGAN 0600GMT 941109. For the four axes of approach (Benguela, Huila, Waku Kungo, and Bie), see BBCWS/Portuguese, 2030GMT 941107. For fighting on the Catengue–Chongoroi axis, see RN 1900GMT 940901; TPA 940921; VORGAN 1200GMT 940924; BBCWS 1515GMT 940928; RN 1900GMT 941018; BBCWS/Portuguese 2030GMT 94110.
52. For the eastward FAA advance from Longonjo on the 29th toward Londuimbali on 1 November, despite heavy UNITA minefields, see Reuters 2001GMT 01 November 1994. By this time the FAA had captured all of northern Huila from UNITA, and had managed to recapture all sites in Benguela province that UNITA had taken in mid-October (Lisbon RDP 1 Radio, 0900GMT 941102). On 4 November the FAA occupied Caala (Lisbon RTPI TV, 1200GMT 941104), in preparation for its final push on Huambo.
53. By 7 November UNITA had withdrawn from Huambo toward Bailundo, leaving the FAA to complete their occupation of the city (BBCWS/Portuguese 2030GMT 941101; Reuters, 1440GMT 4 November 1994; Maputo TVM TV 1800GMT 5 November 1994; Reuters, 1154GMT 6 November 1994; Maputo RMN 0500GMT 941107; Luanda RN 1900GMT 941107). For foreign confirmation of the fall of Huambo to the FAA, see Lisbon, RDP Antenna 1 Radio Network 1600GMT 941109.
54. VORGAN 0600GMT 941129.

Chapter Seven

The Chadian Insurgencies, 1975–1991

Insurgency and low-intensity conflict have marked the history of Chad, especially its desert north, since 1965. However, the situation never caught world attention until 1975, when the then-President, Ngarta Tombalbaye (ex-François) was killed in a coup led by the Army. By 1979 northern Chadian tribesmen had come to dominate the government and its military forces, and the history of Chad since then has been one of coups and military conquests by opposing northern factions. This dreary history would even still be of limited interest to the outside world were it not for the interests of France (the former colonial ruler of Chad) and Libya – whose leader, Muammar Qadhafi, seeks to dominate it and thus ensure the security of his southern border, as well as pursue his various aims to regional influence – and the interests of the United States and other Western countries in containing Libyan expansionist aims.

In 1987, the conflict was for the time resolved in favour of the Chadian regime of Hissein Habré and its French and United States backers. The Libyans suffered a series of crushing defeats in northern Chad and were expelled from the country. Even the 1990 overthrow of the government by a dissident faction led by the current President, Idris Deby, failed to permit the Libyans to recoup their earlier losses. However, at the time of writing Chad is again entering a period of uncertainty as the government has still not made promised democratic reforms to end the power of northern desert nomad leaders, and has been unable to reduce the size of the armed forces. Despite continuing problems, including growing unrest and discontent in the south, Deby's government has neverthe-less been able to successfully thwart challenges to its power by insurgent factions linked not only to the former government of President Hissein Habré but also threats by dissi-dent factions of Deby's own supporters.

PHASES OF THE CONFLICT
The Chadian conflicts divide themselves fairly easily into a number of successive phases that mark (1) the decline of the post-independence rule of the southerners and political collapse, (2) civil war and Libyan intervention, and then two fairly stable regimes, that of (3) Habré and (4) Deby, that mark the 1980s and 1990s. The phases of the conflict are thus:

■ A period of incipient insurgency, which ended with the fall of the Tombalbaye regime in 1975;
■ The spread of the northern insurgency, progressive collapse of the central govern-ment, the loss of political power by southerners, and the takeover by northern nomads amid destructive civil war and continued Libyan involvement, from 1975 to 1982;
■ The regime of Hissein Habré, 1982–1990, which restored some stability, gained inter-national support to expel the Libyan presence in the north, but finally fell prey to military dissidents led by Idris Deby;
■ The current regime of Idris Deby, from 1990, which began with major reforms on its agenda but which has proved unable to follow through on them, a victim of the same ethnic political-military dynamics which brought it to power. However, at the time of writing his regime has managed to reconcile itself to its main insurgent opponents.

The main focus of our discussions below will be the rise of the northern insurgents under the FROLINAT movement and the struggle of Habré's forces in 1986-1987 against Libyan-backed rivals in northern Chad. The military history of the country is very rich indeed, enough for many volumes, and only the most important military episodes can be discussed below.

KEY MILITARY FACTORS IN THE CONFLICT

In the following overview of the insurgency and the opposing forces, the main focus will be upon:

■ Strategy and tactics of the major armed factions;
■ Libyan intervention and tactics used against Chadian insurgents and light forces;
■ French and other foreign support to successive Chadian governments, especially for COIN warfare in the north.

Military high points of the troubled history of Chad include:

■ The insurgency that intensified after 1975 into civil war and which by 1979 destroyed most of the government institutions of the country;
■ The Libyan invasion of 1980-1981 to support the claims of Goukouni Oueddei to power;
■ The Libyan invasion in support of its northern Chadian allies in 1983, an unsuccessful bid to drive Hissein Habré from power (Habré was subsequently supported by the French in Operation 'Manta');
■ The expulsion of Libyan forces from most of northern Chad in a series of astounding victories in 1986-1987 (this was connected with the French Operation 'Epervier');
■ Habré's overthrow in 1990 by the forces of Idris Deby.

These highlighted periods are of military interest due to the lessons they yield for insurgent warfare and war between armed groups using desert nomad tactics.

OVERVIEW OF THE CONFLICT

THE EMERGENCE AND SPREAD OF INSURGENCY, 1965-1975

Chad's internal woes began with the policies of President François Tombalbaye, who ruled the country from independence to 1975. Tombalbaye, a southerner, relied upon his region as a support base. In the sparsely populated Muslim northern and central regions of Chad, discontent grew as the southern-dominated government suppressed dissent and favoured its own. By October 1965 the discontent of many Chadians was reflected in rebellions in the Sahelian middle part of the country. The initial rebellion began with uprisings by Moubi tribesmen at Mangalame in the mountains of the Guera prefecture; despite harsh reprisals by the government, uprisings then spread to Batha prefecture by the end of the year.

Early stage of the insurgency

At first the rebellions against the central government resembled the uprisings against the Congo government that had occurred some years earlier. Local peasants, alienated from the central government, armed themselves with traditional weapons and an assortment of old World War II arms and directed their anger against officials of the central government. The major issues were not only the measures designed to curb local traditional rulers but also corruption and abuses in collecting taxes (including an increase in the cattle tax and the imposition of a new civic tax) by agents of the Tombalbaye regime.

From the start, the central government harshly repressed the rebellions. In the Guera rebellion at least 500 died, many of them reputedly killed by government troops, in addition to government officials who died at the hands of angry peasants. Despite these measures, the rebellion spread to Batha prefecture and over the next two years to Ouaddai (by mid-1966) and Salamat (February 1967) prefectures. By 1967 the rebels, under the recently-organised FROLINAT (see below) had about 3,000 personnel loosely organised throughout central Chad, most still armed with antiquated weapons, which, however, still allowed them to assassinate government officials and their suspected sympathisers and conduct ambushes and raids. The Chadian Army, with about 8,000 personnel at this time, was unable, despite its advantage in firepower and mobility, to contain the spread of the insurgents, as the latter were well-entrenched in the difficult terrain of central Chad.

Formation of FROLINAT; spread of the insurgency to the BET The disadvantage the Chadian Army suffered was increased by the support neighbouring countries gave the insurgents. Muslim countries such as Algeria, Libya, and Sudan offered refuge to Chadian insurgents, and Sudan allowed the organisation (22 June 1966) of the Chadian National Liberation Front (Front de Libération Nationale du Tchad, FROLINAT) on its territory at the village of Nyala. The first leader of FROLINAT, Ibrahim Abacha, sought to take advantage of the refuge offered by Sudan to use the latter to base cross-border raids against government garrisons in contested areas of Chad. Under Abacha, FROLINAT's political programme advocated a popular, national democratic government of socialist direction; nationalisation of the cotton industry and other key economic sectors; non-alignment and rejection of any foreign military presence; the territorial integrity of the country; and the use of Arabic and French as national languages.[1]

In the meantime, more ominous events were taking place in northern Chad. There, in the Saharan prefecture of Borkou-Ennedi-Tibesti (BET), the French had withdrawn their last troops from Chad in 1965. In February 1968 Ibrahim Abacha was killed by the Chadian army near Abéché, but the local FROLINAT structure survived. Indeed, by that time a second FROLINAT group had formed in the BET area of the country following the arrival there of Mahamat Ali Taher in 1968 to organise the local Toubou tribesmen. The group organised by Taher emerged as the Second Liberation Army of FROLINAT, and was dominated by the Toubou. Yet a third entity further west, the Third Liberation Army, was organised at about this time in Kanem province among the ethnic groups there under the leadership of Aboubaker Abderrahmane. Discontent with the central government's policies had spread to the north-east and far north of Chad as well, prompting the outbreak of insurgent activity there from March 1968. In August 1968 a mutiny of the Toubou-dominated National Guard and Nomad Guard broke out at the garrison of Aozou, and gave the insurgency renewed impetus. By the end of the year government authority was restricted to the garrisons of Faya Largeau, Fada, Bardai, and Ounianga Kebir. The nomad Toubou and other desert groups to the east such as the Zaghawa and Bideyat controlled the countryside and made government administration impossible.

The rebellion of BET was a serious development that was the culmination of years of discontent arising from their ill-treatment by the Tombalbaye regime. The BET was dominated by the Toubou (Teda and Daza ethnic groups). Their spiritual leader, or Derde, Oueddei Kichidemi, who had held the office since 1939, had been persecuted by the Tombalbaye government and forced into exile in Libya. The latter country, at this time ruled by King Idris II, had ties to northern Chad as the ethnic groups there extended into southern Libya; so did the spiritual authority of the Derde.

With the spread of the rebellion, President Tombalbaye was forced (March 1969) to request direct assistance from the French government. The latter had already sent para-troopers into Aozou in late August 1968 to protect its interests, and this deployment was increased to an expeditionary force of 1,600, deployed in April 1969. 1,000 belonged to the 1st Parachute Regiment of the Foreign Legion. This intervention lasted to mid-1971. With French support, the Chadian Army was able to contain the rebellion to the BET. Part of the reason for this success included concessions Tombalbaye's government was forced to make – political reforms, abolition of many of the new taxes, and reinstatement of local leaders, especially in the Sahelian prefectures. Chadian internal security in 1970 and 1971 was less problematic for the central government, in part due to the French presence and in part due to government reforms. But this was the calm before the storm.

The rebellion of the nomads in BET continued, however, and on 1 September 1969 a fateful event was to occur in Libya that was to involve the two countries in war for over two decades. On that date Colonel Muammar Qadhafi and his supporters took power from King Idris II. Subsequently the king's bodyguard, consisting of Toubou nomads, was disbanded. Its members were permitted to return to northern Chad with their weapons. Qadhafi subsequently sought to expand the regional influence of Libya, with Chad the prime target of opportunity.

Emergence of splits within FROLINAT; Libyan involvement deepens FROLINAT had grown under Ibrahim Abacha and united the disparate rebels throughout the Sahelian prefectures of Chad, but his death in early 1968 had thrown the movement into turmoil. It was two years before the movement was to re-emerge under the leadership of Dr Abba Siddick, one of FROLINAT's founders but also a Marxist and self-proclaimed ideologue for FROLINAT. In the meantime, the FROLINAT Second Liberation Army in the BET became increasingly autonomous from the mainline FROLINAT of Abba Siddick and his First Liberation Army, and followed the leadership of Goukouni Oueddei, son of the Derde, and his lieutenant, French-educated Hissein Habré. While the latter emerged as the military leader of the Command Council of the Armed Forces of the North (Conseil de Commandement des Forces Armées du Nord, CCFAN), one of the FROLINAT successor factions to the Second Liberation Army, Goukouni sought the leadership of FROLINAT itself. Abba Siddick was ultimately restricted to the leadership of FROLINAT in the area controlled by its First Liberation Army in eastern Chad near the Sudan border. The Third Liberation Army of FROLINAT was operating in western Chad among the Kanembu people there.

French presence in Chad may have deterred Qadhafi temporarily from making any move against his southern neighbour. But with the beginning of the departure of the French from the BET in January 1971 (completed by the end of the year), he began to actively support FROLINAT as well as subversion within Chadian government and military circles against Tombalbaye himself. Relations were broken in August 1971 after an abortive coup attempt traced to Libya. This accelerated Qadhafi's assistance to FROLINAT. However, the Chadian government gradually sought a policy of accommodation, with Chad breaking relations with Israel in November 1971 and once more recognising the regime in Libya. However, in 1972 Libyan police and gendarmes occupied parts of the contested Aozou strip as Qadhafi sought to justify claims by citing a treaty made by Vichy France with Mussolini during World War II. By 1973 Libyan troops were present in the Aozou strip, and the following year the Chadian government was forced to admit that it had lost control of the area. By this time most of the BET had been effectively abandoned to the insurgents.

The concessions by the Tombalbaye government had their effect. While the French assisted the Chadian Army in bottling up the Second Liberation Army of FROLINAT in remote pockets of the BET, the improved relations with Libya allowed further gains against the insurgents. Libya restricted deliveries of supplies to the northern FROLINAT fighters, and this prompted fighting in 1973 and 1974 between the First and Second Liberation Armies. The Second Liberation Army (by now under control of Hissein Habré and renamed the FAN) was forced out of Ennedi by early 1974 and retreated to the Tibesti Massif. The First Liberation Army was left in control in the Ennedi. Its leader, Abba Siddick, with his heavily Arab base, was a firm ally of Qadhafi. The Second Liberation Army, however, had not been defeated but only checked by the combination of a supply cutoff and military attacks. A major split in the Second Liberation Army emerged, however, with factions taking sides along pro- and anti-Libyan lines. The latter faction was led by Hissein Habré, a Paris-educated former Chadian official of Toubou Daza (Anakaza clan) extraction who had defected to the rebels in 1971. Goukouni, however, maintained a pro-Libyan stance despite Qadhafi's obvious attempts at manipulation. Habré, however, decided to force the issue of French support to the Chadians by taking foreign hostages and hoping to split French policy toward Chad by forcing Paris to talk directly with FROLINAT's Second Army.

It was in the taking of hostages that FROLINAT and Second Liberation Army leader Hissein Habré first came to the world's attention. The Second Liberation Army by late 1973 had lost control of the Ennedi area and was forced back into the Tibesti massif itself. In April 1974, however, it took three foreigners hostage, including Françoise Claustre, a French archaeologist, and Major Pierre Galopin, a French military officer, later killed on Habré's orders. While the hostage crisis was eventually resolved, it had finally brought the insurgents into the world spotlight and had exposed the weakness of the Tombalbaye regime. It also created a major rift within Second Liberation Army ranks as Goukouni and Habré disagreed over the usefulness of taking foreign hostages. The two men, already at odds over relying on Libyan support, were from different branches of the Toubou ethnic group and had a personality conflict as well.

Last days of the Tombalbaye regime Tombalbaye, in the meantime, had taken the country in a new, disastrous, direction. The alienation of the north from the regime was followed by crisis in the southern support base. Political and economic reforms were abandoned in 1971, ostensibly for security reasons. In June 1973 Felix Malloum, the armed forces chief of staff, and others were arrested on charges of 'political sorcery' and other political figures were killed, arrested, or driven into exile. Tombalbaye subsequently replaced his ruling Parti Progressiste Tchadien, or PPT, with a new entity, the National Movement for the Cultural and Social Revolution (Mouvement National pour la Révolution Culturelle et Sociale, MNRCS). Looking to Zaire and its leader, Mobutu Sese Seko, and the latter's policies of 'Zairian authenticity,' Tombalbaye attempted to imitate this example. Local place-names were changed (Fort-Lamy, the capital, became Ndjamena; Fort-Archambault became Sarh); Government employees were ordered to replace their Christian names with 'indigenous' names; Tombalbaye replaced his Christian name, François, with Ngkarta. Many foreign missionaries were forced out of the country. France and its policies were attacked.

However, Tombalbaye went further. Chadian non-Muslim candidates for the civil service, government, and higher military ranks were all required to undergo the initiation into the Sara yondo rites. These harsh initiations, which were widely perceived as pagan and peculiar to the Sara ethnic group, only one of a number of southern peoples upon whom the Tombalbaye regime relied for its military and administrative support, were resented by many Chadian southerners on religious and ethnic grounds. They served to further alienate Tombalbaye's main sources of support for his increasingly crisis-ridden government. Further poor performance by the army against FROLINAT led to Tombalbaye's increased criticism of its leadership. Continued army involvement in alleged plots against the government resulted in growing alienation of the military and the loss of Tombalbaye's military support base. Finally, in March 1975, arrests of senior military officers seen as behind another coup plot resulted in junior military officers staging a mutiny and ordering gendarmerie units in the capital to overthrow and kill Tombalbaye on 13 April 1975. Malloum, released from prison, became the new President of Chad. French support was reaffirmed and many thought that the government would be able to carry the fight against the northern insurgents forward once more.

After Tombalbaye: chaos and civil war, 1975-1979

The post-Tombalbaye era marked Chad's descent into a period of political instability and economic ruin from which, over twenty years later, it has yet to recover. The weak government of Felix Malloum that took power after Tombalbaye's assassination attempted to enlist one of the northern insurgent factions, led by Hissein Habré, to counter the threat by the Libyan-backed faction led by Goukouni Oueddei. However, Habré's ambitions to power and Goukouni's access to support by Qadhafi resulted in the northeners effectively taking power by 1978 and then fighting among themselves, bringing Chad to ruin.

The civil war prompted direct Libyan military involvement, which resulted in Habré's defeat and flight from the capital. In 1980 Goukouni became president of Chad, backed by Libyan forces and a coalition of various groups that called itself the Transitional Government of National Unity (GUNT). Goukouni, however, soon began to lose control of the situation. Habré and his supporters had begun to operate from the Sudan border area, and by late 1981, with the departure of Libyan troops, he began to push toward the capital. The Libyans had been replaced by a peacekeeping force drawn from various African countries, but these proved ineffective in preventing hostilities, and stood by as Habré's forces continued their advance. Habré's forces occupied Ndjamena on 7 June 1982, dispersing Goukouni's forces defending the city. Goukouni himself, along with some of his key supporters, fled across the border to Cameroon and later resurfaced in Libya. Habré's forces subsequently gained control of southern Chad, which had remained under the control of the former Chadian army.

Habré declared himself president of Chad on 21 October. Although Goukouni's forces remained in control of parts of the north, especially the far north of the BET, Habré's lobbying in the world arena and assistance by opponents of Libyan expansion in the region resulted in most African countries recognising the government by the end of the year and Habré's government taking the country's seat at the United Nations. Habré, despite the animosity and outright hatred of many other Chadian political leaders, was now the country's strong man and immediately set about strengthening his position and preparing for the inevitable showdown with Libya.

The 'Toyota Wars' in northern Chad (1986-1987)

After consolidating his control of the remainder of Chad, Habré turned his attention to unifying the country. He was well aware of the diversity of Chad's peoples, the widespread disaffection and resentment in the wake of the civil war, and the need to give them a sense of national identity, and mobilise them behind him to face Goukouni and the remnants of GUNT and, beyond them, the Libyans themselves. His political capabilities were quite successful in forming a new national army as well as a new national political party. In doing so, he attempted to rally as many former enemies to his cause as possible, both internal and external. Many groups were ultimately reconciled to him, although into the mid-1980s most of the leaders of Libya-backed factions remained aloof. It was not until 1986 that the unity of the GUNT began to crumble, and was promptly taken advantage of by Habré.

In the meantime, Habré faced the first threat to his power, namely a resurgent GUNT, backed by Libyan troops. Goukouni, with Qadhafi's support, invaded northern Chad in April 1983. Despite tenacious resistance from Habré's forces, the Chadian government lost northern Chad to the invaders. This was after a brilliant campaign by Habré that recaptured Faya Largeau from Goukouni (30 July 1983) and prompted direct Libyan ground and air support to their allies. Habré was forced to relinquish his gains and retreat southward in August. By this time France and the United States had intervened to prevent any further southward push by Goukouni and the Libyans.

France's military intervention, codenamed Operation 'Manta', started on 9 August; United States and French aircraft began to lift in the first of 3,500 troops. They were equipped with state-of-the-art anti-armour and anti-aircraft defences as well as a range of offensive weaponry. Air assets backing ground forces included both fixed- and rotary-winged elements at various central Chadian airfields. Operation 'Manta' had the mission of containing the Libyan/GUNT expansion, to train Chadian forces, and to provide other assistance as required, including humanitarian. French and US equipment deliveries to the FANT soon followed.

In the face of the French deployment and United States military assistance to the Habré regime, Qadhafi refused to make any concessions to withdraw Libyan forces or persuade the GUNT to negotiate. By late September the French began to fix their positions on the 'Red Line' (the 16th Parallel), which, after some military incidents in which the Libyans and GUNT came out second, became the de facto demarcation line and the southern limit of the French 'zone d'exclusion', with any Libyan forces south of the line subject to immediate attack whenever and wherever detected. Qadhafi, though not overtly challenging the French move, still refused to make any serious movement toward negotiations. Meanwhile, Habré, well aware that Operation 'Manta' put off the inevitable contest with Goukouni and Qadhafi, began to rebuild his forces and equip them with French and US-supplied weaponry.

The cost and growing unpopularity of Operation 'Manta' with the French public and some sectors of government was a far greater threat to the continuation of the operation than any Libyan-GUNT threat. The French Defence Ministry was under continuing government pressure to ensure that not only the minimum military contingent necessary for the task remained in Chad, but that the entire force stayed only as long as was absolutely necessary. Many argued that France had a permanent presence, both air and ground, in neighbouring Central African Republic, and that any permanent deterrent capability should be stationed there.

Libya's forces remained at a disadvantage as long as the French deployment remained in Chad, threatening Libyan ground and air forces as well as the GUNT. Operation 'Manta', however, bolstered the Chadian forces in a number of ways. It not only provided a real air capability against the Libyans, as well as state-of-the-art air–ground support, but it also put into place an effective logistical system that could be used by the FANT as well. Against the Libyan threat the FANT would have been at a disadvantage without French assistance. Habré used his military aid to good advantage in 1984-1986 in southern Chad, where the new Chadian army, the Chadian National Armed Forces (FANT), were utilised to suppress rebellions by a number of commando, or codo, groups there still loyal to former Chadian military commanders such as Colonel Abdelkader Kamougue.

Qadhafi's response to the French deployment was both military and political. On the military front, Libya began to build or upgrade airstrips in northern Chad, especially at Tanoua (Aozou), Ouadi Doum, Faya Largeau, and Fada. The airfields were intended to be part of a network that included Sebha, Kufra, and Matan es-Sara in Libya to support Libyan-GUNT operations against Habré and the French. Qadhafi also re-equipped the GUNT and formed it into a force of about 4,500 personnel. However, the continuing major problem faced by the GUNT was the disaffection between the FAP of Goukouni, a Toubou, and the CDR of Achiek ibn Oumar, a Chadian Arab. GUNT forces remained light, vehicle-mounted formations deployed in the Tibesti and areas immediately south at Faya Largeau and Fada. In addition to the GUNT deployment, there were about 5,000 or so Libyan mechanised forces deployed in northern Chad, with key bases at Fada, Ouadi Doum, and Faya Largeau. By 1986 the Libyan buildup was effectively completed.

While France did not feel threatened by any Libyan military moves, Qadhafi's political offensive resulted in negotiations between Libya and France on a mutual troop withdrawal. On 17 September 1984 the two countries agreed on a mutual withdrawal of combat troops. While French withdrawal was completed on 10 November, Libyan troops remained. When Qadhafi refused to remove them after a second conference, France decided to retaliate for its being misled by preparing the way for any future interventions. It recognised Chad's claim to the Aozou Strip, and further stated that it would intervene if either the Libyans or the GUNT advanced on Ndjamena. The continuing French presence in the Central African Republic ensured that forces could be deployed almost immediately to effect this. French President Mitterand, however, said that France would not force out Libyan troops from northern Chad, or intervene in a civil war.

The military situation in the aftermath of Operation 'Manta', though not ideal for Habré, was still advantageous. Habré could still build up the FANT under the aegis of French forces in the Central African Republic; French and United States military aid–weapons, equipment, and training – still flowed into Chad. Meanwhile, the GUNT, despite its Libyan outfitting, was increasingly riven by leadership disputes on the personal and ethnic level as well as a steady stream of defections due to growing Libyan domination of northern Chad. By 1985 it was evident that a major confrontation was inevitable; it was merely when, that remained in question.

Renewed fighting; the FAP revolt against Libyan rule The long-awaited GUNT attack on FANT positions finally took place in February 1986. With heavy Libyan support, GUNT forces moving southward from Faya Largeau and Fada attacked FANT positions along the 'red line' from 11 to 16 February. All of these attacks were repelled by the FANT amid heavy fighting. By the 16th the fighting had escalated as French aircraft based at Bangui in the Central African Republic bombed the main Libyan airfield at Ouadi Doum. In retaliation Libyan aircraft made a desultory attack on Ndjamena airport on 17 February, with one bomb hitting the runway and closing it for two days.

France responded to the Libyan attacks by announcing a new operation to support the Chadian government, namely 'Epervier' ('Sparrowhawk'), that soon deployed 1,400 troops (later raised to 2,500 or so) along the 16th Parallel and a detachment of Mirage and Jaguar aircraft, as well as air defence assets, at Ndjamena airport. The United States also reacted to the incident, furnishing the Habré regime with an additional $10 million in military aid. The French deployment was in progress as another GUNT-Libyan attack against Oum Chalouba on 5 March took place. This was also repulsed by the FANT with no French assistance being required. Subsequently the FANT raided the Libyan base at Chicha, destroying it and capturing a number of Libyans, who were displayed to the international press on 20 March. The Libyans, discredited by the failure of their Chadian allies in the February–March attacks, were subsequently preoccupied with the confrontation with the United States in the Gulf of Sidra, beginning with initial exchanges on 24–25 March and culminating in the 15 April bombing of Libyan military facilities at Tripoli, Benghazi, and other sites. Qadhafi found little time to fix his attention at the moment to Chad, where his forces were under threat of French air strikes if they moved south.

The failure of the offensive impacted heavily on GUNT, and set in motion its effective disintegration over the following year. Habré's propaganda and his agents worked to undermine GUNT unity and exploit the hostility to the Libyans that had developed among many of Goukouni's supporters. Following another refusal by Goukouni to meet with the government, GUNT vice-president Kamougue resigned. He had earlier rallied to Habré along with a number of other opposition figures, including many southerners. This effectively ended the rebellion in southern Chad, and deprived the Libyans of a southern opposition to support against the central government. The breakup of the GUNT continued into the autumn of 1986, with Achiek ibn Oumar ending his 'condominium' with Goukouni and the FAP in the GUNT. Goukouni's forces had grown increasingly restive, with many dissatisfied with his leadership. The subsequent rebellion of most of his FAP forces was followed by news of his wounding in Tripoli in the course of a battle between his bodyguards and Libyan security forces on 10 October.

By this time the Libyans were faced by a full-scale rebellion of the FAP throughout northern Chad. Starting in August, elements of Goukouni's forces began to rally to Habré, especially in the wake of the split between Achiek ibn Oumar and Goukouni in August. Libyan forces in support of Achiek ibn Oumar assisted the CDR, heavily Arab, in attacking the Toubou FAP at Fada and elsewhere, using mechanised units and aircraft. Most of the FAP then withdrew into the Tibesti massif. The GUNT thus lost about two-thirds of its effective strength with the FAP changeover, and the Libyans, so long supporters of northern insurgents, found themselves faced with insurgent activity against their forces. Despite a temporary truce, the few FAP who remained on the GUNT side went over to the rebels on the news of Goukouni's wounding and capture in Tripoli in October. Libya's position had thus become untenable. Despite the presence of as many as 5,000 of Qadhafi's troops in the BET, concentrated at Fada, Faya Largeau, and Ouadi Doum, all heavily armed and with air assets, the Libyans were faced with an increasingly hostile population and the loss of their secure LOCs into the Aozou Strip through the Tibesti.

The FAP rally to Habré took place in November, and initially caught the Libyans by surprise. After taking Libyan garrisons at Bardai, Zouar, Yebbi Bou, and even Aozou itself (with an air base), the FAP consolidated its gains briefly before the Libyans deployed three separate combat groups to recapture the towns starting on 11 December. By the 20th they had done so, subsequently forcing the FAP into the massif itself, from where it continued raids against the Libyans. Qadhafi by now had about 6,000 troops in the region; these included Libyan forces in the main BET bases as well as in the Aozou Strip.

By the end of 1986 the Libyan disarray was virtually complete, despite control of the air. Libyan garrisons in the BET were virtually cut off from the Aozou Strip and the main overland resupply lines remained subject to FAP attacks. Libyan attempts to starve out the rebels in the Tibesti failed as French aircraft made parachute drops of arms, ammunition, and provisions to the FAP. The latter continued their hit-and-run attacks from their Tibesti hideouts, retreating afterwards into the rugged terrain where armoured and mechanised formations could not follow, and where air attack was virtually impossible.

The 'Toyota Wars' and the reconquest of the north 1987 – the year of the 'Toyota Wars' in Chad – saw some of the most remarkable fighting the continent has seen. Habré's forces, in three months, defeated Libyan forces inthe BET in lightning strikes and recaptured most of the Aozou Strip from the Libyans. Qadhafi's forces were expelled from Chad with heavy losses. Despite subsequent Libyan countermoves, Chad stood firm and maintained control over its conquests.

By early January Habré's forces were ready, assembling at Kalait and Ziguei for thrusts north of the 16th Parallel. The FANT was equipped with a variety of highly mobile and rugged vehicles. These included 4WD pickup trucks on which anti-armour and anti-aircraft weapons were mounted, and more conventional but somewhat slower light armoured vehicles for additional firepower. The FANT formations thus optimised speed, manoeuvrability, and firepower. The 1986 victories against GUNT-Libyan probes south of the 16th Parallel had improved morale and given FANT confidence in its tactics.

The Fall of Fada[3]

During the FAP rebellion in Tibesti, Habré bided his time for the right moment to launch his attack against Libyan forces. This came at the end of 1986, when on 31 December FAP units near Zouar inflicted a serious defeat on Libyan forces. Qadhafi's forces in northern Chad were dispersed to protect a variety of sites. However, a large concentration of Libyan and CDR troops had assembled at Fada, making a tempting target for Habré.

Early on 2 January the FANT struck against Fada using a series of classic desert nomad tactics in their attack. The FANT columns, attacking at high speeds, penetrated the armoured cordons protecting the base and then fired at them from the rear, often from virtual point-blank range. With the outer cordon of tanks and armoured vehicles destroyed, the Libyans withdrew the two remaining cordons closer to the Fada base and airfield. However, these were also overrun by noon, with the Libyan headquarters element escaping by air. 784 Libyans were killed and 81 captured. The FANT destroyed 92 T-55 tanks and 33 BMP-1s, capturing thirteen and sixteen respectively. A huge amount of weapons, including artillery and logistical vehicles, was captured as well – all this at the cost of eighteen killed, 54 wounded, and three vehicles destroyed on the FANT side.

The victory at Fada and the utter rout of the Libyans fixed world attention on Habré's FANT, which had fought against overwhelming odds and against far heavier weaponry. Libyan morale, by this time already low, was further damaged by the debacle. Although Libya reacted with air strikes by MiGs based at Ouadi Doum against Fada, Zouar, and Arada, as well as overflights of other Chadian towns, Qadhafi's forces could in reality do little. French air defences around Ndjamena as well as the presence of 'Epervier' air assets made any Libyan venture risky at best. French aircraft retaliated for the Libyan air attacks by destroying the air traffic control and air defence radar systems at Ouadi Doum on 7 January.

The Libyans received a second defeat on the 21st when FANT forces moving north from Ziguei attacked and destroyed a Libyan force in the Zouar area that was attempting to push out FAP elements who had established themselves nearby from the 13th. The Libyan rout was complete, with subsequent counterattacks on 23 January and 6, 15-16, 20, and 28 February repulsed. In the meantime, Libyan aircraft conducted air strikes with little success against FANT units in the Zouar and Fada areas. By this time FANT forces were raiding from bases on the central axis to the west of Faya Largeau. Libyan forces in the southern part of the BET had lost the main route into western Libya, and had to rely on the central and eastern routes from northern Chad into Sebha Oasis for overland resupply; even these were no longer secure from FANT interdiction.[4]

The Battles at Bir Koran and Ouadi Doum[5] After Fada, the Libyans responded by sending in more troops to Chad, many through the airfields at Ouadi Doum and Faya Largeau. By March there were at least 14,500 Libyans in the country. However, these troops remained beset by poor morale and organisational problems. The FANT retained Zouar in the north-west and Fada in the east, and was raiding from the central axis against the Faya Largeau region. Libyan aircraft still used the airfields at Faya Largeau and Ouadi Doum, but air strikes against FANT targets were increasingly risky due to improved Chadian anti-air capabilities. Thus a major ground attack by Libyan forces at the huge base was prepared at Ouadi Doum in early March against Fada.

The Libyan attack, launched by two mechanised columns in an attempted envelopment of the FANT position, was detected by the FANT. Using nomad tactics that had been so effect-ive at Fada, they struck at 07:00 on the 19th at the first Libyan force at Bir Koran, 50km south-east of Ouadi Doum, routing it and killing 384, capturing 47, and capturing or destroying a wide assortment of armoured vehicles and weapons. The following day, the second forma-tion, which had come to the aid of the first, was also defeated, losing 467 killed and 89 captured, and a similar assortment of weapons and equipment captured or destroyed.

The Libyans retreated across the desert to Ouadi Doum, with the FANT in pursuit. Ouadi Doum was protected by minefields, and had not been previously attacked by the FANT because of this. However, as the returning Libyans passed through gaps in the minefields, the Chadians, following behind, thus ascertained the safe path into the base, and advanced through the gaps, attacking the remnants of the fleeing force as well as the other Libyan troops based there. In a battle lasting 25 hours, the FANT captured the base and inflicted the worst single defeat of the war on the Libyans 22-23 March. 1,269 Libyans were killed and 438 captured. These included the Libyan zone commander, Colonel Khalifa Haftar, who was captured, and his deputy, Colonel Gassim Ali Abou Naour, who was killed. 89 T-55 tanks and 120 BMP-1s were destroyed or captured, and much other material was captured or destroyed. Sixteen Libyan aircraft, including three combat helicopters, were destroyed on the ground and sixteen captured. A range of air defence and air defence radar equipment (including SA-6s and SA-10s) was captured.

The loss of Ouadi Doum sealed the fate of the remaining Libyan occupation of northern Chad. Close air support of ground troops was no longer possible and the remaining Chadian allies of the Libyans rallied to Habré. Libyan forces began a slow and difficult withdrawal northward into the Aozou Strip. The FANT harried them as Libyan aircraft bombed Ouadi Doum, Faya Largeau, and other towns, in most cases to prevent Chadian use of the captured equipment. However, these strikes were generally unsuccessful but did cause civilian casualties. By 27 March the FANT reoccupied Faya Largeau; on 30 March, Ounianga; and on 1 April, Gouro.

In three months of fighting a relatively small, lightly-armed (by conventional standards) force had defeated a large, well armed mechanised one with air support, in a series engagements that had cost the Libyans dear. Official FANT records for the period 20 December 1986 to 30 March 1987 show 4,469 Libyans killed and 936 captured against FANT losses of 77 killed and 132 wounded. The Libyans lost over a billion dollars' worth of equipment, much of it appropriated by the FANT for its own use.[6]

Fighting in the north; the aftermath Despite Habré's victories, most of the Aozou Strip remained under Libyan occupation. Following the consolidation of the FANT positions, Habré chose to ignore the French request to bring the Aozou Strip issue before an international tribunal. Instead, on 8 August 1987 he sent Mahamat Nouri and a 400-strong FANT force against the town of Aozou, which was captured. However, the Libyan base and airstrip at Tanoua remained in Qadhafi's hands, and from this they counterattacked, using light forces under Colonel Ali Sharif al-Rifi armed in the same 4WD vehicles used by the FANT and backed by close air support by aircraft based in southern Libya. The Chadians were driven from Aozou on 29 August, but remained in the mountains south of Aozou.[7]

Despite appeals to France, Habré received no military support against Libyan air attacks. FANT air defence capabilities were increasingly ineffective against Libyan aircraft, which delivered their ordnance above the effective range of the SAMs available to Habré's forces. However, this did affect the accuracy of bombing and other air support activity. Confident that the military tide was turning in his favour, Qadhafi continued to refuse to negotiate with Habré.

Habré, exasperated by the continued impasse with Qadhafi, finally decided on a bold military move. On 5 September 1987 FANT forces based north of Ounianga and led by Habré's most able general, Hassan Djamous, struck across the Libyan border at the airfield and military post of Matan es-Sara. This was a major base for Libyan aircraft providing support to operations in the Aozou Strip, and the only major installation in the land LOC between the Chad border and the Libyan oasis of Kufra.

The attack on Matan es-Sara gave the Libyans no warning. The FANT completely destroyed the base, killing or capturing over 2,000 Libyans, and destroying 22 aircraft and

100 armoured vehicles. An enormous amount of military equipment was captured by the FANT, which took it post-haste back across the border, vacating the base before the Libyan air response, which bombed the facility nevertheless. Subsequent Libyan actions were impulsive and equally unproductive. Libyan aircraft attacked Chadian sites on 8 December. One bomber reached Ndjamena, but was shot down by French air defences. Qadhafi finally agreed to a ceasefire on 11 September.[8]

Habré to Deby, 1989-1990, and subsequent developments

By the late 1980s it became evident that Habré, entrenched firmly in power, was ever more unwilling to make needed reforms, even though he no longer had a credible Libyan threat to worry about and use as an excuse to end his virtual military dictatorship over the country. The end of the conflict with Libya also meant that military assistance by Chad's western supporters, especially France and the United States, had less leverage with the Habré regime. However, Habré and his Gorane supporters were becoming increasingly uneasy as rumours of dissent from within the military began to surface. Habré's power rested on the military, and it was the latter who could unseat him. Allegations of an attempted coup by two of his most trusted military commanders, Hassan Djamous and Idris Deby, in early 1989 began the cycle of events that were to unseat him less than two years later.

In April 1989 Habré moved against his opponents, charging them with coup plotting and apprehending Hassan Djamous, who was later killed. Idris Deby, however, escaped to Sudan, where he organised a successful resistance against the regime, called the Patriotic Salvation Movement (Mouvement Patriotique du Salut, MPS). With Libyan support and French refusal to prop up the Habré regime, Deby first successfully resisted government attempts to destroy him. Finally, in a series of military actions from 10 November to 2 December 1990, Deby was able to inflict major defeats on Habré's forces and drive him from Ndjamena.

Habré's supporters later resurfaced in Niger, but have remained generally too weak to pose a threat to the Deby regime. However, the Chadian government has been beset by various insurgent threats in the north-east and the south since 1991. The Deby regime successfully pursued a major foreign policy objective of Chadian governments, namely the return of the Aozou Strip. The case was put before the International Court of Justice at the Hague, with the case finally decided in Chad's favour on 3 February 1994. Libya agreed to withdraw its forces from the contested area in April of that year, and by 31 May had done so.[9]

NOTES

1. *NA*, November 1977, pp. 1057-8.
2. See *ARB*, 8312a-8313b; 8336a-8337c.
3. See *ARB*, 8370a-8371b.
4. *ARB*, 8401a-8402a.
5. See *ARB*, 8432a-8434a.
6. *ARB*, 8468b-c.
7. *ARB*, 8588c-8591a.
8. *ARB*, 8617b-8618a.
9. *ARB*, 11319a-11320a; 11393a; 11427a-b.

Chapter Eight

Insurgencies in the Horn of Africa

The second great theatre of Cold War conflict in Africa was the Horn. This vast area, almost as large as Europe itself, is home to a large number of ethnic groups that have in many cases long-standing and implacable enmities. The region, with its rugged terrain and vast, undeveloped areas with little or no infrastructure, is tailor-made for insurgency, rebellion, and banditry and difficult for conventional military operations.

Two insurgencies are discussed here. The first are the northern Ethiopian insurgencies from 1975 to 1991 that brought down the quasi-communist dictatorship of Mengistu Haile Mariam, in which the chief insurgent groups were Eritrean and Tigrean. The second is Somalia, where insurgency has combined with civil war and anarchy to reduce the country to a shambles since the 1990 overthrow of president-turned-dictator Siad Barre.

ETHIOPIAN INSURGENCIES

When Emperor Haile Selassie I was overthrown in 1974 Ethiopia had but one insurgency, that in Eritrea. By the mid-1980s there were at least a half-dozen major insurgent groups and many smaller ones. It was the TPLF, one of the insurgencies that originated after the imposition of the Mengistu regime, that ultimately brought it and its strong man to ruin.

PHASES OF THE WAR, 1975–1991
Despite the simultaneous activity of two major insurgent groups in northern Ethiopia, the conflicts collectively fall into a sequence of fairly well-defined phases that reflect the security impact on the Mengistu regime. Four major phases can be identified:

Phase One: Eritrean ascendancy and tactical defeat; emergence of the TPLF, 1975–1978
During this period the new Ethiopian regime of Mengistu Haile Mariam and the Provisional Military Administrative Committee (PMAC), which had inherited the Eritrean problem from the last Emperor, Haile Selassie, fought to recapture gains by the insurgents. It was marked by the following events:

■ The struggle between the new Ethiopian government and the Eritrean People's Liberation Front (EPLF), which resulted in first the victory and then the tactical defeat of the EPLF and other Eritrean groups and their withdrawal from the major urban centres;
■ The foundation of the Tigrean People's Liberation Front (TPLF) in Tigray;
■ The start of massive Soviet and other communist-country assistance to Mengistu and the PMAC:
■ The rapid expansion of the Ethiopian Army and Air Force, spurred by the Ogaden War, to cope with both external and internal threats;
■ Initiation of major annual offensives against Eritrea;
■ Sudanese and other Arab country assistance to the Eritrean rebels.

Phase Two: The struggle for Eritrea; spread of conflict through Tigray, 1978/9–1984
This period was one of intense fighting in Eritrea as the EPLF battled the government in defence of its holdings there and attempted to expand operations throughout the rest of Eritrea; in Tigray the TPLF expanded its operations as well. It included:

■ Beginning of Eritrean offensives against the central government;
■ Establishment of territorial control by the EPLF in northern Sahel zone (with the main insurgent centre near Nakfa and areas immediately north), and its successful defence against the Ethiopian Army and Air Force;
■ By 1981, the ascendancy of the EPLF as the principal Eritrean liberation movement, with the defeat of the ELF in Barka zone;
■ The TPLF spread of operations throughout Tigray province;
■ Continued expansion of the Ethiopian military, especially the Ethiopian Ground Forces (EGF);
■ The start of a major period of famine in northern Ethiopia, subsequently exploited by the Mengistu regime as a weapon against the northern insurgents.

Phase Three: The initiative passes to the insurgents, 1984–1988
This period was initiated by the March 1984 capture of Mersa Teklay by the Eritreans and ended by the catastrophic defeat of the Ethiopian Army at Af Abet. However, already as early as 1984 it was apparent that the central government could not defeat the insurgents, who had become too well-established in the north. This phase was marked by the following developments:

■ The virtual alienation of the northern Ethiopian population from the Mengistu regime by its use of the famine as a weapon against the insurgents in 1984–1985;
■ The increase in logistical capabilities of the EPLF with the capture of the port of Mersa Teklay (March 1984) and the Sudan border post of Teseney (January 1984);
■ Establishment of the EPLF throughout most of Eritrea and control of the entire Eritrean border with Sudan;
■ Unsuccessful annual offensives against the Nakfa area by the EGF, launched from bases in the Keren-Asmera corridor;
■ Collapse of the government military strategy with the catastrophic defeat of the Ethiopian Second Army at Af Abet in March-April 1988;
■ In Tigray, establishment of TPLF territorial control over most of the province by the end of 1988.

Phase Four: Destruction of the Mengistu regime, 1988–1991
After Af Abet, it took the EPLF and TPLF insurgents a little over three years to inflict ever more devastating defeats on the Ethiopian military and advance to Addis Ababa, finally capturing the capital and putting Mengistu to flight in May 1991. This phase of the war was marked by:

■ Virtual isolation of the Second Army in the Massawa Asmera-Keren corridor by the end of 1988 and its cutting off from the sea in March 1990 with the EPLF capture of Massawa;
■ Complete control of Tigray by the TPLF by the end of 1988 and expansion of TPLF operations south and eastward;
■ Loss of most Soviet and other communist aid and the virtual exhaustion of Ethiopian manpower by early 1991;

179

■ From September/October 1989, the progressive advance of the TPLF-led Ethiopian People's Revolutionary Democratic Front (EPRDF) southward to the capital.

HIGH POINTS OF THE CONFLICT, 1975–1991

Discussed here are salient aspects of the conflict in the north, emphasising major military events. The reader should also keep in mind that as the Ethiopian government forces fought with Eritrean and Tigrean forces, other insurgent groups concurrently challenged Mengistu's regime with varying degrees of success, though never as significantly as the EPLF and TPLF.

The spread of insurgency in northern Ethiopia, 1975–1978/9

Following the military takeover of 1974, the PMAC inherited a rapidly-spreading armed resistance throughout Eritrea, which had had its autonomous status illegally abrogated by the previous imperial regime. In early 1975 the central government had approximately 2,500 troops in Eritrea, many busy preventing the capture of the towns of Ak'ordat and Teseney by the rebels. These key towns dominated the main route across the Sudanese border; the regime of Sudanese President Gafaar Nimeiri was said to be assisting the Eritrean rebels, many of whom were Muslims.[1]

The situation up to 1975 remained fairly static. Despite an offensive by the Eritrean Liberation Front (ELF) and its allied faction the Popular Liberation Front (PLF) in February, little changed in the first half of the year. However, later fighting spread to southern Eritrea and involved other ethnic groups. Locally the main groups involved were the Tigreans and the Afars or Danakils south of Eritrea. The Afars, who had a semi-autonomous state ruled from the town of Asahita by Sultan Ali Mireh, resisted attempts by the PMAC to impose its rule, and in the ensuing fighting the sultan was forced to flee to the neighbouring French Territory of the Afars and Issas (TFAI), where he established the Afar Liberation Front (ALF). The Afars continued to resist PMAC attempts to impose its rule, and gradually developed an attitude of mutual live-and-let-live which held through the remainder of the war.[2]

Meanwhile, in nearby Tigray province similar attempts by the PMAC to impose land reforms and increase government control over the lives of the local peasantry resulted in widespread discontent. A local member of the nobility, Ras Mengesha Seyaim, raised the banner of revolt by April of 1975, forming the Tigrean Liberation Front (TLF); this move-ment was to be later taken over by and subsumed into the Tigrean People's Liberation Front (TPLF), with the TPLF leader, Meles Zenawi, usurping the TLF insurgent role, killing Mengesha Seyaim, and advocating a radical Marxist agenda. Later the TLF joined a number of other resistance movements in forming the Ethiopian Democratic Union (EDU), a blanket opposition faction best represented in the northern part of the nation. However, the TPLF continued to dominate northern armed opposition outside Eritrea.[3]

From the start the PMAC had attempted to persuade the general population in Eritrea to negotiate its differences with the central government but the Eritreans remained suspicious. Despite a direct invitation from PMAC chairman General Teferi Banti to meet with its representatives, the Eritreans (ELF) refused to attend. The latter, concerned over rival movements and convinced of the central government's weakness, felt it could do better on the battlefield than at the negotiating table.

1976–1977 marked the beginning of the long conflict in Eritrea as insurgents rejected co-option by the PMAC and resisted its military efforts. The PMAC, for its part, subse-quently abandoned reconciliation in favour of a military solution. Belief in the feasibility of a military option was reinforced by the switch from the United States to the Soviet Union as the principal military supplier. The emergence of the hard-liners in the PMAC, led by Colonel Mengistu Haile Mariam, was the result of a violent power struggle within the revolutionary government that had far-reaching implications not only for Eritrea and Tigray but also for the rest of the Ethiopia as well as the entire region. The dominance of Mengistu in the PMAC aligned Ethiopia with the USSR and was to result in the buildup of an enormous military force armed by the Soviets. So armed, the central government was determined to crush all opposition to its social and economic reforms throughout the country by force. As time went on it was to become apparent that military force as an answer was increasingly less effective and that the population was progressively alienated from the central government and sympathetic to the insurgents. Despite this, Mengistu remained to the end a believer in the military option.

1976 opened with renewed attempts by the PMAC to negotiate. The threat of war grew in the Horn as border disputes with Somalia became ever more common, and the central government feared being forced to fight a two-front war. At the time, the major military supplier for the PMAC was the United States, and this patron was wary of some of the extreme steps being taken by the central government in both its social reforms as well as its treatment of internal minorities. On 16 May General Teferi Banti, in a special radio broadcast, outlined a nine-point proposal for Eritrea, which included a general ceasefire with the insurgents, the end of the state of emergency imposed to combat the Eritrean rebels, and cooption of the Eritrean 'progressive' agenda by incorporating that element of its leadership into the PMAC.[4]

The PMAC backed up the nine-point peace proposal with military action in hopes of making gains against a disunited Eritrean resistance unsure over the response to the central government's offer. On 15 May it launched an offensive in the Asmera area, western Eritrea (Ak'ordat corridor), and southern Eritrea. The PMAC also assembled a large army of poorly armed and trained conscripts from among the peasantry in the central highlands and deployed them in western Eritrea with the aim of marching into and occupying the rebellious province. The peasants had about 40,000 in their ranks by late May and over 100,000 by the end of June. However, this rag-tag army fell apart in northern Tigray near Adwa when it was attacked by the Eritreans. On 19 June government forces, stalled at Humera, formerly called off the campaign.[5]

Repercussions of the fiasco reached the highest ranks of the Ethiopian military and the PMAC. Some within the latter boldly stated that the central government should have been much more sympathetic to the Eritreans' demands. However, the main policy advocates of reconciliation were gunned down by central government troops under the pretext of 'plotting against the government' and 'economic sabotage'. Dissent within the PMAC over the Eritrean question was henceforth much more subdued.[6]

October 1976 gave the Eritreans further cause to worry about central government intentions. On the 9th a sweeping administrative reform package implemented the kebele (sub-district) system throughout the country. These jurisdictions gave considerable power at the local level for government organs to enforce the PMAC agenda. They also served as instruments of control, allowing the PMAC to have eyes and ears in practically every city ward and village in the country.[7]

1977 opened with most land routes in Eritrea as well as the population controlled by the Eritrean People's Liberation Front (EPLF), a new faction of ELF breakaways, based in northern Sahel. Early 1977 was spent by the EPLF in gaining and consolidating territory. By 22 March the town of Nakfa in the very difficult hilly terrain of northern Eritrea was taken by the EPLF while the ELF concentrated on gains in the lowlands further south-west and south.[8]

Meantime sensational events took place in Addis Ababa. On 3 February General Banti was killed in a gun battle near his home by rival PMAC elements led by Mengistu. Central government hostility toward Eritrea became more pronounced as the USSR promoted its agenda within the PMAC and assisted its client Mengistu. Soviet and Cuban influence grew until in March the PMAC announced it had made an agreement with the USSR to obtain Soviet weapons and equipment, thus sealing Ethiopia's alliance with the East Bloc.[9]

The central government believed it had finally found a way around the need for negotiations to settle its border dispute with Somalia in the east and its differences with internal dissidents. Negotiations as a condition for military assistance were part of the United States aid policy; with the USSR now a patron providing unqualified military aid, the PMAC was finally able to begin arming a growing military force with the aim of first repelling the Somali invaders in the east and then turning its attention to the Eritreans and other internal enemies.

As Ethiopia began to arm its rapidly growing army, the Eritrean opposition met in Khartoum in October to agree on common courses of action between the ELF and the EPLF. By this time the insurgents controlled over 90 per cent of Eritrea. The EPLF's agenda called for independence from Ethiopia, despite the latter's need for access to Red Sea ports. The first EPLF congress, from January to March of 1977, developed this agenda, which remained an article of faith for the movement through the collapse of the Mengistu regime in 1991.[10]

Military action, especially by the EPLF, increased in 1978 in anticipation of later attacks by government forces. The war with the Somalis in the Ogaden was being prosecuted with Soviet and Cuban aid, and the EPLF rightly feared that once scores were settled in the east, Eritrea would be the regime's next target. Even before the end of the Ogaden fighting Ethiopian troops, ferried by Soviet transport aircraft, were airlifted into Asmera, capital of Eritrea, starting in March. The ELF and ALF were also busy in the north; the latter cut the road inland from Aseb to the highlands in November, although government forces soon reopened it.[11]

Soviet military assistance by late 1978 began to transform the Ethiopian Army from the relatively small pre-revolution force (four divisions) equipped with Western equipment to a much larger force armed with Warsaw Pact equipment. Major ground systems acquired by the Ethiopian forces included tanks (T-34s and T-54/55s), APCs, artillery (including D-30 122mm and M-46 130mm cannon), and multiple rocket launchers (MRLs) (122mm BM-21), plus logistical vehicles. Also supplied were extensive amounts of small arms and ammunition, as well as training. In the Ogaden, the Cubans had provided actual ground troops to assist the Ethiopian Army. By 1978 the USSR also began to assist the Ethiopian military in air operations, agreeing to provide 48 MiG-21s in September of that year.[12]

The EPLF withdraws to the north, 1978/9

The inevitable assault in Eritrea took place in March–December 1978. A government force of at least 75,000 advanced into Eritrea along several fronts, recapturing most towns from the insurgents. The ELF, based in the lowlands of central and western Eritrea, was hardest hit, however, while the EPLF simply withdrew to its mountain strongholds around Nakfa. Through December repeated operations by the Ethiopian Army and Air Force failed to dislodge the EPLF, despite the temporary loss to the latter of its corridor to Sudan (Ak'ordat fell on 15 August 1978; Keren on 27 November).[13]

The central government, now dominated by Mengistu (the PMAC had been replaced by the governing council known as the Derg, of which Mengistu was head) and its Soviet and Cuban supporters, advocated a military solution to the insurgencies. From July 1979 to January 1980 the Ethiopian Army mounted two major offensives to take Nakfa and drive the EPLF from its strongholds in northern Eritrea into Sudan. The organisation and tenacity of the EPLF had already made a sobering impression upon the Mengistu regime; already, in early 1979, the insurgents were besieging the towns that the army had earlier recaptured from them.[14]

The limits of the Ethiopian military's capabilities were reached in the summer of 1979. From 16 to 31 July the EPLF threw back a major offensive against Nakfa. The following month the Tigrean People's Liberation Front (TPLF), which had replaced the TLF in Tigray, made its first major gains in the province (July–August) despite a major Ethiopian Army campaign there. The final military action in Eritrea, which closed 1979, was a two-pronged offensive by the EGF. The first battle of the campaign took place from 1 to 15 December in the Nakfa area, and resulted in the repulse of Ethiopian forces; the second major battle took place from 5 to 10 January 1980, during which time the EPLF turned back an attempted attack along the coast and then inland east of Af Abet. Following this reverse, central government forces retreated to bases near Asmera. The losses to the Ethiopian ground forces in Eritrean offensives alone were immense; at least six army divisions had suffered extensive casualties – over 15,000 – with one and possibly two divisions virtually annihilated. Losses of armour and other vehicles numbered in the hundreds.[15]

The extent of government losses is reflected in the low level of military activity during the remainder of 1980. In October the EGF undertook another attack against the EPLF in the Af Abet area, but this was apparently a diversionary move to allow forces elsewhere to open roads closed by insurgents. A similar campaign took place in Tigray, with little result. The insurgents avoided contact with the army, which withdrew leaving much of the province in control of the TPLF with a few enclaves of government garrisons on the main roads. 1980 and most of 1981 saw little military action by the government as the Mengistu regime sought to build up its forces for another major offensive.[16]

The significance of the 1979 victory of the EPLF was that the movement had success-fully defended territory it had captured and secured against three concerted EGF assaults. Continued successful defence of the Nakfa area, a rugged, remote region, against further EGF assaults ensured a secure base area for the insurgents. They subsequently used this base to expand their area of operations throughout the north. The subsequent history of the war is one of repeated unsuccessful EGF attacks against the base area, and EPLF coun-terattacks that progressively enlarged its area of control. Thus by the mid-1980s large areas of Eritrea were 'no-go' zones for the EGF, regardless of the size of the force that attempted to break into EPLF strongholds. The Tigrean insurgency, not as developed at this time, later used the EPLF insurgency as a model.

The Mengistu regime responded to the EPLF successes with a measures to deny the insurgents bases or resources. This turned into a mere scorched-earth programme, enforced by aerial bombing or artillery shelling of inhabited villages likely to be used by the insurgents, destruction of crops and livestock, destruction of transport and other infrastructure, and levelling of all dwellings outside government zones of control. The regime's aim was to depopulate those areas it could not hold militarily. The EPLF responded by moving much of the population in liberated areas to Sudan, and by protecting the rest in fortified village complexes designed to evade detection, or, if discov-ered, to resist aerial bombing or shelling by ground forces.

With government forces temporarily at bay, differences between the EPLF and ELF began to emerge again. These were over conflicting areas of operations, resentment over past fail-ures to cooperate or coordinate, and ideological or personal differences between comman-ders of the opposing forces. From 28 August to late September 1980 the EPLF drove the ELF from the highlands into the lowland area of Eritrea along the Baraka River, effectively ending its role as a major force in the conflict. During early 1981 the EPLF renewed its attacks on the ELF, driving it into Sudan, where government forces disarmed the remnants. The EPLF, with its secessionist agenda, thus gained control of the Eritrean liberation struggle. The EPLF enjoyed increasing popular support and advocated a plebescite in Eritrea under international supervision to choose autonomy, confederation with the central government, or complete independence. The EPLF agenda and war fighting style had prevailed.[17]

The war, 1981–1988

There was a major drought and famine in Ethiopia which lasted from 1984 to 1987/8. Military events must be viewed in light of the prevailing famine. As large areas of northern Ethiopia, including Tigray and parts of Eritrea were hard-hit, the regime was quick to seize upon famine relief, or denial of it, as a weapon to force the population affected by the famine into areas of government control. At the same time it denied access of food provided by relief agencies into insurgent-held areas. However, there were major difficulties in supplying most government-held areas as well. Had it not been for international relief efforts, the Mengistu regime would have likely collapsed. As it was, much famine relief once under government control was directly diverted to supplying government garrisons and operational units, and undoubtedly prolonged the war. Despite the famine, both sides continued to fight on, with the insurgents continuing to make gains, albeit more slowly than they would otherwise have.[18]

The answer of the Mengistu government to reverses at the hands of the EPLF was more war. 1982 began with the launching of the ambitious Operation 'Red Star' that was intended once again to attempt the capture of Nakfa. At least ten divisions – 140,000 men – were marshalled in preparation for this offensive, begun in January. However, by the end of the fighting season (October–November), government forces were in retreat. They managed to penetrate within 10km of Nakfa before being forced to withdraw by determined EPLF counterattacks. Attacking forces lost almost fifteen per cent–20,000 men–as casualties in the fighting.[19]

Having failed in its attempts to win by force, the Mengistu regime tried in 1983 to negotiate. Talks were held in Rome with the EPLF, with little concrete result. At the same time the central government mounted another attack against the TPLF in February, which lasted to November. In return the TPLF as well as the EPLF increased the level of fighting against the central government, with the TPLF mounting operations in Wello and Gonder provinces for the first time.[20]

Despite advocating negotiations, actions by the Mengistu regime pointed to more military conflict. On 3 May it promulgated a national service decree that made males aged 15 to 30 eligible for active military service, and males up to the age of 45 liable for call-up as well.[21]

In 1984 the EPLF followed up January gains with an offensive, in which it used captured EGF tanks, APCs, and artillery. In concerted attacks along the 60km Nakfa Front from 19 to 22 March, the insurgents overran EGF defences and captured Karora and Mersa Teklay, defeating in the process an EGF task force consisting of an infantry division, a mechanised brigade, two tank battalions, four field artillery battalions, and six air defence battalions, killing 4,000 EGF soldiers and capturing 2,500.[22]

As March drew to a close, it became evident that the EPLF was winning some of its most impressive victories since 1978. Towns in central and southern Eritrea were attacked and encircled. Alghena was captured in late March, to be followed by Mersa Teklay, Senafe, and Addi Caleh; in all, the EPLF claimed it had 7,500 EGF prisoners as a result of these actions. The capture of Mersa Teklay was a particular blow to government forces, as this was the port from which resupply by sea from Dahlak and Mitsiwa had been made to support EGF offensives in northern Eritrea; the EPLF could now use the captured port in its turn.[23]

The capture of Mersa Teklay was militarily significant for another reason: the EPLF made use of captured tanks and APCs to mount a successful brigade-sized combined arms attack on the town. EPLF air defence was effective, shooting down an EAF MiG-23.[24]

Little or no change in the Mengistu regime's desire to militarily crush the Eritrean resistance was apparent through 1985. In the face of this threat the Eritrean factions continued to pool their resources and seek agreements with one another, forming in January the

Eritrean Unified National Council (EUNC). The new movement sought support from other anti-regime movements, and supported the Western Somali Liberation Front (WSLF). It claimed to be equal in manpower to the EPLF. However, non-EPLF Eritrean factions were to figure little in the subsequent history of the war.[25]

The government renewed the 1985 fighting on a vicious note. On 24 and 25 March Ethiopian Air Force (EAF) fighters descended upon the town of Abi Adi in Tigray, where TPLF members had gathered to celebrate the tenth anniversary of the movement. The town, whose normal population of 4,000 had swollen to 20,000, was severely damaged and several hundred people, mostly civilians, were killed. Evocation of this event subsequently became a rallying cry for the TPLF.[26]

The TPLF, spurred to revenge for the attack, pressed regime forces hard. The subsequent TPLF campaign took the fighting south into Wello province. This fighting, which pitted the lightly-armed TPLF insurgents against mechanised EGF units with combat helicopter and air support, marked the first major TPLF campaign south of Tigray.[27]

The EPLF summer campaign was less successful, gaining and losing the town of Barentu but nevertheless still inflicting heavy losses on the EGF. In capturing Barentu, the attacking EPLF force defeated two EGF divisions and a mechanised brigade during a three-day battle, killing 2,000 EGF personnel. This was the second-largest battle fought by the EPLF to date (the largest had been at Mersa Teklay in March 1984).[28]

In reaction to EPLF victories, the regime forces launched a counteroffensive in August to recapture Barentu, in which they had the cooperation of the Kunama people of Barentu, who supported the central government and opposed the EPLF secessionist agenda.[29]

1986 still saw no softening of the central government position even though the EGF had suffered considerably. It spent most of the year training and reorganising. New insurgent groups appeared at this time in the northern fighting, including the Ethiopian People's Democratic Movement (EPDM). This group cooperated with the TPLF to take Sekota in Wello province on 6 November, defeating a relief force as well.[30]

Another group active in the north was the Ethiopian People's Revolutionary Party (EPRP), which on 27 December attacked a work camp in the Gotam region, overrunning and scattering the EGF and militia force defending it. Two Italian technicians, who were later released, were abducted by the insurgents.[31]

Fighting was at a subdued level through Eritrea in 1987 as government forces continued to build up supply depots and reinforce garrisons. The famine continued, and international relief efforts worked hard to feed populations in Eritrea, Tigray, and Wello provinces. Often relief convoys were not permitted by the government to supply insurgent-held areas. Conflict picked up later in the year; on 23 October the EPLF attacked and destroyed a food relief convoy, citing government practices of using such convoys to cover troop and equipment movements. Similar attacks followed.[32]

In December fighting resumed in earnest as the EPLF halted the eighth major EGF offensive against Nakfa. Breaking through the EGF lines south of the town, the EPLF forces inflicted over a thousand casualties on government forces. The counterattack was subsequently announced as the first move of an EPLF offensive designed to drive the 120,000-man Second Army from Eritrea. It was to be accomplished with only 30,000 EPLF insurgents.[33]

Af Abet and afterwards: 1988–1989

In Eritrea, the EPLF braced itself for a major offensive by government forces on the basis of late 1987 fighting. The regime had formed a new command, the Nadew ('Destruction') Command at Af Abet, a major logistics and support base, to coordinate the new offensive, the twelfth of the war and the ninth major one to be directed against the EPLF stronghold around Nakfa. The advancing force consisted of three infantry divisions reinforced with armour and artillery – perhaps a third of government forces in Eritrea. The offensive began in late February, but the EPLF preempted the attack and outmanoeuvred it. The largest ground combat yet seen in the war continued from 17 to 23 March, with the most intense fighting taking place from the 17th to 19th. Ground forces advancing against Nakfa were turned back, encircled, trapped in a valley near Af Abet, and then subjected to repeated artillery bombardments followed by mechanised and infantry sweeps. Nearby EGF units were also outmanoeuvred and defeated in detail. By 19 March the Nadew Command had been annihilated, as had its subordinate units – three infantry divisions, a mechanised division, and support units. 50 tanks, 60 artillery pieces, 200 vehicles, and much other equipment were captured intact. 15,000 Ethiopian Army personnel were killed or captured, and 3,000 others sent fleeing southward. Three Soviet advisers were captured and a fourth killed in battle, out of a total of thirteen supporting the regime in Eritrea.[34]

As a result of the fighting the EPLF occupied Af Abet on 19 March, and fighting continued as the Eritreans pursued retreating EGF units to north of Keren. The latter town, a main base for the government forces in Eritrea, was endangered, and EGF units abandoned nearby towns to reinforce it. Near the coast the EPLF attacked logistical lines from the port of Massawa to Asmera, attacking three army camps west of Massawa on 21 March and shelling the port city itself. In response to EPLF gains, the Mengistu regime imposed a state of emergency in Eritrea and Tigray in a vain attempt to control the situation. In addition, two 10km-deep strips of land along the Ethiopian border with Sudan in Eritrea and Tigray, as well as the Red Sea coast of Eritrea, were designated 'prohibited areas' where normal movement by the civilian population was not permitted. Inhabitants of areas affected by this cordon sanitaire were to be evicted and resettled elsewhere within fifteen days.[35]

The EPLF followed up the Af Abet victory by forcing the EGF from large areas of Eritrea. By the end of March government units were forced from Barentu and Keren was shelled after the EPLF broke through government lines in fighting at Genfalom. EPLF artillery units were located 10km from Keren by 1 April. The main regional supply depot at Keren was hit by EPLF artillery on 1 April and burned for two days. On 2 April EGF units withdrew from Agordat. Later fighting broke through EGF positions on the Halhal front, in the mountains north of Keren, forcing the troops back to 20km north of the city. EPLF operations continued through May.[36]

In Tigray, fighting in the first two months of 1988 finally garnered results with the TPLF capture of four towns, including two key food distribution centres. The TPLF followed up its victories by the end of March by taking Aksum.[37]

Concurrent with EPLF victories in Eritrea, the TPLF attacked EGF logistical lines in Tigray. By late May the TPLF also attacked retreating EGF units fleeing the fighting in Eritrea.[38]

Despite the debacle at Af Abet, government forces continued to transfer units into Eritrea to reinforce Keren and Asmera. By 28 May the Mengistu regime claimed that Keren had been 'stabilised' as the result of government defensive operations in the area.[39]

In Tigray, government forces were reinforced and began a major counteroffensive in the province by the end of May to retake a number of towns, including Korem, captured by the insurgents. This campaign was marked by bitter fighting and atrocities by central government forces. For instance, on 22 March the town of Hauzien, 550km north of Addis Ababa, was hit by EAF bombers and Mi-24 helicopter gunships. The attack came on market day, and 360 people, practically all of them civilians, were killed and much of the town, including the mosque and school, destroyed or severely damaged. The TPLF claimed that the air force used cluster bombs and napalm in its attack.[40]

Despite EGF attempts to regain control of the situation, it was obvious to most observers that the central government had lost the initiative. In Eritrea a major command had been completely destroyed and the fighting front pushed back to the Keren–Asmera corridor and to Massawa. The EPLF was able to form and outfit a number of complete mechanised and artillery units with the equipment taken intact at Af Abet and other battles, and repair a considerable amount of other equipment that had been damaged and captured. Despite the regime's claims of success in Tigray after government forces recaptured the larger towns, the TPLF refused to join battle with the EGF. Instead, it abandoned towns to advancing government forces and retained control of the countryside, later retaking most towns and villages except for some heavily garrisoned sites. For the remainder of 1988 no major combat activity was reported throughout northern Ethiopia.

Later the central government offered to grant limited autonomy to Eritrea, but on its own terms. Eritrea would be partitioned into two self-governing regions. The EPLF, seeing this as the attempt to divide and conquer that it was, rejected the suggestion in early 1989.[41]

The long march to Addis Ababa, 1989–1991

In early 1989 both the EPLF and TPLF initiated offensives against government forces to pre-empt any new EGF operations. In Eritrea, an EPLF offensive in January killed over 3,000 EGF personnel, and targeted LOCs between Asmera and Massawa.[42]

In Tigray, the TPLF offensive begun in January continued into February with major campaigns to the south of Tigray proper. Now TPLF forces began to threaten northern Gonder province. As of 25 February Mekelle and Maychew remained the only large towns in Tigray under government control, Inda Selassie having been lost. TPLF operations had pushed south into northern Gonder and Wello provinces.[43]

As February 1989 drew to a close the TPLF continued its victories. Most of Tigray was now untenable for the EGF, and on the 27th it evacuated Mekelle, the provincial capital. As many as 20,000 EGF soldiers left in the town retreated south, fighting their way back through TPLF-held territory as they did so. Demoralisation had set in, and the abandonment by the EGF of bitterly-contested Tigray was a further blow to morale. The towns of Maychew (Tigray) and Korem (Wello) had been the only remaining strongpoints on the whole EGF front against the Tigreans, blocking an advance further south into Wello.[44]

EGF operations in Tigray, including the whole military support structure, had been dealt a setback with the capture of Mekelle and its EAF air base. The TPLF ability to muster, move, and resupply forces throughout the province free from air attacks out of Mekelle was of considerable benefit to its capabilities.[45]

In Eritrea, EPLF forces continued to hem in regime forces in the Massawa–Asmera–Keren corridor. Overland transport south through Tigray was now impossible, so the principal supply port for the central government was Aseb, to the south near the Djibouti border. Massawa was of use only to resupply the EGF Second Army in the Asmera–Keren corridor. The EPLF, perhaps taking a cue from the recently-ended Gulf War, began using speedboats along the Red Sea coast to harass at Massawa.

In the meantime, the central government was beset with internal troubles. Two developments in particular spelled impending doom. An abortive coup attempt against Mengistu and his circle by senior EGF commanders in May had failed, and in reprisal Mengistu had a number of senior officers involved in the plot killed. This deprived the troubled EGF of experienced commanders at a time when they were needed most. In addition, support from communist countries began to wane. The USSR openly questioned the wisdom of supplying military equipment to client states that repeatedly failed in the most basic attempts to maintain internal security. Cuba, a staunch supporter of Mengistu and his policies since 1977, announced that it would withdraw the last 2,000 of its troops by 30 September 1989. This was due to the unwillingness of the USSR to finance continued Cuban 'internationalist' operations in Africa or elsewhere.[46]

The EPLF reaction to these two events, which both served to debilitate Ethiopian military efforts in Eritrea, was measured. Little was done to interfere with the withdrawal of the Cubans, while on 18 May the EPLF announced a unilateral ceasefire 'in support of the movement for change by the Ethiopian armed forces.'[47]

In August EPLF and TPLF representatives met in Eritrea to work on further cooperation in military and civilian areas. On 7 August the principal Eritrean movements (EPLF and ELF) agreed on a common policy for the future of Eritrea. The insurgents, especially the TPLF, indicated a willingness to negotiate with the Mengistu regime from newly-found positions of strength, but the central government proved unwilling to do so. The government in Addis Ababa continued to believe that a military solution was possible, despite all evidence to the contrary.[48]

The new-found strength of the TPLF was reaffirmed in September with the announcement of another string of victories from the latest Tigrean offensive, named 'Peace in Struggle.' The latter began on 28–29 August and resulted in the capture of Maychew and the large-scale invasion of northern Wello by TPLF units. The military force responsible for this now called itself the Ethiopian People's Revolutionary Democratic Front (EPRDF), which was an umbrella group for most non-Eritrean northern insurgencies. The main components were the TPLF and the Ethiopian Democratic Movement (EDM), although its military operations were generally led by Tigreans.[49]

The situation for the central government forces was now quite serious. The Third Revolutionary Army found itself in central and northern Wello facing TPLF units that had broken through defensive lines and who were now attacking the Kobo–Weldiya road. By mid-September northern Wello was overrun and Lalibela evacuated; this put the road west from Weldiya into Gonder in danger, as EPRDF troops could now interdict its traffic and outflank EGF positions in the Weldiya area. Kobo was firmly in EPRDF hands by mid-September.[50]

Fighting took place during August and September to the west, with the EPRDF forces of Operation 'Peace in Struggle' making substantial gains in northern Gonder.[51]

October 1989 continued the string of EGF military defeats. A major advance southward along the general line of the Kobo–Weldiya road broke through EGF lines in October and threatened Dese, which lay at the junction of the main north–south road to Addis Ababa and the road coming east-south-east from the port of Aseb, the Mengistu regime's only remaining link to the sea.[52]

Also active during late 1989 was the military arm of the Oromo Liberation Front (OLF), the Oromo Liberation Army (OLA). In a number of widespread actions in the Gimbi and Kelem regions of Welega province, which the OLF had renamed 'Western Oromia,' the OLA was able to defeat elements of EGF units operating in the area. By this time the OLF and other Oromo movements were loosely coordinating actions with the EPRDF. During the next eighteen months Oromo insurgent movements were to increase in frequency and extent. Operations of the OLF/OLA, however, still centred in and around Welega province.[53]

The situation was now extremely grave for the Mengistu regime and the EGF. As the EPRDF victories continued, the central government decided to withdraw units from the Second Army in Eritrea and redeploy them north of Dese. To do this passenger airliners of Ethiopian Airlines, the national carrier, were used. By the 21st the redeployed 3rd Division halted advancing EPRDF forces. However, further attacks by the 3rd Division were stopped by the EPRDF's Hayk Front command and the tactical situation stalled north of Dese.[54]

Throughout 1991 the situation in north-central Ethiopia was one of a gradual loss of territory along the fighting front by the EGF, which bitterly contested any ground lost. However, the EPRDF advance, though gradual, was ever southward. The Mengistu regime reacted to the EPLF victories by implementing massive recruitment drives for military personnel in Addis Ababa and elsewhere to replace units lost in the past year's fighting.[55]

As 1989 ended, the prognosis for the central government's forces was not favourable. In Eritrea the EPLF had continued its policy of gradual gains and consolidation, closing in on the reduced Second Army units there. The main threat to the Mengistu regime remained on the Dese–Hayk Front. There the EPRDF began an outflanking move in mid-December, pushing south-west of Dese and threatening the road from Dese to Addis Ababa.[56]

Through early 1990 fighting see-sawed in Gonder and Wello provinces, with the EGF temporarily able to resist the EPRDF. Part of the reason, it was claimed, for EGF success was Israeli aid, which reportedly provided several hundred T-55 tanks, a number of fighter planes, and other weapons to the Mengistu regime.[57]

In the meantime fighting in Eritrea resumed. In February the Mengistu regime was once again faced with a two-front war in the north. A long (almost nine months') ceasefire of the EPLF with the central government came to an end on 8 February 1990. Fighting resumed along the Keren–Asmera–Massawa corridor.[58]

The EPLF claimed it had pre-empted an impending EGF attack that it claimed was in preparation since early January.[59]

Concurrent with the land offensive came a new tactic by the EPLF, namely attacks on shipping in the Red Sea. These actually began in January, designed to prevent arms shipments from coming into the port of Massawa. Coastal artillery and rockets were used against ships at sea; other tactics included the use of speedboats mounted with machine guns and rocket launchers to interdict shipping. On 1 January a Polish freighter was boarded and the crew taken into custody. The ship, originally bound for Massawa, was set afire with rockets and beached. The crew was released on 15 January. Other ships were warned away by weapons fire or boarded and told to leave Eritrean waters.[60]

The main EPLF objective was Massawa, the link of the EGF Second Army for sea resupply. A pincer attack from the north-west and south-east starting on 8 February broke through EGF lines and entered Massawa on the 10th. Two EGF divisions and eight brigades were either destroyed or rendered combat incapable in the fighting. Subsequent to the EPLF victory elements of the EGF, which had withdrawn to the Dahlak Archipelago, made two attempts in February to recapture Massawa. Both failed, and the invaders lost nine ships sunk and two captured. By 15 February the EPLF was in unchallenged possession of the town, despite repeated government air attacks.[61]

The loss of Massawa was a fatal blow to the Ethiopian military effort in Eritrea. The link to the sea had been cut and the only supply means was by air into Yohannes IV airport near Asmera. 120,000 EGF troops of the Second Revolutionary Army were surrounded and their long-term sustainability depended solely upon a recapture of the lost port. The Mengistu regime was left with the port of Aseb near the border with Djibouti, with a tenuous road link, via Kombolcha near Dese, to the capital, plus the Djibouti–Addis Ababa railway, as the only links to the sea. In addition, relief aid to 4.5 million people in Eritrea and Tigray was interrupted by the fall of the port. Despite the EPLF offer to let international agencies use Massawa to offload relief supplies, the famine relief effort, begun in late 1989, was halted on orders of the Mengistu regime. It refused to let the port be used and the EAF continued to bomb it; food supplies were destroyed in the attacks.[62]

By early April the EGF was ready for a major attempt to recapture Massawa. The attack, on three fronts, failed by late April 1990 with at least 40 per cent of the attacking forces lost as casualties, to include 6,500 dead and 9,000 wounded.[63]

On the heels of news of the failed Second Army offensive in Eritrea news came to Addis Ababa of further EPRDF gains against the Third Army in northern Shewa. In its advance southward, the EPRDF stratagem to bypass Dese had succeeded. On 25 May the EGF launched a counteroffensive to drive EPRDF forces back. It failed, and in the process the EGF 3rd Division was largely destroyed. As of 21 June 1990, the EPRDF was about 75km north of the capital.[64]

The overall strategic situation for the Mengistu regime was very grave. To defend a frontier that ran from east of Dese in an arc through central Gonder, almost 200,000 troops of the Third, Fourth, and Fifth Revolutionary Armies had been committed. The vast extent (over 750km) and rugged terrain made the battle line almost impossible to adequately defend against the continuous and intensive probes by EPRDF and other insurgent groups. The EPRDF claimed further victories in late May and June, killing nearly 22,000 EGF troops. Compounding the continuing EGF problems of poor training, ineffective support, and poor morale was the late May announcement of the execution of twelve generals responsible for the failed coup attempt of May 1989.[65]

In the early summer of 1990 fighting was centred in northern Shewa and south-eastern Wello provinces. The see-saw fighting in the area gradually coalesced into a defined 'front' near Fiche. The importance of the Fiche front lay with its defence of the northern border of Selale district (northern Shewa) and southern Merhabete district against advancing EPLF forces. The only main route still open to government forces that ran from Addis Ababa into Gojam and Gonder provinces ran through Selale, and made possible resupply of Third Army units stationed along the Fiche front. EGF tactics on the Fiche front to hold back EPRDF forces sometimes showed initiative and aggressiveness, but generally failed due to the inability of Third Army Headquarters to provide follow-up and proper support. However, the EGF defensive operations were generally successful and were able to help the government hold out until the following year.[66]

In Eritrea, the war in 1990 remained at a stalemate, marked by attempts by the Second Army to break out of the Keren – Asmera corridor. The EPLF made further slight gains against the EGF in the area, but had few major victories. The war in the Red Sea continued as well. Ethiopian forces – about 500 EGF and naval units–still held the Dahlak archipelago and shipping continued to go into the government-held port of Aseb on the southern Eritrean coast. Sporadic fighting off the Eritrean coast took its toll of shipping as EPLF coastal artillery attacked two ships in mid-November, burning one and damaging the other.[67]

On 18 December, Massawa was finally reopened to relief shipments. The move was welcomed by famine relief organisations that had been using overland routes from Sudan and airlifted food shipments into Asmera airport. The two-year drought, compounded by the fighting throughout northern Ethiopia, had resulted in the worst famine in living memory. However, few believed that the Mengistu regime would let the Second Army passively wait and let itself be progressively hemmed in and ultimately overwhelmed by the EPLF.[68]

The expected EGF offensive in Eritrea began on 25 December 1990, launched along the Ginda front by units of the Second Revolutionary Army. Within three days the attack, directed at EPLF positions near Ginda, had faltered, and a number of subsidiary attacks had also failed. This was to prove the last major attempt by EGF forces to break out of its encirclement.

The 1991 spring offensive: Operation 'Teodoros'

The end, when it finally came, came surprisingly quickly – following a campaign by the EPRDF and EPLF of three months and five days. At the end of February 1991 both the EPRDF and the EPLF initiated new offensives against the EGF Third and Fifth Armies, which together had upwards of 175,000 personnel along the Gonder, Gojam, north Shewa, and Wello front. The EPLF on 28 February began a push down the Eritrean coast to Tiyo, which soon fell. By 11 March the EPLF was 60km north of Aseb, having taken the coastal town of 'Ed. Ethiopia's only remaining port, defended by elements of the 5th Division, was in danger of falling to the Eritrean insurgents.[69]

However, the direct threat to the regime came in northern Shewa and Gonder. There EPRDF forces, led by four newly-formed TPLF divisions reinforced with mechanised elements contributed by the EPLF, initiated Operation 'Teodoros' on 23 February. This was an attack along the entire government front, including the Third Army front in Northern Shewa and south-eastern Wello as well as that of the Fifth Army in South and Central Gonder. The main push came from the east. In late February the EPRDF pushed through government defences, advancing southward along the eastern shore of Lake Tana and into Gojam, bypassing EGF defences at Gonder.[70]

Meanwhile the EPLF continued its advance along the coast, and on 7 April took Beylul and Beriasole, defeating four EGF brigades. By the end of the month Aseb was threatened. The fall of Aseb would cut off the Mengistu regime from any direct outside sea resupply, and force it to rely solely upon the Djibouti–Addis Ababa railway. To control the latter, the central government had armed several local militias formed from the Afar (Danakil) population of the region opposite the Djibouti border.[71]

By April the EPRDF had moved south of the Blue Nile from Gojam province into northern Shewa, and taken Gojam province. In the west the remnants of the EGF Fifth Army had been driven from Gojam south into the Nekemte area of Welega province (mid-March). The EPRDF, following them, penetrated Welega and on 1 April captured Nekemte, the provincial capital, giving them effective control of the province and the main road east to Addis Ababa.[72]

Through the rest of the month the EPRDF steadily advanced eastward, reaching Ambo, 80km from the capital on 25 April. Despite the ongoing negotiations that had been taking place between the Mengistu regime and the EPRDF, the fighting continued into May. EPRDF efforts were now directed at the Third Army, which had been reinforced with units of the First Army from eastern Ethiopia as well as elements of the Second Army airlifted from Asmera. In the face of repeated attacks by the EPRDF, now backed up with mechanised units supplied by the EPLF, the Dese front crumbled. On 15 May Dese itself fell and Kombolcha, Third Army Headquarters, was captured as well. Within the week Mengistu, aware of the hopelessness of the situation, abandoned Addis Ababa and fled to Zimbabwe, leaving a caretaker government to face the advancing insurgents. On 22 May Addis Alem fell, on 26 May Air Force Headquarters and the garrison at Debre Zeit. On 28 May EPRDF troops finally entered Addis Ababa, formally bringing to an end the sixteen-year civil war.[73]

INSURGENCY AND CIVIL WAR IN SOMALIA, 1988–1991

At first glance Somalia appears an unlikely place for deep-rooted ethnic strife. No other African nation has the degree of ethnic unity as does Somalia. Over 99 per cent of its people are ethnic Somalis, and one would think that this situation would prevent much of the internal warfare Somalia has suffered since independence. Other factors supporting unity include Islam (all Somalis are Muslims) and way of life (most Somalis are pastoral cattle and camel raisers). Somalis have a reputation for independence, ethnic pride, and devotion to family and clan, all within the context of deeply-felt belief in Sunni Islam.

Despite this, Somali society has been historically riven by feuds between the major clan families, a situation that has been exacerbated by foreign rule and the late Siad Barre regime (see below). Descent is a major factor in Somali ethnic consciousness and personal identity. The root of Somali descent is the affiliation with a clan family, of which six exist. The first four, called the Soomal, are subdivided into two large groupings, the Irir and the Darod. The Irir comprise the Dir, Isaak, and Hawiye, while the Darod include the Majertain, the Ogadeni, and other clans. Their members dwell for the most part in northern and central Somalia, and trace their ancestry from medieval unions of Somali women with Arabs from Yemen in the nearby Arabian peninsula. The remaining two clan families, the Saab, are the Digil and Rahanwein, who dwell in the southern part of Somalia.

191

SOMALI INSURGENCIES IN THE SIAD ERA

Mohamed Siad Barre took power in a military coup in 1969. He subsequently aligned the country with the USSR and its communist allies, receiving large quantities of military aid with which he armed the vastly increased security services. In 1977–1978 Siad realigned with the West after the Somalia suffered a defeat during the Ogaden war with Ethiopia. As retaliation for Siad's use of the Western Somali Liberation Front (WSLF) as a surrogate during the war, Ethiopia supported anti-Siad Somalis who sought his overthrow. Most armed opponents of the regime organised themselves under the Somali National Front (SNM, which represented the northern Isaaks) and the Somali Salvation Democratic Front (SSDF, which was supported by the Majertain). Throughout most of the 1980s Siad Barre was able to contain the SNM and SSDF. He received considerable western military assistance to support himself against Ethiopia and its Somali surrogates, and at the same time supported the WSLF against the Mengistu regime.

Siad's rule

Siad Barre's government exploited divisions within Somali society and attempted to rule by force where it could not prevail by manipulation. The government sought to make all Somalis members of the ruling Somali Revolutionary Socialist Party (SRSP) and force all youths into its youth group, or Guludayeel. It formed local militias to ensure control over the clans in rural areas. Siad was able to utilise favouritism and manipulate the representation of clan members in the government to gain allegiance. Where such measures failed, the government utilised coercion and intimidation by a large security apparatus, dominated by military intelligence or Hangash, the Somali National Police, and the National Security Service (NSS).[74]

Siad Barre is remembered with bitterness by many Somalis as the man who exploited and manipulated clan divisiveness to the point where open conflict between Somalis resulted from his machinations. His method of rule was to build dependence upon his personal power, and then exploit that dependence by apportioning governmental offices and positions to reward those who supported his agenda. However, his constant shifts of favour to factions and individuals gradually drove away but a small inner circle. Toward the end of Siad Barre's rule even members of the military and security services deserted en masse to the insurgent side.

Insurgency and the growth of internal unrest

By the late 1980s most of Somali society had become alienated from the Siad Barre government and its methods of rule. In addition, Somalis from the north had begun to actively resist the central government. The SNM and SSDF, both of which had been founded in the 1970s and backed by Ethiopia, grew in power as discontent within Somalia grew. Much popular discontent was found in the north, whose people suffered continued discrimination by the Siad Barre regime. In May 1988, fighting broke out throughout the north between government security forces and Isaak clan members supported by insurgents of the SNM. As the fighting escalated, government repression became harsher. It culminated in the bombing by the Somali Air Force of the city of Hargeisa, which destroyed large parts of the city and killed hundreds of civilians. Following this, resistance and rebellion intensified and spread throughout the north. Popular support for the SNM throughout the north was almost universal.

Following the spread of fighting, two new factions emerged to garner support against Siad Barre. These were the Somali Patriotic Movement (SPM), which drew its support from Ogadenis (mostly Darods), and the United Somali Congress (USC), which drew upon the Hawiye clan family. In mid-1990 these two groups joined forces with the SNM to act against Barre. By this time most of the country was in virtual anarchy, with most rural areas controlled by either insurgents or bandits and with all but the largest urban areas contested between Siad Barre's forces and the insurgents. In the cities, too, there was trouble, with unrest even in Mogadishu; security forces used increasing brutality to suppress opposition.

INSURGENCY AND THE OVERTHROW OF THE SIAD REGIME, MAY 1988–JANUARY 1991

From May 1988 to the end of 1990, the Siad Barre regime fought a long and unwinnable war against an insurgency that spread to most of the Somali clans. The SNA directed its operations against local clan groups that it perceived as supporting the insurgents, not against the insurgents themselves. However, the SNA, SSDF, and other newer clan-based groups of fighters were able, despite Siad's war against segments of the Somali population, to never lose their focus of attacking and destroying the regime that fought an increasingly savage, ethnically-motivated war against its own people.

SNM attacks and government response, May 1988–March 1989

1988 marked the beginning of the end for the Siad regime. The coalition that the Somali President had built following his seizure of power in 1969 lost its raison d'être with Somali defeat in the Ogaden War (1977–1978), but government manipulation of clan rivalries and the doling out of favours managed to keep a tenuous base of support for another decade. The acceptance of the colonial administrative boundary as the border with Ethiopia through the 3 April 1988 treaty as well as the open hatred in which Siad was held by northern Somalis shattered any doubts as to the true priorities of the regime. The reconciliation with Ethiopia cost the regime its support from the Ogadeni clan, which laid its hope on the ability of the Somali military to recapture the Ogaden from Ethiopia.[75]

Not only did the agreement with Ethiopia put Siad's political base in disarray, it had the immediate effect of starting the war in the north. With the demilitarisation of the border there the Somali National Movement (SNM) took advantage of the situation to infiltrate its fighters back into the north rather than risk their forced repatriation by Ethiopia to Somali security authorities. This came at a time when the Mengistu regime could ill-afford to support the SNM following its massive defeat by the EPLF at Af Abet in Eritrea and its inability to contain the growing TPLF insurgency in Tigray. Ethiopia, therefore, was apparently willing to accommodate Siad Barre's demands with regard to the SNM. At the same time, the Somali government, faced with dwindling military aid from abroad, could ill afford to support anti-Mengistu insurgents in eastern Ethiopia.

The SNM did not wait for the Somali government to make the first move, but struck first, in a series of initially effective, wide-ranging, and coordinated attacks. The first town hit was Burao, on 27 May, followed by Hargeisa on 31 May. In both cases the SNM was initially successful in occupying the town, although nearby SNA garrisons were not overrun and government forces eventually reoccupied both towns. The latter actions were accompanied by massive atrocities against the civilian populations, including looting, murder, and rape. Ethnic hatred of northeners by the predominantly southern SNA was clearly evident in such actions. Civilians in cities not attacked by the SNM, including Berbera, Erigavo, Borama, and Sheikh, were set upon by government forces at first word of the SNA attacks and subjected to similar human rights violations. Civilians attempting to flee the fighting by crossing the Djibouti and Ethiopian borders were attacked by SNA units. Ogadeni refugees in camps throughout the north joined government forces in attacking Isaaks and any suspected SNM sympathisers.[76]

By 25 June the Somali government claimed its security forces had reasserted control throughout the north.[77]

However, fighting continued, as did atrocities against the civilian population, as the SNA sought to kill any and all suspected SNM sympathisers and control the population by preventing any movement outside the major towns. The nomad population was especially targeted, as it was believed that this provided the major support for the SNM. SNM fighters who took over Hargeisa and Burao wore no uniforms and sought to conceal themselves among the urban population. This provoked indiscriminate government air attacks and artillery bombardments of the towns. At least 70 per cent of Hargeisa was destroyed in this manner.[78]

The operational history of the conflict in northern Somalia to January 1989 was marked by:

■ Air operations against SNM concentrations in towns and villages;
■ Operations by SNA garrisons against the people of the neighbouring towns and villages;
■ Air and ground operations against SNM or suspected SNM units in the rural areas.

The main effort of these operations was to control and terrorise the population, especially Isaaks. At least 50,000 to 60,000 were killed as the result of government bombardments, abuse, and murder. The actions had the effect of polarising the north and its Isaak population as well as leading to a cut-off of most foreign military assistance, including that by the US. The SNM in its turn attacked refugee camps, especially those with Ogadeni populations that it believed had assisted the government security forces, also attacking any armed non-Isaaks as allies of the government. Eventually the government banned journalists from northern Somalia, hoping a news blackout would minimise criticism of abuses by the security forces there.[79]

At the end of 1988 the government had been unable to prevent SNM movement throughout the north despite extensive use of air and ground operations to counter the insurgents. Most towns and larger villages lay in ruins as the SNA could not prevent insurgent infiltration and the security forces in turn relied on air and artillery bombardments to dislodge the SNM. The net effect of these actions was the dislocation of almost 850,000 northeners, 400,000 of whom fled to Ethiopia, at least 40,000 of whom fled to Djibouti, and of whom the rest fled the cities and the fighting there to live in the countryside.[80]

From 1 to 20 December the Somali Minister of Defence toured the north, visiting in addition to Hargeisa the town of Burao (Todheer region) as well as the Nogaal valley. The latter area was the centre of the Majertain clan group, who continued to support the anti-regime Somali Salvation Democratic Front (SSDF). The government statements on the visit stressed the need for improving the economy and general welfare, as well as political reconciliation. However, subsequent reporting indicated that the repressive measures against the Isaak population throughout the north were continuing and that the SNM insurgency still operated there.[81]

The central government's poor image on human rights received a further blow at the end of the year. On 22 December 1988 the Somali consul in Damascus requested asylum in Sweden, claiming that the Siad Barre regime had obtained chemical weapons from Libya.[82]

As of late January 1989, the government continued to deny use of chemical weapons and claimed that the fighting was over, with Burao and Hargeisa held by the government. The SNM, on the other hand, claimed that it had 95 per cent of the north in its possession and that it was continuing to fight to capture Hargeisa and was shelling Berbera every day.[83]

By the end of the year the restiveness among supporters of Siad Barre had grown to the point where a special session of the ruling Somali Revolutionary Socialist Party (SRSP) was held in January. The SRSP session recommended amending the constitution to allow freedom of personal political expression and curb extra-legal abuses of such by the security forces. The SRSP Central Committee recommended a political solution to the problems in the north and the extension of amnesty programmes. It also recommended an extensive programme of economic reconstruction there. Despite these measures, the UNHCR announced on 22 January that it was terminating assistance programmes in northern Somalia due to the general lack of security there. It noted that as many as 840,000 resided in 44 camps throughout Somalia; 400,000 alone were in thirteen camps in the north.[84]

On 6 March the Somali government set up a special committee to administer northern Somalia. This included Todheer and areas west to the Djibouti border. The purpose of the body, which was under direct control of the President, was to coordinate political, social, and economic programmes. The agency, promulgated by presidential decree, thus sought to unify security management for the area and at the same time escape legal or constitutional controls recommended by an increasingly less supportive SRSP.[85]

Government collapse in the north

On 22 March 1989 there was a mutiny of Ogadeni SNA personnel at Kisimayo. Rebellious troops, about 600 total, captured vehicles, weapons, and ammunition, and occupied the Kisimayo–Afmadu road. The government sent personnel to negotiate with them; they demanded Siad Barre's resignation due to resentment over the growing influence of the President's clan in the Army as well as the peace treaty with Ethiopia in 1988 that let the Ogaden remain in Ethiopian hands. Although SNA representatives went to Kisimayo to negotiate with the rebels, discontent continued and was ultimately to result in the organisation of the Ogadeni-based SPM.[86]

The mutiny at Kisimayo came at the same time that the SNM announced (23 March) that its forces had captured Erigavo, the administrative centre of Sanaag, as well as two other government strongpoints. The SNM claimed control of '95 per cent' of the north, according to its London office.[87]

On 14 July there were riots in Mogadishu prompted by the arrest of religious leaders the previous day. They had criticised the ongoing civil war, the progress of which the Siad Barre regime attempted to keep secret, and the failure of the government to negotiate an end to it. As a consequence of the rioting 46 were reportedly massacred and 2,000 others detained. Although the government subsequently claimed 23 killed and 59 injured, there may have been more than 400 killed and 1,000 injured as troops fired upon crowds of civilians.[88]

Despite ongoing restrictions that prevented journalists from covering the progress of the insurgency, reports came out in August that troop desertions were continuing and even of mutinies of whole units.[89]

The events reported in news media indicated an army on the verge of disintegration, where ethnic purges of non-Darod elements were becoming common, and where many local populations in the interior of central Somalia were suffering at the hands of Siad Barre's troops. Fighting continued to spread southward.

The insurgency spreads southward

As of September 1989 the rebellion had spread to southern Somalia, especially the Belet Weyne area and the upper Juba River (Webi Juba) valley around Luuq. The security situation at Kisimayo was also very poor. To prop up its deteriorating military, the central government purchased large amounts of aid from Libya, mostly small arms and ammunition but also, it was claimed, chemical weapons. The latter, however, if indeed purchased, were never used.[90]

By September it was increasingly evident that each major clan group in Somalia was developing its own political arm. Any post-Siad settlement would therefore have to be a series of very delicate power-sharing agreements among these organisations. The major ones included that of the SNM of the Isaak clan group in the north; the Somali Salvation

Democratic Front (SSDF) of the Majertain (Darod) clan group further east; the Somali Patriotic Movement (SPM) of Ogadeni Darods along the southern border with Ethiopia; and the United Somali Congress (USC) of the Hawiye clan group in central Somalia. Of all of these, the SNM took the lead in consolidating its power. In mid-September government forces suffered a major defeat at the hands of the SNM near Burao (Burco), in a battle which effectively liberated most of the north from Siad's forces.[91]

Potentially more serious were the actions of the Somali Patriotic Movement (SPM) on the Kenyan border near Liboi (September–October 1989). The insurgents, pursued by government forces, crossed the border. SNA elements in armoured cars and jeeps then followed but were engaged by Kenyan police; four of the latter were killed. The SNA claimed it had been fired upon. The incident drew an angry reaction from the Kenyan government, which threatened cross-border raids to pursue SNA elements in the future. However, beyond the immediate damage to relations with the Kenyan government was the fact that a major faction of insurgents had become established in the south, had taken territory, and had been successful in repelling SNA attempts to recapture it.[92]

October 1989 saw the beginning of a multi-pronged offensive by the SNA against SPM positions in the south. In the fighting the SNA used armoured columns supported by Hawker Hunter aircraft based at Bale Dogle and reportedly flown by ex-Rhodesian mercenaries. The town of Asmado, the centre of the SPM, was recaptured. The SNA offensive had its desired effect of regaining at least some territory and causing the SPM to split into at least two opposing factions. However, this was done at the cost of hundreds of civilian casualties.[93]

On 19 November the SNM and the SPM issued a joint communiqué announcing the coordination of operations against the central government, as well as the provision of mutual assistance where possible. Other political movements also soon joined the anti-Siad coalition, including the USC and SSDF. The anti-Siad agreement followed the government loss of the key town of Galcaio in mid-November. The town's garrison mutinied and the SNM came to its assistance. Desertions to the SPM side were also reported from the south.[94]

The period through mid-1990 is marked by continuous warfare in northern and central Somalia. During this period the SNA lost control of most of the area, retaining only a few garrisons at major airfields that permitted resupply. The clan groups in north and central Somalia completed the formation of militias to back their new political organisations. In many cases militias were formed from deserting SNA elements. The widespread nature of this phenomenon as well as the simultaneous weakening of the SNA meant that the latter was unable to counterattack to recapture lost posts or territory.

Major areas of clan group control began to emerge at this time. The largest and most compact was the SNM-dominated area inhabited by the Isaak clan family. Further east, in the area of the Majertain, was the SSDF or SDSF. To the south, in the vast areas inhabited by the Hawiye clan family, was the USC, which by this time had come under the military leadership of a former SNA general, Mohamed Hasan Farah 'Aideed', a member of the Habr Gedr clan. His main rival was Ali Mahdi Mohamed of the Abgal clan. Both of these groups were located in the Mogadishu area, but as long as the Siad regime remained alive put aside differences and concentrated on the overthrow of the central government. Further to the south smaller clan-based parties, including Omar Jess's SPM, operated. Along the border with Ethiopia elements of the Marehan clan continued to assist the regime and its interests.

Final days of the Siad Barre regime; fall of Mogadishu

By June 1990 most of the north was in the hands of the SNM. A few isolated SNA garrisons held out, but the insurgents claimed the north for themselves. Support for the SNM claim was given by reports of subsequent military action to the end of 1989 and into 1990. On 5

May 1990 SNM forces attacked an SNA unit near the Djibouti border at the town of Loyada. SNA losses were substantial, to include several senior officers and dozens of soldiers. As the SNA were returning from a meeting with the Djibouti military, the Siad regime claimed that Djibouti had complicity in the matter, which was, however, denied. The incident was reflective of the loss by the SNA of effective border control and the free use of border-crossing operations by the SNM to strike at will against remnants of the SNA.[95]

On 7 August 1990 the three main Somali insurgent groups operating in the south, the SNM, the SPM, and the USC, joined forces. They agreed to coordinate future operations against the SNA. (The SSDF, on the other hand, having gained effective control of Majertainia, opted out of large-scale fighting for the time being.) Through the next three months the newly-unified insurgents made rapid advances in the central part of Somalia, prompting Siad to name his son-in-law General Siad Hersi 'Morgan' as the new Minister of Defence and later Chief of the Army (15 November). However, by this time the situation was too far gone to save militarily, and the insurgents would have no part of any future government that included Siad.[96]

In November 1990 the insurgents continued their advance toward Mogadishu, and by the 3rd were only 50km from the city. Mogadishu dissolved into anarchy as local gangs and groups of military deserters battled with security forces as well as groups of Siad Barre's ethnic Darod supporters. Starting on the 8th with the United States, foreign nations advised their nationals to leave the country as the insurgents, now led primarily by elements of the USC, encircled Mogadishu. On the 21st the airport was attacked, the first in a series of violent conflicts as the USC penetrated Mogadishu, taking advantage of the fighting that had broken out between security forces and elements of the local population backed by infiltrated USC guerrillas. By 28 December the USC forces had moved into the capital itself, dislodging Siad Barre's troops there.

Siad Barre finally fled Mogadishu on 31 December 1990, as USC-led forces continued to advance on the capital. Fighting, both interfactional as well as between insurgents and the remnants of government forces, continued, with casualties numbering in the thousands. Several hundred people, civilians and military, were killed at the end of the year in the takeover of Mogadishu. Perhaps a half million lives had been lost since the outbreak of fighting in 1988.[97]

The USC was quick to fill the power vacuum left by Siad, although it lacked the legitimacy of national rule as well as the security forces capable of restoring order. On 23 January a new interim government was established under the auspices of the Committee of National Salvation, made up of the USC, the SSDF, and Somali Alliance Movement (SAM), and the Somali Democratic Movement (SDM). On the 29th Ali Mahdi, a Hawiye Abgal, was named interim president by the USC and representatives of other factions present in Mogadishu. On 3 February he announced the new government. But from that time on things began to fall apart. It was clear to all that the new interim government was dominated almost entirely by the USC of the Hawiye, who also wanted to form the bulk of the security services. This had already sparked violent conflict in Mogadishu on 10 February between the USC and the Ogadeni SPM. But Mogadishu was in the centre of Hawiye territory, and the SPM was forced to withdraw. In addition to the fighting, a major refugee crisis was taking shape; 18,000 had fled to Ethiopia to escape the fighting in the south and 20,000 other refugees were gathered across from the Kenyan town of Mandera, waiting to cross to safety.[98]

POST-SIAD SOMALIA

The new USC President, Ali Mahdi Mohamed, named Omar Arteh Ghalib as Prime Minister. From the start, however, there was insufficient support for the new regime, which was dominated by the Hawiye clan family. In addition, other parts of Somalia were dominated by separate insurgent groups, among whom the SNM, SPM, and SSDF held the largest chunks of territory. The new government soon found itself unable to control much of the country, and was hard pressed to maintain order in Mogadishu itself as Hawiye clans and sub-clans began to clash over their share of power in the new government. A major round of fighting broke out in June as former general 'Aideed' emerged as the main USC rival to Ali Mahdi. The latter had the support of the Abgal Hawiye clan while Aideed was backed by the Habr Gedr clan. While the Ali Mahdi government professed a democratic agenda, no practical way to advance it could be found. Much effort was expended in trying to restore basic services and food shipments to Mogadishu. Foreign assistance remained problematic, as only the Egyptian and Italian embassies remained open. In addition, continued fighting between Hawiye and Darod clan militias as well as representative armed factions plagued the south throughout the summer.[99]

In neighbouring Ethiopia the first half of 1991 saw the Mengistu regime go the way of the Siad Barre government. By May there was considerable unrest throughout the Somali–Ethiopian border areas as the central government in Addis Ababa collapsed; this aggravated the new government's problems in border control and maintaining order in the areas it ruled. Refugee problems multiplied as well.

June and July were marked by continuing efforts to reconcile the feuding Somali factions. Meetings were prompted by the concerns of Djibouti president Hassan Gouled. Djibouti, which was home to the Somali Issa clan family, had been flooded with Somali refugees. In a preparatory stage for a national conference held in Djibouti from 5 to 12 June, conferees agreed on a full-fledged national conference in July, also in Djibouti. This conference called upon the northern part of the country, which had seceded, to rejoin Somalia. Representatives from the north (i.e., from the SNM) did not attend, although representatives from six other factions (USC, SSDF, SPM, SDM, SPA, and USF) did.[100]

The North: Secession

On 16 May 1991 northern Somalia announced its secession from the rest of the country, and on 5 June announced the formation of a 21-member government headed by Abdul-rahman Ahmad Ali, the provisional prime minister. Most of the new cabinet were members of the Somali National Movement, which had prompted the secession. The new state was called the Republic of Somaliland, and comprised the area of former British Somaliland.[101]

While not recognised by other governments, the breakaway state had by June formed its own military force and police, who had succeeded in restoring security throughout most of the new republic. The main priority was the rebuilding of the shattered economy and making the remnants of the infrastructure work once more. Livestock exports to the Arabian peninsula resumed in May following the reopening of the port of Berbera.[102]

For the foreseeable future, it is likely that the self-proclaimed Republic of Somaliland will continue to rebuild the north and at the same time remain aloof from the south and its problems. However, it is unlikely that the breakaway regime will receive foreign recognition as the legitimate government of Somalia (which it does not represent itself to be), nor will it receive recognition as a separate state (which would violate Organisation of African Unity principles of territorial integrity). Despite this, the Republic of Somaliland has received and will probably continue to receive assistance from a number of nearby Muslim states; this, and the peace now at hand in the north, will ensure that the secessionist state undergoes at least a moderate economic recovery.

The South: Anarchy

Meanwhile, the southern part of the nation continued in turmoil. While the Mahdi government tried and failed in its effort to govern Somalia, Siad Barre, who had retreated to the border and formed his Somali National Front (SNF), continued his attempts to destabilise the new regime. His repeated raids from the Luuq and Bardera (Bardheere) regions were unsuccessful in capturing Hawiye-held areas. However, the latter were plagued by continued in-fighting. In the process, the main farming areas of the lower Juba and Shebelle Rivers suffered heavily and local food sources for Mogadishu and other cities were thus lost.[103]

The heart of the problem for the south was the lack of support for the Mahdi government, including from among many Hawiyes. No progress had been made since the talks in June and July toward reconciliation of the USC with other Somali groups. At least six main factions controlled southern and central Somalia at the year's end. President Mahdi, backed by his Hawiye Abgal clan, refused to relinquish power after the breakdown of negotiations to forge a compromise among the USC factions. With the support of his faction of the USC, he had himself inaugurated President of Somalia on 18 August.[104]

Complicating efforts to make peace and rebuild the south was the continued presence of Siad Barre in the Kenya-Somalia border area. It was alleged by many Somalis that the former President received support from the Kenyan government that allowed him to maintain himself in the region. Siad Barre had withdrawn with the remnants of his forces toward the interior of the country and throughout mid- and late 1991 attempted to break through to the Somali coast and gain access to the port of Kisimayo. Failing in this, he attempted to promote further discord among the various factions throughout the south, according to many Somalis, hoping to take advantage of the strife to return to power.

The USC factional fighting, UN intervention, and aftermath, November 1991 to date

Most of the history of the period from November 1991 is one of anarchy and inter-clan violence. Through late 1991 and 1992 the main security problem in Somalia was the continued infighting in Mogadishu between the forces of Ali Mahdi and Aideed, as well as conflict in the hinterland that disrupted food production and distribution to many urban centres. International media seized upon the events and world public opinion soon put pressure on the major powers to act. This precipitated the US-led United Nations intervention that started in December 1992. The ill-fated UN intervention, marked by Aideed's continued harassment of its forces, especially those of the United States, following a decision in 1993 to first exclude him from the peace process and then to apprehend him, met its moment of crisis in October, when United States and other forces suffered heavy casualties in fighting in central Mogadishu. Aideed remained at large and continued to direct resistance against the UN, now considered by many Somalis as invaders.

NOTES

1. For the fighting in general, see *ARB*, 3498a–3499b; 3530a–3531c; 3529a–4598a; 3627a–3628b; 3695a; 3731a–3732a, and references cited below.
2. *ARB*, 3659b–3660a. By the end of the war, the Mengistu regime had armed the Afars in an attempt to buy at least their non-cooperation with anti-regime rebels.
3. *ARB*, 3597b–c; 3794b–3795b.
4. *ARB*, 4024c–4026c; the nine-point plan is outlined on 4025a–b.
5. *ARB*, 4025a–4026c; 4059c–4060a.
6. *ARB*, 4088b–4089b.
7. *ARB*, 4193b.
8. *ARB*, 4282a, 4361a.
9. *ARB*, 4323b–4324c (Death of General Banti); 4361a; 4393a–4395a.
10. *ARB*, 4361a–b (EPLF 1st Congress); 4602c–4603a.
11. *ARB*, 4469b; 4507a–4508a; 4535c; 4675b. For ALF actions, see 4634b. The insurgents had taken Kerora in January and Nakfa in March; on 6 April they took Af Abet; later that month they took Teseney. Through the summer other towns fell to the EPLF: Dekemhare (6 July), Keren (18 July), and Ak'ordat (30 August).

12. *ARB*, 4558c-4559c.
13. *ARB*, 4925b-4926b; 4960a-c; 5027b-5028a; 5064b-5065a.
14. *ARB*, 5152b. Similar actions were also undertaken by the ELF, but to a much more limited degree.
15. *ARB*, 5342b-c; 5378b-c; 5541a-b.
16. *ARB*, 5829c; 5830a.
17. *ARB*, 5829b-5830a; 5993b-c.
18. See the essay by Alex de Wall, 'Intervention Unbound,' in *Military Intervention in Africa* (InterNet, Hornet/mil_intv.html).
19. *ARB*, 6313a-b; 6345a-6346b.
20. *ARB*, 6803c-6804b.
21. *ARB*, 6842c.
22. *ARB*, 7183b-c; see also 7709b-c. See also Lionel Cliffe's prescient article, 'Dramatic Shifts in the Military Balance in the Horn: The 1984 Eritrean Offensive', in *RoAPE*, 30, September 1984, pp. 93-7.
23. *ARB*, 7212c-7213b.
24. *ARB*, 7213a-b.
25. *ARB*, 7505b-c.
26. *ARB*, 7572c.
27. Ibid.
28. *ARB*, 7709b.
29. *ARB*m 7749a.
30. *ARB*, 8313c-8314a.
31. *ARB*, 8372b-c.
32. *ARB*, 8673b-c; 8703b-c.
33. *ARB*, 8730b-c.
34. *ARB*, 8815a-c; *FBIS*, FBIS-AFR-88-054, 21 March 1988, pp. 3 ff; 88-055, 22 March 1988, p. 1; 88-056, 21 March 1988, p. 1; 88-058, 25 March 1988, p. 2. See also 'EPLF captures Soviet military officers following biggest victory to date', EPLF news release, 21 March 1988; '20,000 Ethiopian soldiers were put out of action', EPLF news release, 24 March 1988. For a detailed description of the action, see 'Ethiopia on the ropes', *The Middle East*, June, 1988, pp. 13-16.
35. *ARB*, 8836c-8837a; 8885a-b. See also 'Ethiopian army withdraws from three towns', EPLF news release, 28 March 1988, and FBIS-AFR-88-059, 28 March 1988, p. 3.
36. *ARB*, 8885c-8886b.
37. *ARB*, 8814c-8815a.
38. *ARB*, 8886a-b.
39. Ibid.
40. *ARB*, 8915c-8916b.
41. *ARB*, 9147b-c.
42. *ARB*, 9147c.
43. *ARB*, 9190b-9191a; *AD*, April 1989, p. 8.
44. *ARB*, 9222c-9223c; *AD*, April 1989, p. 8.
45. Ibid.; *AD*, May 1989, pp. 8-10.
46. See *ARB*, 9422b-c.
47. 'EPLF Announces Unilateral Ceasefire', EPLF Press Release, EPLF Washington DC office, 18 May 1990.
48. *AD*, October 1989, p. 8.
49. *AD*, October 1989, pp. 8-9.
50. Ibid.; *ARB*, 9433a-b.
51. *AD*, November 1989, pp. 22-3.
52. *ARB*, 9453c-9454c; *AD*, December 1989, pp. 22-4.
53. Ibid.
54. *ARB*, 9453c-9454c; *AD*, December 1989, p. 24.
55. *ARB*, 9491a-9493b; *AD*, January 1990, pp. 16-17.
56. *ARB*, 9526c-9527b; *AD*, February 1990, pp. 19-20.
57. *ARB*, 9661a-c; *ADJ*, April 1990, pp. 21-22; May 1990, p. 20.
58. *ARB*, 9592b-9594b.
59. 'Statement on the Red Sea Situation', EPLF Press Release, EPLF Washington DC office, 13 January 1990.
60. *ARB*, 9556a-b.
61. 'Eritreans Liberate Massawa; Offensive Continues', EPLF Press Release, EPLF Washington DC office, 12 February 1990; 'EPLF Liberates Massawa', *Adulis*, Volume VII, No. 3, March 1990, pp. 1-3.

62. *ARB*, 9593a-9594b.
63. See *ARB*, 9661a; *ADJ*, May 1990, p. 20; *ADJ*, June 1990, p. 22.
64. *ARB*, 9732b-9733c.
65. *ARB*, 9769a-b; *ADJ*, July 1990, p. 22.
66. *ADJ*, July 1990, p. 22.
67. *ARB*, 9910a-b.
68. *ARB*, 9949a-b.
69. *ARB*, 10020c-10021b; 10054c.
70. *ARB*, 10020c-10021b.
71. *ARB*, 10093b-10094a.
72. *ARB*, 10093b-10094a.
73. *ARB*, 10054c-10056b; 10093b-10094a; 10093c-10094a; 10130b-10135c.
74. The Hangash was the vocalisation of the HNG, or Hayada Nagadgelyada Gaashaandhiga. The NSS was an acronym for the Nabadsugida Soomaliyeed, or Somali Security Service. (see Africa Watch's *Somalia: A Government at War with its Own People* (New York/Washington, 1989, pp. iii and 47-8), henceforth abbreviated as 'Africa Watch, *Somalia*'.
75. See the discussion in *ARB*, 9390c-9391b, and the sources cited there. Siad Barre's attitude toward SNM and other security service abuse of northeners, originally one of concern, underwent a marked change after the 3 April treaty was signed (see Africa Watch, *Somalia*, pp. 127-128).
76. See *ADJ*, July 1988, p. 24; August 1988, p. 30. The fighting and its immediate consequences are documented by Africa Watch, *Somalia*, pp. 127-70. See also the report by Robert Gersony, 'Why Somalis Flee: Synthesis of Accounts of Conflict Experience in Northern Somalia by Somali Refugees, Displaced Persons and Others', US Department of State, Bureau for Refugee Programs, August 1989.
77. *ADJ*, August 1988, p. 30.
78. Africa Watch, *Somalia*, pp. 7-10; 127-70.
79. Africa Watch, *Somalia*, pp. 127-70, 193-9. The strategy of denying access by journalists and others was not successful in preventing loss of foreign military aid. The government apparently reversed its policy by the time US State Department consultant Robert Gersony researched displaced persons in northern Somalia in February 1988 ('Why Somalis Flee', pp. 1-2).
80. Africa Watch, *Somalia*, pp. 9-10. The government admitted 'terrorist' damage in the north, but only in September. It claimed that 60 per cent of all property there was destroyed but attributed it all to the SNM (*ADJ*, November 1988, p. 29).
81. *ADJ*, February 1989, p. 25. For the continuation of the government efforts to stamp out the SNM, see Africa Watch, Somalia, pp. 127 ff. and 'Why Somalis Flee', especially pp. 60-2.
82. *ADJ*, February 1989, p. 25.
83. *ARB*, 9151b.
84. *ADJ*, March 1989, pp. 25-6.
85. *ADJ*, April 1989, p. 20.
86. *ARB*, 9256c-9257b.
87. *ADJ*, May 1989, p. 21.
88. *ARB*, 9347b-9348a.
89. See, for instance, *ARB*, 9390a-b, for the Dobli incident, July-August 1990. This occurred when rebel soldiers took over the town of Dobli at the Kenya border. They were there with at least 6,000 civilian refugees from settlements earlier raided by the Somali army. As of 31 July a SNA attack, though unsuccessful, killed 27, and an army battalion had been sent against Dobli. The mutiny was eventually suppressed in August 1990.
90. *ARB*, 9424c-9425a. The claim was made by the SNM and in part substantiated by some international organisations.
91. Ibid.
92. Ibid.
93. *ARB*, 9457b.
94. *ARB*, 9496c-9497a.
95. *ARB*, 9676b-c. The incident coincided with outbreaks of fighting between elements of the Issa and Gadabursi clan groups in Djibouti city in June 1990 (ibid.). By this time the Issa and Gadabursi were beginning to organise and arm their own political movements with armed wings, the United Somali Front (USF) and Somali Patriotic Alliance (SPA), respectively.
96. *ARB*, 9804c.
97. See *ARB*, 9737c.
98. *ARB*, 9738b,
99. *ARB*, 10101a-b; 10180c.
100. *ARB*, 10180a-b.

101. *ARB*, 10142a-b.
102. *ARB*, 10180b-c. See also 'The Struggle to Survive in Somaliland', *Washington Post*, 14 November 1992, p. A18.
103. *ARB*, 9842c-9843a.
104. *ARB*, 10228a-b.

Chapter Nine

Insurgencies in Sudan, Uganda and Zaire

The insurgencies that have plagued southern Sudan, northern Uganda, and eastern and south-eastern Zaire have taken place in some of Africa's most inaccessible and undeveloped areas. They are often poorly documented and, with the exception of the most recent regime in Uganda, government security forces have shown little or no capability in effectively countering the insurgents. While Cold War politics plays a part in the fighting in these countries, the real roots of discontent leading to insurgency lie in ethnic and regional differences that have persisted for generations if not centuries.

THE INSURGENCY IN SOUTHERN SUDAN, 1983 TO THE PRESENT

Sudan's insurgency has not only split the country but has destroyed what little stability that was restored throughout the country following the resolution of an earlier conflict, that of the Anya Nya (AN), which ended in 1972 after fifteen years of war throughout the south. The latest round of insurgency began in 1983 and continues throughout Sudan's south. The roots of the conflict are not only political but also religious and cultural, pitting the Muslim Arab north against the Christian and Animist African south. Repeated failure by the central government either to militarily suppress the SPLM or come to terms politically with the southerners' demands has resulted in the destabilisation of the central government and its increasing dominance by radical militant Muslims of the National Islamic Front (NIF), since the mid-1980s the main vehicle for political expression of militant Islamic views in Sudan. The civil conflict has taken on an international dimension, as the regime in Khartoum seeks to spread militant Islam not only in the southern part of the country but also regionally.

The following discussion covers the background to the current insurgency, its origins and early history to the end of 1985, and then divides the insurgency to date into phases. It should be emphasised here that the civil war to date now affects more people than any other on the continent, in terms of deaths and displacement. Starvation and disease due to man-induced famine have repeatedly hit the populations of the war zones. The conflict is also perhaps Africa's cruellest, which says much in a continent marred everywhere by the brutality of insurgent war.

BACKGROUND: THE ROOTS OF REBELLION

The roots of southern discontent, first expressed in the Anya Nya rebellion, lay in the deep-seated differences between the Muslim north and the Christian and Animist south. Historically, the Muslims from the north had been seen as invaders and exploiters of southern agriculturalists and cattle raisers. Under the rule of the Mahdists (1889–1898), the imposition of Islamic rule upon non-Muslims throughout the south was accompanied by great barbarity. The establishment of the Anglo-Egyptian Sudan and British administrative techniques served to end the widespread and brutal warfare the south had known for decades, but old memories remained and cultural and religious differences persisted. Another historical form of dominance by the north over the south was the former's tolerance and even encouragement of raids by northern tribes, many of them relatively recent Arab immigrants, against the south to steal cattle and slaves. As with attempts at forced Islamicisation, this was halted during Anglo-Egyptian rule.

The settlement of the Anya Nya rebellion in 1972 was through a series of compromises, including especially a unified government for the southern region to represent southerners' interests at Khartoum. Former Anya Nya insurgents, many of them local Dinka and Nuer tribesmen, were integrated into the national army. There was also supposed to be tolerance by the Muslim north of southerners' religious beliefs. The success of such a settlement was dependent on the degree to which the north was willing to curb radical Islamic pressures, however. As it turned out, it could not do so.

Continued north-south tensions after 1972

It was hoped that peace in 1972 would enable economic recovery to take place from the shambles of the rebellion. However, recovery was slow, and further international debt accrued from costly development schemes. Chief among these was the Jonglei Canal project, which aimed to cut through the Sudd, a huge swampy area of the southern Nile basin, and improve the river's flow and downstream volume. It was one of several Nile Basin development projects designed to regulate water supply and improve flood control. However, southerners were wary of the projects, fearing that consequent ecological changes would endanger their farming and herding economy. Nevertheless the central government persisted in costly development schemes. Regardless, economic conditions grew worse through the late 1970s and early 1980s.

Domestic difficulties continued, exacerbated by two major problems. First was the deepening economic crisis, aggravated by the terrible droughts of the early 1970s. Agricultural land in the central and western part of the country was abandoned, and many pastoralists could no longer find water or grass for their animals. Many tribesmen were forced into northern cities and helped create a large group of discontented, impoverished urban unemployed. Radical Islam as well as socialist and Marxist ideas found fertile ground there. The government, led by General Jafaar al-Nimeri, had come to power by a military takeover and its legitimacy was questioned by many. The government was well aware of the potential destabilisation that could result from the growing discontent; it moved against the radical Marxists and other leftist elements but sought to appease the growing radical Islamic community, which was too large to confront directly. In regional policy Sudan supported the Eritrean freedom fighters, who from the mid-1970s fought the Marxist central government of Ethiopia. The latter was claimed by Khartoum to be supporting domestic Marxists and radicals. The generally pro-Western (at the time) Nimeri government had another enemy in the person of Libyan strongman Qadhafi, who also supported anti-regime dissidents.

A second problem was continued north-south differences. In the growing climate of political Islam that was sweeping much of Sudan, tolerance for Christian and Animist religious practice, never strong to begin with, diminished rapidly. Local unrest, often due to radical Muslim-instigated violence against southerners in general and non-Muslims in particular, grew. Armed raids by northern tribes against the south were on the increase. Many were assisted by local militias armed and trained to preserve security in rural areas by the central government. Southerners, including former Anya Nya guerrillas, felt the Sudanese government could not or would not protect them. Northerners in military units in the south were perceived as supporting government attempts to Islamicise the region.

Situation in the south, early 1980s

By the early 1980s, the situation had become very tense and only the right catalyst was needed to precipitate a full-scale revolt. Tensions were high among former Anya Nya in military units in the south, as the Sudan People's Armed Forces (SPAF) sought to rotate units in which they served to the north and replace them with northeners. This was an easier process with units that had integrated northeners and southerners, but many garrisons remained completely southern in composition. For the latter, to be moved out of the area was a major concern. Former Anya Nya had local family and community ties and feared what would happen once their protective presence was removed. In addition, SPAF salaries were quite low – between US$10 and $45 – and soldiers augmented their incomes with farming and cattle raising. To forfeit families, cattle, and farms was too great a price.

Conflicts between the SPAF and southerners were not uncommon. Since 1972 rejectionist members of the old Anya Nya (AN), mainly Nuers, refused to join the central government forces and had set up their own Anya Nya II (AN-II) movement. However, they were small in number and their actions were disparate and had relatively little effect during the 1970s. But with increasing economic problems and spread of discontent they found increasing support. AN-II operated throughout eastern Bahr el-Ghazal and Upper Nile as far east as the Ethiopian border. Some AN-II personnel were given Libyan-funded training in a number of camps in the Gambela region of Ethiopia.

ORIGIN OF THE SOUTHERN SUDANESE INSURGENCY (1983–1984)

In 1983 the issue of rotation/transfer of former AN units became critical. What would have been a routine operation in other circumstances now threatened to split Sudan's army. However, the central government persisted in its rotation efforts, and by January many units, such as the large garrison at Bor, flatly refused to be moved. In early March a small garrison at Wangkay, 160km west of the military base at Bentiu, mutinied, killed their commanding officer, and fled to the bush. Northern troops were sent to Bentiu in mid-March to locate the mutineers, who linked up with AN-II units in the area. The SPAF force from Bentiu was ambushed as it moved toward Wangkay. At about the same time, police stations at Warop (Tonj area) and Ganylid (Rumbek area) were attacked by AN-II units. Amazingly, the SPAF ignored these warning signs and persisted in efforts to rotate former AN units. Finally, at the end of March another southern garrison at Raga, about 300km north-north-west of Wau, scheduled for reassignment to el-Fasher, rebelled and fled to the bush with their weapons.

The situation could yet have been salvaged, but influential former AN personnel in the Sudanese Army such as US-educated Colonel John Garang de Mabior, a Dinka and highly regarded among southerners, were not called upon to mediate. Nor was the troop rotation policy modified. The Bor garrison continued intransigent, and as a result the parent garrison at Juba withheld pay. Only in mid-May was Garang sent to Bor, and by that time the unit had openly rebelled and fled into the bush with its weapons, defeating an SPAF force sent to prevent its flight. The second great southern rebellion had begun, and Garang and other southern officers with him joined the insurgents.

At first resistance was poorly coordinated and lacked direction as units rebelled and former AN units fled into the bush. Many sought refuge in Ethiopia. However, it was soon evident that AN-II did not dominate the new movement. Units from key garrisons soon joined the resistance, but for the remainder of 1983 the insurgency pattern was one of unit mutinies followed by wholesale desertion to the bush. Some insurgent elements began kidnapping expatriate workers for ransom. One such group called itself the Southern Sudanese Liberation Front (SSLF). Its members had training in Ethiopia and financing from Libya; some came from the Boma plateau area near the Ethiopian border.

Other rebel elements laid siege to the garrison at Naser near the Ethiopian border in late summer. Only on 21 December did the SPAF break the siege. This followed an armed clash at Malwal (Malwal Gahoth) near Naser, in which the SPAF claimed 480 insurgents killed at the cost of seven SPAF killed and thirteen wounded; the rebels fled toward the Ethiopian border. The Sudanese government claimed that rebel operations were supported by (and based in) Ethiopia, and that wounded insurgents were treated in hospitals at Gambela and Addis Ababa. Already on 9 December Sudanese Vice-President General Omer Muhammad Tayeb publicly asserted that Ethiopia and Libya supported the unrest. The SPAF subsequently received some Egyptian air force air–ground support by late December.

The SPLA version of events of 1983 differs considerably and is probably more accurate, but the differences in the accounts reflect the propaganda war that already marched side by side with the military one. According to John Garang the first SPLA offensive was initiated on 16 May 1983, and culminated in the capture of Malwal on 17 November. In the fighting there were 120 SPAF killed and 60 wounded at the cost of twelve SPLA killed and 30 wounded, from an attacking force of 150 personnel. The campaign continued with the attack on Naser on 12 December, in which the insurgents captured the eastern part of the town and held it for seven days; during the siege the SPAF had 267 killed and 173 wounded at the cost of four insurgents killed and nine wounded. The SPAF lost one helicopter at Malwal and three at Naser, plus three river boats and assorted vehicles at Naser.

This first SPLA offensive, initiated even before the name of the force or of the parent SPLM had been widely publicised, was consistent with the strategy of Colonel John Garang and others: to form a cohesive organisation from a force of AN-II, former AN, and southern Sudanese Army deserters, and work quickly to capture and consolidate territory in the south. Building the organisation involved a combination of negotiations and some outright fighting with elements of AN-II still active in the south. Some joined while others remained hostile. According to Garang, over 60 per cent of the first five SPLA battalions formed were former AN-II. The major issue was between those who wanted a secessionist organisation similar to the old AN while Garang and others wanted a unified, democratic, secular Sudan instead. While some AN-II and their leaders refused to join with Garang, the new organisation and its military arm were a cohesive unit by May 1983.

In 1984 the rebellion spread, with the second insurgent offensive initiated on 8 February. Malakal was bombarded on 22 February; subsequently Ayod was overrun. On 10 February the Jonglei Canal project was attacked and the base camp destroyed in a five-hour operation. Steamer traffic on the Nile between Bentiu and Malakal (Tonga area) was also attacked, as were garrisons near Tonga in mid-February. It was estimated at the time that since the troubles began in early 1983 over 2,500 soldiers, police, and security officials of southern origin had openly rebelled and deserted. From January to April the insurgents took a number of key towns throughout Bahr al-Ghazal and Upper Nile.

EMERGENCE OF THE SPLA

By early 1984 the rebels identified themselves as belonging to a new organisation, the Sudanese People's Liberation Movement (SPLM), the military arm of which was the Sudanese People's Liberation Army (SPLA). The SPLM, with external (political) headquarters in London, claimed its foundation from shortly after the Bor rebellion. It was headed by Colonel John Garang, also head of the SPLA. Assisting Colonel Garang were Korbino Kuanyin, Lieutenant Colonel William Nyuon Bany, and Major John Gordon Kong, all former AN officials who had joined the SPAF in 1972. The SPLA charter reflected southern concerns over northern economic and political domination and called for a democratic, secular Sudan – directly conflicting with the Islamic parties Sudanese President Nimeri attempted to placate. Khartoum reacted to the disastrous situation developing in the south by imposing a State of Emergency, directed against southern rebels as well as 'enemies of Islamicisation.' In a 29 April 1984 speech, Nimeri publicly accused the SPLM of Marxist-Leninist leanings and claimed it was a tool of Ethiopia and the USSR, claims which the SPLM denied.

By June Khartoum claimed it had stabilised the situation, and the SPAF chief of staff, General Abd ar-Rahman Suwar ed-Dhahab, said that the south was under control. However, Naser remained under siege and the second battle in seven months had just taken place with the SPAF again failing to break through SPLA lines. Naser was resupplied via air despite the earlier loss of two helicopters to SPLA SAMs.

To most outside observers, it was apparent as early as 1984 that the SPAF could not win militarily. The SPLA had tied down SPAF personnel and units and reduced its effectiveness. In addition, other factors gave the SPLA an advantage:

■ It was an insurgent force largely of former guerrillas and military men with combat experience;
■ The SPLM enjoyed support from the southern public, which was hostile to Khartoum;
■ The SPAF were demoralised and poorly equipped;
■ The terrain was very difficult for comprehensive, large-scale operations needed to prosecute the war.

Throughout the remainder of the year, SPLA operations continued to put the SPAF at a disadvantage. Many southerners continued to join the force. These included prison and police force personnel with their weapons, as well as some regular army members. As of late 1984 SPLA radio was instructing clandestine cells in Juba army, police, prison, and wildlife service units to defect as intensified fighting was imminent.

Continued success of the SPLA; overthrow of Nimeri

By early 1985 the SPLA controlled large parts of the south, and continued to capture government outposts cut off from resupply and reinforcement. It showed it could directly confront SPAF units in early January when it destroyed a SPAF battalion in a two-day battle near Winjibol near the Ugandan border. The SPLA did not enjoy an unbroken string of victories. In February 1985 a large force of 3,500 in the Bor area moved southward against Juba. The two-pronged attack met stiff resistance from the Mandari militia and SPAF forces, and was forced back. However, in a third major SPLA offensive, strategic areas such as the Boma plateau and Yirol were captured. SPLA efforts were assisted by the newly-formed Radio SPLA, which began broadcasting on 2 November 1984 from a site believed to be in neighbouring Ethiopia.

The major event of 1985 was the April coup d'état that overthrew President Nimeri. A military government headed by SPAF Chief of Staff General Suwar ed-Dhahab took power and promised to hand over power in the future to a civilian regime. The coup was caused by increasing internal unrest over Nimeri's attempts to control the militant Muslim factions as well as general discontent over the declining economy and the lack of success in resolving the southern war. Despite initial favourable reaction by the SPLA, the lack of progress in negotiations soon saw the resumption of hostilities after a short-lived truce. Bor was attacked by the SPLA from 29 May, and other garrisons came under renewed siege.

In July 1985 the central government acknowledged that it had begun to receive logistical and training support from Libya. Although Libya claimed it wished to promote negotiations between the government and the SPLA, hopes by the latter for a settlement dimmed; it was apparent that Libya's shift in support from the SPLA to the new regime was a bid by Qadhafi for influence in Khartoum.

Despite the election of Sadiq el-Mahdi to replace Suwar ed-Dhahab in Khartoum, and the new Sudanese leader's stated interest in a reconciliation with the south, for the rest of 1985 fighting continued as the SPAF attempted to break the siege of Bor and keep the Bor–Juba road open. The insurgents also maintained their pressure in southern Upper Nile and central Equatoria into the fall. Bor was finally relieved by a force from Malakal on 4 November. Elsewhere, fighting continued throughout December 1985, and by this time had spread into south-eastern Blue Nile along the Ethiopian border, where the SPLA operated south of Kurmuk by the end of the year. Fighting continued in eastern Bahr al-Ghazal state as well.

During August and September 1985 the el-Mahdi government undertook a campaign to arm local tribesmen in western Sudan, setting an unfortunate precedent. Arms were given to loyal tribes in northern Darfur and Kurdufan, despite criticism in both government and rebel circles. The implications of this policy were still being felt in the early 1990s with tens of thousands of modern weapons in the hands of tribesmen in the west, despite ongoing SPAF attempts to control the situation. The availability of modern small arms to local militias in a setting where long-standing ethnic grievances exist has only served to exacerbate conflict and result in widespread human rights abuses.

In his 1986 New Year's broadcast, John Garang noted that Khartoum had determined the coming year to be a 'year of war.' The SPLA had grown to where the government was forced to admit it was the major threat to the regime. 1986 saw widespread pre-emptive offensives by the SPLA against government forces, including another attempt to capture Juba. Although unsuccessful, this attack shook government advocates of a military solution to the conflict, and both sides decided to attempt negotiations. However, talks between el-Mahdi and Garang were initiated but soon collapsed and were not revived despite later Libyan attempts at mediation. Shortly thereafter (August) the fighting resumed, marked by an attack on Wau by the SPLA. Sudanese government officials noted in January 1987 that the SPLA had a field force of 12,000, organised in at least twelve battalions, as well as a reserve of 10,000, or ten battalions.

OVERVIEW OF THE SUDANESE CIVIL WAR SINCE 1986

Since 1986 the history of the civil war in southern Sudan was marked by cycles of fighting between government forces and the SPLA. The SPAF usually had the advantage during the dry season (late November through April–May), but the insurgents had generally made most of their gains during the rainy season, when many roads are under water, weather prevents air–ground support to government troops, and the lush vegetation offers concealment for SPLA forces.

Although the relatively short duration of the war does not allow for firm division into phases, it is possible to distinguish three main ones. The first, which extended to the end of 1987, saw the SPLA establish itself in Bahr al-Ghazal and Upper Nile and consolidate its positions; the second, from early 1988 through late 1991, was a period of SPLA expansion in which the insurgents took the initiative and established control throughout most of the south; the final period, from late 1991 through 1995, saw a reversal of SPLA fortunes and the success of government operations.

Consolidation of SPLA positions to the end of 1987

This period was marked by:

■ The rebellion of southern military units and the founding of the SPLM/SPLA;
■ Formation of a regular SPLA force in territorial zones of deployment;
■ The replacement of the Nimeri government by first a military council and then a civilian government, neither of whom could or would negotiate peace with the SPLA;
■ The firm establishment of SPLA power in Upper Nile and in Bahr el-Ghazal;
■ Continued attempts to destabilise SPAF positions in western Equatoria through attacks on Bor and Juba;
■ Probes against SPAF control in western Bahr el-Ghazal and Blue Nile to test government defences there.

Due to its strong position in Upper Nile, in November 1986 the SPLA was able to success-fully counter a large government dry-season offensive (five battalions plus reinforce-ments) along two axes of approach from Malakal. The SPAF had as its objective the Nasir–Akobo–Pachala area. In a series of engagements from 23 to 27 November at Anatyer near Malakal the SPLA was able to rout the offensive. Although unsuccessful, the pattern set by the SPAF for this offensive was to persist to the end of the war: large task forces based on several infantry battalions reinforced with armour and extra logistics attempted to penetrate as far into SPLA-held territory as possible while dry-season conditions permitted, and capture SPLA-held towns or relieve towns under insurgent siege. The SPLA, for its part, countered with the effective tactics it has used ever since: to draw the SPAF into SPLA territory and attack the invaders at the end of their logistics lines, later recouping any losses by operations during the rainy season.

SPLA successes under 'Bright Star' and follow-on operations (early 1988–late 1991)
This period was marked by:

■ The overthrow of the civilian government by a military junta backed by radical Islamic elements;
■ The organisation of SPLA units into 'Bright Star' task forces, each entrusted with terri-torial responsibilities;
■ The establishment of SPLA rule throughout Equatoria, with insurgent control estab-lished to Sudan's southern borders;
■ Spread of the insurgency to southern Darfur and Kurdufan states in western Sudan;
■ The siege of Juba and the isolation of remaining government garrisons.

1988 marked the beginning of a change in SPLA strategy. The insurgent movement organ-ised a series of task forces that worked in a coordinated fashion to gain territorial control and capture government garrisons. The overall operation was called 'Bright Star,' and it worked in conjunction with other SPLA forces responsible for smaller, more local opera-tions. The first major success of the campaign was in June and was directed against a SPAF task force moving from Juba to Torit and Kapoeta, defeating it decisively on 25 and 26 June and halting the offensive.

Intense fighting continued through the rest of the year and saw steady SPLA gains in numerous engagements. On 12 July Garang could say with confidence that the SPLA had effectively taken territorial control of the south. All major land and water routes were interdicted. SPLA recruitment was continuing and even rising, with new recruits from Blue Nile and southern Kurdufan. The SPLA was holed up in garrisons in the south at Juba, Wau, Torit, Malakal, Bentiu, Uweyl, Rumbek, Gogrial, Naser, Akubu, Yei, Bor Maridi, Mundri, and a few other sites.

During early 1991 the 'Bright Star' operations were engaged in taking SPAF garrisons and extending insurgent control to the southern border of Sudan with the Central African Republic, Zaire, Uganda, and Kenya.

Continued success of the SPLA and the ineffectiveness of the SPAF were contributing factors in the overthrow of the central government in 1989. A group of officers heavily influenced by the radical Muslim National Islamic Front (NIF) of Muslim militant leader Hassan el-Turabi ousted Prime Minister el-Mahdi. The group, which called itself the National Salvation Revolutionary Command Council (NSRCC), or Revolutionary Command Council (RCC) for short, was headed by Brigadier Omar Hassan Ahmad al-Bashir. It suspended the constitution and assumed all offices of government. Bashir, a northerner from Shendi, had been a senior officer in the war. He claimed that the spirit behind the coup was nationalist and in support of the sacrifices the military had made in the southern war. He and the RCC blamed Prime Minister el-Mahdi for the inability to decisively end the war. Bashir and others on the RCC were heavily influenced by the radical Muslims, however, and no one saw any hope that peace negotiations would seriously take place until another military solution was tried. These concerns were justified by continued fighting.

The SPLA was at the peak of its power in mid-1991. It controlled most of southern Sudan and its personnel strength approached 40,000. Its continuing military success was a major embarrassment to the Sudanese government, which sought military assistance from Iran and China, and announced plans to expand the regular force and augment it with a paramilitary militia, the People's Defence Force (PDF), modelled after the Iranian Revolutionary Guards. Khartoum continued its intransigence toward negotiations, backed by the increasingly influential NIF, which also used the government to further its agenda of Islamicisation of Sudanese society. The combination of SPLA success in the south and growing NIF control of the government in Khartoum began to have a destabilising effect upon the Bashir regime, which suppressed several coup attempts by disaffected military officers.

However, a major change in the situation took place in October 1991, ostensibly along ethnic lines. At that time Riak Machar and Lam Akol, a Nuer and a Shilluk respectively, began a rebellion that soon involved the town of Naser as well as most of Upper Nile state. This breakaway faction sought secession from the central government and wished to open negotiations with Khartoum. The outbreak of fighting between Garang's forces and the Naser faction at the end of the rainy season came at a time when the central government had massed a huge force to mount a multi-pronged dry season offensive for early 1992. Taking advantage of internal SPLA divisions, Khartoum made agreements with the Naser faction to allow passage through Upper Nile state while a major attack was also mounted from Juba toward Torit, the SPLA's main centre. Indeed, many observers believe that agents of the central government were instrumental in inciting the initial split by the Naser faction from the SPLA.

Fighting continued through the late summer of 1982 as government forces captured a number of garrisons throughout the south from the SPLA, including Bor, Kapoeta, and even Torit. The onset of the rainy season halted further government attempts to penetrate to the Kenyan and Ugandan borders. However, starting in July the SPLA began a series of attacks on Juba which inflicted significant damage but failed to capture the town.

The fighting at Juba followed close upon talks between the government and the insurgent factions at Abuja, Nigeria, which saw a strategic realignment of both SPLA groups against the government, which by now admitted that it would grant peace to the south only on its own terms. Amid the continuing siege of Juba and the weakening position of government troops in outlying posts, the SPLA in October 1992 underwent another split, this time marked by the departure of William Nyuon Bany, Garang's deputy military commander. The Bashir government, emboldened by earlier successes and by these further internal SPLA problems, publicly announced that its 1993 dry-season offensive would end the insurgency once and for all. Despite this, SPLA forces from the Naser faction and others attacked Malakal in late October, raising doubts about SPAF capabilities to successfully initiate any new military actions. While the attack was unable to dislodge the SPAF from Malakal, it did dispel Khartoum's claims that it had firm control of those parts of southern Sudan it had ostensibly reoccupied.

UGANDA, 1981–1992

Uganda has seen almost continuous warfare since the later days of the Idi Amin regime. Following its overthrow in 1979, a new government was set up, led by Yusufu Lule, with many of former president Milton Obote sympathisers and opportunists among its ranks. The tenuous political structure was supported by about 8,500 Tanzanian People's Defence Force (TPDF) troops. Prominent in the new government were Paulo Muwanga, Interior Minister, who controlled the internal security services, and Yoweri Museveni, the Defence Minister, who was tasked to build a new army from the core of exiles who returned from Tanzania.

PHASES OF THE UGANDAN INSURGENT CONFLICTS

There are two main phases to the Ugandan fighting since 1981:

First phase: NRA resistance and overthrow of the Obote and successor regimes, 1981–1986 The struggle of the NRA against the Obote regime began in 1981 and developed during 1984 when Museveni's forces established secure bases in western Uganda. In 1984–1985 the NRA gradually consolidated its territory and advanced on Kampala, and caused the overthrow of Obote in 1985. In 1985–1986 it completed its conquest of Uganda, putting to flight the successor military regime.

Second phase: Ugandan government versus northern insurgents of the HSM and successor movements, 1987–1992 This phase was dominated by the gradual re-imposition of order throughout Uganda by the new government and the expulsion of the remaining armed movements in northern Uganda. During this period the government was faced with a new resistance movement led by Alice Lakwenya, whose Holy Spirit Movement (HSM) proved quite difficult to suppress. However, by 1992 security had been generally restored to the north.

DEVELOPMENT OF THE NRA AND FIRST YEARS OF THE INSURGENCY, 1981–1983

Museveni's task in creating a new Ugandan army was a formidable one. In May 1979, Uganda's forces consisted of about 1,000 troops trained in Tanzania, many of them at Camp Musoma, and brought into Uganda with the TPDF by Lieutenant Colonel Oyite-Ojok, who became armed forces Chief of Staff. The rival to it, and later to the occupying Tanzanian troops, was a force being formed by Museveni, which consisted of several thousand youths that he had armed and trained. This was the first indication that Museveni was beginning the implementation of his own separate agenda. Incidents were reported between members of this force and TPDF troops in the western part of Uganda as early as May 1979.[1]

The differences between Museveni and his opponents in the defence establishment were supplemented by other conflicts which only served to promote strife within the Uganda National Liberation Army (UNLA). President Lule could not control the differences within the UNLA between Museveni's supporters and his own. Many of the latter were also plants by the TPDF to further Tanzanian President Nyerere's, and by extension former Ugandan President Obote's, interests. Lule strove for proportional representation within the armed forces by region, and also pushed for uniform educational standards for UNLA personnel, as well as an age minimum. This ran counter to Museveni's goals, and was not implemented. Museveni wished not only to build a large group of BanyaNkole and BaTutsi in the UNLA, but also to ensure that he continued to have the support of the many youths that he had cultivated and indoctrinated under his guidance.[2]

As noted above, the conflict with the Lule government and later with that of Geoffrey Binaisa (who replaced the deposed Lule in June 1979) provided Museveni with a vehicle to advance his personal agenda. A MunyaNkole from the Rwanda border area with family connections to the BaTutsi Rwandan exile community, he was already a recognised leader of the Ankole as well as of the Tutsi exiles, who fought for the UNLA against Amin. By some accounts, Museveni saw in the BaTutsi world-view a basis for his own power goals: the ultimate formation of a confederation centred in Africa's central Rift valley under hegemonic control by BanyaNkole-BaTutsi rulers in Uganda, Rwanda, and Burundi. However, in 1979 Museveni's agenda was not yet known, and his power in the Ugandan government, under

211

siege since his conflicts with Lule, ended when he was fired as Defence Minister. When Museveni was ousted by Binaisa and the Tanzanians, his BaTutsi supporters left the UNLA along with him and began to forge links with southern groups such as the Baganda in preparation for future active resistance against a projected return of Obote.

During November 1981 UNLA operations against insurgents in West Nile and north-west of Kampala resulted in numerous claims of human rights violations. By this time two leading insurgent factions had emerged as the major challengers of the regime. These were the Uganda National Rescue Front (UNRF), which claimed about 3,000 fighters under Brigadier General Moses Ali in West Nile, and the National Resistance Movement (NRM), with its armed element, the National Resistance Army (NRA), which claimed about 1,000 fighters in a number of camps in southern Uganda. Its leaders were Museveni (in Uganda), the military commander, and, in London, Yusufu Lule.[3]

Throughout the remainder of 1981 UNLA operations continued in southern Uganda north-west of Kampala. Atrocities were claimed by the insurgents as the UNLA took reprisals against civilians. Assisting government security forces at this time were training teams from Tanzania, North Korea, Cuba, and Ethiopia.[4] Military training was further augmented in early 1982 by the arrival of a Commonwealth team composed of British and Sierra Leonean troops. By this time the UNLA had grown to somewhat over 10,000 soldiers.[5] Early 1982 saw continued insurgent action in West Nile and in the areas around Kampala. The UNLA continued vain efforts to contain the insurgency by both urban and rural sweeps in southern Uganda.[6] In May 1982 UNLA operations in the 'Luwero triangle' began. These infamous activities by Ugandan security forces were to result in the deaths of at least 300,000 Ugandans by 1985. Security forces, including the UNLA, police, internal security personnel of the National Security Agency (NASA), and the youth militia of Obote's party, the Ugandan People's Congress (UPC), all participated in the activities. The security forces, dominated by northern Ugandans, imposed collective punishment on the residents of the Luwero area, virtually depopulating many regions as any who did not flee were killed.[7] The September 1982 Amnesty International report on human rights abuses by the UNLA was predictably rejected by the government; however, Obote did admit 'indis-cipline' in UNLA ranks.[8] As of mid-1983, continuing reports of human rights violations murders of civilians by government security forces, arbitrary detentions, and torture continued. Many of them were attributed to the UPC Youth Wing, which was used as an unofficial militia by the UNLA.[9] In July 1983 the UNLA undertook the first of a series of major offensives against the NRA. Directed against the Luwero triangle, it forced at least 100,000 civilians to flee. Another offensive was also undertaken against West Nile.[10]

NRA on the offensive, 1984–1985

By 1984 Museveni and the NRM had established secure bases in central Uganda that were 'no-go' areas for government forces. With the general consolidation of the NRA position in the west and on the borders of the Luwero Triangle, Museveni began to attack government positions throughout western Uganda. The most notable of the early 1984 attacks was that of 20 February on Masindi Barracks, which was overrun by the insurgents. In the fighting, 178 soldiers, 27 police, and eighteen prison guards were killed at the cost of five NRA soldiers. Many other government personnel were captured, including the local police commissioner. More important for the NRA, 765 rifles, 140 mines, ten machine-guns, 100,000 rounds of ammunition, and numerous mortars, mortar bombs, rockets, uniforms, and radio sets were also taken. The blow to government morale with the loss of Masindi, a major garrison, was telling.[11]

As the NRA was making its gains in an increasingly disciplined and professional manner, the UNLA still exhibited all the signs of lack of control. This was indicated by its behaviour following the 25 May NRA attack on Namugongo. UNLA troops arriving on the scene indiscriminately killed at least 87 local civilians. The Obote government later admitted its troops had committed the atrocities, but took no measures to punish those responsible nor to prevent any further such actions.[12] Even though the UNLA was unable to curb the abysmal behaviour of its troops, attempts were made at the national level to address the problem of human rights abuses, which were by now garnering international attention. On 22 June Parliament withdrew the power of military police to unilaterally detain civilians, which had been granted under the Amin regime in 1973 and never withdrawn. At the same time, this measure was balanced on the negative by 6 July actions that decreed the death penalty for 'terrorism' and life imprisonment for cattle theft. 'Terrorists' were members of illegal organisations, and the Interior Ministry was empowered by the same action to declare organisations illegal and its members thus terrorists.[13] As operations continued in and around the Luwero Triangle during the summer of 1984, the mass killings of civilians continued and finally generated the condemnation of the United States Government and of international organisations. It was claimed in early August that at least 200,000 civilians had been massacred in the Luwero Triangle, with many of the killings methodically planned and undertaken at Kireka and Lubiri Barracks, east and west of the capital respectively. The Obote government denied the charges. However, its frustration was clearly evident in the November 'anti-terror' drive in Kampala itself, which netted few results. Insurgent activity continued in the Luwero Triangle through the remainder of the year and into early 1985.[14] On 23 January 1985 Yusufu Lule died in London, and his death placed Museveni in full charge of the NRM/NRA. Museveni's style was entirely different from that of Lule, and he committed the NRA to the offensive.[15] In the meantime, news of the extermination camps of the Obote regime continued to leak to the outside world. In March the influential Manchester *Guardian* newspaper detailed the security forces' methods of fighting insurgents by acting against the population that it believed supported them.[16]

According to the *Guardian* article, the UNLA set up five special detention camps in the Luwero triangle that were distinguished from the more common detention camps by a more selective intake process. Special measures were established to determine probable insurgent supporters and anyone in the local Baganda population who was a leader or professional of any sort. The camps, at Katikamu, Boma, Kabungata, Bukomero, and Mitgana, were supplemented by the Luwero police station. The camps were run by the Special Brigade, a unit directly under the control of Obote himself. At these sites the detainees were carefully screened as to their background. The Ugandan National Security Agency (NASA) agents assigned to the camps would carefully check the intakes for known or suspected insurgents or their supporters, and take them away to be killed. The NASA men were known as 'computers' for the printouts they carried to assist them in their work. The arrest process itself was called 'panda gari', 'get in the car', after the common phrase used during security roundups.[17]

The purpose of the security sweeps and the camp system established by the security forces was to clear the Luwero triangle of any possible support for dissidents. The sweeps and camp detentions were accompanied by wholesale slaughter by UNLA and other security forces of entire villages believed to support the NRA. The latter was not affected by Uganda government efforts, and continued its operations in the Luwero triangle. 50,000 were forced from their land between 1981 and 1984, and, as it later turned out, at least 200,000 were killed by the security forces. Elsewhere during 1984–1985, the worst-affected area was Bunyoro west of Masindi and Hoima.[18]

The war in 1985 saw steady gains by the NRA and other insurgent forces throughout western and northern Uganda. The primary reason was the UNLA's atrocious and brutal treatment of the population outside some areas of the north and its almost total lack of discipline and control. Police and paramilitary forces, although somewhat more organised, behaved with similar brutality. By mid-1985 at least half of the population of the Luwero triangle, about 300,000 in total, may have been killed. 280,000 were refugees, of which 200,000 were in Sudan, 30,000 in Rwanda, and the rest in Zaire. The UNLA was increasingly unable to fight the war effectively, even using terror as a weapon.[19]

Meanwhile, NRA pressure continued as it moved eastward. On 23 June the UNLA barracks complex at Jinja was attacked; at the same time Magamaga, 18km to the east, was also hit. Other key sites were also targeted throughout the country at this time, provoking brutal reprisals by the NRA against the population. By the end of June it had become apparent that the Obote government could not prevent the steady advance of the NRA. All this happened while UNLA and other security forces were under severe attack by international agencies for their human rights abuses; 36 mass graves were reported in the Luwero-Kampala area alone.[20] By July the situation was untenable for Obote as the security forces began a series of bitter internal recriminations over the conduct of the war. Acholi-Langi rivalry built up to the point where fighting erupted in the streets of Kampala. Finally, on 27 July Obote was again driven from power, his place taken by Brigadier General Basilo Olara Okello, an Acholi, supported by the Army Commander, Major General Tito Okello (no relation). Power was given to a military council made up of representatives from the various security forces. However, the security situation in and around the capital remained dangerous as rival groups claimed control of parts of Kampala and fought turf wars there. Worse yet, the change in leadership failed to help UNLA and other security organs in their fight against the NRA.[21]

NRA victory, July 1985–January 1986

The NRA, which had attempted negotiations with the new Okello government, soon found the latter unwilling to share power. It thus went again on the offensive by the third week of August in a series of major operations designed to consolidate power in the west, forcing UNLA units there to surrender and be disarmed; Kasese and Fort Portal fell.[22]

Throughout October fighting continued, for the most part small operations designed to force back UNLA units from NRA areas as well as larger operations designed to capture isolated UNLA garrisons. By November the NRA extended its control to the Nile River in the east and south to Kampala and Lake Victoria. NRA patrols and systematic mining of all roads into insurgent territory formed a cordon sanitaire that government forces could not breach.[23]

The NRA advance was marked by a few major battles. These generally resulted from UNLA attempts to penetrate NRA-held areas. The UNLA forces, if successful in their drives forward, would invariably suffer logistics problems and come under intense fire by the NRA when they lost their forward momentum. Casualties were usually heavy. Such was the case when the NRA repulsed a major drive by the UNLA in late November toward Katonga Bridge near Masindi. In this campaign, the UNLA massed 10,000 troops in an attempt to reopen the Kampala–Masaka road as well as that to Masindi. The attacks were repulsed with heavy casualties and the NRA counterattack took Masaka.[24]

The UNLA and the Okello regime were now in desperate straits, and tried to arrange a peace pact, which failed (17 December). By this time, in the Kampala area, at least 10,000 NRA, well-armed, well-organised, and with high morale and discipline, were facing 15,000 UNLA and affiliated forces whose quality varied considerably but which was generally far below the NRA standard. The NRA's final push in January was thus destined to succeed. On the 26th the capital fell to Museveni's forces as the Okellos and their troops fled northward into Sudan. Their retreat was marked by indiscriminate atrocities against civilians, even fellow northeners.[25]

The war was not yet over. By 1 February the NRA controlled as far as the Nile, the Masindi area, and the axis running east from Kampala through Jinja to the Kenyan border.

The NRA, with 30,000 troops, was making steady progress against remnants of UNLA units in the north. Lira fell on 28 February; Gulu on 9 March after heavy fighting. On 19 March Kitgum was deserted by UNLA troops who fled northward into Sudan. The NRA shortly thereafter occupied the border posts and was thus left in control of the entire country.[26]

1986–1992: THE NRM/NRA AND UGANDAN INTERNAL SECURITY

The NRM aftermath

The NRA following the NRM victory was enlarged considerably and took on a different character as an army of mostly young men and teenage boys augmented by fighters from FUNA (Former Ugandan National Army) and FEDEMU (Federal Democratic Movement of Uganda). By 1987 the NRA had grown in numbers and complexity to where a division structure was introduced. NRM civil government was also expanded to the local level throughout the country. Each political subdivision had its own level of Resistance Councils (RCs).

Key to the implementation of civil support to the military was the formation of Local Defence Units (LDUs). An example of LDU operations as they had evolved by the early 1990s is found in the support they were tasked to provide the NRA proper in Teso in July 1992. 4,000 LDUs and former rebels, or 'reporters', were being deployed in groups of 300 for each county, evenly distributed by sub-county, to help preserve civil order. The NRA 3rd Division, Brigadier General Shef Ali commanding, was overseeing the process. Local governments were involved in the process as well. The nineteen sub-counties in Soroti district in particular were the focus of the effort. The LDUs went beyond regular RC activities in that they were an armed militia or paramilitary force that was a first line of defence against residual insurgents. How well LDUs would have worked against the large, well-organised bands of insurgents in the late 1980s is another question, however.[27]

Ironically, in the wake of the NRM takeover and Museveni's consolidation of power, the regime was itself beset by another insurgency. This was begun by a self-professed prophetess and medium, Alice Lakwenya, and her associate Joseph Kony. The insurgents, calling themselves the Holy Spirit Movement (HSM), began their activities throughout northern Uganda in late 1986 and early 1987, attacking government forces in human waves. The HSM leadership convinced its adherents that they were bullet-proof and had special powers. After heavy casualties the movement was pursued around most of central Uganda, appearing to confront local NRA units and then moving onward to attack targets some distance away.

The strife within the UNLA and the Ugandan defence establishment took place as resistance against the new regime persisted. As of late 1987, remnants of the old UNLA remained throughout the northern part of the country, and consisted of the hard-core elements of the former Ugandan national army (later FUNA). They numbered about 3,000 to 4,000 personnel, and were a primarily infantry force capable of carrying out attacks against forward NRA outposts. UNLA attacks had increased in 1986, with Kitgum and Gulu attacked. The occupying TPDF forces were unable to prevent insurgent activity, and extreme measures that they often took, including reprisals against the local population, further served to alienate the Tanzanians. The latter were seen as foreigners supporting a distant government in Kampala that had no real interest in northern Ugandan affairs.

Uganda's security situation 1989–1992

In the 1989 New Year's address, President Museveni announced the formation of a new police force, the Administrative Police. This force was deployed in each district and was under the control of each NRA district administrator. Their function was to assist the civil authorities to maintain order and support NRA operations as necessary.[28]

In February the first stages of the general elections were interrupted in two areas of northern Uganda by insurgent unrest. The first was in northern Gulu, where HSM insurgents still controlled parts of the countryside. The other was in eastern Usuk, where Karamajong tribesmen, angered over the confiscation of cattle by the NRA, raided the area in an attempt to recapture them. The raid was accompanied by reports of robbery, murder, rape, and kidnapping of local women.[29]

During the last three weeks of May the NRA conducted a large-scale offensive against the HSM in northern Gulu. The COIN operations killed at least 370 insurgents and disrupted supply lines to Sudan. At the same time, NRA units drove HSM insurgents from Murchison Falls Game Park. The operation was accompanied by claims that NRA soldiers killed civilian villagers.[30] At the same time the Museveni government NRM attempted to pass legislation allowing it to establish special courts in areas affected by the insurgency that would expedite trials of suspected NRA personnel. Such a move, it was felt, would obviate the need for long periods of detention for the many suspects awaiting trial. However, the bill faced opposition within parliament and would have made it easier for the government to convict suspects.[31]

In mid-summer 1989 the NRA conducted a sweep campaign against Uganda People's Army (UPA) insurgents in the Kumi area of Teso, 250km north-east of Kampala. The operations netted 276 youthful suspects, who were detained and locked in rail cars for three days awaiting interrogation. At least 50 died of suffocation in the incident (10 July), which was condemned by Amnesty International and other humanitarian organisations. This accompanied condemnations of NRA operations as being characterised by rape, torture, murder, and unlawful detention of civilians.[32] HSM insurgent activity continued in Gulu. On 13 July the insurgents attacked the town itself.[33]

To deny insurgents cross-border access and resupply, the Museveni regime undertook some regional security management efforts. On 7 September, Uganda restored diplomatic relations with Zaire, which had been suspended since April due to the increase in border incidents involving the Uganda-based Congo Liberation Party (Parti Congolaise de Libération, PCL), and Zairian armed forces. Commerce between the two countries had suffered as a result.[34] In early April 1990, the Bashir regime in Sudan signed a mutual non-aggression pact with Uganda. The aim of the pact was to ensure that neither country could be used as a base for operations against the other. The pact called for monitors to supervise each other country's borders for violations.[35]

In other regional efforts Museveni was not as successful. Following the abortive Rwanda Patriotic Front (RPF) invasion of Rwanda from Uganda in October 1990, the Ugandan government received considerable criticism from the fact that evidence indicated that most of the RPF was composed of current or former NRA members of Rwandan Tutsi origin. The fighting along the border and alleged Rwandan reprisals against Tutsis drove more refugees across the border. Refugees from Sudan continued to come into Uganda from the north. By the end of 1990 there were 20 per cent more refugees in the country than there had been in December 1989, and Uganda had to cope with a tenacious insurgency on its southern borders that challenged the French-backed and Belgian-backed Rwandan government.[36]

Internal security remained the main preoccupation of the Museveni regime, however. The government did suffer some setbacks. December 1990 saw a major defeat of the NRA by northern rebels in which many government troops were killed. In the ensuing fall-out, two NRA commanders were executed for cowardice and the army undertook a severe series of reprisal attacks that incurred the condemnation of Amnesty International.[37] The poor security situation in the north continued into 1991. In an ironic incident, President Museveni in his New Year's message stressed the peace that the NRM had brought to the country. On the same day, elements of the UPA abducted 40 youths, wounded others, and stole or destroyed property in villages near Kumi in south-east Teso. Insurgent activity continued in the Kumi and Kitgum areas.[38]

In early 1991 a new insurgent movement surfaced in northern Uganda, called the Uganda Christian People's Democratic Alliance (UCPDA), led by Joseph Kony. In a statement to the Ugandan magazine *New Vision* on 19 February, the NRA commander discussed the movement and said that it was a new manifestation of the HSM. Kony was a mystic like Alice Lakwenya, and a follower of the latter.[39]

The movement had caused an increase in security incidents throughout the north. The UCPDA's actions were directed mainly against the civilian population as a source of supplies and recruits. The UPCDA, according to the NRA, kept its ranks filled by abducting youths.[40]

In response to the rise in insurgent activity the NRA initiated a major operation in March in north and central Uganda. The operations of 1991 were to prove quite effective on the government side, due especially to a new emphasis on Museveni's part to upgrade training and weapons for the NRA. As a result of the 'cordon-and-search' procedure, 400 insurgents, most UPCDA/HSM, were reported killed and 500 weapons recovered by mid- to late-May.[41]

NRA operations continued into the summer in northern Uganda. What the NRA called 'mopping up' operations killed 155 insurgents from 28 June to 5 July; 100 were arrested. The Minister of State for Defence, Major General David Tinyefuza, had been placed in charge of the operations. Tinyefuza discussed the operations, saying that the UPCDA/HSM was the primary target. Speaking in Lira, the general criticised northern Ugandan leaders for not discussing insurgent atrocities against the civilian population. What was not stressed, however, was the fact that there was a widening gulf between the government in Kampala and the northern Ugandan ethnic groups.[42]

On 30 July 1991 Major General Tinyefuza summed up operations against the UPCDA/HSM since the latter began its offensive in March. 1,500 insurgents and 80 NRA soldiers had been killed. As of late July the NRA judged the situation in the north to be safe enough to reopen the roads that had been closed in the 'cordon-and-search' operations; routes to and from Lira, Kitgum, Gulu, and Apach were to be reopened as soon as possible. Despite claims that the insurgents had been eliminated as a threat, there was an attack on 26 July when UPCDA/HSM attacked for the second time Nyetta Teacher's College 3km from Lira, killing three NRA soldiers.[43]

Although the NRA made much of UPCDA/HSM atrocities against the civilian population, including murder, rape, mutilation, and robbery, Amnesty International (London) in August 1991 accused the NRA itself of atrocities, including the summary executions of at least 70 Ugandan civilians in the course of its cordon-and-search operations. The Catholic bishops of Uganda also protested about the NRA's extensive human rights abuses throughout the north. They made these charges in a statement released at the conclusion of their annual 1991 conference.[44]

In fact, by summer the effectiveness of NRA operations in the north was tempered by the adverse publicity it received. Tinyefuza had a reputation for aggressive tactics and charged his subordinate commanders with producing results against insurgents in Gulu, Kitgum, and Teso regions. As a result, extensive human rights violations were perpetrated by the NRA. The case of Gulu, cordoned in late April, is illustrative. The males of the town were detained during house-to-house searches and imprisoned in the soccer stadium. Those without proper identification documents and others were arrested, including a number of former UNLA personnel or returned rebels. The threat from the insurgents was accompanied by one from internal 'subversives' according to some members of the NRA, and accordingly some northern opposition politicians were also detained. The net result of the 1991 operations was a questionable military situation as of early August and a lingering record of human rights violations by the NRA that received wide publicity not only in Uganda but also abroad. In addition, civil authority was often disregarded by NRA members engaged in operations, and it was widely felt that members of the Acholi ethnic group were especially targeted for humiliation and harassment.[45]

In an interview published in July 1991, Museveni answered claims about human rights abuses in the north and about NRA treatment of its own personnel charged with such abuses. He stressed that no organised insurgencies remained: 'There is no insurgency in the north or east. There are still gunmen around. Many of these terrorised villages during Obote's time. Now they are terrified of returning to their villages. They have become lawless brigands and we have a duty to hunt them down.' As for NRA members found guilty of human rights abuses, Museveni stressed that the guilty had been executed, but only after a court martial found them so.[46]

In mid-March 1992 the NRA resumed operations against insurgents throughout northern Uganda. The two groups targeted were those of Joseph Kony in the Kitgum and Lira areas, with operations scheduled to be completed by late March/early April, and those of the UPA in Teso. The three military officers entrusted by Ugandan President Yoweri Museveni for this task were Army Commander Major General Mugisha Muntu, 2nd Division Commander Lieutenant Colonel Leuben Ikondere, and 5th Division Commander Lieutenant Colonel Santos Okecho Okecha. Directives published at the time stressed that careful guidance had been issued for the conduct of NRA troops, in large part to avoid alienating the population as had taken place in the cordon-and-sweep operations of 1991.

By late March 1992 the operations against the remaining northern insurgents had been completed, to the satisfaction of the central government. The last actions against the UPCDA/HSM were fought near Lira and Kitgum. The NRA apparently exercised highly professional behaviour, with no incidents of abuse against the local population reported. In addition to the NRA troops of the 2nd and 5th Divisions, LDUs also participated in the action. These forces, similar to local militia, had been trained to back up civil authorities, to whom responsibility for future anti-insurgent operations was transferred at the conclusion of the campaign.

By the end of spring it appeared that the long northern insurgency was finally at an end. Although the NRA had begun the contest with its own institutional knowledge of insurgent fighting, it had passed through several painful stages of learning by experience. Only in the end did the increasing professionalism of the force and the careful attention of higher echelons – up to the President himself–ensure the successful conclusion of the campaign. As of mid-1992 the Ugandan NRA had finally appeared to have hit upon the right mix of counterinsurgency combat technique and civil relations that not only eliminated the last guerrilla fighters but displayed the restraint necessary to permit the continued support of the population for the insurgents to end.

ZAIRE, MID-1970S–EARLY 1990S

Throughout most of Zaire's independence, the vast country (the size of the United States east of the Mississippi River) has been plagued with banditry, insurgencies, and episodes of extremely destructive rebellions. Following a series of such unrest during the early and mid-1960s, which brought President Mobutu to power, a modicum of internal stability was established throughout the country. However, the declining economic situation as well as governmental malfeasance and the encroachment of autocratic rule through the 1970s and 1980s promoted continuing insurgent opposition, most of it in the eastern part of Zaire. The incidents in Shaba in 1977–1978 and at Moba in 1984 were only the most visible manifestations of the situation. Further north, along Zaire's border with Uganda and

Sudan, low-level insurgencies have persisted for decades. As of the early 1990s, the break-down of civil order and military capabilities threatened the widespread destabilisation of the entire region.[47]

The insurgencies of eastern Zaire in the 1980s have been poorly documented. It is difficult even to know to what degree they have been successful, although some gauge of their success has been their survivability. However, much of this has been due to the corruption and ineptitude of the Zairian military (Forces Armées Zairoises, or FAZ). Until 1990, most insurgent movements have been preoccupied with mere survival in remote areas of north Shaba and Kivu. With the beginnings of political liberalisation a few of the insurgents in eastern Zaire (such as the PRP, MNC, and the FNLC – see below) linked themselves with legitimate political opposition in the country, and have apparently attracted growing numbers of recruits. However, it is unlikely that the various movements can unite to mount an armed attack against the central government. The poor infrastructure throughout the country (which has deteriorated markedly since the last great rebellion in the area in the 1960s) will not allow an armed force to march cross-country against the seat of power. Nor do the insurgents have any capability to sustain large-scale operations against FAZ units. Should large numbers of government troops rebel and join with insurgents, however, it is likely that the rebels could extend their control over large areas of eastern Zaire and even defend against a FAZ counterattack.

The Zairian government response to the rebels has been on the whole counterproductive. Although some attempts were made in 1984–1985 to maintain control over FAZ troops in north Shaba, more recent COIN efforts further north have been without effective control or coordination. Left to their own devices, isolated FAZ units who have not been paid or otherwise supported by the central government engage in rampages of pillage and destructive violence against the local populace. Many of the latter join the rebels in response to these excesses. When FAZ troops mount operations against insurgents, the campaigns are short-lived and marked by looting and extortion against the populace in areas thought to support the rebels. Anti-guerrilla operations are conducted with little or no COIN expertise; the morale of government forces is quite poor. Even such basic requirements for COIN as border control and effective intelligence gathering are inadequate.

FAZ counterguerrilla operations in eastern Zaire have consisted of light infantry operations, with the exception of a few airborne operations to rapidly deploy troops (as in November 1984). Armour and mechanised units cannot operate well in the rugged terrain, and a lack of roads and support infrastructure would make it all but impossible to sustain operations should they even be deployed. The FAZ FT (infantry) and GN troops deployed to the area lack most support, such as resupply and maintenance, and suffer from low personnel availability rates and poor maintenance of the small arms, infantry support weapons, and communications equipment that they do have on hand. Under such circumstances the FAZ is quite limited in its capability to react to reports of insurgent activity.

Although some air support was available to the FAZ during the mid-1980s fighting against PRP rebels in north-east Shaba (Moba I and Moba II), during the late 1980s and into the early 1990s the decline of the Zairian Air Force (FAZA) meant almost no air–ground combat support or any but the most basic transport capabilities. The extreme corruption prevalent in the FAZA often meant that routine supply missions suffered from the private commercial dealings of FAZ officers. FAZA aircraft were used to support such activities. At the time of writing the FAZA has only a few small cargo aircraft for supply and transport. None of its C-130 cargo aircraft are operational. Thus the FAZA cannot support any COIN efforts in the interior of the country.

With the degradation of FAZ capabilities the insurgents have been able to thrive on the eastern border. Making their living by smuggling, however, they still apparently prefer to avoid confrontation wherever possible and in true Zairian style seek to bribe officials to look the other way at their activities. In more remote areas away from the border posts and large towns, insurgent groups operate but can be little distinguished from ordinary armed bandits. They make their living by poaching and exactions from the local population. Although insurgent activity is widespread (through an area roughly the size of England), most make no effort to promise any benefits to the population and exist only because there is no effective civil or military power to keep them in check.

BACKGROUND TO REBELLION

After the terrible ravages of internal revolts in the mid-1960s, Zaire, then the Democratic Republic of the Congo, enjoyed a brief period of relative calm. Much of this was under the increasingly autocratic rule of President Joseph Desire Mobutu (who later changed his name to Mobutu Sese Seko in a move toward Africanisation of the country's personal and place names), who had taken power in 1965. Mobutu mortgaged development of the country to the fortunes of world mineral prices, especially copper, from the country's rich Shaba (ex-Katanga) province. Mobutu's gamble failed, however, as world copper prices sharply fell in 1974 and have remained depressed ever since. This miscalculation has deprived the country of potential income from Shaba's minerals and has kept it poor. The pervasive corruption and official mishandling of the nation's resources has not helped the situation.

Although Mobutu was able to triumph over the rebels in eastern and central Zaire in the 1960s with the assistance of mercenary troops, he later purged them from the ranks of his security forces, and built up an indigenous military force, the Forces Armées Zairoises (FAZ), or Zairian Armed Forces. This force, which consists of a large army augmented by much smaller air and naval wings, plus a large gendarme force, has been noted for its ineptitude and corruption. Control of the FAZ and the Zairian civilian intelligence and security services has in great part enabled Mobutu to remain in power. Assistance (equipment and training) to Zaire's military forces from Belgium France, Israel, China, and the United States has maintained the FAZ through the late 1970s and the 1980s.

In the course of settling the rebellions of the 1960s, Mobutu drove into exile a number of armed oppositionists. These included the remnants of Lumumbist rebels, who continued to conduct sporadic actions in eastern Zaire, as well as former Katangese gendarmes, who fled in 1967 when Mobutu destroyed the growing power of their allies, the mercenary troops who had earlier helped him retain power. The ex-Katangese gendarmes formed an organisation known as the National Front for the Liberation of the Congo (FNLC, Front National pour la Libération du Congo), which was based at camps in Zambia and Angola. Zaire's vast, undeveloped interior and long, poorly patrolled borders made it almost impossible to prevent infiltration by oppositionists, many of whom engaged in smuggling and poaching to survive. In the early 1990s many of these armed oppositionists began to pose a growing low-level insurgent threat in the more remote parts of the country.

Despite the extensive foreign military assistance described above, Zaire's military has repeatedly proven a paper tiger. The intervention by Mobutu in northern Angola in October–November 1975 was a classic debacle. Having invaded the area to support Holden Roberto's National Front for the Liberation of Angola (FNLA), the FAZ began to commit acts of pillage, rape, and even murder as they advanced toward Luanda. At the battle of Quifandongo, on 11 November 1975, the combined FNLA-FAZ force was routed by Cuban-backed MPLA forces and fled in disarray back toward the border. Of two battalions of FAZ troops, only half were ever accounted for again; the rest who were not casualties deserted or fled and never reported back to their units. The MPLA was subsequently the victor in Angola.[48]

SHABA I AND SHABA II (1977–1978)

In retaliation for the ill-fated FAZ intervention the MPLA supported two attempts by ex-Katangan rebels of the FNLC to invade their former homeland, Shaba province, in 1977 and 1978 – 'Shaba I' and 'Shaba II.' Although most of the 'rebel' activity associated by the Zairian government in Shaba I is still open to some question, Shaba II was a genuine invasion by a force of several thousand insurgents who infiltrated through Zambia. It had the support of a significant part of the local population and was aimed at capturing or destroying the critical mining infrastructure in Shaba. FAZ ground force (FT) units stationed in Shaba fled in complete disarray. The high point of the insurgent invasion was the capture of the mining centre of Kolwezi and the taking of several hundred expatriate European hostages. Rapid intervention by a force of Belgian, French Foreign Legion, and allied African forces soon enabled the FAZ to recapture Kolwezi and drive the invaders out.

A comparison of the two episodes is instructive. Shaba I began on 8 March 1977 when 1,500 to 2,000 armed FNLC under its General Nathanael Mbumba crossed the Shaba border at Dilolo and advanced eastward. By 12 April FNLC claimed Mutshatsha, Kisengi, Kasaji, Sandoa, and Kapanga as additional gains. The 3,000 to 4,000 FAZ in Shaba were deployed north and east, at Kamina Base and Lubumbashi. The few troops on the border fled in the face of the FNLC attack. However, Zaire, aided by other African countries, especially Morocco (which sent 1,500 troops) was able to regroup and subsequently counterattack. The main force, based at Kolwezi, advanced westward on 14 April. By 25 April Mutshatsha was regained; on the 27th Kapanga and Sandoa were retaken. Zairian and Moroccan troops regained the border on 21 May with the recapture of Dilolo. Kapanga, the object of a 'second front' attack, was the last major town to be retaken, on 26 May.[49]

Zaire subsequently made bitter charges against Angola for supporting the insurgents. Although the MPLA denied any connection with the FNLC, it was obvious that the only staging base for the ex-Katangese could have been Angola west of the Dilolo border area. It was also apparent to most observers that the Shaba incursion was a retaliation by Angola for Zaire's help to the FNLA in 1975. The insurgents had not been defeated in any major battles, but had fallen back toward the border in good order. Most of the invaders reportedly spoke Lunda, the language of the populations of Shaba and adjacent parts of Zambia and Angola, and enjoyed the support of the locals. Although things were quiet for almost a year, more trouble was to come.

The most devastating insurgent attack since the 1960s was made against Shaba on 11 May the following year. About 2,000–2,500 FNLC, having infiltrated through Angola and Zambia across the Zairian border, captured the key mining centre of Kolwezi and took hostage most of the European expatriates there. This precipitated intervention by Belgium and France on the side of Zaire. On 19 May the 2nd Parachute Regiment of the French Foreign Legion was airdropped on Kolwezi and two days later had regained the city. The 20th Belgian Parachute Battalion later took control of the airport. The insurgents avoided direct contact but still incurred high losses and fled, after committing atrocities against both European and African hostages. The ex-Katangese recrossed the border on 23 May, moving across the north-west salient of Zambia back to their camps in Angola. The French subsequently withdrew, although the Belgians kept a 700-man parachute strike force at Kamina base. However, the FNLC had had enough for the time being and this plus international pressure against the invasions helped to ease the ex-Katangese threat.[50]

THE PRP AND OPERATIONS IN NORTHERN SHABA (1984–1985)

With the repulse of the ex-Katangese gendarmes, Shaba enjoyed relative peace until late 1984. At least half of all Zairian FT troops were deployed in southern Shaba around Kolwezi and Lubumbashi. Northern Shaba, however, remained the site of low-level unrest by the Popular Revolutionary Party (Parti de la Révolution Populaire, PRP). This group, led by Laurent Kabila, a former 1960s rebel commander, had been active in the region, especially in the Mount Mitumba region west and south-west of the towns of Kalemie and Moba. The FAZ, in an attempt to counter the insurgents, formed an operational zone, 'Secteur Tanganyika', which comprised Kalemie zone and areas of adjacent Kivu region. By the early 1980s the unrest had subsided as the PRP and its supporters engaged in smuggling with neighbouring Tanzania, apparently with the approval and/or collusion of local security authorities. Another insurgent group active in the area included the Congolese Liberation Party (Parti de Libération Congolaise, PLC), which reportedly was supported by Libya.[51]

In November 1983, tensions between the PRP and the local authorities were raised apparently due to increased demands by local officials to permit the PRP-affiliated smugglers to remain in business. By this time the PRP was composed of a network of loosely affiliated groups in north Shaba and south Kivu. On 13 November local PRP elements based north-west of Moba captured the town and held it through the 15th before fleeing as the elements of the FAZ 31st Parachute Brigade (troops from the 311th and 312th Battalions) and the Zairian naval 13th Brigade at Kalemie drove them from the area. The FAZ troops claimed 122 insurgents killed but other, more credible, accounts indicate that these were all probably local people upon whom government forces took reprisals for their alleged support to the PRP.[52]

Throughout the remainder of 1984 and into mid-1985 FAZ troops conducted local anti-guerrilla operations in the mountainous area from Moba northward along the west bank of Lake Tanganyika into Kivu region. In general, the operations were inconclusive. A subsequent attack by insurgents crossing Lake Tanganyika against Moba on 16–17 June 1985 ('Moba II') was repulsed with little effort by FAZ troops stationed there, according to an official account. Other reports claim that the 2,500 FAZ troops operating in the area were also conducting simultaneous anti-guerrilla operations against localities north-west of Moba.[53]

Subsequent counterguerrilla operations in north Shaba and south Kivu continued to the end of 1985. However, they were costly in their logistical demands and produced few results. The troops from the 31st Brigade initially used for the operations later returned to base at Kinshasa and Kamina and left local responsibility to the FAZ 13th Infantry Brigade based at Kalemie. The latter unit lacked the support capability and equipment to conduct effective operations against the PRP and activity in north Shaba subsided to the pre-crisis level. Some counterguerrilla operations continued, however, managed by Mobutu's new military security organ, the Service d'Action Militaire et de Renseignment (SARM), and by early 1986 the armed aspect of the PRP movement was all but defunct. In January 1986 up to 524 former PRP insurgents surrendered to Zairian authorities after leaving the rest of the group following a dispute in the Fizi area. For all practical purposes the armed PRP threat had ended.[54]

UNREST AND INSURGENCY IN NORTH-EASTERN ZAIRE

North-eastern Zaire (Kivu region and adjacent areas of Haut-Zaire region) has always been isolated from the Zairian capital. More accessible from the eastern coast of Africa via Mombasa, Nairobi, and Kampala, this vast area has a relatively large population that has suffered since the crushing of the great eastern rebellion in 1965. Mobutu's policies in this region, designed to punish its people for support to the rebels, denied it the necessary resources to develop or even rebuild. The already heavily damaged infrastructure of the colonial era as a result deteriorated even further to where almost all paved roads disintegrated into rutted, almost impassable trails. The other infrastructure was similarly neglected. LOCs were so bad in the 1980s that in 1988 this area, the Kivu region (about two-thirds the size of France) was split into three new regions that could better be administered locally! Commerce with the outside world was and remains difficult, with cross-border smuggling routine. As with the PRP in northern Shaba, such arrangements always involve the local security forces, who, like the government officials, are rarely paid.

In addition to reprisals against the population, Mobutu had another reason for not encouraging development. The almost non-existent LOCs meant that any enemy trying a major invasion in force would face almost insurmountable obstacles before he could even penetrate to the largest city in the area, Kisangani (ex-Stanleyville). An infantry unit, the 41st Commando Brigade, along with units of the Zairian GN, was responsible for protecting the borders. None of the security force units there was particularly effective and indeed these units were more preoccupied with smuggling and other illegal activities than border defence. A vast, three-cornered informal trade zone existed where the Zairian, Sudanese, and Ugandan borders converged, all with the collusion of local authorities. Throughout the early and mid-1980s it was profitable to all.

As with north Shaba, many of the smugglers in Kivu were former insurgents and part-time bandits. Some included elements of the National Congolese Movement (Mouvement National Congolais – Lumumbist, MNC/L), which claimed affiliations with the armed opposition of the 1960s in the area. Sporadic actions by its armed wing, the Lumumba Patriotic Army (Armée Patriotique Lumumba, APL), which claimed 1,500 fighters, extended from the eastern border of Zaire through the Ituri Forest to Kisangani. In mid-February 1988 the APL made an attack on the headquarters and garrison of the 41st Brigade at Kisangani. Its operations were allegedly directed by Nathanael Mbumba, based at Kampala, Uganda. APL personnel were reportedly trained in Libya, and had some forces based in both Angola and Uganda. Another movement, which also operated in eastern Zaire, was that of the Democratic Force for the Liberation of Congo-Kinshasa (Forces Démocratiques pour la Libération du Congo-Kinshasa, FODELICO), led by the 1960s rebel Antoine Gizenga.[55]

Most insurgent activity, however, was along Zaire's border with Uganda. This region had had a troubled history through the 1980s. Refugees from both Uganda and Sudan crossed the border to flee from wars in their own nations. Although there was considerable cross-border trade much was illicit and the local officials on both sides of the border were involved. Zairian authorities, however, made successful efforts to keep out the weapons that were found almost everywhere in Sudan and Uganda. Under such conditions local insurgent groups did not necessarily thrive as they did further south, but did manage to survive government operations by both Zairian and Ugandan troops designed to maintain civil order and ensure local officials' illicit trade interests. The basis for the security arrangement between the two countries was developed in January 1986, later revised and periodically renegotiated since.[56]

Of the insurgent groups in the area the above-mentioned Lumumbist groups were active. In the Ruwenzori the group led by Amon Bazira was active through the 1980s and into the 1990s, and in 1992 had coalesced into the National Army for the Liberation of Uganda (NALU), directing its insurgent efforts eastward rather than competing with political and insurgent groups to the west. Bazira's group, however, had an extensive support structure in areas of Kivu and Haut-Zaire regions immediately west of his area of operations. Another group was the Congolese Liberation Party (Parti Libération Congolaise, PLC), founded in the early 1980s by Antoine Kibungu, who left the MNC/L. The movement, which at most probably had only 300–400 effectives, was responsible for cross-border attacks against Zairian military positions in the summer of 1987, for which actions the FAZA undertook several air strikes on the Uganda-Zaire border. During the latter 1980s PLC headquarters was reportedly near Kasese, Uganda, near the border with Zaire.

For the Ugandan border, the most troubled period appears to have been the summer of 1987. During this time Zaire repatriated over 90,000 Ugandan refugees to West Nile but the two countries also had a number of border clashes due to local causes. On 12 June the NRA attacked the Bazira group in the Ruwenzori and overran a base camp. Two captured insurgents claimed affiliation with Lumumbists committed to overthrowing Mobutu's regime. Apparently these operations were part of a joint effort with Zaire to contain the insurgents, as on 31 July representatives of the two nations met in Kasese to discuss common border security problems; the Ugandans assured Zaire that they would not harbour its insurgents. An even more serious insurgent incident, however, had occurred in early July, during which MNC guerrillas attacked Watsa in Haut-Uele subregion; subsequently another attack was made (11 July) on Kisindi.[57]

To the end of the 1980s banditry, smuggling, and outright insurgency continued on the rise along the border. This was despite a series of agreements by both Uganda and Zaire to promote better border control. However, insurgents still claimed to operate freely in eastern Zaire. In January 1988 the MNC/L and its military wing, the APL, claimed to be operating from Makaone in the Ituri forest and to have political operatives working against the Mobutu regime in eight of Zaire's regions.[58] Insurgent activity in the Ruwenzori also continued. This remained an item of concern for both Uganda and Zaire, as by now the guerrillas were raiding both countries at will. 15 March and 13 November 1988 agreements on combating border 'crime' and illegal commercial activities indicated the desire of both nations to cooperate to curb insurgents who would jump the border to attack targets in one country or the other. This effort even extended to the lakes, where on June 20 1988 it was announced that the FAZN would begin patrols on Lake Edward to interdict 'pirates' and others. Not only the Ruwenzori but also Arua, to the north of Lake Edward, had been an area of concern for both countries, with cross-border banditry and smuggling compounding the efforts against low-level insurgency. Uganda, for its part, undertook border operations against insurgents and apprehended some who claimed affiliation with the Lumumbist PLC.[59]

The Ugandans, empowered by anti-rebel legislation and attempts to restructure and reform the police force, began to undertake a hearts-and-minds campaign on its side of the border to persuade insurgents and self-proclaimed rebels to surrender, with some success.[60]

With Zairian political liberalisation from May 1990, former oppositionists based in Uganda, Angola, and other countries returned to eastern Zaire and founded political parties. Many of these began to recruit youth wings ('jeunesse') to support their political activism. Although in the 1960s such groups engaged in inter-party fighting, little threat was seen until September 1991. At that time, the civil and military unrest that started in Kinshasa spread throughout Zaire. Members of the FAZ mutinied and attacked the local populace, looting towns, including many in eastern Zaire. In the confusion, arms and ammunition were stolen from government armouries and found their way into the hands of opposition groups in the east. The Kivu border area had already suffered considerable security difficulties as a result of the insurgency of the Rwandan Patriotic Front (RPF) against the Rwandan government. The latter had been an ally of the Zairian central government since the 1960s and was a major partner in regional security pacts.[61]

As for guerrilla operations, the greatest trouble spot continued to be in the Kivu and Haut-Zaire regions bordering Uganda and Sudan. The major government security concern was from armed Lumumbist groups who reportedly still operated there and who now had an openly legal support base among some elements of the population. On 12 October 1990, Nathanael Mbumba, the FNLC commander and head of the ex-Katangan gendarmes in Angola, returned to Zaire from Tanzania. His return was under an amnesty for former external opposition leaders and Mbumba announced his desire to prepare for the return of his followers.[62]

However, negotiations subsequently broke down, although by early 1992 many of the FNLC partisans had moved to the Kivu-Haut Zaire border area. Some remained in Angola;

indeed, these troops, known as 'Tigres', were used by the MPLA regime in special units that operated in northern Angola.[63]

Amon Bazira's insurgent group still remained active as well, by late 1991 and early 1992 perhaps receiving assistance from anti-Museveni regime sources to incite trouble in the Ruwenzori area.[64]

A new cycle of insurgent activity in eastern Zaire began in late December 1992. On 22 December soldiers of the 41st Brigade, with its headquarters at Kisangani, revolted and looted the city due to lack of pay. The MNC/L took advantage of this development to intensify its operations against Zairian government centres in eastern Kivu. Although the rebellion was quelled by Christmas 1992, the MNC/L continued its insurgent operations in the east. The FAZ remained unable to contain the guerrillas.

Continued chaos in Zaire's central government, the steady deterioration of the security situation, and the increasing availability of small arms to any who could purchase them, portended further trouble ahead. Cheap weapons and lack of government control in eastern Zaire were a contributing factor to continued low-level insurgency for the foreseeable future.

NOTES

1. *ARB*, 5301.
2. *ARB*, 5261.
3. *ARB*, 6255b–6257a.
4. *ARB*, 6289b–c.
5. *ARB*, 6395a–b; 6424b–c.
6. *ARB*, 6424b–c.
7. *ARB*, 6467c.
8. *ARB*, 6593a–b.
9. *ARB*, 6884a.
10. *ARB*, 6912b–6913a.
11. *ARB*, 7147b–c; 7190c–7191a.
12. *ARB*, 7284b–c.
13. *ARB*, 7248c; 7316b.
14. *ARB*, 7388a–c; 7448c.
15. *ARB*, 7502c–7503a.
16. *ARB*, 7583c–7584a.
17. *ARB*, 7583c–7584a.
18. Ibid.
19. *ARB*, 7659a–7660a.
20. *ARB*, 7659a–7660a.
21. *ARB*, 7719c–7724b.
22. *ARB*, 7759c–7761c.
23. *ARB*, 7834a–7836a.
24. *ARB*, 7872a–b; ADJ, January 1986, p. 14.
25. *ARB*, 7909a–7911b; 7948c–7951b.
26. *ARB*, 7951a–b; 7985c–7989b; 8018c–8019c.
27. *New Vision* (Kampala), 24 July 1992, p. 1.
28. *ARB*, 9154c.
29. *ARB*, 9183c.
30. *ARB*, 9295b.
31. *ARB*, 9296b–c.
32. *ARB*, 9355c–9356a.
33. *ARB*, 9356a.
34. *ARB*, 9403b–c.
35. *ARB*, 8646b–c.
36. *New African*, March 1991, p. 20.
37. *New African*, March 1991, p. 20.
38. *New African*, March 1991, p. 20.
39. *ARB*, 10027b.
40. *ARB*, 10027b.

41. *ARB*, 10103b-c.
42. *ARB*, 10217b-c.
43. *ARB*, 10249b.
44. *ARB*, 10249b.
45. Information courtesy of the Uganda Democratic Coalition (Silver Spring, MD).
46. *New African*, July 1991, p. 15.
47. A note on sources: Specific sources are noted wherever pertinent. General information has been provided courtesy of the Heritage Foundation (Washington DC), the International Freedom Foundation (Washington DC), the Uganda Democratic Coalition (Silver Spring MD), the Washington RPF representative, the AFJN, and a number of private individuals.
48. See John Stockwell, *In Search of Enemies: A CIA Story*, Norton, New York, 1978, pp. 213ff.
49. *ARB*, 4348c-4351a; 4399a-4402b; 4435b-c.
50. *ARB*, 4854c-4862c; 4890a-4895c.
51. Amnesty International USA, *Zaire: Reports of Torture and Killings Committed by the Armed Forces in Shaba Region* (New York, 1986), pp. 4-5.
52. See the Amnesty International report, pp. 6-7; *ARB*, 7450a-7541c.
53. See the Amnesty International report, pp. 4-5; *ARB*, 7690a-b. The FAZ claimed eight of twelve boats used by the attackers sunk on the lake; Aeromacchi MB-326K COIN aircraft were reportedly used to attack them as they fled.
54. ADJ, March 1986, p. 22.
55. *Africa Confidential*, Vol. 29/7, 1 April 1988, p. 8. For FODELICO, see *ARB*, 4399a-4402b.
56. *AD*, March 1986, p. 28; see also *ADJ*, March 1986, pp. 22-3. Mobutu and Museveni discussed security issues on 29 January at Goma, days after the NRA took Kampala.
57. *ADJ*, August 1987, p. 19; September 1991, p. 28.
58. *ADJ*, April 1988, p. 21.
59. *ADJ*, May 1988, p. 22; August 1988, p. 24; September 1988, p. 30; January 1989, p. 14; February 1989, p. 22.
60. *ADJ*, October 1988, pp. 15-16. This mission was entrusted to the NRA 75th Battalion, Kasese. It should be noted that much of this internal security effort took place within the context of returns of refugees from Zaire and Sudan, especially the latter, into Ugandan border areas such as West Nile.
61. For the RPF insurgency, see the discussion on Rwanda.
62. *ADJ*, December 1990, p. 22.
63. Information courtesy of the International Freedom Foundation (Washington DC).
64. Information courtesy of the Uganda Democratic Coalition (Silver Spring, MD).

Chapter 10

The Uncertain Future

The 1990s have seen a marked change in the origins and spread of African conflicts. In the post-Cold War era, many African states that were originally firm allies of either East or West have found themselves bereft of further support as their services were no longer needed. Weak and upopular governments have been overthrown, sometimes after protracted periods of war and disruption. Elsewhere, unfinished agendas held in abeyance since independence due to Cold War politics are finally playing out. This chapter is an epilogue of sorts that briefly notes the new conflicts and how they differ from those of the 1970s and 1980s. They mark an era that is by no means likely to end soon and dynamics of unrest and conflict that in many cases are still imperfectly understood.

THE HORN OF AFRICA

The fall of the Mengistu regime in May 1991 was a key event, along with the ceasefire in Angola, in marking the end of Cold War conflicts on the continent. In Ethiopia, the insurgents had finally won, and immediately began consolidating their power. However, elsewhere in the Horn conflict continued as Ethiopia began to rebuild and the new state of Eritrea (independent in 1992) took shape.

Somalia remained the main security problem. There, fighting continued between factions not only in the southern region of the country but also in the new, break-away state of Somaliland (see Chapter 8). Continued fighting in the south into 1993 between the victorious United Somali Congress (USC) factions in Mogadishu garnered world attention. It was in November 1992 that the international community, led by the United States, intervened to provide famine relief and peace-keeping, turning the operation over the following year to the United Nations. The subsequent disastrous confrontations with USC warlord Mohamed Farah 'Aideed' and the growing antipathy of the Somali people to the UN presence forced a gradual scaling down of the operation and a final 1995 withdrawal. Since that time the factions have continued to fight, with no resolution in the foreseeable future likely. As for Somaliland, the dominant Isaaks and their allies continued, amid fits and starts, to consolidate their new state, which continues to have a greater relative degree of stability than the rest of the former Somali Republic. However, few nations recognise it as a separate state.

In Djibouti, conflict erupted shortly after the consolidation of the EPRDF government in May. Through the summer there were continuing problems with various groups along the Addis Ababa-Djibouti railway, which included Afar and Somali factions. One of the latter, the Issa and Gurgura Liberation Front (IGLF), threatened to block the rail line. However, security problems on the Ethiopian side of the border were eventually resolved.

On the Djibouti side, a protracted period of unrest had just begun, however. The continuing discontent of the Afar people with the ruling Issa Somali clan in Djibouti finally escalated into an armed insurgency in October 1991 in which a large group of armed Afars, calling themselves the Front for the Restoration of Unity and Democracy (FRUD), invaded Djibouti. By early 1992 they had taken the northern, Afar, half of the country and resisted initial attempts by the small, Issa-dominated Djibouti military to counterattack. It was only with French assistance that the government was able to rally over the next two years and fight the insurgents to a standstill. However, the Afar cause had gained international attention and support, and the government of Djibouti President Hassan Gouled Aptidon was forced, under French and other foreign pressure to make significant political concessions as part of a final settlement. By 1995 the FRUD insurgency was over, although the prognosis for future conflict erupting again depends heavily on continued political liberalisation.

WEST AFRICA

The end of the Cold War had a significant impact on Liberia, an American "quasi-colony" that was a major client state through the late 1980s. By that time, however, the increasingly corrupt and brutal rule of President Samuel K. Doe and his ruling Krahn tribe (who had come to power in a coup in 1980), had lost most foreign aid and any US military aid. The increasing discontent by the Liberian people over the Doe regime was manifested in several coup attempts. However, at the end of 1989, Charles Taylor, a former Liberian government official, led an invasion of the country from neighbouring Ivory Coast that caught the Doe regime by surprise. Taylor's National Patriotic Front of Liberia (NPFL) made steady progress against the Armed Forces of Liberia (AFL), which took increasingly brutal reprisals against the local populations in areas supporting the revolt. By late summer Taylor's forces were at the gates of Monrovia, and had occupied most of the rest of the country. The fighting in Monrovia caused civilian casualties and suffering that appalled Liberia's West African neighbours, and the Economic Community of West African States (ECOWAS) finally formed an intervention force, primarily drawn from Nigerian, Ghanian, Senegalese, and Sierra Leone troops, that landed in September 1980. Shortly afterwards Doe was captured and killed by a dissident NPFL faction and the intervention force, the ECOWAS Monitoring Group, or ECOMOG, supported an alternative government. This alienated Taylor, who saw the move as thwarting his aspirations to control the entire country, and through late 1992 his forces continued to spar with ECOMOG. In the meantime the NPFL supported itself by various lumbering and mining concessions, and sought to entrench its rule throughout the Liberian hinterland.

In 1991 the NPFL began to attack border areas of Guinea and Sierra Leone to punish them for supporting ECOMOG. Sierra Leone bore the brunt, with NPFL forces invading the country in 1991 and subsequently supporting a rebel movement, the Revolutionary United Front (RUF) in the southern part of the country. The RUF through 1995 conducted a brutal insurgent campaign against government forces, who, despite mercenary and Nigerian military help were unable to contain the RUF's spread. Finally, in 1995 the Sierra Leone government hired the services of the South African-based Executive Outcomes, Ltd., which had been crucial in assisting the Angolan government in 1993-1994 against UNITA. This was a turning point in the war, and although the RUF was not extirpated, its expansion was stopped and it was pushed back to the south. However, civil security had suffered due to the proliferation of banditry and abuses by military personnel. The RUF began to adopt tactics reminiscent of RENAMO in Mozambique, kidnapping civilians to support remote bases in the countryside, and create zones of devastation as a crude *cordon sanitaire*. It was only in late 1995, with the formation of militias recruited from local hunters, called Kamajor, that the government found an effective means of countering RUF in its new defensive mode. By November 1996 the RUF was forced to sign a ceasefire with the government, but unrest continued. A worrisome sign was the increasing rivalry between the Sierra Leone military and the Kamajor, which has since mid-1996 escalated into armed conflict. As of writing the conflict continues in the country, with no sure prognosis.

In the meantime, conflict continued in Liberia. The anti-NPFL forces in 1991 trained and fielded a force based in Sierra Leone called the United Liberation Movement, or ULIMO, that included former AFL soldiers and other opponents of the Taylor regime. By late 1992 they had recaptured large parts of western Liberia and reached Monrovia. However, factionalisation between Krahn former AFL personnel and the Muslim Mandingos eventually resulted in an open break and by early 1994 widespread fighting that prevented further ULIMO gains against the NPFL.

In the meantime open conflict had broken out between the NPFL and ECOMOG, with the latter pushing back Taylor's forces from November 1992 and expanding its perimeter around the capital. Taylor's NPFL, however, continued to resist attacks by the West African force as well as ULIMO factions through 1993. By this time the formation of various local militias and armed groups had continued, with few areas of Liberia free from conflict. Krahns seeking to regain power lost since the fall of Doe formed the Liberian Peace Council (LPC), drawing to it former AFL and Krahn ULIMO members. Elsewhere local militias such as the Lofa Defence Force (LDF) took root, often with the support of other factions (in the case of the LDF, that of Taylor's NPFL).

The history of the Liberian conflict in 1994-1996 has seen continued fighting outside the capital, with the majority of the population either refugees in surrounding countries or internally displaced, mostly to the relative safety of Monrovia. As of writing attempts to forge a lasting peace between the warring factions continue, with some hope of eventual success. However, much of the recent progress seems to have been due to the security provided by ECOMOG, and the future of Liberia after the occupying force and the stability it provides is withdrawn is uncertain at best.

CENTRAL AFRICA I: UGANDA AND SUDAN

Post-Cold War changes in Uganda and Sudan are continuing as of the time of writing, and form part of a major strategic realignment that spans the centre of the African continent. At the centre of the change is Uganda, which emerged victorious in 1991-1992 from its fight with northern insurgents of the former HSM (see Chapter 9). However, gains by the Sudanese government in 1991 and 1992 subsequently allowed the hard-line Islamist backers in the latter to support the insurgents in reprisal for Uganda's support to the SPLA.

The SPLA collapse (see Chapter 9) in 1991-2 was due to the inability of the anti-government factions to resolve the splits that erupted in October 1991. It has since become evident that the Sudanese government actively worked to keep differences and conflicts in the SPLA as active as possible, allowing it to make significant military gains from early 1992 throughout the states of Equatoria, Upper Nile, and Bahr el-Ghazal. Dr John Garang's SPLA was in turmoil all this time, riven by departures of Nuer leaders from the movement and later even by fellow Dinka tribesmen who had significant personal differences with his style of rule. Through this time the Sudanese military continued to push southward, with little substantial resistance in 1992 and 1993 after the failed July 1992 SPLA attack on Juba. It was only when Sudanese forces drew near to the Ugandan border in late 1993 and 1994 that resistance stiffened. This was due, Khartoum charged, to increased Ugandan support to the insurgents.

About this time anti regime insurgents began to increase their activity against the Ugandan government. From mid-1995 there were increasing episodes of cross-border incursions and infiltrations by the reinvigorated Lord's Resistance Army (LRA) of Alice Lakwenya's disciple, Joseph Kony. The LRA employed many tactics used by the insurgents before 1992, and caused a major deterioration in civil order and security throughout northern Uganda.

The period 1994-1995 represented the nadir of SPLA fortunes, and also saw the greatest period of anti-regime insurgency in northern Uganda. However, by the close of 1995 major changes were underway. Sudanese opposition groups that included the SPLA, had formed an umbrella alliance that included groups operating in Blue Nile state and in the Red Sea area. These groups, the Sudanese government claimed, were supported by the Eritrean government. Khartoum claimed that most of its neighbours – Egypt, Eritrea, Ethiopia, and Uganda – were engaged in a conspiracy to destroy it by supporting the SPLA and other rebels.

CENTRAL AFRICA II: ZAIRE

As the conflicts in Sudan and Uganda played themselves out, a related set of conflicts began to loom large to the west. The long-standing ethnic tensions in the Great Rift Valley nations of Rwanda and Burundi between Tutsi former overlords and Hutu peasantry had persisted since the early 1960s. In October 1990, in a move that appeared of limited impact at the time, a large number of Rwandan Tutsi exiles deserted the Ugandan army en masse and invaded northern Rwanda under the aegis of the Rwandan Patriotic Front/Army. The RPF was checked by the Rwandan government with French and Belgian aid. However, the RPF, though defeated, subsequently came under the leadership of Paul Kagame, who led the movement in a guerrilla war that by 1992 had occupied territory in northern Rwanda and forced the Hutu-dominated government to the negotiating table. Meanwhile, pressures for democratic reform in Burundi to the south resulted by 1993 in the Hutus regaining control of the government.

The actions by the Rwandan president, Juvenal Habyarimana, had infuriated extremists in his own government and military, however, who dominated increasingly radicalised militias and youth groups. On 6 April 1994, the plane carrying Habyarimana and Burundi president Ntaryamira was shot down as it returned to the Rwandan capital, Kigali. Subsequently a bloodbath of unprecedented proportions for Africa took place as the Hutu militias, dominated by the Interahamwe, the largest of the organisations, killed up to a million Tutsis and dissident Hutus before the RPF was able to rally, occupy Kigali, and then push the former regime's security forces westward.

In mid- and late July 1994, upwards of 1.5 million refugees fled Rwanda in the face of the RPA advance, and entered Zaire. The government of the latter country was an old ally of the Hutu regime, and allowed the fugitives to take refuge in the eastern part of the country. The subsequent relief operations to feed the fugitives were well-documented by international media. Among the fugitives were members of the militias as well as the Rwandan military (the Rwandan Armed Forces, or FAR, henceforth dubbed the ex-FAR). The militants dominated the refugee camps and prevented any returns to Rwanda, dominating a nation in exile.

Through 1994 and 1995 ethnic conflict in eastern Zaire increased with its spread to Rwandans who had settled in the eastern part of the country. Tutsis who had lived in Zaire for centuries were the main targets. The Zairian government of President Mobutu Sese Seko supported the extremist Hutu factions in their attempts, and local Zairian government and military officials were increasingly hostile to Zairian Tutsis. In the meantime, Hutu extremists who dominated the Zairian camps used them as bases to strike at the Tutsi-dominated government of the RPF as well as the new (since 1996) government of the Tutsi-controlled military in Burundi. Uganda, whose government was sympathetic to the RPF, provided assistance to Rwanda but was hard-pressed by its northern rebels, who were joined in resistance to the government by a new insurgency, that of the West Nile Bank Front, in 1995.

THE NEXUS: A STRATEGIC RE-ALIGNMENT

Through mid-1996 the security situation in the region continued in crisis. The SPLA rebels' progress against the central government in Khartoum continued, but had little effect on the Sudanese government's ability to keep supporting the LRA against the Ugandan regime. In Rwanda, cross-border raids from Zaire were increasingly common, and anti-government rebels also targeted parts of Uganda from Zaire as well. In eastern Zaire ethnic conflict continued as local tribal militias were organised by locals to defend their own property and territory.

Matters finally came to a head in October 1996, when a local Zairian governor told the local BanyaRwanda, called the BanyaMulenge, who numbered about 300,000 and who had lived in the region for centuries, to leave. The BanyaMulenge resisted, organising their own militia and taking up arms against the Zairian military (the FAZ). Through October and November the BanyaMulenge continued a series of victories against the FAZ and occupied much of the Zairian portion of the Great Rift Valley. The Zairian government claimed that the rebels were supported by Rwanda and Uganda, charges these countries denied. In October, the BanyaMulenge and other groups formed a coalition, called the Alliance of Democratic Forces for the Liberation of Congo-Zaire (ADFLCZ), led by PRP head Laurent Kabila (see Chapter 9). Under Kabila's leadership, the BanyaMulenge and other tribal militias continued their gains against the Zairian government, and by year's end had stated their intention to overthrow the Mobutu regime.

Already ADFLCZ had had a major impact on the regional security situation. By the end of November 1996 the Rwandan refugees in Zaire – the manpower base for the Hutu extremists – had been dislocated from the camps in eastern Zaire, with most returning to Rwanda. Others fled westward, joining the FAZ or simply fleeing ahead of advancing ADFLCZ troops. Opposite Uganda, the ADFLCZ dislocated anti-regime rebels, and allowed the government to focus on its northern border security and the LRA. By late 1996 the latter had been effectively pushed back into Sudan where they were on the defensive, along with the Sudanese military, from a resurgent SPLA that was systematically capturing most of the southern part of the country, including the border areas with Zaire and Uganda.

In January the insurgents pushed back an attempted FAZ counteroffensive, and in February made a major push toward Kisangani, Zaire's third city. By mid-March Kisangani had fallen and Kabila announced his next target would be Lubumbashi in mineral-rich Shaba region. On 9 April Lubumbashi fell and the ADFLCZ pushed westward. As of the time of mid-May 1997 the insurgents are posed to attack Kinshasa, the capital, with a battle for the city imminent.

Within a year there have been profound changes in central Africa that suggest a major strategic shift is underway. The tacit alliance evident between the ADFLCZ rebels in Zaire, Rwanda, Uganda, and the southern Sudanese rebels of the SPLA has already significantly changed the political makeup of central Africa, with more changes likely. With a change of government in Kinshasa a likely near-term development and with the Sudanese military continuing to suffer losses in the south, this alliance of relatively new revolutionary regimes is likely to continue as a major force for the foreseeable future. If this is indeed to be so, it portends well for future stability, as they new order is more likely to implement significant social and economic changes regardless of its wariness of too much political liberalisation.

As for continued instability in the Horn and ongoing conflict in West Africa, the near-term prognoses for these areas is not optimistic. Deep-seated ethnic and regional rivalries are likely to continue to fuel current and likely future insurgencies. However, the impending resolution of the crisis in the Great Lakes area may prove an inspiration for others seeking an innovative end to otherwise seemingly implacable conflicts.

Glossary of Terms

The following glossary of terms does not pretend to be complete in its scope, but is provided to give the reader additional information about aspects of insurgency and COIN warfare especially in southern Africa.

African National Congress (ANC) *Rhodesian, Angolan, Mozambican, and Ugandan conflicts.* From the 1960s to 1990 black South Africans who joined the banned ANC organisation fled to camps in Angola, Tanzania, Mozambique, Zambia, and other southern African countries, where many received military training at the hands of Soviet and other communist country personnel. The first major armed venture by trained ANC military cadres was in their assisting ZIPRA guerrillas from 1966 against the Rhodesian government. From 1975 their establishment in Mozambique garnered the ire of South Africa and the SADF, and a number of cross-border raids, including the spectacular Maputo air raid of 1983, were directed at ANC targets inside that country. In addition, the SADF supported the anti-regime RENAMO insurgency against the Mozambican government. Per the terms of the Nkomati Accords of 1984, the latter agreed not to support the ANC or other expatriate groups hostile to the South African government, and most ANC subsequently left the country. In Angola, the ANC was established in camps in the northern and central parts of the country, well away from SADF cross-border strikes, but as a result of the 1988 New York Accords, the ANC had to leave Angola as well. However, a number stayed, hiring themselves as mercenaries to the Angolan military (see 'Mabecos'). Many were moved to Uganda, where they assisted the Ugandan military in its fighting against insurgents in the northern part of that country.

Area Force, Area Force Units (AFUs) *SWA/Namibian conflict.* The Area Force was one of the three main components of SWATF and was modelled after the Territorial (Commando) Force of the SAA. There were a total of 26 AFUs distributed through Sectors 30, 40, 50, and 60. They were comparable in size, structure, and mission to the SAA commandos – area-bound units staffed by reservists and conscripts whose duty it was to provide protection for local infrastructure and other potential targets for SWAPO/PLAN infil-

trators. AFUs were disbanded in 1989 with the disestablishment of SWATF.

Area operations 'Operations carried out with the aim of covering an area with a framework of military organisations, working in close cooperation with the civil authorities, in order to eliminate the enemy who may have established himself in the area, or who may have infiltrated the area.' (Rhodesian ATOPS)

Assimilado *Angolan and Mozambican conflicts.* Used in Portuguese colonial administration, the term referred to Africans and mesticos (i.e., mixed African-Europeans) who qualified as having been formally absorbed into Portuguese (i.e., European) culture. Assimilado status was abolished in 1961, but following the end of Portuguese rule in Angola and Mozambique the former assimilado community, with its education and technical skills, played a major role in the new governments of both countries, as well as in their military leadership.

Beira Corridor *Mozambican conflict.* This strategic corridor in Mozambique is the shortest route to the sea for land-locked Zimbabwe. After the latter replaced the Rhodesian regime in 1980, the increasingly effective attacks by the insurgent RENAMO movement threatened this vital link, which ran between Umtali in Zimbabwe through Chimoio in Mozambique to the port city of Beira. Running along this corridor were a railway, a road, and a pipeline, all considered by Zimbabwe, as use of the corridor gave it an alternative to the otherwise lengthy and costly Tanzania-Zambia (TANZAM) Railway, or dependence upon South African railway transport. Much if not most of the Zimbabwean military effort in Mozambique was thus geared to ensuring the security of the Beira corridor and thus access to a seaport.

Border control operations 'Border control or counter-penetration operations conducted with the aim of securing our own borders and preventing the enemy from crossing, or preventing supplies, reinforcements, etc., from crossing, to support enemy elements that may have succeeded in penetrating. This includes the elimination of the enemy and the destruction of his transit facilities in border areas.' (Rhodesian ATOPS)

Border operations 'Operations designed to deny infiltration or exfiltration of insurgent personnel and materiel across international boundaries.' (US Government, FM 100-20)

Border Operational Area (BOA) *SWA/Namibia conflict*. The BOA, also known simply as the 'Operational Area,' was that part of northern SWA that comprised Kakoland, Ovamboland, Kavango, and West and East Caprivi, organised in 1974 when the SADF took over the COIN war from the police. The BOA was divided into three Operational Sectors: 10 Sector, comprising Kakoland and Ovamboland; 20 Sector, comprising Kavango, part of Bushmanland, and West Caprivi; and 70 Sector, comprising East Caprivi.

Cabinda *Angolan conflict.* The oil-rich enclave of Cabinda was one of the key strategic areas for the MPLA throughout the civil war in Angola. Despite the deployment of both FAPLA and Cuban troops there, insurgent activity increased after the mid-1980s as both the local FLEC guerrillas as well as UNITA operated there. Despite these security threats, the MPLA was able to retain control of the Cabinda oil fields through the war. After the 1991 ceasefire, however, FLEC insurgent activity increased markedly. By November 1991 at least 15,000 FAPLA troops had been deployed in Cabinda to fight the local insurgents. However, the military option has not proven successful for the MPLA and as of the time of writing Cabinda's security situation continues to decline as FLEC makes further gains.

Caprivi Strip *SWA/Namibia conflict.* This narrow neck of land between Botswana on the south, Zambia on the east/north-east, and Angola on the north was part of SWA/Namibia. In the late 1960s-early 1970s the population, collectively called Caprivian, in part supported an insurgent movement allied with SWAPO called the Caprivi African National Union (CANU). This movement was soon contained by the authorities and the remaining Caprivian dissidents joined SWAPO; many subsequently deserted due to what they saw as preferential treatment for the Ovambos. With the formation of SWATF by the security authorities in 1980, Caprivi was divided between two security sectors; the eastern, known as 70 Sector, had its own Caprivian ethnic unit, 701 Battalion.

Casevac *SWA/Namibia conflict.* The term 'casevac', used in South Africa, is generally synonymous with the term 'medevac' used by other countries.

Civil Affairs *(also CA)* 'Those phases of the activities of a commander which embrace the relationship between the military forces and civil authorities and people in a friendly country or area or occupied country or area when military forces are present.' (US Government, JCS Pub 1-02)

Civil-Military Operations *(also CMO):* 'Military efforts to support resistance auxiliary organisation development, undermine government claims, gain support for an insurgent government, and attain national objectives without fighting.' (US Government, FM 100-20)

Civil war 'A war between factions of the same country; there are five criteria for international recognition of this status: the contestants must control territory, have a functioning government, enjoy some foreign recognition, have identifiable regular armed forces, and engage in major military operations.' (US Government, FM 100-20)

Close air support *(also CAS)* 'Air action against hostile targets which are in close proximity to friendly forces and which require detailed integration of each air mission with the fire and movement of those forces.' (US Government, JCS Pub 1-02)

COIN See Counterinsurgency.

COIN Battalion *SWA/Namibia conflict.* With the need to deal with SWAPO/PLAN incursions into northern SWA/Namibia, the SADF formed a number of mostly ethnic battalions that were designed to be able to rapidly respond to reports of insurgent infiltrations and to engage PLAN units, and, if necessary, pursue them back across the Angolan border. In order to do this units were organised as highly mobile motorised infantry that used South African-made armoured cars such as the Casspir as well as the Buffel APC. Line companies in a COIN battalion were often organised into four or more 'Romeo Mike' reaction forces, each consisting of four armoured vehicles mounting about 40 men (101 Battalion, an Ovambo unit, was particularly noted for this organisation). The term 'COIN Battalion' as well as the organisation of some of its elements was based on the unit of the same type in the SADF, which is very similar in organisation and equipment to the standard SAA motorised infantry battalion.

Commando *SWA/Namibia conflict.* In South African usage the term 'commando' referred to a type of army unit of battalion size that was area-bound and staffed by reservists. Its mission was to provide protection to designated civilian and military facilities, known as key points, as well as to assist civilian security authorities in their mission. South African forces in the border war in SWA/Namibia at times included personnel assigned from commando units. In SWA/Namibia, when the South African administration turned over the security establishment to local management in 1980 and formed SWATF, part of the latter included the 'Area Force,' which consisted of 26 commando-like units known as Area Force Units (AFUs). Their mission was to assist with security management in their home areas, a duty that they successfully accomplished until the disestablishment of SWATF in 1989.

COMOPS *Rhodesian conflict.* Acronym for the Rhodesian Combined Operations Headquarters, located in Salisbury. This body, which reported directly to the Prime Minister, coordinated all COIN operations in Rhodesia and planned and developed COIN strategies. COMOPS was represented at the cabinet level by its own minister, the Minister of Combined Operations.

Consolidation programme 'An operation organised in priority areas as an inter-departmental civil-military effort. Normally conducted at the state level, this operation integrates counterinsurgency programs designed to establish, maintain, or restore host nation governmental control of the population and the area and to provide an environment within which the economic, political, and social activities of the populace can be pursued and improved.' (US Government, FM 100-20)

Counterguerrilla operations Operations geared to the active military element of the insurgency only. To this end, counterguerrilla operations are viewed as a supporting component of the counterinsurgency effort.' (US Government, FM 90-8) In the present work 'counterguerrilla operations' refers to such activity taken against insurgents regardless of whether or not they are part of a comprehensive COIN activity.

Counterinsurgency *(COIN)* (1) 'All measures, both civil and military, undertaken by a government, independently or with the assistance of friendly nations, to prevent or defeat insurgency.' (Rhodesian ATOPS) (2) 'Those military, paramilitary, political, economic, psychological, and civic actions taken by a government to defeat insurgency.' (US Government, JCS Pub 1-02)

Counterinsurgency Operations *(COINOPS)* 'Counter-insurgency operations are the military aspects of counter-insurgency. These consist of: a. Anti-terrorist operations (ATOPS); b. Psychological operations (PSYOPS); c. Operations in support of civil authorities (OSCA).' (Rhodesian ATOPS) The southern African (Rhodesian and South African) definition thus parallels closely the concept of 'counterguerrilla operations' defined above.

CSI *Angolan, SWA/Namibia, and Mozambican conflicts.* The SADF Chief of Staff, Intelligence, or CSI, was the joint staff element responsible for military intelligence collection and production. In addition, the CSI was entrusted with covert military operations.Perhaps the best-known CSI effort was the takeover in 1980 from the Rhodesian government of running the RENAMO insurgency in Mozambique. This effort continued at least to 1984, and may have lasted to the early 1990s despite the promises of the South African government in the Nkomati Accords to cease support to RENAMO. CSI operations, both foreign and domestic, were curbed extensively after political reforms in South Africa were initiated in 1990.

Cuito Cuanavale *Angolan conflict.* Through most of the Angolan civil war this town on the Cuito River in Cuando Cubango province was the easternmost point of secure MPLA control against UNITA guerrilla encroachments. With the loss of Mavinga in 1980, Cuito Cuanavale became an outpost of military control and a major staging point for repeated attempts to recapture Mavinga from UNITA. All ended in failure. With the devastating failure of such an attempt in 1985 in which UNITA, with South African help, decimated a FAPLA task force, Cuito Cuanavale was built up for a major strike against Mavinga in 1986. However, a pre-emptive combined UNITA-South African raid, code-named Operation 'Alpha Centauri', in which the latter used their highly effective artillery, caused severe damage and casualties that forced FAPLA to abandon the offensive. The following year (1987), FAPLA assembled a massive task force to recapture Mavinga from UNITA, but suffered a huge defeat when South African air, armour, mechanised, and artillery units intervened to assist UNITA in Operations 'Modular', 'Hooper' and 'Packer'. Subsequently they pushed FAPLA back to Cuito Cuanavale and began a devastating bombardment that lasted from November 1987 to March 1988. Although Cuito Cuanavale was not taken, most FAPLA had to abandon the town to escape the South African bombardment. UNITA and South African efforts were directed to trying to drive FAPLA and Cuban units who had come to their assistance to the west bank of the river. This attempt was not successful due to the heavily entrenched positions, surrounded by minefields, that protected FAPLA and the Cubans. This was later claimed by FAPLA and its Cuban allies as a victory in the 'Battle for

Cuito Cuanavale.' Despite these claims, FAPLA's high casualties and equipment losses debilitated the force for almost two years. Although Cuito Cuanavale was the staging point for yet another major offensive in 1989-1990, the town was not a major site of combat for the rest of the civil war.

Ethnic battalions *SWA/Namibia conflict.* As part of the successful effort to involve the peoples of northern SWA/Namibia in the war against SWAPO/PLAN, the South African administration organised a number of COIN battalions. These seven units were each filled by members of a single ethnic group, with the exception of one multi-ethnic unit (41 Battalion, later the SWATF 911 Battalion, head-quarters Windhoek). Their unit leaders, at first South African officers and NCOs, were gradually supplemented with Namibians trained at Lenz in South Africa. By the mid- and late 1980s the ethnic units had become the backbone of SWATF, and were highly effective COIN battalions that participated in numerous cross-border operations into Angola. Staffed mostly by Permanent Force personnel, these units nevertheless were able to train conscripts and reservists. The ethnic battalions, as other SWATF units, were dismantled in 1989-1990 with the preparations for Namibian independence.

FAM *Mozambican conflict.* The Mozambican Armed Forces (in Portuguese: Forcas Armadas de Mocambique) was the collective term for the FRELIMO government's military forces, and comprised a joint staff plus ground, air, naval, and border guard services. By the time of the 1992 ceasefire the FAM had at least 70,000 personnel. Its original name was the Popular Forces for the Liberation of Mozambique (in Portuguese: Forcas Populars de Liber-tacao de Mocambique), which it carried throughout the long insurgent struggle against Portuguese colonial rule in the 1960s and 1970s. Often the term 'FRELIMO forces' is used as a synonym for the FAM.

FAPLA *Angolan and SWA/Namibia conflicts.* The Popular Armed Forces for the Liberation of Angola (in Portuguese: Forcas Armadas Populares de Libertacao de Angola), or FAPLA, was the collective term for the MPLA Angolan government's military forces in the period 1975-1991. It comprised a joint staff under control of the Ministry of Defence and included ground, air, and naval forces, plus territorial troops and militias. The term 'FAPLA' was often used during the civil war to refer to Angolan ground forces, which numbered about 115,000 or so by the end of the 1980s. Following the civil war and the short-lived ceasefire, FAPLA was disestablished and most of its units disbanded; most experienced personnel were retained as part

of the new Angolan military, the Angolan Armed Forces (Forcas Armadas Angolanas).

FAZ *Angolan, Chadian, Rwandan, and Zairian conflicts.* The Zairian Armed Forces (in French: Forces Armées Zairoises), or FAZ, were renamed in 1971 from the old Congolese National Army (Armée National Congolaise, ANC). In the early 1990s the FAZ consisted of a joint staff reporting to the Zairian Depart-ment of National Defence (DDNST) and four services, the Army, Navy, Air Force, and National Gendarmerie, totalling about 45,000 personnel. Although its prime purpose was to maintain the regime of President Mobutu Sese Seko (ex-Joseph Desire) in power, Mobutu used the FAZ for some foreign ventures, with mixed results. The use of the FAZ to support the FNLA in Angola in 1975 ended in disaster at Quifangongo. In the 1980s Mobutu sent elements of the FAZ 31st Parachute Brigade to Chad to assist the government of Hissein Habré against Libyan-backed insurgents. Elements of the FAZ 31st Brigade were also sent to Togo in 1986 in the wake of a coup attempt. A more controversial use was in October 1990, when FAZ units were sent to Rwanda to assist the government against the RPF invasion. The breakdown of FAZ discipline and the abysmal behaviour of the troops prompted the Rwanda government to request their withdrawal only weeks after their arrival. During the two invasions of Zaire's Shaba region by the FNLC in 1977 and 1978, the FAZ performed poorly and required foreign assis-tance to drive out the attackers. The FAZ has been notorious for highly irregular and gener-ally inefficient command and control, poor and at times almost non-existent logistics, and a high desertion rate due to poor pay and conditions of service.

Fire Force *Rhodesian conflict.* A term applied to rapid intervention/response units in the Rhodesian Army. The Fire Force was a small force of helicopter-borne and airborne units that were deployed around the country and operated under local Joint Operational Centres (JOCs). Their purpose was to quickly respond to insurgent incidents and engage guerrilla forces. Three Fire Force units existed, covering the 'Hurricane', 'Thrasher', and 'Repulse' Oper-ational Sectors. The Fire Force concept in Rhodesia was similar to that of the 'Romeo Mike' forces in SWA/Namibia, and ensured that insurgents, once detected, could be engaged with superior firepower.

FLEC *Angolan conflict.* The tangled history of the Front for the Liberation of the Enclave of Cabinda (in Portuguese: Frente de Libertacao do Enclave de Cabinda) dates back to the colo-nial period and separatist sentiments after the discovery of oil there in 1966. FLEC had been organised in 1963 by Luie Ranque Franque, who later opposed the MPLA during the struggle at the end of Portuguese colonial rule. FLEC was unable to seize Cabinda in 1974 and was defeated by the MPLA; it subsequently splintered into at least five factions. The MPLA garrisoned the oil installations of Cabinda with not only its own troops but also Cuban forces. By the mid-1980s UNITA appeared in the province and began to ally itself with some elements of FLEC to support its operations in Cabinda. Insurgent activity in Cabinda spread through the end of the 1980s into the 1990s. Following the 1991 Angolan ceasefire the insurgency continued in Cabinda, where FLEC resented being left out of peace negotiations. The insurgency continued and even intensified as FAPLA troops were required elsewhere in Angola to battle UNITA after the breakdown of the reconciliation process and the resumption of war in late 1992.

flecha *Angolan, Rhodesian, and Mozambican conflicts.* The flechas, or 'arrows', were members of special COIN forces recruited by Portuguese colonial authorities first in Angola and then in Mozambique from deserters from the anti-colonial insurgents. Their bush skills, insurgent training, and knowledge of local conditions made them excellent counterguerrilla fighters. The flechas still had an impact in the post-colonial period. Extremely important is the inspiration the concept gave to the SADF when it formed 'Bravo Group' in 1976, which later became 32 Battalion (a number of whose personnel were former flechas). Secondly, in post-colonial Mozambique, many former flechas were sought by the FRELIMO government to be killed; these and disgruntled FRELIMO members formed the basis for the RENAMO movement, organised and supported at first by the Rhodesian government. Finally, in the Rhodesian conflict many former flechas who did not join RENAMO joined the Rhodesian forces where their special skills were employed.

FNLA *Angolan and SWA/Namibian conflicts.* The National Front for the Liberation of Angola (in Portuguese: Frente Nacional de Libertacao de Angola) was founded in 1958 as the Union of Angola Peoples (Uniao das Populacoes de Angola, UPA). From the 1960s the FNLA, under its leader Holden Roberto, received support from the Congolese (later Zairian) government. In 1961 it conducted its first major attack, marked by extensive atrocities against Portuguese settlers and African assimilados in northern Angola. Despite early successes, the FNLA's support base remained confined to the BaKongo ethnic group in northern Angola (now Zaire and Uige provinces). In 1962 the UPA, with additional elements, became the FNLA. With the end of Portuguese rule the FNLA's army, the Exercito Nacional de Libertacao de Angola (ENLA) was

supported by Zaire's president Mobutu Sese Seko in a bid to capture the capital and take power, but was defeated by the winning faction, the MPLA, with Cuban assistance. The FNLA subsequently broke up, with many of its fighters being recruited by South Africa to form Bravo Group, predecessor of 32 'Buffalo' Battalion. Through the late 1970s into the 1980s the FLNA was a nonentity as many joined the MPLA or were otherwise coopted as the Angolan government sought support from the BaKongos of northern Angola. With political liberalisation from 1990 on, the FNLA re-emerged as a legal political party in Angola.

FNLC *Angolan and Zairian conflicts.* The National Front for the Liberation of the Congo (in French: Front National de Libération du Congo) has its origins in former members of the gendarmerie force of the secessionist Congolese province of Katanga (see Katangese ex-gendarmes). After fleeing the Congo (now Zaire) in fear of reprisals by its leader Lieutenant General Joseph Mobutu, the gendarmes, under their leader Brigadier General Nathaniel Mbumba, formed the FNLC in 1968; it had an external office in Paris. The force was composed mainly of members of the Lunda and Chokwe ethnic groups. After serving the Portuguese Angolan colonial administration, the FNLC became a client, after Angolan independence, of the MPLA, which had come to power by defeating the Mobutu-supported FNLA. The invasions of the Zairian region of Shaba (former Katanga) in March 1977 and May 1978 were seen by Mobutu as an attempt by the MPLA to use the FNLC insurgents to overthrow him. Although defeated, the FNLC returned to camps in Angola where it assisted the Angolan military in various operations in the north-east of the country. Other FNLC groups reportedly entered Zaire in the 1980s and established enclaves in its eastern province of Kivu. Through the 1980s the FNLA in Angola, numbering perhaps no more than a few thousand, declined as a viable threat to Mobutu's regime as various ageing ex-Katangese left the organisation, died, or moved elsewhere. Following political liberalisation in 1990, some elements of the FNLC, including those still led by Mbumba (by this time living in Tanzania), returned home to again participate in Zairian political life. Some, however, remained in Angola while yet other elements remained as anti-regime insurgents in remote eastern parts of Zaire.

'Fred'/'Freddie' *Rhodesian conflict.* The nickname 'Freddie' (or 'Freddie-Moe') was applied by Rhodesian forces to FRELIMO (Mozambican) military forces in general. In specific usage, 'Fred' was the brigade-sized reaction force, in Manica province, tasked to respond to Rhodesian cross-border COIN operations against ZANLA base camps. This unit included a battalion of tanks and two battalions of motorised infantry, backed up with artillery and trained by Cuban advisers. Despite its impressive armament and potentially lethal firepower, response by 'Fred' was usually poorly coordinated and more a nuisance than a threat to the Rhodesians.

FRELIMO *Mozambican conflict.* The Front for the Liberation of Mozambique (in Portuguese: Frente para a Libertacao de Mocambique) was founded in 1962. After fighting a long insurgent war against Portuguese colonial rule, it finally took power in 1975 under Samora Machel, forming the government and instituting a one-party state. Almost immediately its social and economic programmes began to alienate large sectors of Mozambican society, and allowed RENAMO, a creation of the Rhodesian security forces and later backed by South Africa, to rapidly garner support throughout the country. FRELIMO subsequently was forced to reconcile with South Africa with the Nkomati Accords of 1984; following the death of Samora Machel in 1986, his successor, Joaquim Chissano, began a series of reforms that resulted in political and economic liberalisation that accompanied renewed military efforts against RENAMO. By 1992 a military stalemate had set in and a ceasefire apparently signalled the beginning of peace negotiations.

Front *Rhodesian, SWA/Namibia, and Angolan conflicts.* The term 'Front' was used by ZIPRA for its war zones inside Rhodesia. Each front was subdivided into military regions where designated ZIPRA units operated. In the SWA/Namibia conflict, PLAN, the armed wing of SWAPO, used this term for its staging areas inside Angola. In the late 1970s PLAN organised fronts north of the SWA border with Angola, each commanded by a central headquarters and a network of base camps that provided logistical support to groups of insurgents attempting to cross the border. In the Angolan civil war, UNITA organised its war zones into fronts; each front (frente in Portuguese) was subdivided into military regions and in turn into military sectors. In 1988, the MPLA organised Angola into four (later five) 'political-military Fronts' that were designed to coordinate the total war fighting resources available to it.

Gorongosa *(Serra Gorongosa) Mozambican conflict.* A forested, mountainous massif in central Mozambique south of the Zambezi River on the border of Manica and Sofala provinces. The immediate vicinity is a game park, and it and the Serra Gorongosa itself have a poor infrastructure and sparse population. This area was chosen in the late 1970s by RENAMO as one of its refuges as well as main centres of operations. In and around the

Gorongosa massif were about a dozen RENAMO base camps, some with airfields that could accommodate light aircraft and even a C-47 Dakota cargo aircraft. The Gorongosa was repeatedly attacked by FAM and ZNA troops, with much of it overrun in operations in 1985 and 1989. However, in each case RENAMO soon returned to ensconce themselves in the area. Through the 1980s it was the main insurgent centre for Mozambique; RENAMO also controlled most of its operations in Zambezia, Manica, and Sofala provinces from there.

'Gorongosa Documents' *Mozambican conflict.* This term refers to documents captured in August 1985 at a number of base camps and other sites in the Serra Gorongosa. The documents, published over the following year or so, indicate a pattern of South African support, including training, logistics support flights, and other activities.

Guerrilla warfare 'Military and paramilitary operations conducted in enemy-held or hostile territory by irregular, predominantly indigenous forces.' (US Government, JCS Pub 1-02)

Homoine Massacre *Mozambican conflict.* The 18 July Homoine massacre was the largest of several massacres committed by to RENAMO in the period July-October 1987. The mass killings of civilians at Homoine, Manjacaze (10 August), and Taninga (16 October) captured the attention of the outside world and fixed international public opinion against RENAMO. Although RENAMO denied responsibility in the incident, the evidence indicates that these were terror killings designed to be an example to the local population in southern Mozambique. Furthermore, they apparently took place in the context of military operations by RENAMO in the southern Mozambican provinces of Gaza, Inhambane and Maputo, which in general supported the Mozambican government. Far from its traditional bases and support population, RENAMO by its actions apparently was trying to terrorise at least part of the local populations in southern Mozambique to support it and reject government authority.

Infrastructure 'In an insurgency, the leadership organisation and its system for command and control. In a broader sense, the systems of communications and the institutions which support the political and economic functions of a society.' (US Government, FM 100-20)

Insurgent 'An indigenous or foreign national not recognised as a belligerent by international law, aiming to overthrow a government by force. In revolutionary war the terms "guerrilla", "revolutionary", "terrorist", or "insurgent" are used on occasion to indicate differences in the opposition. When it is not necessary to indicate specific differences, however, "insurgent" is used to cover all the roles implied by the foregoing terms.' (Rhodesian ATOPS)

Insurgency (1) 'A form of rebellion in which a dissident faction instigates the commission of acts of civil disobedience, sabotage, and terrorism, and wages irregular war in order to overthrow a government. In its ultimate stages it could escalate to a conflict on conventional lines. Although insurgency often starts internally, it has seldom been known to succeed without outside assistance, support, and encouragement.' (Rhodesian ATOPS) (2) 'An organised movement aimed at the overthrow of a constituted government through use of subversion and armed conflict.' (US Government, JCS Pub 1-02)

Joint Monitoring Commission *(JMC) Angolan and SWA/Namibia conflicts.* As a consequence of Operation 'Askari' (December 1983-January 1984), a Joint Monitoring Commission (JMC) of FAPLA and SADF representatives was established to monitor the withdrawal of the South Africans by May of 1984 from Cunene and at the same time ensure that PLAN units did not re-establish themselves there. The JMC consisted of both SADF and FAPLA forces assigned to southern Angola specifically for this purpose. The first meeting of the JMC was held on 26 January at Cuvelai, the scene of the major battle of Operation 'Askari', in response to SADF concerns about the continued infiltration of SWAPO/PLAN operatives into northern Namibia. While SADF had begun a general withdrawal from Angola on 8 January, many of the same troops eventually returned or remained as part of the South African component of the JMC. Headquartered at Ngiva in the southern part of Cunene province, the JMC was for all practical purposes divided into SADF and FAPLA components, with their areas of influence separated by an east-west line at the latitude of Ngiva. Joint forces patrolled on both sides of the line, but often the military initiative or lack of such on the part of the FAPLA component of the JMC meant that action against SWAPO/PLAN violations rested with the SADF in the southern part of the JMC area. Angolan forces were supposed to have taken control of areas from which the SADF withdrew, but in reality PLAN units soon re-established themselves, and within months had started infiltrations and raids once more. With the disbandment on 16 May 1985 of the JMC, FAPLA was left in control of large areas of Cunene province previously occupied or denied to them by the South Africans. SWAPO, which subsequently continued its attempts to penetrate into SWA/Namibia, prompted three major responses by the security forces by the end of that year.

Joint Operational Centres *(JOCs) Rhodesian conflict.* Established during the Rhodesian conflict, JOCs coordinated all security force actions in their areas of control, which corresponded to Operational Sectors (OPS). Local JOCs operated under a main JOC in Salisbury at Defence Headquarters. Sub JOCs existed for each of the main JOCs.

Katangese ex-gendarmes *(see also FNLC): Angolan and Zairian conflicts.* The Katangese gendarme force organised by the Belgian Congo government of Katanga province has had a long and chequered history. The force, augmented by mercenaries from Europe and southern Africa, was used by Katangese leader Moise Tshombe to resist attacks by the Congolese National Army (ANC) aimed at ending his secessionist attempts. With the collapse of the secession many of his Katangese force fled across the border to Northern Rhodesia (later Zambia) and Portuguese-ruled Angola. In the latter place many were hired by the Portuguese government to fight insurgents there. Tshombe subsequently returned from exile to head the Congolese government, crushing major rebellions with hired mercenaries as well as Katangese forces. But Tshombe's subsequent fall from power, the coup by Lieutenant General Joseph Desire Mobutu (who replaced him in 1965), the rebellion of Katangese units of the ANC in 1966, and the subsequent purge of mercenaries and their rebellion in 1967 prompted many Katangese soldiers to flee the Congo and Mobutu's reprisals. Many ended up in Angola, where, under one of their military leaders, Brigadier Nathaniel Mbumba (who founded the FNLC in 1968), the Katangese ex-gendarmes became part of the counterguerrilla forces of the Portuguese colonial administration. With the end of Portuguese rule Mbumba and his group, still vehemently anti-Mobutu, became clients of the new MPLA government, which was later accused of supporting FNLC attempts to invade Shaba (ex-Katanga) in 1977 and 1978. With the defeat of the invasion the Katangese ex-gendarmes returned to Angola and later fought for the MPLA regime. After political liberalisation in Zaire in 1990, some ex-Katangese, under Mbumba's leadership, returned home while others remained in Angola, where, under the nickname of 'Tigres', they fought for the Angolan military in special units.

Koevoet *SWA/Namibia conflict.* One of the components of the SWA Police COIN force. Also known as Ops-K, the unit was founded in 1981 using white officers and former SWAPO personnel. Mounted in Casspir ACs, Koevoet units were used as a rapid response force to SWAPO penetrations in a manner similar to that of the SWATF 101 and 201 Battalions. In the course of the COIN war in SWA/Namibia this unit's aggressive tactics and high success rate earned considerable international opprobrium, most due to a successful disinformation campaign launched by SWAPO and its supporters. The unit was disbanded in 1989 prior to Namibia's independence but many personnel were simply reassigned to the SWA Police.

Lancaster House Agreement *Rhodesian conflict.* This accord, reached in London on 21 December 1979 after long discussions among all parties to the conflict, was the settlement that brought the long insurgency to an end. The agreement resulted in a ceasefire, the drafting of a new constitution for Rhodesia-Zimbabwe, and elections within six months of the agreement.

Lomba River *Angolan conflict.* A river in Angola's Cuando Cubango province, tributary to the Cuando River (which, as the Chobe, flows into the Zambezi at the eastern tip of the Caprivi Strip in Namibia). The Lomba was the site of three major battles (1985, 1987, and 1990) during the Angolan civil war as FAPLA task forces based on Cuito Cuanavale attempted to cross it and capture the UNITA-held town of Mavinga. In 1985 and 1987 FAPLA attempted to outflank the river but was driven back with great loss. In 1990 a strong FAPLA force succeeded in crossing the Lomba despite a series of intense battles there in late January and penetrating to Mavinga in early February before being halted and ultimately forced to retreat in early May.

Low intensity conflict *(LIC)* 'Political-military confrontation between contending states or groups below conventional and above the routine, peaceful competition among states. It frequently involves protracted struggles of competing principles and ideologies. Low intensity conflict ranges from subversion to the use of armed force. It is waged by a combination of means, employing political, economic, informational, and military instruments. Low intensity conflicts are often localised, generally in the Third World, but contain certain regional and global security implications.' (US Government, JCS Pub 1-02)

Luena, Battle of *(April-May 1991) Angolan conflict.* The attempt by UNITA to capture the city of Luena in Moxico province was the final major battle of the first Angolan civil war. Despite UNITA's repeated attempts to isolate the town and launch major attacks against it, Luena was well-defended and resisted the attacks. Although UNITA forces used artillery to support the mainly infantry attacks, the lack of mechanised or armoured units prevented it from being able to penetrate FAPLA lines.

Lusaka Accord *Angolan and SWA/Namibia conflicts.* The Lusaka Accord of February 1984 followed a major SADF incursion into Angola in pursuit of SWAPO/PLAN insurgents. The accord provided for the withdrawal of South African forces from Angola, the establishment of a neutral zone monitored by a Joint Monitoring Commission (JMC) (q.v.) composed of SADF and FAPLA, and the relocation northward of PLAN camps north of the zone, also known as the Area in Question (AIQ), which comprised most of Cunene province.

Mabecos *Angolan conflict.* 'Mabecos', which refers to the wild dogs that roam Angola's countryside, is the popular term for members of the special units attached to FAPLA that are composed of expatriate black South African personnel of the ANC who remained in Angola following the movement of ANC camps from the country during 1988-1990. See the entry under African National Congress (ANC).

MARNET Radio System *SWA/Namibia conflict.* The acronym stands for Military Area Radio Net, and was a system developed in the RSA and in SWA in the 1980s to support civilian home defence. Families in isolated farms and settlements would be provided with radio sets organised into an area network which would be monitored by security forces. In the event of an insurgent sighting or other incident, the net was used to alert the local security force headquarters, which would send a reaction force in response to the call.

Mavinga *Angolan conflict.* Mavinga, a town in Angola's Cuando Cubango province south-east of the large government base at Cuito Cuanavale, was controlled by UNITA after 1981. In that year and in a series of almost annual campaigns thereafter, Angolan government forces attempted to capture the town from UNITA. Mavinga was a local logistics hub for UNITA and the centre of a major agricultural area supporting the insurgents. It was also the main town between Cuito Cuanavale in the government-controlled area and the UNITA capital of Jamba, and was intended by government forces as a springboard against the latter. Major campaigns launched from Cuito Cuanavale against Mavinga took place in 1985, 1987, and 1990. In the first two attempts FAPLA was repulsed by UNITA with South African assistance. A 1986 attempt failed before an attack could be launched due to a pre-emptive UNITA and South African attack. In February 1990, however, FAPLA was able to penetrate to Mavinga but its attacking forces were halted and in turn besieged by UNITA, forcing their withdrawal in May 1990.

Mine countermeasures *Rhodesian and SWA/Namibia conflicts.* Extensive communist country support to anti-regime insurgents included the provision of anti-vehicle and anti-personnel mines,the purpose of which was to restrict security force mobility by rendering them unwilling to venture on patrols from garrison. The countermeasures to mine warfare included the development of mine-resistant and mine-protected vehicles, mine-detecting vehicles, and mine exploders.

Mine-resistant and mine-protected vehicles *Rhodesian and SWA/Namibia conflicts.* The use of mine-protected vehicles began in Rhodesia and Namibia to counter the insurgent strategy of laying anti-vehicle and anti-personnel mines on the roads. Both South Africa and Rhodesia produced several families of mine-resistant vehicles used not only by security forces but also by civilians (these vehicles are discussed in the pertinent chapters in the text). The most important result of fielding mine-resistant vehicles was to prevent the insurgents from restricting security force mobility thus rendering them a 'garrison force' unwilling to venture on patrols. The fielding of mine-resistant and mine-protected vehicles in the Rhodesian conflict was but one facet of mine counter-measures, and probably the most successful; it was improved upon by the South Africans in SWA/Namibia and had an even greater success rate. With the South Africans, such vehicles as the Ratel IFV, the Buffel APC, and the Casspir armoured car enabled security forces to move rapidly and with little hesitation on SWA roads. Eventually the security forces in both SWA as well as in South Africa proper were equipped with mine-protected vehicles. Despite the use of more sophisticated anti-vehicle mines by PLAN insurgents in SWA in the late 1980s designed to counter the anti-mine engineering, their attempts did not pose a serious threat to security forces through to the end of the war.

Military civic action 'The use of preponderantly indigenous military forces on projects useful to the local populace at all levels in fields such as education, training, public works, agriculture, transportation, communications, health, and sanitation, and others contributing to economic and social development, which would also serve to improve the standing of the military forces with the population.' (US Government, JCS Pub 1-02)

Mujiba *Rhodesian conflict.* 'Mujibas' were insurgent sympathisers, primarily in Shona areas, who acted as cadres for guerrilla forces in African areas. They acted as informers, intelligence gatherers, and logistical assistants, and performed other tasks as required to support ZANLA activities. The mujiba system was implemented by ZANLA after 1972 and by war's end 50,000 sympathisers were claimed by ZANLA.

Musseques *Angolan conflict.* These were shanty towns surrounding the larger Angolan cities, especially Luanda and Huambo. The musseques swelled through the 1980s as many Angolans fled the countryside and fighting there between FAPLA and UNITA. The newcomers overstrained the urban infrastructure, which often collapsed under the weight of so many newcomers. FAPLA recruited heavily from the musseques, whose inhabitants, normally unemployed, found the military a ready source of employment.

Nkomati Accords *Mozambican conflict.* By early 1984 RENAMO had clearly bested the FAM, not only in promoting the South Africans' agenda of destabilising the FRELIMO government, but in its own members' desire to rid themselves of any traces of central government rule. FRELIMO's inability or unwillingness to moderate its programmes for restructuring Mozambique's social and economic life continued to arouse considerable antipathy among the population, especially that in rural areas. The FAM, armed and trained for conventional war, was increasingly unable to protect RENAMO targets. Security forces were tied down guarding priority towns and facilities, while the insurgents were free to roam the countryside and strike at will. South Africa, for its part, desired Mozambique to cease harbouring operatives of the African National Congress (ANC) on its territory. Thus, by late winter 1984, FRELIMO decided to open serious negotiations with the South African government designed to ensure that each government would cease support for the other's dissidents. On 16 March 1984, Mozambique and South Africa signed the Nkomati Accords, designed to normalise relations between the two governments under the conditions noted above, at a ceremony at the border town of Nkomati (near Komatipoort, RSA). Despite the Accords, both sides found it difficult to adhere to them. Mozambique could not entirely eliminate the ANC from its territory, although it was able to suppress much of its activity. On the other hand, the South African government's agreement was apparently compromised within the security forces as elements of the intelligence staff as well as many members of South Africa's Portuguese community still supported RENAMO. This support continued into the late 1980s. Despite this, the Nkomati Accords gave FRELIMO the breathing space it desperately needed, and helped it hold out through mid-1985, when neighbouring Zimbabwe was able to intervene in the conflict, sending in combat troops in August of that year.

Operational Sectors *(OPS) Rhodesian and SWA/Namibian conflicts.* Also known as Joint Operational Commands, these were areas of territorial responsibility for COIN forces. Each Sector was administered by a Joint Operational Centre (JOC) that coordinated all security force actions in its AOR. In the Rhodesian conflict Operational Sectors were established starting in late 1972. By early 1977 the entire country was covered by six such sectors ('Hurricane', 'Thrasher', 'Repulse', 'Tangent', 'Grapple' and 'Salops'). During the SWA/Namibia conflict, the Operational Area was divided from 1980 into three Operational Sectors each responsible for border control and maintaining area security. By the late 1970s the complexity of JOC operations became such that fifteen (by 1980, seventeen) 'sub JOCs' were established to coordinate more local joint security activities.

Operations in support of civil authorities (OSCA) 'Any military operation in support of civil authorities, which involves primarily the maintenance of law and order and essential services, in the face of civil disturbance and disobedience.' (Rhodesian ATOPS)

PBs *SWA/Namibia conflict.* Acronym for the Afrikaans term plaaslikebevolking, 'local population', used by security forces. Another term used less commonly was 'the povo', from the Portuguese word povo, 'people'. Security forces devoted considerable time to maintaining good relations with the PBs, who in return often provided valuable intelligence as to PLAN operations in the immediate locality.

Peacekeeping operations 'Military operations conducted with the consent of the belligerent parties to a conflict, to maintain a negotiated truce and to facilitate diplomatic resolution of a conflict between the belligerents.' (US Government, FM 100-20)

Peacemaking operations 'A type of peacetime contingency operation intended to establish or restore peace and order through the use of force.' (US Government, FM 100-20)

Peacetime contingency operations 'Politically sensitive military operations normally characterised by the short-term, rapid projection or employment of forces in conditions short of war.' (US Government, FM 100-20)

Psychological operations *(PSYOPS)* (1) 'An action conducted over a predetermined period of time and consisting of the application of various coordinated measures, directed at the population in general or the inhabitants of a specific area or social group, own armed forces, or at the enemy in accordance with determined doctrines and techniques. They are conducted by military forces, civil authorities, or by both in conjunction with each other, to achieve an objective of psychological action.' (Rhodesian ATOPS) (2) 'Planned opera-

tions to convey selected information and indicators to foreign audiences to influence their emotions, motives, objective reasoning, and ultimately the behaviour of foreign government, organisations, groups, and individuals. The purpose of psychological operations is to induce or reinforce attitudes and behaviour favourable to the originator's objectives.' (US Government, JCS Pub 1-02)

Reaction Force *SWA/Namibia conflict.* As opposed to the 'Romeo Mike' units found in COIN battalion companies, the term 'reaction force' (in its full form) was used by the SAA and SWATF for their mobile reserve. In general, 61st Mechanised Group at Operet was the reaction force for SAA units in SWA.

RENAMO Mozambican conflict. The Mozambican National Resistance (in Portuguese: Resistencia Nacional de Mocambique), also known as the Mozambican Resistance Movement (MRM) and by RENAMO's English acronym NRM, was begun by the Rhodesian government after the establishment of FRELIMO in Mozambique in 1975. Due to widespread popular discontent with FRELIMO policies the movement grew rapidly and by 1980 involved large parts of central Mozambique. When Rhodesia became Zimbabwe, support to the movement shifted to South Africa and the SADF (1980). Continuing its successful operations, RENAMO by 1984 had debilitated Mozambican economic capabilities as well as threatened the existence of the FRELIMO regime. After the Nkomati Accords, SADF direction and support supposedly ceased. From 1984, RENAMO attempted to defeat the government militarily, a strategy which failed as FRELIMO recouped losses by the end of 1987. However, from that time to the 1992 ceasefire, the initiative in the war shifted back and forth between government forces and RENAMO, and finally to stalemate.

'Romeo Mike' *(RM) SWA/Namibia conflict.* RMs were COIN reaction force teams (hence their name, derived from the Afrikaans term reaksie mag, abbreviated RM) from the SWATF 101 Battalion (Ovambo). A typical Romeo Mike team included two officers and 20 to 40 enlisted soldiers mounted in four Casspir armoured cars with a logistics vehicle in support. Their mission was rapid response to PLAN sightings with the aim of engaging and neutralising the insurgents.

South African Police *(SAP) Rhodesian and SWA/Namibia conflicts.* The SAP figured heavily in the early days of both of these insurgent conflicts. In Rhodesia, the SAP provided patrols to assist Rhodesian security forces until their withdrawal in February 1974. In SWA, the SAP assumed border protection in 1966 when the conflict began and held it through 1974, when the military took over security management in the Operational Area. The SAP nevertheless continued to perform regular police functions throughout SWA/Namibia until the formation of SWAPOL in 1980.

South-West Africa Territory Force *(SWATF)* *SWA/Namibia conflict.* Formed on 1 August 1980, it was disbanded prior to Namibia's independence in 1990. This force was designed to be a SWA/Namibian fighting force, and was composed of units recruited from local ethnic groups to fight PLAN insurgents. The force included a number of South Africans who had been seconded to SWATF. Never more than 30,000 personnel in total, with only about 12,000 or so full-time soldiers, the force nevertheless was highly successful in its mission of defending the border area and reacting to PLAN incursions. SWATF included a Reaction Force, an Area Force, and an infrastructure or support element. The Area Force was similar to the SAA Territorial (Commando) Force. The Reaction Force included a conventional motorised brigade plus six COIN battalions, all ethnic units drawn from the Namibian population.

Special Forces (Angola) *Angolan conflict.* FAPLA Special Forces (Portuguese: Forcas Especiais) were Army (EPA) units under control of the Army staff. They were used to support FAPLA combat operations as well as to conduct special missions, such as reconnaissance. They were also known as the 'Red Berets' (Portuguese: Boinas Vermelhas).

Special Forces (Rhodesia) *Rhodesian conflict.* Rhodesian Army Special Forces constituted a separate headquarters from the regular army and comprised three and later five elements. These included the Rhodesian African Rifles (RAR), the Rhodesian Light Infantry (RLI), the Special Air Service (SAS), the Selous Scouts, and the Grey's Scouts. Both the RAR and RLI were originally under Army Headquarters but due to their increasing participation in, and proficiency in, special operations, they were by the late 1970s included among the Rhodesian Army Special Forces, and also were parcelled out to the Joint Operation Commands (JOCs). After 1977 Special Forces were under the direct control of COMOPS.

Special Forces (South Africa) Angolan and SWA/Namibia conflicts. South African Special Forces were directly under the SADF staff. The highly trained personnel were organised into at least four elite units known as Reconnaissance Regiments, and were also known as 'Recce Commandos'. In the SWA/Namibia and Angola conflicts their mission was to conduct long-range reconnaissance operations and undertake or provide support to special missions and covert operations.

SWAPO *SWA/Namibia conflict.* The South-West Africa People's Organisation, or SWAPO, began insurgent operations in 1962. The insurgency grew sporadically into the mid-1970s as members of the primarily Ovambo movement sought to use Angola as a base. With the end of Portuguese rule in Angola, the new government and its Cuban allies supported SWAPO by providing its military forces with bases and logistical assistance. SWAPO's military arm, the People's Liberation Army of Namibia, or PLAN, thus grew emboldened and increased its cross-border attacks. In May 1978 Operation 'Reindeer' signalled the initiation of a new policy by SA authorities of pre-emptive moves against SWAPO infrastructure in southern Angola. SADF and SWATF operations against PLAN infiltrations continued through late 1988. Despite its setbacks, SWAPO support among the Ovambo populations of northern Namibia continued to be strong, and, after independence, the former insurgents were voted into power in the new government.

SWAPOLCOIN *SWA/Namibia conflict.* This English abbreviation corresponds to SWAPOLTEIN in Afrikaans, and both refer to the South-West Africa Police Counterinsurgency wing. SWAPOLCOIN had three elements, including the COIN unit proper, known as Ops-K or 'Koevoet'; the SWAPOL Task Force, which patrolled the Botswana border; and an office that oversaw the recruitment, training, and employment of special constables.

Tactical group *Angolan conflict.* This FAPLA formation (in Portuguese: grupo tactico, GT) was a mechanised unit built around a BMP-1 company and support elements; it typically had about 300 personnel. GTs were fielded for the first time in 1987, but were commonly used for the first time in 1989 and were a critical part of the FAPLA force structure up to the 1991 ceasefire. Although some GTs were independent, attached directly to military zone headquarters, most were found in groups of two to four under task force headquarters. GTs, with their capability for rapid movement using the BMP-1s, were used to punch through UNITA defensive lines and allow slower infantry formations to exploit the breakthrough. Tanks could be added to GTs to provide extra firepower, but this usually slowed down the unit's advance.

Task force *Angolan and SWA/Namibia conflicts.* In SWA/Namibia: The use of task-organised forces in military operations has always been practised by South African forces. All major cross-border operations against SWAPO into Angola from SWA/Namibia have been undertaken by elements selected from a number of different unit headquarters and combined to make a force specially fitted for the task. These forces, which the SADF called by the English term 'task force', were usually built around a battalion or in some cases a brigade headquarters. The operations were characterised by high mobility and firepower, and were generally highly successful. By the mid-1980s the use of battalion-sized task forces of 800 to 1,000 men in mechanised and motorised formations was common for both the SADF and SWATF. In Angola: By contrast, FAPLA task forces were more standardised formations. The late 1980s were a period of extensive FAPLA reorganisation in the face of a growing UNITA threat. Consequently FAPLA began to experiment with task-organised forces, ultimately developing an organisation which would be highly mobile, logistically self-sustaining, and firepower-intensive. This formation, called a task force (in Portuguese: agrupamento), consisted of a headquarters that controlled a combat and support element base of about 300-400 personnel, plus two or more highly mobile mechanised elements called tactical groups (q.v.). After May 1990 an increasing number of task forces were formed, most of them from former FAPLA motorised brigades. At least one task force was employed by FAPLA in Cabinda in late 1990 against FLEC insurgents there. FAPLA's success rate for task forces was mixed. Some were effective, being composed of highly-trained and disciplined soldiers, but many formations were not very effective due to breakdowns in support and poor troop control.

Territorial Army *(Rhodesia) Rhodesian conflict.* The Territorial Army was the main vehicle for training National Servicemen (NSMs), who served as conscripts in the Rhodesian Army for a tour of eighteen months, as well as retraining former NSMs who had been called up for reserve duty. The principal unit to which these personnel were assigned was the Rhodesian Regiment (RR), in whose territo-rial battalions the personnel would train and serve when mobilised.

Territorial Forces *(Angola) Angolan conflict.* Territorial troops (tropas territoriais, TTs) were area-bound Army units that were under direct command of the local military district (later military zone), and who were responsible for area protection against UNITA. TTs were under the same national-level command as militia units and the two groups normally coordinated operations.

Territorial Force *(SWA/Namibia)* See Area Force.

UNITA *Angolan conflict.* The National Union for the Total Independence of Angola (in Portuguese: Uniao Nacional para e Independencia Total de Angola), headed by Dr Jonas Savimbi, has been one of the most successful insurgent movements in Africa. It was founded in 1966 and fought against Portuguese colonial rule; despite its defeat in 1975-1976 at the hands of Cuban troops assisting the MPLA, it regrouped and by the late 1970s had once again gone on the offensive. Its armed wing was FALA, the Armed Forces for the Liberation of Angola. Throughout the 1980s the movement grew and spread its area of control, inflicting, with South African help, a number of major defeats on government forces and finally forcing the MPLA government to a ceasefire in 1991. Since the breakdown of the election process and the outbreak of further hostilities in November 1990, UNITA has scored a number of successes against the MPLA and its forces, culminating in the defence of Huambo from January to March 1993. As of the time of writing UNITA controls over three-quarters of Angola and its operations continue to further restrict MPLA control to coastal areas and a few inland enclaves.

Chronology

THE FIRST ANGOLAN CIVIL WAR, 1975-1991: CHRONOLOGY

1974	April	Military coup in Portugal and announcement that Angola and other Portuguese possessions will be granted independence.
1975	October	Operation 'Savannah' begins, in which UNITA forces, backed by South Africa, capture two-thirds of Angola by November.
	November	MPLA, in possession of Luanda, becomes by default the recognised government of Angola and establishes the People's Republic of Angola (PRA).
1976	February	South African forces withdraw, followed by Cuban and MPLA defeat of UNITA and FNLA.
	March	Cuban-backed MPLA offensive against UNITA begins.
	May	Savimbi regroups UNITA forces on Cuanza River and begins a guerrilla war against the MPLA and Cubans.
1976-7		Continued MPLA and Cuban campaigns against UNITA in central and southern Angola.
1978	May	South African raid on SWAPO base areas, including Techamutete, initiates a long period of cross-border raids.
	May	FNLC guerrillas invade Zaire's Shaba province from bases in Angola in a second attack ('Shaba II'), prompting Zaire to support UNITA.
1979	December	Savimbi locates his capital at Jamba in Cuando Cubango.
1982-3		UNITA operations in Moxico push its zone of control to the Benguela Railway.
1983		UNITA begins operating north of the Benguela Railway.
	July-Sept	UNITA operations in Cuanza Sul province.
	August	Capture of Cangamba.
	November	UNITA campaigns to extend operations into north-west Angola and the Lundas, concluded April 1984.
	November	Reorganisation of FAPLA.
	December	Start of South African Operation 'Askari' in Cunene province against SWAPO; FAPLA and Cuban forces assisting SWAPO suffer defeats.
1984	March	UNITA capture of Sumbe on the Atlantic coast.
	March-April	UNITA operations in eastern Angola reach Zaire border.
	April-Oct	Two major FAPLA offensives against UNITA both fail.
1985	Aug-Oct	FAPLA Operation 'Second Congress' against Mavinga fails; South African assistance to UNITA a factor in defeating a FAPLA attack against Mavinga.
1986		Summer offensive by FAPLA on three fronts is generally unsuccessful despite increased Soviet and other communist country military assistance to FAPLA.
	August	South African Operation 'Alpha Centauri', in which FAPLA base at Cuito Cuanavale is heavily damaged, preventing it from staging an offensive against Mavinga.
1987	August	Initiation of another major FAPLA offensive against Mavinga.
	September	Initiation of South African Operation 'Modular' to counter FAPLA attack; major FAPLA defeats.
	Oct-Dec	Major battles between South Africans and FAPLA in south-eastern Angola; Operation 'Modular' evolves into Operation 'Hooper'; FAPLA driven back to Cuito Cuanavale.
1988	Jan-April	Siege of Cuito Cuanavale and involvement of Cuban troops in war; Operation 'Hooper' becomes Operation 'Packer'; Cuban advance south-

		ward toward Namibian border.
	April-July	Operation 'Displace' shifts South African troops to north-west Namibia.
	September	Withdrawal of South Africans from Angola.
1989	December	Following stalled peace negotiations, FAPLA launches Operation 'Final Assault' against Mavinga.
1990	Jan-May	FAPLA forces reach Mavinga and stall; UNITA begins major operations in northern Angola.
	May	FAPLA retreat from Mavinga; FAPLA establishes a separate Cuanza-Bengo Front to counter UNITA attacks north-east of Luanda.
	June-Aug	FAPLA attempts to dislodge UNITA from Uige and northern Malange provinces and disrupt UNITA bases east of Luanda.
1991	January	Capture of Munhango.
	March	Capture of Cuemba.
	April-May	Siege of Luena by UNITA.
	May	Ceasefire takes effect.

THE SECOND ANGOLAN CIVIL WAR, 1992-1995: CHRONOLOGY

1992	September	MPLA declared winner in general election tainted by fraud despite United Nations supervision.
	October	Fighting between UNITA and MPLA spreads throughout Angola.
	November	Fighting in Luanda; UNITA attacks urban centres; beginning of major civil conflict throughout Angola.
1993	January	UNITA in control of Uige, Negage, and Soyo; Huambo, Kuito, Malange, and Menongue put under siege.
	March	Huambo falls to UNITA; Soyo recaptured by FAA.
	May	UNITA recaptures Soyo; FAA fails to recapture Cuango Valley diamond areas.
	Aug-Nov	FAA advance on Huambo.
	September	UN security council embargo on arms and fuel to UNITA.
	November	Resumption of talks in Lusaka.
1994	Jan-Feb	Major FAA offensive in Bengo.
	March	Start of FAA offensive against Cuango Valley diamond area and Cafunfo.
	April-May	FAA offensive in Cuanza Norte and capture of Ndalatando.
	July	Cafunfo taken by FAA; siege of Kuito broken.
	September	FAA offensive in Huila.
	Oct-Nov	FAA offensive against Huambo, captured 6 November.
	November	Lusaka peace protocol signed on 16th.
	December	Fighting continues in north-eastern Angola.
1995	Jan-Feb	Fighting in Bengo, Uige, and Cuanza Norte provinces.

CHAD CIVIL WARS AND INSURGENCIES: CHRONOLOGY

1960	August	Chad independent.
1965	November	Riots in Mangalame in Guera mark beginning of insurgency.
1966	June	FROLINAT founded at Nyala, Sudan.
1968	August	Mutiny in Aozou of Nomad Guard and National Guard units.
1969	February	FROLINAT leader Ibrahim Abatcha killed in combat.
1971		Chad breaks relations with Libya, August; Libyan overt support to FROLINAT.
1972-3		Libya begins to deploy forces in Aozou Strip.
1975	April	Tombalbaye killed; Felix Malloum heads new government.
1976-7		FROLINAT gains in northern Chad.
1978	August	National Union Government with Malloum as President and Habré as Prime Minister.
1979	February	Civil war begins; Goukouni's forces enter Ndjamena.
1979-82		Period of civil war.
1980	May	French forces depart Chad.
	October	Goukouni requests military assistance from Libya.

	December	Libyan forces control Ndjamena.
1981	January	Goukouni and Qadhafi announce steps toward 'complete unity' between Chad and Libya; international outcry.
	Oct-Nov	Libyan forces depart Chad.
	December	Deployment of Inter-African Force in Chad.
1982	June	Habré's forces capture Ndjamena.
1983	January	Formation of FANT by Habré government.
	June-Aug	Fighting between Habré government and Libyan-backed GUNT in northern Chad.
	August	France initiates Operation 'Manta', deploying troops and aircraft in Chad; Libyan advance halted.
1984	August	Alphonse Kotiga leads southern commandos in a rebellion against the government.
	November	French troops of Operation 'Manta' depart Chad.
1986	February	Kotiga and his forces rally to the Habré regime, ending the southern rebellion.
	Feb-March	Libyan-backed GUNT attacks on FANT fail. France subsequently deploys troops and aircraft in Operation 'Epervier'.
	August	Rebellion of FAP troops in northern Chad against Libyan and other GUNT forces begins.
1987	January	Commencement of major FANT attacks against Libyan forces; Fada captured.
	March	Battles at Bir Kora and Ouadi Doum, captured by FANT.
	August	FANT attacks into Aozou Strip; Libyan counterattacks.
	September	FANT raid against Matan es-Sarra in Libya.
1989	March-April	Alleged coup plot and flight of Idris Deby to Sudan.
1990	Nov-Dec	Defeat of Habré and FANT by Deby's forces; flight of Habré and takeover of Chad by Deby and the MPS.
1991	December	Fighting between ANT and MDD around Lake Chad.
1992	Jan-June	Continued fighting in Lake Chad region.
1993-4		Unrest in southern Chad.
1994	February	International Court of Justice rules in Chad's favour in Aozou Strip dispute; Libyan troop withdrawal claimed in May 1994.

CHRONOLOGY OF EAST AFRICAN/HORN INSURGENCIES:

1974	Coup in Ethiopia; Emperor Haile Selassie I deposed and later killed; beginning of two decades of internal unrest and insurgency.
1976-7	Fighting between Ethiopia and Somalia; Ogaden war; power shift in Horn.
1979	Ethiopia/Eritrea: Failure of Ethiopian government forces to recapture Nakfa; start of territorial control of northern Eritrea by the EPLF.
	Uganda: Idi Amin overthrown and ultimately succeeded by Milton Obote as president.
1983	Sudan: Start of SPLM insurgency.
1986	NRM attains power in Uganda.
1987	Spread of Holy Spirit Movement (HSM) in northern Uganda.
1988	Eritrea: Major defeat of Ethiopian army at Af Abet by EPLF.
	Somalia: Start of SNM insurgency throughout north.
1989	Sudan: Coup puts NIF as power behind new regime.
1990	Eritrea: EPLF captures Massawa.
	Rwanda: RPF invasion.
	Somalia: Fall of Siad Barrç regime.
1991	Ethiopia: EPRDF overthrows Mengistu regime.
	Sudan: Major splits in SPLM lead to internecine fighting.
	Somalia: Formation of breakaway Somaliland Republic.
	Somalia: Beginning of civil war between USC factions.
	Djibouti: Start of FRUD insurgency (Afars).
1992	Sudan: Siege of Juba.
	Somalia: UN intervention.
1994	Rwanda: Civil war; widespread massacres; UN intervention.
1995	Sudan: Resurgence of SPLM.

MOZAMBIQUE INSURGENCY, 1975-1992: CHRONOLOGY

1975	June	Mozambique becomes independent with FRELIMO the ruling party; subsequently support is provided to Rhodesian and South African insurgent movements; internal dissent develops to FRELIMO policies.
1976		Broadcasts by clandestine Voz da Africa Libre at Gwelu to Mozambique; Rhodesians begin training Mozambican dissidents.
1977		Rhodesian SAS take over training of RENAMO, now headed by AndrÇ Matsangaisse.
1979	March	RENAMO attack near Beira.
	April	FAM attack on RENAMO camps in Gorongosa follows alleged RENAMO attack on Tete-Mutarara rail line.
	Sept-Nov	More FAM attacks on RENAMO camps in Gorongosa and surrounding area.
	October	Death of Matsangaisse at Gorongosa.
	December	RENAMO capture of Espungabera.
1980	February	RENAMO support infrastructure and radio clandestinely moved from Rhodesia to South Africa.
	May	Espungabera recaptured by RENAMO.
	July	FAM capture of Sitatonga headquarters of RENAMO.
	October	RENAMO sabotage of Umtali-Beira Railway.
	October	Security pact between Zimbabwe and Mozambique to counter RENAMO activity.
	November	RENAMO attack on Cabora Bassa power line.
1981	July-Aug	Renewal of widespread RENAMO military activity throughout central Mozambique; emergence of Afonso Dhlakama as president and successor to Matsangaisse.
	December	FAM capture of Garagua base in Manica.
1982	March	FAM reorganised.
	May	ZNA-assisted FAM operation to keep Beira corridor open.
1983	August	Major FAM offensives in Zambezia and in southern Mozambique.
1984	March	Signing of Nkomati Accord between South Africa and Mozambique, 16th; South African assurance that it will cease supporting RENAMO.
1985	July-Aug	Deployment of ZNA troops in Mozambique to provide support to FAM.
	Aug-Sept	Joint FAM-ZNA operation captures RENAMO HQ at Casa Banana, Gorongosa; other FAM operations target RENAMO base areas throughout Mozambique.
1986	February	RENAMO reoccupies Casa Banana.
	April	ZNA recaptures Casa Banana from RENAMO.
	October	President Machel killed in a plane crash near Maputo; RENAMO declares war on Zimbabwe for the latter's assistance to FRELIMO; RENAMO relocates its HQ to Zambezia province as a new major RENAMO offensive is launched from Malawi-Mozambique border area.
1987	Jan-March	Joint FAM-ZNA offensive in Zambezia recaptures lower Zambezi towns lost to RENAMO earlier.
	July-Oct	RENAMO operations in southern Mozambique; massacres at Homoine, Manjacaze, and Taninga.
1988	December	Mozambican government renews amnesty programme for RENAMO deserters.
1989	June	Mozambican government decision to liberalise political activy and commerce, and seek international mediation to conflict.
1990	July-Aug	RENAMO-FRELIMO negotiations in Rome begin peace process.
1992	August	Rome agreement calling for ceasefire on 1 October.

RHODESIA INSURGENCY CHRONOLOGY, 1962-1980

1962		First armed infiltration by ZAPU recorded.
1963		ZANU founded by ZAPU dissidents; first ZANLA recruits sent to PRC for training.

1964		First killings by ZANLA 'Crocodile Gang' of a white Rhodesian.
1965	November	Unilateral declaration of independence (UDI), with Ian Smith of the Rhodesia Front party as Prime Minister.
1966		Imposition of first UN sanctions.
	April	First major battle between security forces and insurgents at Sinoia.
	May	Viljoens killed by ZANU.
1967		Fighting at Wankie between security forces and mixed ZIPRA-ANC group.
1968	November	FRELIMO activity in Mozambique spreads to Tete province.
1969		ZANU-FRELIMO agreement to use Mozambican bases for raids into Rhodesia.
1970		FRELIMO activity crosses Zambezi River, extending the potential area of insurgent basing south along the Rhodesian border with Sofala province.
1972		First major infiltration into Rhodesia from Tete; ZANU establishes bases in north-east Rhodesia.
	December	Major upswing in war begins as Altena Farm is attacked.
		Operation 'Hurricane' zone established in north-east Rhodesia.
1973	September	First major SAS external operation (Macombe, in Mozambique).
1974	April	Coup in Portugal begins independence process for Mozambique, opening border to infiltration by ZANLA.
	November	Release of nationalist leaders from prison.
1975		Robert Mugabe becomes leader of ZANU.
1976		Major resumption of hostilities by ZANLA from bases in Tete, Manica, and Gaza.
	February	Operation 'Thrasher' (eastern highlands) begun.
	March	Mozambique border closed.
	May	Operation 'Repulse' (south-east) begun.
	August	Operation 'Tangent' (Botswana border) begun.
1977	March	Combined Operations (COMOPS) established.
	August	First ZANLA bombing in Salisbury.
	August	Operation 'Grapple' (Midlands) begun.
	November	Operation 'Dingo' against Chimoio area ZANLA bases.
1978	June	Operation 'Splinter' (Lake Kariba area) begun.
	September	ZIPRA shoot down a civilian passenger plane.
	October	Zambia reopens border.
1979		Rhodesian SAS begins training of Mozambican insurgents (RENAMO).
	February	Second passenger plane shot down by ZIPRA.
	June	First black African government installed in Rhodesia.
	September	Operation 'Uric' in Mozambique's Gaza province.
	September	External operations destroy infrastructure in Zambia and prevent ZIPRA 'invasion' of Rhodesia.
	December	Settlement agreement signed implementing Lancaster House Conference provisions.
1980	April	Zimbabwe becomes independent with Mugabe as its first Prime Minister.

RHODESIAN CROSS-BORDER OPERATIONS AGAINST ZIPRA

Operation name	Date	Intended target/remarks
Cross-border 'hot pursuit'	Feb 1978	ZANLA groups in Botswana.
'Elbow'	June 1978	Zambia/Kabanga Mission area.
'Gatling'	Oct 1978	Zambia/Mkushi Camp.
'Bastille'	13 Apr 1979	Zambia/Lusaka. Major raid that ended ZIPRA capabilites to invade Rhodesia.
'Dinky'	13 Apr 1979	Zambia/Botswana border area.
'Carpet'	26 June 1979	Zambia/Lusaka. Capture of ZIPRA NSO HQ.
'Chicory'	July 1979	Zambia/Lusaka. Destroyed ZIPRA arms depot at JZ Camp.
'Tepid'	October	Various sites in central/northern Zambia.

RHODESIAN CROSS-BORDER OPERATIONS AGAINST ZANLA

Operation name	Date	Intended target/remarks
'Dingo'	Nov 1977	Mozambique/Manica province, Chimoio area, ZANLA camps ('New Farm', aka Vanduzi or Chimoio). Camp destroyed; 2,000 ZANLA killed.
ZANLA barracks attack	May 1978	Mozambique/Tete city. 'Snoopy' Sept 1978 Mozambique/Manica province, Chimoio circle area.
'Shovel'	15 Dec 1978	Mozambique/Tete airfield and nearby RR net.
'Inhibit'	17 Dec 1978	Mozambique/south-eastern area.
'Neutron'	Feb-Mar 1979	Mozambique/Vanduzi Circle near Chimoio.
Beira fuel depot raid	23 Mar 1979	Mozambique/Beira.
'Bouncer'	Various in 1979	Mozambique/Maputo ZANLA HQ. Generally unsuccessful attempts to target key ZANLA leaders.
'Uric'	5-8 Sept 1979	Mozambique/Gaza province. Targets along Chicualacuala RR.
'Norah'	12 Sept 1979	Mozambique/infrastructure at Beira port.
Second Beira attack	18 Sept 1979	Beira port.
'Miracle'	Oct 1979	Mozambique/Chimoio area ZANLA camps. Major ground operation; camp destroyed but later reoccupied by ZANLA.
'Cheese'	12 Oct 1979	

RHODESIAN COIN STRUCTURE, 1978-1979

COMOPS NJOC	HQ Salisbury	**OPS 'Hurricane' (NE Mashonaland)**	
		JOC	HQ Salisbury
Rhodesian Army	HQ Salisbury	2 Brigade	HQ Salisbury
Armoured Car Regt		Sub-JOC	HQ Mount Darwin
Artillery Regt		Sub-JOC	HQ Bindura
Rhodesia Defence Regt		Sub-JOC	HQ Mtoko
Rhodesian Special Forces	HQ Salisbury	**'Salops' (Salisbury environs)**	
Selous Scouts		JOC	HQ Salisbury
Grey's Scouts			
Special Air Service		**OPS 'Tangent' (Matabeleland)**	
		JOC	HQ Bulawayo
Police	HQ Salisbury	1 Brigade	HQ Bulawayo
		Sub-JOC	HQ Wankie
Guard Force	HQ Salisbury	Sub-JOC	HQ Victoria Falls
		Sub-JOC	HQ Gwanda
OPS 'Thrasher' (Manicaland)			
JOC Thrasher	HQ Umtali	**OPS 'Grapple' (Midlands)**	
3 Brigade	HQ Umtali	JOC	HQ Gwelo
Sub-JOC	HQ Rusape	Sub-JOC	HQ Gokwe
Sub-JOC	HQ Grand Reef	Sub-JOC	HQ Gatooma
Sub-JOC	HQ Chipinga	Sub-JOC	HQ Enkeldoorn
OPS 'Repulse' (Victoria)		**OPS 'Splinter' (Kariba shoreline)**	
JOC	HQ Fort Victoria	JOC	HQ Kariba
4 Brigade	HQ Fort Victoria		
Sub-JOC	HQ Buffalo Range		
Sub-JOC	HQ Rutenga		
Sub-JOC	HQ Shabani		

SOUTH-WEST AFRICA INSURGENCY CHRONOLOGY, 1966-1990

1966	August	SWA police attack PLAN camp at Ongulumbashe and kill or apprehend the insurgents there following three infiltrations since September 1965.
	December	Major PLAN infiltration and recruiting campaign in Ovamboland and Caprivi; quickly suppressed by security forces.
1968	Jan-March	Major PLAN infiltrations into East Caprivi from Zambia countered by security forces.
	August	Two groups of PLAN enter Caprivi from Angola contained by year's end; this action effectively ends insurgent activity until early 1971.
1971	April	First mine incident recorded near Katima Mulilo.
1974	April	SADF assumes security responsibility for SWA border.
	April	Coup in Lisbon that leads to Angolan independence by November 1975.
	June	A number of Ovambo leaders, among them PLAN, flee SWA and relocate into Angola.
	June	First SADF casualty in SWA border war.
1975	April	First Cuban instructors for MPLA show up in Angola; subsequently Cuban weapons and supplies are recovered by SADF and SWA police from PLAN insurgents.
	August	SADF occupies Calueque and dam area.
	September	South African support to UNITA begins.
	October	Operation 'Savannah' initiated.
	November	Angola independent under the MPLA.
	December	PLAN begins operations with FAPLA/Cuban support and cover.
1976	January	Withdrawal of Operation 'Savannah' troops begins; completed in March.
	May	PLAN-initiated incidents begin to increase in frequency and intensity along the SWA border.
1977		PLAN begins construction of base camps north of SWA border.
	July	UNITA controls areas north of SWA border as far west as Cuangar.
	October	PLAN attempts large-scale penetrations in Ovambo; contained by security forces in battles that extend into Angola.
1978	May	Operation 'Reindeer' against Cassinga and Cunene PLAN installations.
	August	Katima Mulilo incident and subsequent SADF border strike into Zambia.
1979	March	Operations 'Rekstok' and 'Safraan' disrupts PLAN recovery from 1978 border strikes.
	December	UNITA established at Jamba in south-east Angola opposite Caprivi Strip.
1980	May	Operation 'Sceptic' initiated against Smokeshell and other PLAN complexes in Cunene.
	August	SWATF founded.
1981	August	Operation 'Protea' launched against PLAN sites in Cunene; establishment of a SADF-occupied area north of the SWA border.
	November	Operation 'Daisy' against Bambi and Cheraquera.
1982	March	Operation 'Super' north of Kakoland.
1983	February	Operation 'Phoenix' initiated, lasting through April.
	August	Claims of SADF involvement in the UNITA capture of Cangomba.
	December	Initiation of Operation 'Askari' (concludes 15 January).
1984	February	Lusaka Accords establish the JMC.
1985	May	JMC disbanded.
	June	Operation 'Boswilger'.
	September	Operation 'Egret'.
	September	Claims of SADF intervention in Angolan civil war near Mavinga.
1986	August	Major SADF intervention to assist UNITA at Cuito Cuanavale.
1987	August	Initiation of major FAPLA assault on UNITA.
	September	Operation 'Modular' opened to support UNITA.
1988	March	Movement of Cuban troops to SWA border in Cunene.
	June	SADF/SWATF force defeats Cubans and FAPLA at Techipa.
	July	New York Accords providing for Namibian independence as well as a schedule for Cuban troop withdrawal from Angola.
	August	Withdrawal of South African forces from Angola completed.
1989	April-May	Security forces defeat last PLAN incursion.
1990	March	Namibian independence; SWAPO government installed.

SOUTH-WEST AFRICA: COIN STRUCTURE AND UNITS IN THE BORDER OPERATIONAL AREA, MID- TO LATE 1980S

10 Sector	HQ Oshakati	*20 Sector*	HQ Rundu
101 Battalion	HQ Ondangwa	201 Battalion	HQ Omega Base
102 Battalion	HQ Opuwa	202 Battalion	HQ Rundu
1 SWASPES	HQ Oshakati (Otavi)	203 Battalion	HQ Luhebu
51 Battalion	HQ Ruacana	55 Battalion	HQ Nepara
52 Battalion	HQ Oshakati	32 Battalion	HQ Buffalo Camp
53 Battalion	HQ Ondangwa	SWAPOL	Regional HQ Rundu
54 Battalion	HQ Eenhana	SWAPOLCOIN	Sub-HQ Rundu
61 Mechanised	HQ Omathiya		
	(Oshivelo)	*70 Sector*	HQ Katima Mulilo
	Battalion Group	701 Battalion	HQ Mpacha
		Armoured Car Sqn	HQ Mpacha
SWAPOLCOIN	HQ Oshakati	Artillery Bty	HQ Mpacha
	Sub-HQ Opuwa	SWAPOL	Regional HQ Katima Mulilo

251

Appendix 1

Principal African Insurgent Factions and Groups, 1975 to Date

Overcoming the alphabet soup of abbreviations and acronyms is but one hurdle for the student of African conflicts. An even greater challenge is met in attempting to understand the intricacies of insurgent movements – their ethnic and political basis, leadership, and agendas. In a few cases, such as Angola or Mozambique, there are only a few insurgent organisations. Usually, though, the situation is much more complex. Many groups have split into factions, some of which have emerged as entirely new groupings. In other cases the national armed forces, defeated by the insurgents, degenerate into a faction themselves. This was the case in Chad and Liberia. In the following table I have attempted to group the various insurgent entities as logically as possible, supplied a few explanatory notes, and where I felt necessary referred the reader to more complete discussions.

ANGOLA

Frente Nacional de Libertacao de Angola (National Front for the Liberation of Angola), FNLA
Founded: 1962.
Leadership/major personalities: Holden Roberto, Daniel Chipenda.
Ethnic basis: Primarily Kongo, the movement had connections to the Uniao das Populacoes do Norte do Angola, UPNA, founded in 1957.
Armed element: Exercito Nacional de Libertacao de Angola (National Army for the Liberation of Angola), ENLA.
Agenda: Pre-1975, independence of Angola from Portugal; post-1975, anti-MPLA.
Factionalisation: Major split between Roberto and Chipenda in 1975-1976.

Frente de Libertacao do Enclave de Cabinda (Front for the Liberation of the Enclave of Cabinda), FLEC
Founded: 1963 from three smaller movements, MLEC, CUNCC, and Alliama.
Leadership/major personalities: Luis Ranque Franque, Henriques Nzita Tiago, Antonio Eduardo Sozinho, Auguste Tchioufou.
Ethnic basis: Cabinda (primarily Kongo).

Armed element: Each FLEC group had its own armed element, that of FLEC-FAC perhaps being the largest in the late 1980s.
Agenda: Separatist, i.e, independence or autonomy for Cabinda.
Factionalisation: The movement, riven by internal disputes, split after Angolan independence into a number of splinter groups, the most important of which are:

Front for the Liberation of the Enclave of Cabinda/Original
Leadership/major personalities: Luis Ranque Franque.
Ethnic basis: Cabindan.
Agenda: Separatist.

Front for the Liberation of the Enclave of Cabinda/Renovada (FLEC/R)
Leadership/major personalities: Jose Tiburcio Zinga Bumba.
Ethnic basis: Cabindan.
Agenda: Separatist.

Front for the Liberation of the Enclave of Cabinda/Armed Forces of Cabinda (FLEC/FAC)
Leadership/major personalities: Henriques Tiago Nzita.
Ethnic basis: Cabindan.
Agenda: Separatist.

Uniao Nacional para Independenca Total de Angola (National Union for the Total Independence of Angola), UNITA
Founded: 1964.
Leadership/major personalities: Dr Jonas Savimbi.
Ethnic basis: Mixed, but Savimbi's Ovimbundu ethnic group held many important positions.
Armed element: Forcas Armadas de Libertacao de Angola (FALA).
Agenda: Pre-1975, independence of Angola from Portugal; post-1975, end to government alliance with Soviet/East bloc countries and withdrawal of Cuban troops from Angola.
Factionalisation: Negligible, with the most significant known dissident move, that of Tito Chingunji and Wilson dos Santos in

the late 1980s, suppressed with little difficulty.

BURUNDI

Conseil National pour la Défense de la Démocratie (CNDD)
Founded: 1993.
Leadership/major personalities: Leonard Nyangoma.
Armed element: Forces pour la Défense de la Démocratie (FDD).
Agenda: Replacement of Burundi government by a Hutu regime.
Factionalisation: PALIPEHUTU expelled from CNDD in January 1995; CNDD itself is a breakaway movement from the Front pour Démocratie en Burundi (FRODEBU) party that began armed action against the Burundi government following the assassination of President Ndadaye which later formed an umbrella organisation of Hutu resistance parties.

Front de Libération Nationale (FROLINA)
Founded: 1993.
Leadership/major personalities: Joseph Karumba.
Agenda: Replacement of Burundi government by Hutu regime.
Factionalisation: None.

Parti pour la Libération du Peuple Hutu (PALIPEHUTU)
Founded: 1972
Armed element: Forces de Libération Nationale (FLN).
Agenda: Extreme Hutu nationalist movement.
Factionalisation: None.

CHAD

Of all the African countries afflicted by insurgency, Chad holds the record for the number and variety of its insurgent movements. The original FROLINAT, founded in 1966 from a number of already pre-existing dissident groups, soon split into various fighting factions. Most of the military history of Chad in 1985 was marked by fighting between FROLINAT factions and splinter groups and the Chadian Army (FAT) and its various successor groups. However, in the late 1980s and into the 1990s a number of new groups emerged, listed below. The listing here supplements Appendix B of *Chad: A Country Study*, 2nd edition, 1990, pp. 219ff. See also Decalo, *Historical Dictionary of Chad*, for details of the late 1970s insurgent movements.

FROLINAT and its descendants to the late 1970s

Front National pour la Libération du Tchad (FROLINAT)
Founded: 1966 in Sudan from three pre-existing groups (the Mouvement National de Libération Tchadien, MNLT, of Hassan Ahmed Moussa; the Union Nationale Tchadienne, UNT, of Mahamat Ousman, Abba Siddick, and Ibrahim Abatcha; and the Association des Enfants du Tchad, based in Cairo).
Leadership/major personalities: Ibrahim Abatcha, Abba Siddick, Mahamat Ousman, and Hassan Ahmed Moussa.
Ethnic basis: Originally a confederation of northern ethnic groups.
Armed element: FROLINAT Liberation Army.
Agenda: The 1966 FROLINAT platform (see text).
Factionalisation: The movement began to see its first major divisions in the early 1970s, and by the middle of the decade the FROLINAT groups in the Tibesti area and nearby had begun to be affiliated with the Toubou ethnic groups there. The main split took place in 1971 when Goukouni Oueddei and Abba Siddick took their factions their own separate ways.

Principal FROLINAT groupings and their descendants to the late 1970s

Première Armée de Libération du FROLINAT ('FROLINAT First Army')
Founded: This was FROLINAT's original Liberation Army.
Leadership/major personalities: Ibrahim Abatcha, General Mohamed Baghalani, Abba Siddick.
Ethnic basis: Eastern Chadian groups, dominated by Arabs.
Armed element: See also the 'Volcan Armies' below.
Factionalisation: After Baghalani's 1977 death, First Army personnel joined either the First Volcan Army of Adoum Dana or the New Volcan of Acyl Ahmat.

Première Armée Volcan (First Volcan Army)
Founded: 1977.
Leadership/major personalities: Adoum Dana.
Ethnic basis: Arabs from central Chad.
Agenda: Pro-Libyan

Nouveau Volcan (New Volcan)
Founded: 1977.
Leadership/major personalities: Acyl Ahmat.
Ethnic basis: Arab, especially Awlad Suleiman.
Agenda: Pro-Libyan, anti-Habré; predecessor of CDR (see below).

Conseil Démocratique Révolutionnaire (Democratic Revolutionary Council), CDR

Founded: 1978.

Leadership/major personalities: Acyl Ahmat (founder), Achiek ibn Oumar.

Ethnic basis: Arabs from Ouaddai or Batha prefectures.

Agenda: Pro-Libyan, anti-Habré; oppose Toubou factions in GUNT.

Deuxième Armée de Libération du FROLINAT ('FROLINAT Second Army')

Founded: Organised by Mahamat Ali Taher in 1968 who arrived in the Tibesti to unite anti-regime opposition there.

Leadership/major personalities: Goukouni Oueddei, Hissein Habré.

Ethnic basis: Toubou.

Agenda: FROLINAT organisation for the Toubou of the BET.

Factionalisation: The Toubou groups within the Second Army split along internal lines, following Goukouni (Teda) or Habré (Daza), who formed the FAP and the FAN respectively.

Conseil de Commandement des Forces Armées du Nord (Command Council of the Northern Armed Forces), CCFAN

Founded: 1971.

Leadership/major personalities: Goukouni Oueddei, Hissein Habré.

Ethnic basis: Toubou.

Forces Armées Populaires (Popular Armed Forces, FAP)

Founded: 1972

Leadership/major personalities: Goukouni Oueddei.

Ethnic basis: Toubou, primarily Teda.

Forces Armées du Nord (Northern Armed Forces, FAN)

Founded: 1976.

Leadership/major personalities: Hissein Habré.

Ethnic basis: Toubou, primarily Daza.

Troisième Armée de Libération du FROLINAT ('FROLINAT Third Army')

Founded: 1975.

Leadership/major personalities: Aboubaker Abderrahmane.

Ethnic basis: Kanembu.

Agenda: The FROLINAT element representing the peoples of Kanem prefecture and adjacent areas

Factionalisation: The group later changed its name to the Popular Movement for the Liberation of Chad (MPLT, see below); later a splinter group, the Western Armed Forces (FAO) emerged.

Mouvement Populaire pour la Libération du Tchad (Popular Movement for the Liberation of Chad), MPLT

Founded: Renamed c. 1977.

Ethnic basis: Kanembu.

Forces Armées Occidentales (Western Armed Forces), FAO

Founded: 1979.

Leadership/major personalities: Moussa Medela.

Ethnic basis: Kanembu.

Chadian Armed Forces and factional groups to 1986

Forces Armées Tchadiennes (Chadian Armed Forces), FAT

Founded 1960 as the national army of Chad. It emerged as a faction in 1979 following its defeat at Ndjamena and withdrawal to the south.

Leadership/major personalities: Colonel Wadal Abdelkader Kamougue.

Ethnic basis: Sara and other southern ethnic groups.

Armed element: 3,500 or so in 1980-1981.

Agenda: Support southern interests as a member of a national coalition government and defend its holdings in southern Chad.

Factionalisation: After the 1982 defeat and exile of Kamougue, some FAT rallied to Habré while others formed local factions in the south as 'commandos' or 'codos'.

Commandos ('Codos')

Founded: Emerged in 1982 following the defeat and subsequent disintegration of the FAT.

Leadership/major personalities: Colonel Alphonse Kotiga.

Ethnic basis: Sara and other southern ethnic groups.

Armed elements: Armed elements rallying to the regime as of 1986 totalled 14,000.

Agenda: Represent southern interests; defend local areas in the south against attempts by the regime to occupy them.

Factionalisation: The codos tended to be fairly coherent groups at the local level but eventually all rallied to the regime by 1986 following Kotiga's reconciliation with Habré in February of that year. Major commando elements included the Red Commando, Green Commando, the Commandos of Hope, the Green Eagle Commando, the Black Commando, and the Coconut Palm Commando; these united under Kotiga in January 1985. There were a number of additional groups as well, but of minor importance.

Dissident groups from the late 1989s through the mid-1990s

In the wake of Habré's victory over the Libyans and their Chadian surrogates, little opposition remained. However, there were a few dissident movements still active in Chad.

Mouvement pour la Salut National du Tchad (Movement for the National Salvation of Chad), MOSANAT

Founded: In Ndjamena in October 1986.
Leadership/major personalities: Lieutenant Moldom Bada, Godi Donanga.
Ethnic basis: Hadjerai, Boulala, Baguirmi, and other ethnic groups in Guera prefecture.
Armed element: 2,000.
Agenda: Resistance to Habré regime; vague programme of political reform.

Mouvement Patriotique du Salut (Patriotic Salvation Movement), MPS

Founded: 1989; renamed 1990.
Leadership/major personalities: Idris Deby.
Ethnic basis: Zaghawa and Bideyat.
Armed element: 2,000 members of the Forces Patriotiques du Salut in October 1990.
Agenda: Opposition to Habré regime by military force; democratic reform.

Following the ousting of Habré by Deby in 1990 a number of new insurgent groups began to form, with the first significant activity, that of the MDD, beginning in late 1991. Subsequently a number of additional groups emerged. No comprehensive study of the groups has yet been made, but the dissidents as of mid-/late 1994 are discussed by Geraldine Faes: 'Tchad: La Carte de la Rebellion', *Jeune Afrique*, No. 1766, 10-16 November 1994, pp. 22-3.

Front National Tchadien (Chadian National Front), FNT

Leadership/major personalities: Dr Ali Harris Bachar (Executive Secretary), Ibrahim Zahab (military CoS).
Ethnic basis: Ethnic groups in the Ouaddai prefecture.
Armed element: Consisted of about 1,100 in early 1994.
Agenda: Anti-Deby, and an ally of other opposition movements (with the exception of Habré's).

Comité National de Redressement du Tchad (National Committee for the Redress for Chad), CNRT

Leadership/major personalities: Abbas Koti, its former leader, was killed on 24 October 1993 at Ndjamena a few weeks after rallying to the government; his brother Hissene later took his place.

Ethnic basis: Zaghawa, other groups in Bilitne and Lac prefectures.
Armed element consisted of several hundred personnel in late 1994.
Agenda: Seek union with the FNT and the MDD against Deby's regime.

Comité de Sursaut National pour la Paix et la Démocratie (Committee of National Revival for Peace and Democracy, CSNPD)

Founded: 1992.
Leadership/major personalities: Lieutenant (later Colonel) Moise Nodji Kette.
Ethnic basis: Southern Chadian ethnic groups.
Armed element: Numbered perhaps as many as 1,000.
Agenda: Protest over government actions against Chadian Human Rights activists; opposition to government slowness in making democratic reforms.

Mouvement pour la République Federal (Movement for a Federal Republic), MRF

Founded: 1994.
Leadership/major personalities: Laokein Barde.
Ethnic basis: Sara and other populations in Logone oriental.
Armed element: Believed to be about 2,000 or so in late 1994: Forces Armées pour la République Fédéral (FARF).
Agenda: Seeking union with other groups to resist the regime; represent southern Chadian ethnic interests, primarily Sara.

Mouvement pour la Démocratie et le Développement (Movement for Democracy and Development), MDD

Founded: 1991.
Leadership/major personalities: Issa Moussa Medela (President), Brahim Ala, Adoum Yacoub, Goukouni Guet (killed 1993), Barkaye Oguy (killed 1992).
Ethnic basis: Kanembu groups (MDD-Medela), Toubous formerly allied with Habré regime (MDD-Habré).
Armed element: Consisted of 3,000-4,000 in the Lake Tchad region and in Cameroon.
Agenda: The Medela faction's objective was to bargain for major guarantees of security before agreeing to rally to the Deby regime; the MDD-Habré supporters remained hostile to the central government with the aim of maintaining resistance, but had little hope of finding any other pro-Habré groups in opposition to Deby's regime.
Factionalisation: The two main groupings were MDD-Medela, which held out for ultimate reconciliation with the regime, and MDD-Habré, led by Adoum Yacoub, which remained hostile to it.

DJIBOUTI

Front pour la Restauration de l'Unité et de la Démocratie (Front for the Restoration of Unity and Democracy), FRUD

Founded: 1991 from three pre-existing Afar nationalist groups, the Action pour la Revision de l'Ordre Ô Djibouti (AROD), the Front des Forces Démocratiques (FFD), and the Union pour la Démocratie et de la Justice Sociale (UDJS).

Leadership/major personalities: Adoyta Youssef, Abbate Ebo Adou, Ahmed Dini (chairman), Ali Mohamed Daoud (chairman after March 1994).

Ethnic basis: Afar.

Agenda: Autonomy for Afar region; equality for Djibouti Afar population.

Factionalisation: A major split in the movement emerged in March 1994, when Ougoureh Kifleh Ahmed formed a faction advocating negotiated settlement; reconciliation was made with the mainstream and Ali Mohamed Daoud was elected chairman. At this, Ahmed Dini, head of the Addis Ababa-based faction of FRUD, split and formed a separate faction.

ETHIOPIA

The Horn of Africa was awash with insurgent groups in the 1980s. I have grouped the main insurgent factions according to their regional/ethnic orientation. Splinter groups existed for most, and they remain extremely hard to track.

Eritrean Groups

Eritrean People's Liberation Front (EPLF)
Ethnic basis: Eritrean.

Armed element: Eritrean People's Liberation Army (EPLA).

Agenda: Independence for Eritrea; Marxist through late 1980s.

Factionalisation: EPLF-PLF broke away.

Eritrean Liberation Front (ELF)
Ethnic basis: Eritrean.

Agenda: Independence for Eritrea, but prepared to settle for autonomy.

Factionalisation: Subsequent to 1978 offensive lost many members to the EPLF.

Eritrean Liberation Front-Popular Liberation Forces (ELF-PLF)
Ethnic basis: Eritrean.

Agenda: Independence for Eritrea.

Somali Groups

Western Somali Liberation Front (WSLF)
Ethnic basis: Somali, primarily Ogadeni.

Agenda: Reunion of Somali areas of Ethiopia with Somalia.

Somali Democratic Salvation Front (SDSF)
Ethnic basis: Somali, heavily Majertain.

Agenda: Majertain autonomy.

Somali-Abo Liberation Front (SALF)
Ethnic basis: Somali.

Agenda: Union with Somalia.

Issa and Gurgura Liberation Front (IGLF)
Founded: 1991

Ethnic basis: Issa clan family (Somali); Gurgura.

Agenda: Local autonomy for Issa and Gurgura inside Ethiopia; opposition to dominance of Issa in Djibouti by the Mamasan.

Afar Groups

Afar Liberation Front (ALF)
Leadership/major personalities: Sultan Ali Mireh.

Ethnic basis: Ethiopian Afars.

Agenda: Afar autonomy.

Factionalisation: The ALF, founded by Sultan Ali Mireh of Asahita, remained relatively quiescent during the 1980s and consisted of regional groupings. Most had no territorial ambitions outside Afar territory, and the Ethiopian central government, which never fully controlled the Danakil and other Afar regions, generally left them unmolested as long as access to the port of Aseb was not interfered with.

Afar National Liberation Movement (ANLM)
Ethnic basis: Ethiopian Afars.

Agenda: Afar autonomy; Marxist entity.

Other Groups

Tigray People's Liberation Front (TPLF)
Ethnic basis: Tigrean.

Armed element: Tigray People's Liberation Army (TPLA).

Agenda: Autonomy for Tigray region.

Ethiopian People's Revolutionary Democratic Front (EPRDF)
Ethnic basis: Mixed, but dominated by Tigray groups from the TPLF.

Armed element: Ethiopian People's Revolutionary Democratic Army (EPRDA).

Agenda: Overthrow of Mengistu regime and replacement with a revolutionary government.

Ethiopian People's Revolutionary Party (EPRP)
Ethnic basis: Tigray and Gonder.

Armed element: Ethiopian People's Revolutionary Army (EPRA).
Agenda: Overthrow of Mengistu regime and replacement with a revolutionary government.

Ethiopian Democratic Union (EDU)
Ethnic basis: Various, but heavily represented by Tigray, Gonder, Gojjam.
Agenda: Overthrow of Mengistu regime and replacement with a democratic government.

Oromo Groups

Oromo Liberation Front (OLF)
Ethnic basis: Oromo.
Agenda: Autonomy for Oromo areas.
Factionalisation: The OLF was a diffuse, far-flung organisation of a number of regional groups, many with differing local agendas. It survived the fall of the Mengistu regime only to rapidly expand and then factionalise along regional and agenda lines.

LIBERIA

National Patriotic Front of Liberia (NPFL)
Founded: 1989 (though some organising of the resistance had taken place earlier).
Leadership/major personalities: Charles Gankay Taylor, Tom Woweiyu.
Ethnic basis: Nimba County ethnic groups, especially Gio and Mano.
Agenda: Overthrow of Doe regime; establishment of NPFL rule in Liberia with Taylor as president; anti-ECOMOG.
Factionalisation: Major splits took place in 1994, following defeats by ULIMO.

Independent National Patriotic Front of Liberia (INPFL)
Founded: 1990.
Leadership/major personalities: Prince Yormie Johnson.
Ethnic basis: Various, but included a number of Johnson's followers from the NPFL.
Agenda: Anti-ECOMOG; attempted power broker between ECOMOG and NPFL.

United Liberation Movement (ULIMO)
Founded: 1991.
Leadership/major personalities: Raleigh Seekie, Albert Karpeh, Roosevelt Johnson, Alhaji Kromah.
Ethnic basis: Krahn and Mandingo.
Agenda: Anti-NPFL; support the formation of a national unity government.
Factionalisation: By late 1992 a split took place between the Krahns, led by Roosevelt Johnson, and the Mandingos, led by

Kromah; by late 1993 the split was irreconcilable (see below).

ULIMO-Johnson Faction (ULIMO-J)
Emerged: 1993.
Leadership/major personalities: Roosevelt Johnson.
Ethnic basis: Krahn.
Agenda: Anti-NPFL.

ULIMO-Kromah Faction (ULIMO-K)
Emerged: 1993.
Leadership/major personalities: Alhaji Kromah.
Ethnic basis: Mandingo.
Agenda: Anti-NPFL.

Lofa Defence Force, LDF
Founded: 1993.
Ethnic basis: Lofa County ethnic groups.

Liberian Peace Council (LPC) (aka National Peace Council)
Founded: 1993.
Ethnic basis: Krahn.
Agenda: Represent Krahn interests in any peace settlement.

Armed Forces of Liberia (AFL)
Emerged: As a separate faction in late 1991 following the death of President Doe.
Leadership/major personalities: Hezekiah Bowen, Moses Wright.
Ethnic basis: Krahn and allied groups.
Agenda: Support IGNU.
Factionalisation: From late 1993 many AFL personnel left the force to join the LPC.

MALI

Front Islamique Arabe de l'Azaouad (Arab Islamic Front of the Azawad) (FIAA)
Founded: 1990
Leadership/major personalities: Ahmed Ould Sidi Ahmed; Zahabi Ould Sidi Mohamed; Moulaye Souleymane (former POLISARIO Front officer and commander of the FIAA armed element).
Ethnic basis: Tuareg; some Saharawis, including Arabs.
Armed element: 2,000 or so under command of Moulaye Souleymane; based in Mauritania.
Agenda: Attracted Tuaregs with strict Muslim views; had links with other conservative organisations.

Mouvement Populaire de l'Azaouad (Popular Movement of the Azawad) (MPA)
Founded: 1990.
Leadership/major personalities: Iyad Ag Ghali, Bilal Salloum.
Ethnic basis: Tuareg.

Armed element: Based in northern/north-east Mali; c. 1,500 or so under Iyad Ag Ghali.

Front Populaire de la Libération de l'Azaouad (Popular Front for the Liberation of the Azawad) (FPLA)
Founded: 1991.
Leadership/major personalities: Rhissa Ag Sidi Mohamed (Secretary-General); Youssouf Harish.
Ethnic basis: Tuareg.
Armed element: About 1,500, including some former POLISARIO Front fighters; leadership based in Burkina Faso.

Armée Révolutionnaire de Libération de l'Azaouad (Revolutionary Army for the Liberation of the Azawad) (ARLA)
Founded: 1991.
Ethnic basis: Tuareg.

Mouvements et Fronts Unifés de l'Azaouad (Unified Movements and Fronts of the Azawad) (MFUA)
Founded: 1991.
Ethnic basis: Tuareg.
Armed element: Included at least 1,500 active fighters.
Agenda: Implementation of the Mopti Accord.
Factionalisation: Formed in 1991 from MPA, FIAA, and ARLA.

Mouvement Patriotique Malien Ghanda Koy (Patriotic Malian Ganda Khoy Movement) (MPM) aka Ghanda Koy
Founded: 1994.
Ethnic basis: Songhai and allied ethnic groups.
Agenda: Anti-Tuareg militia action.

MOZAMBIQUE

Resistencia Nacional de Mocambique (National Resistance of Mozambique) (RENAMO)
Founded: 1977.
Leadership/major personalities (internal): André Matsangaisse, Afonso Dhlakama.
Leadership/major personalities (external): Jorge Jardim, Orlando Christina, Domingos Arouca.
Ethnic basis: Varied, but Ndau dominated most higher ranks of the organisation.
Armed element: Peaked at 18,000-20,000 in the late 1980s.
Agenda: Overthrow of central FRELIMO government.

Naprama
Founded: 1989.
Leadership/major personalities: Manuel Antonio.

Ethnic basis: Nampula province ethnic groups.
Agenda: Generally anti-RENAMO, pro-FRELIMO.

Uniao Nacional de Mocambique (Mozambican National Union) (UNAMO)
Founded: 1986.
Leadership/major personalities: Drawn from CUNIMO; includes Gimo M'Phiri, Gilberto Magid Fernandes, Marcelo Cardoso, Carlos Reis.
Ethnic basis: Zambezia-based groups.
Agenda: Nationalist; both anti-RENAMO and anti-FRELIMO, 'third-party' alternative to both; recognised in 1990 as a legitimate political entity by the government.

Commte de Uniao de Mocambique (Committee for Mozambican Union) (CUNIMO)
Founded: 1986.
Leadership/major personalities: Artur Vilankulu.
Ethnic basis: Various: CUNIMO stressed its role as an umbrella organisation.
Agenda: 'Third party' in Mozambique peace process.
Factionalisation: The movement fell prey within a short time to the ethnic and regional agendas of its various component groups; some, with most of the leadership, went on to form UNAMO.

NIGER

Front National pour la Libération de Niger (National Front for the Liberation of Niger) (FNLN)
Leadership/major personalities: Abdoulaye Diori, Kamed Moussa.
Ethnic basis: Tuareg.
Armed element: Reportedly backed by Libya.

Front pour la Libération de l'Air et de l'Azaouad (Front for the Liberation of the Air and the Azawad) (FLAA)
Founded: 1991.
Leadership/major personalities: Rhissa Ag Boula, Mohamed Moussa, Mano Dayak.
Ethnic basis: Tuareg.
Factionalisation: Spilt in mid-1993 between Mano Dayak faction of the FLAA and the new FLT (see below) of Rhissa Ag Boula.

Armée Révolutionaire pour la Libération du Nord-Niger (Revolutionary Army for the Liberation of Northern Niger) (ARLN)
Founded: 1993.
Leadership/major personalities: Attaher Abdoulmoumin and other FLAA breakaways.
Ethnic basis: Tuareg.

Coordination de la Résistance Armée (Coordination of Armed Resistance) (CRA)
Founded: 1993.
Ethnic basis: Tuareg.
Factionalisation: Formed by the FLAA, ARLN, and FLT as a negotiating body.

Front de Libération de Tamoust (Front for the Liberation of Tamoust) (FLT)
Founded: 1993.
Leadership/major personalities: Rhissa Ag Boula.
Ethnic basis: Tuareg.

Front Patriotique de Libération du Sahara (Patriotic Front for the Liberation of the Sahara) (FPLS)
Founded: 1994.
Ethnic basis: Tuareg.

RHODESIA/ZIMBABWE

Zimbabwe Africa People's Union (ZAPU)
Founded: 1961.
Leadership/major personalities: Joshua Nkomo.
Ethnic basis: Ndebele.
Armed element: Zimbabwe People's Liberation Army (ZIPRA).
Agenda: Overthrow of white Rhodesian government and replacement by a black nationalist regime.

Zimbabwe Africa National Union (ZANU)
Founded: 1963.
Leadership/major personalities: Reverend Ndabaningi Sithole, Robert Mugabe.
Ethnic basis: Shona.
Armed element: Zimbabwe African National Liberation Army (ZANLA).
Agenda: Overthrow of white Rhodesian government and replacement by a black nationalist regime.

Front for the Liberation of Zimbabwe (FROLIZI)
Founded: 1971.
Ethnic basis: Mixed.
Agenda: Overthrow of white Rhodesian government and replacement by a black nationalist regime; sought to be an umbrella movement, especially with exiles; supported by Zambia.
Factionalisation: FROLIZI soon fell victim to the ethnic factionalisation that beset other movements.

Zimbabwe People's Army (ZIPA)
Founded: 1976.
Ethnic basis: Mixed.
Agenda: Overthrow of white Rhodesian government and replacement by a black nationalist regime; sought to unify ZAPU and ZANU members hitherto at odds with one another.
Factionalisation: ZIPA proved ineffective after failing to reconcile ethnic differences between Ndebele and Shona members.

RWANDA

Front Patriotique Rwandais/Rwandan Patriotic Front (FPR/RPF)
Founded: 1987 from the Rwandese Alliance for National Unity (RANU).
Leadership/major personalities: Fred Rwigyema, Peter Bayingana, Chris Bunyenyezi, Paul Kagame.
Ethnic basis: Tutsi, although the movement claimed not to have an ethnic basis.
Armed element: Armée Patriotique Rwandais/ Rwandan Patriotic Army (APR/RPA).
Agenda: Repatriation of Rwandan refugees, especially Tutsi exiles, and equal rights for both ethnic groups.

Le Peuple en Armes pour Libérer le Rwanda (PALIR)
Founded: 1996.
Leadership/major personalities: Hutu exiles in Zaire based at Cyangugu.
Agenda: Hutu nationalist movement advocating the overthrow by force of the RPF government in Kigali.
Factionalisation: None, although the movement may represent an umbrella organisation that includes militias and groups with a range of agendas.

SENEGAL

Mouvement des Forces Démocratiques de la Casamance (Movement of the Democratic Forces of the Casamance) (MFDC)
Founded: Became an armed insurgent movement in 1993.
Leadership/major personalities: Abbé Augustin Diamacoune Senghor, Sidi Badiji.
Ethnic basis: Diola.
Armed element included at its height probably no more than 1,000 active insurgents.
Agenda: Casamance separatists.
Factionalisation: By 1992 a split had developed between the 'Front Nord' of Sidi Badiji and the 'Front Sud' of Diamacoune Senghor (based in Guinea-Bissau).

SIERRA LEONE

Revolutionary United Front (RUF)
Founded: 1991.

Leadership/major personalities: Foday Sankoh.
Ethnic basis: Various.
Agenda: Vague anti-regime agenda.
Factionalisation: RUF's vague anti-regime agenda and the regionalisation of activities has led to the existence of various agendas for local commanders as well as heavy bandit activity.

SOMALIA

Somalia's numerous factions have figured prominently in news accounts of the 1990s. However, through late 1990 there were only four main anti-regime factions to speak of. They are listed here, with later groups following.

Somali insurgent factions emerging through late 1989

Somali National Movement (SNM; in Somali, Midnimadda Dhaqdhaqaaqa Soomaliyeed, or MDS)
Founded: 1981.
Leadership/major personalities: Hassan Adan Wadadi, Ahmed Ismail Abdi, Mohammed Egal.
Ethnic basis: Isaak clan family.
Agenda: Advocacy of neutral political stance by regime in world affairs; against ethnic discrimination toward northern Somalis; later favoured secession.
Factionalisation: The SNM presided over the 1991 formation of the independent Somaliland Republic. However, the latter has continued to be beset by internal dissension by various Isaak clans.

Somali Salvation Democratic Front (SSDF; in Somali, Jabhada Babaadinta Demogratiga Soomaliyeed, JBDS)
Founded: 1976.
Leadership/major personalities: Abdullahi Yusuf Ahmad, Osman Nur Ali.
Ethnic basis: Majertain clan family.
Agenda: Opposition to Siad regime; later secessionist, forming a de facto state from 1989 in north-east Somalia.

Somali Patriotic Movement (SPM; in Somali, Dhaqdhaqaaqa Wadaniyinta Soomaliyeed, DWS)
Founded: 1989.
Leadership/major personalities: Ahmad Omar Jess, Omar Moallem.
Ethnic basis: Ogadeni.
Agenda: Anti-Siad.

United Somali Congress (USC; in Somali, Golaha Midnimadda Soomaliyed, GMS)
Founded: 1989.
Leadership/major personalities: Mohammed Farah Hassan 'Aideed'; Ali Mahdi Mohammed.
Ethnic basis: Hawiye clan family.
Armed element: By 1990 several different armed elements, each affiliated with a Hawiye clan, had emerged.
Agenda: Anti-Siad.
Factionalisation: The USC led dissident forces into Mogadishu in December 1990, and subsequently the movement, as well as the capital, were split by factions loyal to Aideed or Ali Mahdi. This continued conflict precipitated the UN involvement in late 1992.

Somali factions emerging since 1990

After the collapse of the Siad regime and the breakup of the national administration, Somalia devolved into a patchwork of various movements, each of which was dominated by a particular ethnic group. In addition to the four main movements described above, the remnants of the Siad regime and other contenders dominated the country. These movements were subject to their own internal stresses and factionalisations, and the listing below covers Somalia as of late 1992. Each of the groups had their own defence forces, little more than makeshift militias. Shifting alliances and disintegration of political-military groups has taken place constantly since then.

United Somali Front (USF; in Somali, Midnimadda Jabhada Soomaliyeed, MJS)
Leadership/major personalities: Abulamen Dual Ali.
Ethnic basis: Issa.

Somali Democratic Association (SDA; in Somali, Demogradiyeed Ururka Soomaliyeed, DUS)
Leadership/major personalities: Mohammed Abdallahi.
Ethnic basis: Gadabursi.

Somali Democratic Movement (SDM; in Somali, Dhaqdhaqaaqa Demogradiyeed Soomaliyeed, DDS)
Leadership/major personalities: Abdulqadir 'Zoppu'.
Ethnic basis: Rhanwein.

Somali National Front (SNF; in Somali, Dhaqdhaqaaqa Jabhada Soomaliyeed, DJS)
Leadership/major personalities: Ahmed Warsame, Mohamed Hashi Ganni.
Ethnic basis: Marehan.
Armed element: Remnants of the old Somali

National Army (SNA), led by Mohamed Hersi 'Morgan'.

Agenda: The SNF was the remnant of the old regime's Marehan power base, and held power along the Ethiopian border and in the Somalia-Kenya border area; Siad, who headed the movement, was defeated and driven from the country in early 1992 by a coalition led by the USC and Mohammed Farah 'Aideed'.

Southern Somali National Movement (SSNM; in Somali, Dhaqdhaqaaqa Midnimadda Koonfurta Soomaliyed, DMKS)
Ethnic affiliation: Biyemal Dir.

SUDAN

Sudan People's Liberation Movement (SPLM)
Founded: 1983.
Leadership/major personalities: John de Mabior Garang, William Nyuon Bany, Keru-bino Kwanyin Bol.
Ethnic basis: Southern Sudanese ethnic groups, especially Dinka and Nuer.
Armed element: Sudan People's Liberation Army (SPLA).
Agenda: Equality of treatment for southern Sudanese by the national government; evolution into move for southern autonomy.
Factionalisation: Riven by major splits since October 1991 along mostly ethnic lines, with Garang retaining Dinka support and many Nuers joining William Nyuon and others; the SPLM element in the Nuba Mountains has always been semi-autonomous.

Sudan People's Liberation Movement-Main-stream (also known as the Naser Faction); later reconstituted as the Southern Sudan Independence Movement (SSIM)
Founded: 1991.
Leadership/major personalities: Dr Lam Akol, Dr Riek Mashar Teng-Dhurgan, and Gordon Koang Chol.
Ethnic basis: Mainly Nuer.
Agenda: Secessionist; anti-Garang.
Factionalisation: The Naser Faction of the SPLA was ultimately riven by personality differences that hampered its effectiveness and caused it to splinter along ethnic and regional lines.

SOUTH-WEST AFRICA/NAMIBIA

South-West Africa People's Organisation (SWAPO)
Founded: 1957 as the Ovambo People's Congress, later the Ovambo People's Organisation.
Leadership/major personalities: Herman Toivo ja Toivo, Sam Nujoma, Tobias Hanyeko, Dimo Hamaambo.
Ethnic basis: Ovambo.
Armed element: People's Liberation Army of Namibia (PLAN).
Agenda: Independence for South-West Africa/Namibia, by early 1970s using Soviet/East bloc assistance to fight South African rule in SWA.

UGANDA

Uganda National Liberation Front (UNLF)
Founded: 1979.
Leadership/major personalities: Dr Yusuf Lule.
Ethnic basis: Varied, but mostly southern.
Armed element: Supported armed anti-Amin groups.
Agenda: Overthrow of Amin regime.
Factionalisation: Conflict between Lule and radicals led to the latter persuading the Tanzanians to replace him with Geoffrey Binaisa.

National Resistance Movement (NRM)
Founded: 1981.
Leadership/major personalities: Yoweri Museveni.
Ethnic basis: Southern Ugandan.
Armed element: National Resistance Army (NRA).
Agenda: Overthrow of Obote regime.

Holy Spirit Movement (HSM)
Founded: 1986.
Leadership/major personalities: Alice Lakwenya, Joseph Kony.
Ethnic basis: Northern Ugandan.
Agenda: Anti-Museveni regime.

Lord's Resistance Army (LRA), formerly the Uganda (or United) Christian People's Democratic Alliance (UCPDA, also known as the United Democratic Christian Move-ment, UDCM)
Founded: 1991.
Leadership/major personalities: Joseph Kony.
Ethnic basis: Northern Ugandan.
Agenda: Anti-Museveni regime.

Former Uganda National Army (FUNA)
Founded: 1979.
Leadership/major personalities: Comprised former elements of Amin's military opposed to Obote regime.
Ethnic basis: Northern Ugandan.
Agenda: Anti-Obote.

Uganda National Resistance Front (UNRF); Uganda Freedom Movement (UFM); Federal Democratic Movement of Uganda
Founded: 1979-1980.
Leadership/major personalities: Dissident southern Ugandans opposed to Obote regime.
Ethnic basis: Southern Ugandan, primarily Bugandan.
Agenda: Anti-Obote.

West Nile Bank Front (WNBF)
Founded: May 1995.
Leadership/major personalities: Colonel Juma Oris; comprised of elements of Amin's military opposed to Museveni regime.
Ethnic basis: West Nile peoples, including Kakwa.
Agenda: Return of Amin to Uganda.

ZAIRE

Front National pour la Libération du Congo (National Front for the Liberation of the Congo) (FNLC)
Founded: 1967.
Ethnic basis: Katangese (Shaba) exiles in Angola.
Armed element: Armée National pour la Libération du Congo (ANLC).
Agenda: Resistance to Mobutu regime.

Parti de la Révolution Populaire (Popular Revolutionary Party) (PRP)
Founded: Late 1970s.
Leadership/major personalities: Laurent Kabila.
Ethnic basis: North-east Shaba ethnic groups.
Agenda: Resistance to regime.

Mouvement National Congolais-Lumumba (Congolese National Movement/Lumumba) (MNC-L)
Founded: 1964.
Leadership/major personalities: Nathanien Mbumba.
Ethnic basis: Eastern Haut-Zaire ethnic groups.
Armed element: Armée Patriotique Lumumba, APL, claimed 1,500 fighters in late 1980s.
Agenda: Resistance to regime.

South African Cross-Border Operations Undertaken from Northern Namibia, 1978–1987

Operation	Dates	Objective	Remarks
'Reindeer'	4-6 May 1978	PLAN base 'Moscow' near Cassinga 'Vietnam' camp complex near near Chetequera	Operation composed of separate but coordinated raids: (1) Airborne force striking 'Moscow' Cassinga, c. 250km north of the border. (2) Mechanised force striking 'Vietnam' complex, 28km north of the border. (3) Several smaller stopper and area operations associated with the preceding. Units participating included elements of all three battalions of 44th Parachute Brigade.
'Saffron'	23-7 Aug 1978	PLAN bases in SW Zambia opposite eastern Caprivi	Response to a PLAN rocket attack on Katima Mulilo base from Zambia.
'Sceptic'	25 May- 30 June 1980	PLAN base area known as 'Smokeshell' (Chifufa)	Mechanised force operation assisted by close air support and follow-up infantry operations.in south-central Angola, Units included 61 Battle Group, precursor of some 65km² in area 61 Mechanised Brigade.
'Klipklop'	30 July- 1 Aug 1980	Chitado, PLAN base N of Kakoland used as PLAN transit point and tactical headquarters/ supply depot	A 'minor external' by a two-platoon infantry force.
'Protea'	24 Aug- 1 Sept 1981	PLAN infrastructure in SE Angola east of a N-S line through Ngiva; main objective was PLAN camps S and SE of Xangongo and PLAN NW Front HQ at Xangongo, then Ngiva, site of PLAN N Front HQ	Largest SADF/SWATF external before 'Askari'. Culmination of a series of foot- mobile search-and-destroy ops in S Angola; one, 'Carnation', in tandem with 'Protea'.Mechanised forces aided by air suppression of FAPLA AD radars preceded attack; extensive helicopter support to mechanised force. Simultaneously undertaken with the foot-mobile Operation 'Carnation' to the E.Units participating included SAA airborne elements, 61 Mech Bn, 32 Bn, SWATF elements. First major FAPLA resistance (brigade level) to SADF/SWATF troops.
'Daisy'	1-20 Nov 1981	PLAN HQ at Bambi; base complex near	Mech force (61 Bn/4 SAI) and SWATF motorised force, supplemented by

		Chetequera. Subsidiary base at Ionde	stopper and area ops forces; some paratroops also involved. Air action between SAAF and FAPA.'Daisy' was a follow-up to 'Protea' to exploit that operation's gains and further disrupt PLAN infrastructure.
'Super'	March 1982	PLAN camp at Iona in Cambeno valley, north of Kakoland	Force comprised 32 Bn personnel airlanded by helicopter. Effectively destroyed PLAN attempts to open a new front in Kakoland.
'Mebos'	22 Jul-13 Aug 1982	PLAN Central and E Front HQ west of Mupa area	Forces included SWASPES and elements of 1 Recce Commando. Considerable search-and-destroy activity required.
'Phoenix'	15 Feb-15 Apr	Destruction of infrastructure supporting PLAN offensive in Kakoland, Ovambo, and Kavango. Main target the PLAN 'Special Unit' based at Cahama and Cuvelai; targets lay on both sides of the border	Series of attacks designed to pre-empt or blunt 1983 PLAN attacks into 10 Sector or western 20 Sector that required pursuit into Angola and attacks on PLAN bases there. Extensive coordination required due to large number of separate actions along a 500km border conducted by various elements of the security forces. Precursor to Operation 'Askari'.
'Askari'	12 Dec 1993-15 Jan 1984	Intended to cripple PLAN intentions for an early offensive for 1984. Object was to disrupt PLAN logistic infra-structure in S/Central Angola, and attack its HQ near Lubango	Triggered by intelligence about a large PLAN force moving south from target areas. Buildup to action with preliminary actions prior to main action. Main force consisted of four battalion-sized mechanised/motorised task forces, including elements of 61st Mech Bn, 82 Mech Bde, 4 SAI, and 32 Bn, much of it CF. Intensified air defence by FAPLA that required several air defence suppres-sion missions; first firings of SA-8s and SA-9s by FAPLA. Direct involve-ment of Cuban and FAPLA forces, including mech and armour, to assist PLAN. Withdrawal from Angola carried out after heavy rains and in unfavourable conditions, but without incident. Largest of the externals mounted by SADF/SWATF from SWA/Namibian bases before 'Modular'.
'Egret'	15-22 Sep 1985	PLAN infrastucture, inc. its 8 Bn, building up for the rainy season offensive	First deliberate external since 'Askari' Main force built around 500 troops from 101 Bn. Main axis of advance Evale-Anhaca-Dova area, moving against Nehone and PLAN base there.
'Boswilger'	28-30 Jun 1985	Exploitation of a follow-up operation that targeted	Used 10 Sector forces moving 40km into Angola and killed 18% of PLAN

		PLAN bases N of 10 Sector	cadres N of border
Unnamed	Feb-Mar 1986	PLAN targets N of eastern part of 10 Sector	Separate attacks against Mucope, Oncocua, and Caiundo.
Unnamed	7 Nov 1986 and following period	PLAN targets N of 10 Sector	Angolan government claim.
Unnamed	May 1989	Follow-up ambushed by FAPLA and PLAN N of 10 Sector	Heavy FAPLA casualties.
Unnamed	12-19 Nov 1986	PLAN training camp N of 10 Sector	Details not available.
Unnamed	12-26 Jan 1987	Exploitation of follow-up north along Mongua axis	Repelled FAPLA Mongua garrison attack 75km N of border. FAPLA casualties heavy after engagement with SWATF.
Unnamed	12 and 19 Jan 1987	Targets in Cunene province	Angolan government claim.
Unnamed	19 Mar-2 Apr 1987	Insurgent force fleeing back to Angola	Engaged from 'Red Line' point on S border of 10 Sector.
Unnamed	Early Jun 1987 (before 8 Jun)	Follow-up by security forces to PLAN base at Anhaca that targeted Kavango	FAPLA engaged security forces near Anhaca. Ngiva reported bombed by SAAF
Unnamed	Before 8 Jul 1987	Unspecified	Angolan government claims; mech forces said used.
Unnamed	27-28 Jul 1987	Follow-up north of 10 Sector incursion by 120 PLAN	SWATF pursuit ambushed by mixed PLAN-FAPLA force, which was defeated before a second engagement took place; heavy FAPLA casualties reported.
Unnamed	30 Oct-1 Nov 1987	PLAN Central HQ N of central Ovamboland	Heavy PLAN casualties.

Source Discussion
and Select Bibliography

African insurgent movements and government counterinsurgency activities are often difficult for the non-area expert to follow due to the nature and availability of source material.
The following discussion should assist interested readers to find further information on
the insurgent movements discussed here.

The conflicts discussed in this book have received frequent press coverage, published
in the collections cited below. However, a word of caution is in order to all who wish to
consult them as source material for African insurgency wars. First, there is often considerable variation in the spelling of names of people and places, forcing the reader to biograph-
ical dictionaries (where they can be of help) and gazeteers. More problematic is the frequent
disagreement in published news accounts of the exact date of a given event or series of
events. Frequently the date given is that when an event was reported by the press, or by one
of the fighting parties to the press. All of the foregoing merely complicates a more general
problem, namely that of reconciling often conflicting accounts of events provided by each
side in the conflict. Precise dates for some events often remain difficult to establish.

For this book I have heavily relied upon the primary news sources, especially broadcasts, to which I refer the reader interested in further details of events. When the latter are
collected and analysed in magazines and news letters, a significant amount of information
normally is sacrificed to the need to produce a concise news story for a given readership.
Often such accounts have a particular slant as well.

The two main periodicals that publish current news about Africa in English that are
available to the general public are that published by the British government, namely *BBC
Summary of World Broadcasts* (abbreviated BBC/SWB; and that published by the United
States government, *Foreign Broadcast Information Service* (FBIS). These publications
summarize world news and have separate sections on Sub-Saharan Africa. Most larger
reference libraries have archives of one or the other of these publications, or can assist
readers to obtain them.

Another valuable reference document is that published by Africana Publications in
New York, namely *Africa Research Bulletin* (ARB). This monthly publication summarises
events for all countries on the continent, itemising political, social, and economic developments for each African nation. It relies upon news broadcasts and newspapers for its
main sources of news, which it cites for each entry. The first volume appeared in 1962 and
since then ARB has been a relatively objective chronicle of events in Africa. Africana also
publishes a yearly update of events in Africa, called *Africa Contemporary Record*,
reviewing (but in less detail than ARB) the previous year's events for each country, and
including essays on special subjects of timely interest. Similarly, Europa Publications
publishes as one of its annual yearbooks for each region of the world the yearly *Africa
South of the Sahara*, with detailed discussions for each country on political, economic,
social, and other topics. The historical discussions for each country are a valuable introduction for the non-specialist into the intricacies of African ethnic and regional politics
that often spawn the insurgencies discussed here.

There are many periodicals that focus on Africa. I will mention but a few of the top
ones that often contain valuable data on military and security affairs. *Africa Confidential*

(London) is the leader in the newsletter category. Prominent among the magazines are *New African* (London), *African Business* (London), *Africa Events* (London-Dar es-Salaam), and *Jeune Afrique* (Paris). These are but a few of scores of news periodicals, many of which are restricted to national readerships on the African continent.

I would also refer the reader to the individual volumes in the series of *African Historical Dictionaries*, published by Scarecrow Press in Metuchen, New Jersey (USA). These works provide valuable background to the history and politics of the countries discussed in this book.

Finally, I want to remind students of African conflicts that the Internet is increasingly important for researching information and receiving current news on the ongoing unrest on the continent. Some conflicts, such as the (as of writing) ongoing war in Zaire, are extensively documented on Internet Web sites. African wars of the future, like such conflicts elsewhere, will be increasingly documented on the Internet. The latter is and will increasingly be an important tool for researchers in this field.

The following select list of titles on southern African conflicts is in no way complete, but is provided to give additional amplification to various facets of COIN warfare. My few annotations are designed to assist the reader or recommend particularly outstanding books.

Abbott, Peter; Botham, Philip; and Chappell, Mike, *Modern African Wars (1) Rhodesia 1965-1980*. London: Osprey, 1986 (Osprey Men-at-Arms, 183).

Breytenbach, Jan, *They Live by the Sword: 32 'Buffalo' Battalion – South Africa's Foreign Legion*. Alberton (S.A.): Lemur Books, 1990. Although heavily edited as a requirement for publication, this account of 32 Battalion by one of its former commanders provides often unique insights into the COIN war in SWA and Angola.

Bridgland, Fred, *Jonas Savimbi: A Key to Africa*. New York: Paragon House, 1987. The standard biography of Savimbi, with much additional material on the Angolan conflict up through the late 1980s.

Bridgland, Fred, *The War for Africa: Twelve Months that Transformed a Continent*. Gibraltar: Ashanti Press, 1990. The best popular account of the South African intervention of 1987-1988, and a useful supplement to Heitman's work on the same subject (see below).

Cillers, J. K., *Counterinsurgency in Rhodesia*. London: Croom Helm, 1985. Perhaps the most concise and systematic study of counterinsurgency tactics in the Rhodesian conflict, this book provides an overview of the evolution of the conflict and the UDI government response to the major security issues as they developed.

Crocker, Chester A., *High Noon in Southern Africa: Making Peace in a Rough Neighborhood*. New York and London: W.W. Norton, 1992. The perspective on the crisis in southern Africa by one of the key figures in the peacemaking process.

Ellert, Henrik, The Rhodesian Front War. Harare: Mambo Press, 1989. A systematic study of the war from an internal security standpoint. It is most valuable for the civilian security force viewpoint and provides valuable insight on the evolution of the conflict.

Finnegan, William, *A Complicated War: The Harrowing of Mozambique*. Berkeley, Los Angeles, and Oxford: University of California Press, 1992. The best first-hand account of Mozambique riven by the RENAMO insurgency.

Heitman, Helmoed-Roemer, *War in Angola: The Final South African Phase*. Gibraltar: Ashanti Press, 1990. The quasi-official SADF account of the war by a leading military correspondent for the region. Essential for understanding South African and Angolan military operations.

Heitman, Helmoed-Roemer, *South African Armed Forces*. Capetown: Buffalo Publishers, 1990.

Heitman, Helmoed-Roemer, *Modern African Wars 3: South-west Africa.* London: Osprey, 1991 (Osprey Men-at-Arms, 242).

Hooper, Jim, *Beneath the Visiting Moon: Images of Combat in Southern Africa.* Lexington (Massachusetts): Lexington Square Books, 1990. Published as *Koevoet!* in South Africa, this book is a first-hand account of operations by the elite SWA Police COIN unit. Another essential book for understanding COIN in SWA.

James, W. Martin, III, *A Political History of the Civil War in Angola, 1974-1990.* New Brunswick and London: Transaction Publishers, 1992. Provides the political dimension to the 1975-1991 Angolan insurgency. Unfortunately, it does not cover the final, critical, two years of the war. Excellent and detailed bibliography.

Legum, Colin, *The Battlefronts of Southern Africa.* New York and London: African Publishers, 1988. The leading work documenting conflicts in the region through the mid-1980s by one of the deans of African scholars.

McCuen, John J. *The Art of Counter-Revolutionary War: The Strategy of Counter-insurgency.* London: Faber and Faber, 1966. With a foreword by Sir Robert Thompson. This work, a model for the South African security forces in Namibia, is key to understanding the concepts of counterinsurgency warfare. The examples used by McCuen are drawn heavily from conflicts in Algeria and Vietnam, but as the South Africans clearly showed, are applicable to the African continent as well.

Minter, William, *Apartheid's Contras: An Inquiry into the Roots of War in Angola and Mozambique.* London and New Jersey: Zed Books, 1994. The account of South Africa's support to insurgency in Angola and Mozambique. Not sympathetic to the South African position, this work nevertheless provides many new insights into the means used by Pretoria to support insurgency, especially in Mozambique.

Norval, Morgan, *Death in the Desert: The Namibian Tragedy.* Washington DC: Selous Foundation Press, 1989. In diametric ideological opposition to Minter, this book, completed just before the COIN war came to a close, is a comprehensive history of the conflict, the forces involved, and operations and tactics.

Pitta, Robert; Fannel, Jeff; and McCouaig, Simon, *South African Special Forces.* London: Osprey, 1993 (Elite Series, 47)

Steenkamp, Willem, *Borderstrike: South Africa hits SWAPO bases in Angola.* Durban/ Pretoria: Butterworths Publishers, 1983. An excellent account of SADF cross-border strikes in the 1978-1980 period by a leading South African military correspondent and writer.

Steenkamp, Willem, *South Africa's Border War, 1966-1989.* Gibraltar: Ashanti Press, 1989. A detailed, chronologically-ordered study of the conflict, lavishly illustrated and containing much hitherto unpublished material.

Stiff, Peter, *Nine Days of War: Namibia - before, during, and after.* Alberton (S.A.): Lemur Books, 1989. A detailed account of SWAPO's final disastrous attempt to force a settlement on its own terms.

Vines, Alex, *RENAMO: Terrorism in Mozambique.* London: James Currey, Ltd., 1991. Essential for understanding how RENAMO works, its origins, and its impact on the civilian population, this is still the best one-volume comprehensive study. Contains extensive references to support further research.

Maps

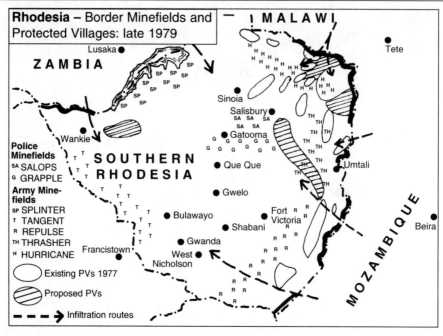

Rhodesia – Border Minefields and Protected Villages: late 1979

ZAMBIA

Lusaka ●

MALAWI

Tete ●

Sinoia ●

Salisbury ●
SA SA SA
SA SA

Gatooma ●
G G G G G
G G G G G

Que Que ●

Gwelo ●

Fort
Victoria ● R
R

Shabani ●

Umtali ●

Beira ●

MOZAMBIQUE

Wankie ●

SOUTHERN
RHODESIA

**Police
Minefields**
SA SALOPS
G GRAPPLE
**Army Mine-
fields**
SP SPLINTER
T TANGENT
R REPULSE
TH THRASHER
H HURRICANE

Bulawayo ●

Gwanda ●

West ●
Nicholson

Francistown ●

Existing PVs 1977

Proposed PVs

Infiltration routes

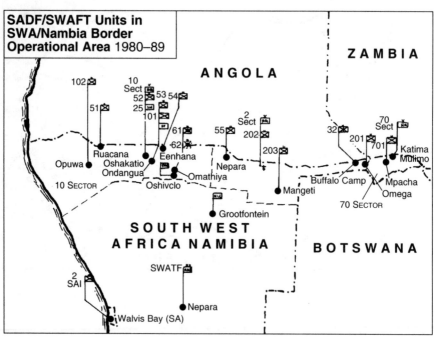

**SADF/SWAFT Units in
SWA/Nambia Border
Operational Area** 1980–89

ANGOLA

ZAMBIA

102

10
Sect
52
51   25
101

53 54

2
Sect

61
62

55

202

203

32

70
Sect

201

701

Katima
Mulimo

Opuwa ●

Ruacana ●
Oshakatio
Ondangua
Oshivclo

Eenhana ●

Omathiya

Nepara ●

Mangeti ●

Buffalo Camp

Mpacha
Omega

10 SECTOR

70 SECTOR

SOUTH WEST
AFRICA NAMIBIA

Grootfontein ●

BOTSWANA

2
SAI

SWATF

Nepara ●

Walvis Bay (SA) ●

Deployment of SADF Forces –
mid to late 1984

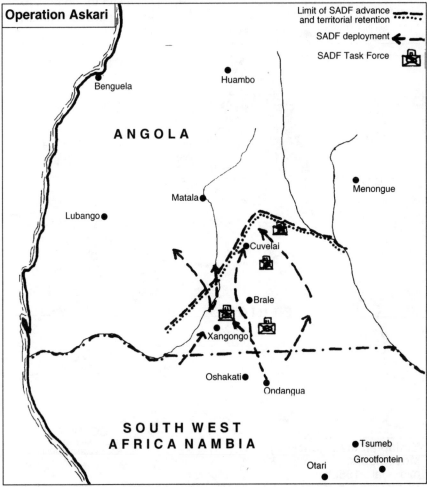

Operation Askari

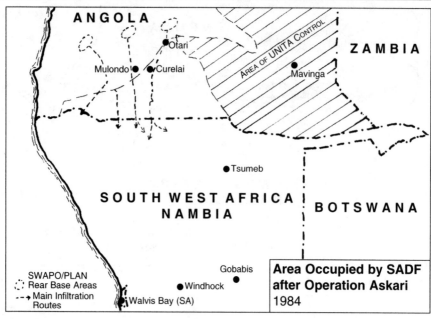

ANGOLA

● Otari

Mulondo ● ● Curelai

AREA OF UNITA CONTROL

ZAMBIA

● Mavinga

● Tsumeb

SOUTH WEST AFRICA
NAMBIA

BOTSWANA

Gobabis
●

● Windhock

Walvis Bay (SA)

SWAPO/PLAN
Rear Base Areas
Main Infiltration
Routes

**Area Occupied by SADF
after Operation Askari
1984**

RED SEA

SAUDI ARABIA

EPLF

Nakfa
Af Abet

EPLF activity,
early 1980s

ERITREANS

NORTH
YEMEN

SUDAN

TPLF

SOUTH YEMEN

AFAR
TERRITORY

Afar Liberation
Front activity

L. Tana

Djibouti

ETHIOPIA

Oromo Libera-
tion Front
Activity

OGADEN
WSLF and Somali
Abo Liberation Front

**Ethiopian Insurgent
Movements,
mid – late 1980s**

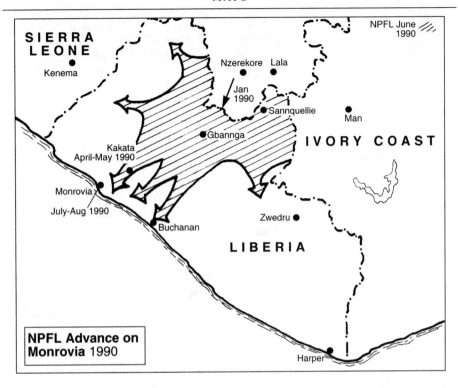

NPFL Advance on Monrovia 1990

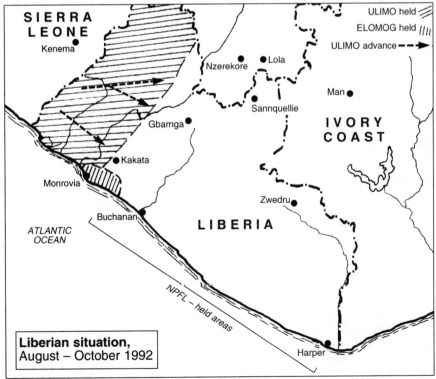

Liberian situation, August – October 1992

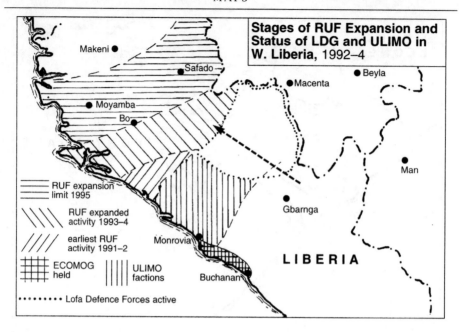

Stages of RUF Expansion and Status of LDG and ULIMO in W. Liberia, 1992–4

Makeni

Safado

Macenta

Beyla

Moyamba

Bo

Man

RUF expansion limit 1995

RUF expanded activity 1993–4

earliest RUF activity 1991–2

ECOMOG held

ULIMO factions

Gbarnga

Monrovia

LIBERIA

Buchanan

•••••••• Lofa Defence Forces active

Index